September 1996-August 1997

# TARBELL'S

## Teacher's Guide

to the International Sunday School Lessons
Includes the NRSV and KJV

Dr. William P. Barker

David C. Cook Church Ministries Curriculum
Colorado Springs, Colorado/Paris, Ontario

Published by David C. Cook Church Ministries Curriculum
4050 Lee Vance View
Colorado Springs, CO 80918
Cable address: DCCOOK
Printed in the United States of America
ISBN: 0-7814-5186-8

# CONTENTS

## LIST OF LESSONS

### SEPTEMBER—NOVEMBER 1996
### GOD'S PEOPLE FACE JUDGMENT

### DECEMBER 1996—FEBRUARY 1997
### NEW TESTAMENT PERSONALITIES

## MARCH—MAY 1997
## HOPE FOR THE FUTURE

## JUNE—AUGUST 1997
## GUIDANCE FOR MINISTRY

# A WORD TO THE TEACHER

No one has ever received a Nobel Prize for teaching a Sunday school class, but teachers are worthy of such respect and honor. Your service in the name of Jesus Christ means so much to those for whom you open the Scriptures, week by week.

Yes, you may feel intimidated by the task, and maybe discouraged at times. For everyone who wants to be taught, there seem to be twenty who don't want to be taught. But hang in there! Remember that the greatest teacher of all, Jesus Himself, sometimes had to teach those not wanting to be taught. Often the disciples were indifferent or slow to understand. Nevertheless, these people were the nucleus of the church, the raw material on which Jesus depended to continue His ministry.

"The mediocre teacher tells," wrote William Arthur Ward. "The good teacher explains. The superior teacher demonstrates. The great teacher inspires." You will inspire a deeper commitment to the Lord as you share your own enthusiasm for the Gospel of Jesus Christ. In spite of the weariness and discouragement you may occasionally feel, your personal joy and gratitude in Christ will spill over into the lives of your students.

And, of course, to be a good teacher requires being a lifelong learner yourself. When you explore the meaning of the Bible's message week after week with your students, you are a fellow learner, growing in your own commitment to Christ. As you yourself are inspired to dig out the jewels from the treasures of God's Word, your teaching will take on a glow and depth that inspires others.

As a fellow teacher (yes, I also regularly teach a Bible class), I salute you as an esteemed colleague in the ministry of Jesus Christ. May you continually discover new measures of meaning in the Scriptures and in your walk with the Lord.

Yours in Christ's service,
William P. Barker

# A NOTE OF APPRECIATION

A special word of appreciation to Mary L. Treisbach and Dr. John B. Barker, who have helped prepare this issue, and whose ministry means so much!

# Use Tarbell's with Material from These Publishers

Sunday school materials from the following denominations and publishers follow the International Sunday School Lesson outlines (sometimes known as the Uniform Series). Because Tarbell's Teacher's Guide follows the same ISSL outlines, you can use Tarbell's as an excellent teacher resource to supplement the materials from these publishing houses.

**Denominational:**
Advent Christian General Conference—*Adult*
American Baptist (Judson Press)—*Adult*
Church of God in Christ (Church of God in Christ Publishing House)—*Adult*
Church of Christ Holiness—*Adult*
Church of God (Warner Press)—*Adult*
Church of God by Faith—*Adult*
National Baptist Convention of America (Boyd)—*All ages*
National Primitive Baptist Convention—*Adult*
Progressive National Baptist Convention—*Adult*
Presbyterian Church (U.S.A.) (*Bible Discovery Series*—Presbyterian Publishing House or P.R.E.M.)—*Adult*
Southern Baptist (Baptist Sunday School Board)—*All ages*
Union Gospel Press—*All ages*
United Holy Church of America—*Adult*
United Methodist Church (Cokesbury)—*All ages*

**Nondenominational:**
David C. Cook Church Ministries—*Adult*
Echoes Sunday School Literature—*Adult*
Standard Publishing—*Adult*
Urban Ministries—*All ages*

# SEPTEMBER, OCTOBER, NOVEMBER 1996

## GOD'S PEOPLE FACE JUDGMENT

## LESSON 1—SEPTEMBER 1

### HOLDING FAST TO THE LORD

*Background Scripture:* II Kings 18—20
*Devotional Reading:* Deuteronomy 10:12-22

| KING JAMES VERSION | NEW REVISED STANDARD VERSION |
|---|---|
| II KINGS 18:1 Now it came to pass in the third year of Hoshea son of Elah king of Israel, that Hezekiah the son of Ahaz king of Judah began to reign. | II KINGS 18:1 In the third year of King Hoshea son of Elah of Israel, Hezekiah son of King Ahaz of Judah began to reign. 2 He |

II KINGS 18:1 Now it came to pass in the third year of Hoshea son of Elah king of Israel, that Hezekiah the son of Ahaz king of Judah began to reign.

2 Twenty and five years old was he when he began to reign; and he reigned twenty and nine years in Jerusalem. His mother's name also was Abi, the daughter of Zachariah.

3 And he did that which was right in the sight of the Lord, according to all that David his father did.

4 He removed the high places, and brake the images, and cut down the groves, and brake in pieces the brasen serpent that Moses had made: for unto those days the children of Israel did burn incense to it: and he called it Nehushtan.

5 He trusted in the Lord God of Israel; so that after him was none like him among all the kings of Judah, nor any that were before him.

6 For he clave to the Lord, and departed not from following him, but kept his commandments, which the Lord commanded Moses.

7 And the Lord was with him; and he prospered whithersoever he went forth: and he rebelled against the king of Assyria, and served him not.

8 He smote the Philistines, even unto Gaza, and the borders thereof, from the tower of the watchmen to the fenced city.

20:16 And Isaiah said unto Hezekiah, Hear the word of the Lord.

17 Behold, the days come, that all that is in thine house, and that which thy fathers have laid up in store unto this day, shall be carried into Babylon: nothing shall be left,

II KINGS 18:1 In the third year of King Hoshea son of Elah of Israel, Hezekiah son of King Ahaz of Judah began to reign. 2 He was twenty-five years old when he began to reign; he reigned twenty-nine years in Jerusalem. His mother's name was Abi daughter of Zechariah. 3 He did what was right in the sight of the Lord just as his ancestor David had done. 4 He removed the high places, broke down the pillars, and cut down the sacred pole. He broke in pieces the bronze serpent that Moses had made, for until those days the people of Israel had made offerings to it; it was called Nehushtan. 5 He trusted in the Lord the God of Israel; so that there was no one like him among all the kings of Judah after him, or among those who were before him. 6 For he held fast to the Lord; he did not depart from following him but kept the commandments that the Lord commanded Moses. 7 The Lord was with him; wherever he went, he prospered. He rebelled against the king of Assyria and would not serve him. 8 He attacked the Philistines as far as Gaza and its territory, from watchtower to fortified city.

20:16 Then Isaiah said to Hezekiah, "Hear the word of the Lord: 17 Days are coming when all that is in your house, and that which your ancestors have stored up until this day, shall be carried to Babylon; nothing shall be left, says the Lord. 18 Some of your own sons who are born to you shall be taken away; they shall be eunuchs in the palace of the king of Babylon." 19 Then Hezekiah said to Isaiah, "The word of the Lord that you have spoken is good." For he thought, "Why not, if there will be peace saith the Lord.

18 And of thy sons that shall issue from thee, which thou shalt beget, shall they take away; and they shall be eunuchs in the palace of the king of Babylon.

19 Then said Hezekiah unto Isaiah, Good is the word of the Lord which thou hast spoken. And he said, Is it not good, if peace and truth be in my days?

20 And the rest of the acts of Hezekiah, and all his might, and how he made a pool, and a conduit, and brought water into the city, are they not written in the book of the chronicles of the kings of Judah?

21 And Hezekiah slept with his fathers: and Manasseh his son reigned in his stead.

and security in my days?"

20 The rest of the deeds of Hezekiah, all his power, how he made the pool and the conduit and brought water into the city, are they not written in the Book of the Annals of the Kings of Judah? 21 Hezekiah slept with his ancestors; and his son Manasseh succeeded him.

**KEY VERSE:** *[Hezekiah] held fast to the Lord; he did not depart from following him but kept the commandments that the Lord commanded Moses.* II Kings 18:6.

## HOME BIBLE READINGS

| Aug. | 26 | M. | II Kings 18:26-36 | Rabshakeh Mocks the Living God |
| Aug. | 27 | T. | II Kings 19:1-7 | Rabshakeh Rebuked by God |
| Aug. | 28 | W. | II Kings 19:14-19 | Hezekiah Prays for God's Deliverance |
| Aug. | 29 | T. | II Kings 19:29-34 | God Promises to Save Jerusalem |
| Aug. | 30 | F. | II Kings 20:1-6 | God Heals Hezekiah |
| Aug. | 31 | S. | II Kings 20:7-11 | The Sign of Hezekiah's Healing |
| Sept. | 1 | S. | II Chronicles 32:27-31 | Hezekiah's Great Riches |

## BACKGROUND

Every community has its identity-defining stories. The little town where I now live was originally a New England fishing village, and the stories of old mariners, storms, and shipwrecks soon become part of the life of everyone who moves here. Without its stories, no group can develop a sense of true community.

God's community also has its stories, and as part of the community, we must hear those stories, again and again. The sacred accounts in God's Word give His people an awareness that they belong to a special group with a special history. When any community forgets its stories, it loses its identity and becomes confused. God's community can also neglect its unique, historical events. Such forgetting brings on a sort of collective amnesia. Therefore, we start this fall series of lessons by recalling some of the stories that have shaped our community as God's people.

This takes us back to the eighth century, B.C. After the reigns of King David and King Solomon, the nation split into two rival monarchies. Israel, the northern kingdom, pursued its irresponsible ways until its capital of Samaria was captured and its people deported by the powerful Assyrians in

722 B.C. Judah, the southern kingdom, managed to survive in the turbulent years that followed as the superpowers of Assyria, Egypt, and later the Babylonians, struggled for supremacy. Our lessons will center on the period of about 135 years after the fall of Samaria to the fall of Jerusalem in 587 B.C. During this period, several kings and prophets in Judah tried to reform God's people. Perceptive leaders knew that the tragedy of Samaria would befall Jerusalem, too, if the people of Judah did not change their ways.

Today's lesson examines the reign of one of the few righteous and God-fearing rulers of Judah, King Hezekiah. His predecessors had permitted various disgusting pagan cults to flourish, allowing true worship of Yahweh to wane. Hezekiah's father, King Ahaz, had also allowed Judah to become a vassal state to Assyria. Young Hezekiah (he was only twenty-five when he began his reign) steadfastly trusted the Lord and managed to lead Judah through some of its most tempestuous times, including a siege by the Assyrian armies.

## NOTES ON THE PRINTED TEXT

*In the third year of King Hoshea son of Elah of Israel, Hezekiah son of King Ahaz of Judah began to reign* (18:1). The writer of II Kings details the succession of Judah's throne. Ahaz ruled Judah about sixteen years, roughly 732 to 715 B.C. He preferred to play international politics, giving expensive gifts to the superpowers of Assyria and Egypt rather than trusting God. He did not listen to Isaiah's advice, and even scorned a sign from God. He also practiced idolatrous cults, leaving his nation morally weak. His son Hezekiah, born about 740 B.C. and designated the heir-apparent in 729, was the exact opposite of his father. *He was twenty-five years old when he began to reign* (18:2). In 715 B.C., Hezekiah became king over Judah, reigning for twenty-nine years. His mother, Abi, a woman of strong and pure religious background, had raised and taught him well. *He did what was right in the sight of the Lord just as his ancestor David had done* (18:3).

The compiler of II Kings detailed Hezekiah's reforms. This faithful king purged idolatry from the land and instituted a religious reformation. *He removed the high places, broke down the pillars, and cut down the sacred pole* (18:4a).

Broken storage jars excavated at Kuntillet Airud, in northeastern Sinai, display figures and contain blessing inscriptions offered to both God and Asherah. Such sacred objects, though popular, became targets of condemnation during Hezekiah's reforms. Yet, despite Hezekiah's reforms, archaeological evidence points to the continuance of pagan elements in Israel's faith and worship.

*He broke in pieces the bronze serpent that Moses had made, for until those days the people of Israel had made offerings to it, it was called Nehushtan* (18:4b). Moses had made a bronze snake as a cure for snakebite during the people's years of sojourn in the wilderness. Kept in the ark of the covenant, it had apparently become a symbol for a pagan cult. The serpent also had long been a fertility symbol associated with the goddess Asherah. Carved reliefs, molded clay incense altars, even a small bronze serpent have all been found by archaeologists. "Nehushtan" could refer to either the serpent or the entire bronze object.

God blessed Hezekiah because he trusted in Him and was obedient to His commandments. *He trusted in the Lord God of Israel; so that there was no one like him among all the kings of Judah after him, or among those who were before him* (18:5). Summarizing his zeal for the Lord, the writer of Kings stated, *For he held fast to the Lord, he did not depart from following him but kept the commandments that the Lord commanded Moses* (18:6). The result of Hezekiah's efforts was success and prosperity. *The Lord was with him; wherever he went, he prospered* (18:7).

Hezekiah also had immediate political success, as he joined in a widespread rebellion against Assyria. *He rebelled against the king of Assyria and would not serve him* (18:7). Yet some kings on the Philistine plain, chiefly Padi of Ekron, remained loyal to Assyria. Padi's people rose against him, choosing to be rid of Assyrian bondage, and Hezekiah marched against Padi and others who supported Assyria. His campaign took him as far as Gaza. *He attacked the Philistines as far as Gaza and its territory, from watchtower to fortified city* (18:8).

Padi was eventually captured and held in Jerusalem, but Assyria quickly crushed the revolt, and the northern kingdom of Israel fell. Hezekiah's southern kingdom of Judah was invaded, and Hezekiah was required to pay a tribute, including gold and silver from the temple. But Jerusalem remained unconquered. From 714 B.C. to 709 B.C. Merodach-baladan of Babylon tried to convince Hezekiah to rebel. In 711 B.C., Merodach-baladan visited Jerusalem and was shown Hezekiah's treasure house with its gold, silver, spices, precious oils, and armaments. Shortly thereafter, Isaiah visited Hezekiah, pressing for Judah to remain neutral.

Upon hearing that Hezekiah had shown Merodach-baladan the treasure, Isaiah pronounced a warning from God. He told Hezekiah that all of his house, including all the things his ancestors had stored up, would be carried to Babylon. *Days are coming when all that is in your house, and that which your ancestors have stored up until this day, shall be carried to Babylon; nothing shall be left* (20:17). More bad news followed: his family would be exiled to Babylon. *Some of your own sons, who are born to you, shall be taken away; they shall be eunuchs in the palace of the king of Babylon* (20:18). Yet Hezekiah heard Isaiah's message as good news, since the calamity would not befall him personally. *Then Hezekiah said to Isaiah, "The word of the Lord that you have spoken is good." For he thought, "Why not, if there will be peace and security in my days?"* (20:19).

*The rest of the deeds of Hezekiah, all his power, how he made the pool and the conduit and brought water into the city; are they not written in the Book of the Annals of the Kings of Judah?* (20:20). In addition to being known for his reforms, Hezekiah was remembered for his public works. Perhaps the writer was recalling an open conduit that brought water from Gihon to the Pool of Siloam. This would have been used to irrigate terraces in the Kidron Valley. Or perhaps the writer recalled Hezekiah's tunnel, as it is referred to today. This was a 1,750-foot underground tunnel that brought water inside the city of Jerusalem.

## SUGGESTIONS TO TEACHERS

Standing up to bullies isn't easy. Sometimes we face the bullying of a threatening tyrant. Other times we experience the brutality of public opinion. Popular culture can also bully us. Young King Hezekiah had to face all three such bullies. The first was the mighty Assyria. The second was indifference toward the Lord among His people. The third was the evil cults that flourished in Judah.

As Hezekiah knew, God is stronger than any threatening bullies, regardless of the form they may take. Your lesson today takes its cue from this youthful king's experience and is meant to help your students hold fast to the Lord in the face of pressures to waver.

1. REFORM AND RENEWAL. Examine Hezekiah's strong effort to bring his people back to obedience, as described in II Kings 18:1-6. What would your class members suggest if asked to point out areas in our society that fall short of what God desires? What could your church do to seek its own renewal?

2. REBELLIOUSNESS AND RUIN. The writer of II Kings 18 reminds his readers of what happened to the northern kingdom of Israel as a result of its arrogant refusal to obey God. Without loyalty to the Lord, a nation is doomed. Take a few minutes to describe to your group members how Samaria, Israel's capital, was finally captured after a terrible siege. The ten northern tribes were deported and dispersed.

3. RELIANCE AND RESISTANCE. The drama of the siege of Jerusalem should come through to your class with vivid reality. Notice the details that flow in II Kings. Try to picture the terror Judah's citizens must have felt. But point to Isaiah's powerful words in II Kings 19:6, 7, too, where he reminded the people of God's might.

Invite your students to focus on Hezekiah's great prayer of reliance on the Lord, found in II Kings 19:15-19. Here is a masterpiece of trust, suitable for every ruler in every age to pray each day. To many in Hezekiah's era, Sennacherib of Assyria seemed stronger than God. But the omnipotent Lord is greater than any bully.

4. RECKLESSNESS AND REBUKE. Hezekiah foolishly showed the Babylonian leaders his treasure house when he was joining with them in a plot against Assyria. Isaiah told Hezekiah that this rash act to get an ally's favor would eventually bring calamity to Jerusalem. Because of Hezekiah's steadfast faith, however, the divine judgment would not come to pass during his reign.

One key point of this episode is that our present actions can sometimes cause dire consequences for future generations. Have your class members list some of the modern-day consequences of past sins.

## TOPIC FOR ADULTS
### STEADFAST FAITH

*Custodian of Faith.* Ken Burns, the creator of the television specials "Baseball" and "The Civil War," commented with dismay on the major league baseball strike of 1994: "The thing I feel most passionately about is that these guys are custodians of something more important than their own bottom line." This phrase might have been spoken by the eighth- or sev-

enth-century prophets about the kings in Jerusalem who failed to be custodians of the nation's faith.

But Hezekiah was an exception. Holding fast to the Lord, he withstood
the taunts and threats of the powerful Assyrian general in a time of personal and national crisis. He proved to be a true custodian of Judah's faith.

*Higher Horizon.* Once when Robert Louis Stevenson was very ill, his wife
came to his room and found that Stevenson had written until his fingers
would no longer respond. He then dictated until his voice was gone. His
body was wracked by pain and fever, and his wife said, somewhat teasing-
ly, "I suppose you will say this morning that all is well?"

"Yes, my dear," came the reply. "I was about to say that. I refuse to make
a row of medicine bottles on the shelf the horizon of my world."

When a person holds fast to the Lord, he or she will not allow threats or
fears, pressures or disappointments to limit his or her horizons. Like
Hezekiah in the face of the terrors of the Assyrians—and Stevenson in the
throes of illness—the man or woman of faith is able to see beyond the
immediate horizons.

*The Reality of Every Situation.* When I begin to believe it's all up to me,
I like to read items that put things in perspective. Here's a recent find:

> While we deliberate, God reigns;
> when we decide wisely, God reigns;
> when we decide foolishly, God reigns;
> when we serve God with humble loyalty,
>      God reigns;
> when we serve God self-assertively,
>      God reigns;
> when we rebel and withhold our service,
>      God reigns—
> The Alpha and the Omega,
> which is, and which was, and which
>      is to come,
> The Almighty.

—Nancy Lindell-Sautter, in Tidings, quoting William Temple.

*Questions for Students on the Next Lesson.* 1. What did Josiah do to bring
about reform in his nation? 2. What was discovered in the temple during
the repairs? 3. What resulted from the covenant that Josiah and his people
made with God? 4. What were the cults like in Josiah's time? 5. Why did
Josiah want to destroy the shrines of these cults?

## TOPIC FOR YOUTH
### IT'S TIME FOR A CHANGE

*All that Glitters.* After years of poor sales, the sparkle has returned to the
jewelry industry. An improved economy, the repeal of the luxury tax, and
the advent of home-shopping television have all spurred the turnaround.

Madison Avenue, though, is largely responsible. It has convinced
Americans that diamonds and gems are the ultimate gift, projecting the

image of wealth. Youth are snapping up diamond earrings, gold rings, chains, baubles and bangles, confident that wearing expensive jewelry is the "in" thing to do.

Actually, youth face a form of idolatry that competes with their potential allegiance to the Lord. Gold, silver, and possessions are finite. What is important—and everlasting—is the Word of God. Put your faith in Him and His eternal promises. Only by knowing Him will you appreciate the beauty and worth of all He graciously gives you.

*Have You Been Assaulted?* Michael Medved, film critic and author of the 1992 book *Hollywood vs. America,* argues that the movie, music, and television industries have created an alien force among us. This force has assaulted America's cherished values and corrupted the nation's children. The industries have become what he terms "poison factories," producing almost nothing but vile, rank-smelling trash posing as art.

Movies, music, and television now mock authority and sensationalize brutality. Traditional standards and values have been pushed aside. Medved believes the public has become numbed to it all, particularly the youth. He worries about how long we can be seduced by such forms of entertainment without paying a heavy societal price. He has called upon the industry to return to the so-called "puritanical" Production Code of 1930. (For that, he was characterized as an angry modern-day reformer, a Martin Luther, nailing his ninety-five theses not to a church door but to a movie marquee.)

Like Medved, do you desire changes for the better? Or are you allowing yourself to be unduly influenced by questionable entertainment? Hold fast to the Lord and His standards. Do not let yourself be victimized.

*Taught the Spectators a Lesson.* The nine contestants at the Special Olympics stood at the starting line for the 100-yard dash, and the Seattle Stadium became quiet. At the gun, the runners all began to move, not at a fast pace, but all with a desire to finish the race and win.

One boy stumbled on the artificial surface, tumbled over several times, and began to cry. The other eight heard the child's cries, looked back, and slowed down. Then, each of them, all eight, turned around and went back to help their competitor. One little girl with Down's Syndrome bent over and kissed the fallen boy saying, "This will make it better." The boy stood— and all nine children held hands and walked together to the finish line.

The spectators rose to their feet in applause, the cheering continuing for several minutes. In one action these young people had reminded the stadium crowd that what truly is important is not winning, but helping others to win—even if it means slowing down, stopping, or changing directions. These handicapped youth pointed the onlookers to a better world.

Hezekiah understood that his ultimate allegiance was to God. He labored to point his people to a better world, where commitment to God and others is the key to life.

*Questions for Students on the Next Lesson.* 1. Who was Josiah? 2. What prompted Josiah's reforms? 3. Was Josiah really a good king? 4. Are your religious leaders committed to the right issues? 5. How do you, personally, demonstrate your obedience to your God?

# LESSON 2—SEPTEMBER 8

## OBEYING GOD'S COMMANDS

*Background Scripture:* II Kings 22:1—23:20
*Devotional Reading:* Deuteronomy 30:15-20

### KING JAMES VERSION

II KINGS 23:1 And the king sent, and they gathered unto him all the elders of Judah and of Jerusalem.

And the king went up into the house of the Lord, and all the men of Judah and all the inhabitants of Jerusalem with him, and the priests, and the prophets, and all the people, both small and great; and he read in their ears all the words of the book of the covenant which was found in the house of the Lord.

3 And the king stood by a pillar, and made a covenant before the Lord, to walk after the Lord, and to keep his commandments and his testimonies and his statutes with all their heart and all their soul, to perform the words of this covenant that were written in this book. And all the people stood to the covenant.

4 And the king commanded Hilkiah the high priest, and the priests of the second order, and the keepers of the door, to bring forth out of the temple of the Lord all the vessels that were made for Baal, and for the grove, and for all the host of heaven: and he burned them without Jerusalem in the fields of Kidron, and carried the ashes of them unto Beth-el.

5 And he put down the idolatrous priests, whom the kings of Judah had ordained to burn incense in the high places in the cities of Judah, and in the places round about Jerusalem; them also that burned incense unto Baal, to the sun, and to the moon, and to the planets, and to all the host of heaven.

6 And he brought out the grove from the house of the Lord, without Jerusalem, unto the brook Kidron, and burned it at the brook Kidron, and stamped it small to powder, and cast the powder thereof upon the graves of the children of the people.

7 And he brake down the houses of the sodomites, that were by the house of the Lord, where the women wove hangings for the grove.

8 And he brought all the priests out of the cities of Judah, and defiled the high places where the priests had burned incense, from Geba to Beer-sheba.

### NEW REVISED STANDARD VERSION

II KINGS 23:1 Then the king directed that all the elders of Judah and Jerusalem should be gathered to him. 2 The king went up to the house of the Lord, and with him went all the people of Judah, all the inhabitants of Jerusalem, the priests, the prophets, and all the people, both small and great; he read in their hearing all the words of the book of the covenant that had been found in the house of the Lord. 3 The king stood by the pillar and made a covenant before the Lord, to follow the Lord, keeping his commandments, his decrees, and his statutes, with all his heart and all his soul, to perform the words of this covenant that were written in this book. All the people joined in the covenant.

4 The king commanded the high priest Hilkiah, the priests of the second order, and the guardians of the threshold, to bring out of the temple of the Lord all the vessels made for Baal, for Asherah, and for all the host of heaven; he burned them outside Jerusalem in the fields of the Kidron, and carried their ashes to Bethel. 5 He deposed the idolatrous priests whom the kings of Judah had ordained to make offerings in the high places at the cities of Judah and around Jerusalem; those also who made offerings to Baal, to the sun, the moon, the constellations, and all the host of the heavens. 6 He brought out the image of Asherah from the house of the Lord, outside Jerusalem, to the Wadi Kidron, burned it at the Wadi Kidron, beat it to dust and threw the dust of it upon the graves of the common people. 7 He broke down the houses of the male temple prostitutes that were in the house of the Lord, where the women did weaving for Asherah. 8 He brought all the priests out of the town of Judah, and defiled the high places where the priests had made offerings, from Geba to Beer-sheba.

*KEY VERSE: (Josiah) made a covenant before the Lord . . . to perform the words of this covenant that were written in this book. All the people joined in the covenant.* II Kings 23:3.

## HOME BIBLE READINGS

| Sept. | 2 | M. | II Kings 22:1-7   | Josiah Ordered Repair of Temple  |
|-------|---|----|-------------------|----------------------------------|
| Sept. | 3 | T. | II Kings 22:8-13  | Josiah Received the Book of Law  |
| Sept. | 4 | W. | II Kings 22:14-20 | Josiah Spared from God's Wrath   |
| Sept. | 5 | T. | II Kings 23:21-25 | Josiah Ordered the Passover Held |
| Sept. | 6 | F. | II Kings 23:26-30 | Josiah's Death                   |
| Sept. | 7 | S. | Psalm 119:1-8     | Keep God's Commandments          |
| Sept. | 8 | S. | Psalm 119:9-16    | Live Righteously                 |

## BACKGROUND

Every generation must renew its commitment to the Lord. The faith of the fathers and mothers must be shown in the lives of the sons and daughters. Although Hezekiah's generation had gone through a time of reform and renewal, a century later Judah was again descending into the depths of corruption and idolatry. A dreary procession of rulers who ignored God and the commandments followed. Palace intrigues, royal debaucheries, and worship celebrations devoted to pagan deities brought the morals of Judah to their lowest levels. The fifty-five year reign of Manasseh in Jerusalem led the people into depths of evil that Judah had never known.

Meanwhile, the international scene was changing. The Assyrian empire had dominated the world for nearly 300 years; however, it had grown too dependent on the booty and slave labor it garnered from conquered countries. Although Assyrian armies had terrorized the Middle East and carved out the largest empire the ancient world had yet seen, they were constantly having to put down revolts from subjugated vassal states. By the seventh century B.C., the great Assyrian power was showing signs of weakening. The Babylonians were ascending as the military force to be reckoned with in the Mesopotamian region. Thus, the Egyptian pharaoh and the Assyrian emperor eventually tried to unite in order to block the Babylonians. However, the Assyrians were finally crushed by the Babylonians in 609 B.C.

King Josiah of Judah came to the throne as a young boy of eight in this period of upheaval. His father, Amon, had been assassinated after a reign distinguished only by unrelenting wickedness. In spite of such miserable times and evil surroundings, young Josiah proved to be one of the few outstanding monarchs during the last century of Judah's existence.

Josiah determined to bring about reform, carrying out a major renovation project on the temple (which had been allowed to fall into disrepair through disuse). Bringing God-honoring worship back to the temple would help call the people back from the heathen shrines erected during the previous centuries.

In the course of the repairs to the Jerusalem temple, someone found a scroll containing words of the covenant between the Lord and His people. This scroll, which we know as (including at least) the Book of Deuteronomy, outlined the responsibilities of the covenant community. When Josiah heard the Word of God, he resolved to carry out its decrees to the fullest. In obedience to God, he destroyed the symbols of false worship, especially the sacred places of the fertility cult of Baal.

## NOTES ON THE PRINTED TEXT

The last, great religious reform before the fall of Jerusalem in 586 B.C. was carried out in Judah by King Josiah. One of his projects was the restoration of the temple. While repairs were underway, workers discovered a book of the law that most scholars believe to be the Book of Deuteronomy. After examining the scroll, the prophetess Huldah warned Josiah that God's day of reckoning was fast approaching—although it would be temporarily delayed because of Josiah's commitment and desire for reform.

Josiah took immediate action. *Then the king directed that all the elders of Judah and Jerusalem should be gathered to him* (23:1). The heads of the families representing all the people were summoned to Jerusalem, and Josiah led them to the temple area. Josiah himself instigated the revival by reading aloud the law, now called the book of the covenant. *He read in their hearing all the words of the book of the covenant that had been found in the house of the Lord* (23:2).

Following proper procedure, the king led the people to rededicate themselves to God by following the commandments in the newly discovered book. The people likely sat or squatted during the reading and stood up as a sign of their assent. They committed themselves to the covenant. *The king stood by the pillar and made a covenant before the Lord, to follow the Lord, keeping his commandments, his decrees, and his statutes, with all his heart and all his soul, to perform the words of this covenant that were written in this book. All the people joined in the covenant* (23:3).

The writer of Kings detailed Josiah's burning zeal for the covenant. First the priests must cleanse the temple, removing and destroying all the symbols of false worship. The vessels were taken to the fields near the Kidron Valley, where they were broken and burned. So complete was Josiah's will to reform that he even gathered the remaining dust and ashes to transport them away from Jerusalem.

The officials of foreign cults were also removed. *He deposed the idolatrous priests whom the kings of Judah had ordained to make offerings in the high places at the cities of Judah and around Jerusalem; those also who made offerings to Baal, to the sun, the moon, the constellations, and all the host of the heavens* (23:5).

The fertility cult of Asherah had even placed an idol in the temple. This, too, was removed. Josiah's men carried the image of the Canaanite mother-goddess over the hill into the Kidron Valley. There, in Jerusalem's garbage dump, it was destroyed. They completed the idol's desecration by throwing its dust on graves, making it unclean and no longer holy. *He brought out the image of Asherah from the house of the Lord, outside Jerusalem, to the Wadi Kidron, burned it at the Wadi Kidron, beat it to dust and threw the dust of it upon the graves of the common people* (23:6).

*He broke down the houses of the male temple prostitutes that were in the house of the Lord, where the women did weaving for Asherah* (23:7). Having stamped out corruption in Jerusalem, Josiah turned his reforming zeal to Judah. He gave the rural priests no option, destroying idolatrous shrines and cult centers throughout the land. *He brought all the priests out of the towns of Judah, and defiled the high places where the priests had made offerings, from Geba to Beersheba* (23:8).

Kathleen Kenyon, the eminent British archaeologist, excavated the east slope of Jerusalem and the terraces of the Kidron Valley. In two caves she discovered cultic artifacts. One cave yielded an incense stand, eighty-four figurines, and hundreds of pots. Many of the figurines had the huge breasts of the fertility goddess Asherah. Kenyon also found clay horses with disc shapes on their foreheads, perhaps the horses of the sun (see II Kings 23:11.) While these particular chariots were not burned (they were dated to an earlier period), they do indicate the kinds of cults Josiah stamped out in his reform.

## SUGGESTIONS TO TEACHERS

When we think of cults, we may recall David Koresh in his Waco commune, or some of the other strange and occasionally dangerous religious fanatics that have seized the headlines in recent years. Such warped forms of devotion are abundant in every age and culture.

Your lesson today shows King Josiah bringing his people back from the religious cults of his own day. The problem in teaching this lesson lies in thinking that "cults" always refer to the bizarre beliefs and weird worship of strange sects. True, you must help your people be on guard against the lure and pressures of these kinds of heresies. But this lesson on obeying God's commands also calls for remembering this: there are other kinds of cults, much more subtle, claiming our loyalty today. For example, consider the cult of violence, the cult of hedonism, the cult of greed. Each of these has devotees, a kind of creed, and a definite appeal. Throughout your lesson, then, bear in mind that obeying God's commands requires a deep and thorough cleansing of God's people, even today.

1. RENOVATING THE TEMPLE. Worship was central in the life of God's people in Josiah's time, and it should have priority in our lives as well. Invite your group members to list ways in which your church's worship services offer praise to God while encouraging spiritual growth in worshipers.

The trend today is to turn Sunday into a day at the shopping mall. What can your students do to encourage fellow church members to be more regular in church attendance? Stress the corporate aspect of worship. Some people say, "I can worship just as well by myself in the woods." Remind your group that such individualism is not true Christian worship.

2. READING THE BOOK. When workers discovered the book we call Deuteronomy, Josiah insisted on having it read in public. Scripture became important again. When love for the Bible wanes, superstition and idolatry creep in. The founders of your own denomination likely placed great emphasis on the role of the Bible in Christian living. Yet is it a neglected book in your church? How faithful are you and your class members when it comes to personal Bible reading?

3. REPORTING THE VERDICT. Focus on Huldah the prophetess for part of your lesson. Point out that women have played key roles in the his-

tory of God's people from earliest times. Then call attention to Huldah's message: her warning of disaster for the nation's apostasy, and her comforting of Josiah with the news that judgment would be delayed because of his penitence. The important point here is that individuals and communities alike are accountable to the Lord.

4. RENEWING THE COVENANT. Josiah and his people publicly renewed their sacred pact with the Lord. Make certain your class members understand what "covenant" means. Review the history of God's covenant making, culminating in the new covenant through Jesus Christ. You may also wish to comment that Communion should be understood as an occasion for Christians to renew their personal covenant with Christ. "The cup of the new covenant" calls believers to obey the Lord and His commands.

5. REFORMING THE WORSHIP. To help make the topic of worship more practical and personal, ask students to take a "temperature test." That is, provide a list of ideas, causes, and objects that enjoy a cultlike following in our society. Some of these things seem to have the feel of a religion. Others may be essentially harmless, but can displace God as the top priority in people's lives. Which of these things do your class members "warm to" the most?

Josiah called his people to allow the Lord back into the center of their lives. We should feel warmest about the Lord.

### TOPIC FOR ADULTS
#### BEGINNING AGAIN

*Restoring the Steeple.* Trinity Episcopal Church in Newport, Rhode Island, was built in 1726. Modeled after the great Christopher Wren buildings in London, the lovely old building was designed and built by a local carpenter named Richard Munday. While Wren's structures were constructed of masonry, Munday and his helpers chose to build Trinity out of wood. One result was that insufficient diagonal bracing was forced to withstand the heavy coastal winds. The problem was compounded when two bays were added in 1762, increasing the wind exposure.

When paint on the steeple and outside walls began flaking in 1987, the congregation decided to call in an expert to determine the original shade of white on the historic structure. The restoration expert, Irving B. Haynes, quickly noted that the peeling paint was the least of the old building's problems. His investigation showed that the south gallery was in danger of collapsing and that the entire building was leaning six inches to the north. The semi-detached tower and graceful spire, pressed by prevailing southwest sea winds, tilted more than a foot to the north.

The congregation quickly embarked on a stabilizing project. At the suggestion of a structural engineer, workers inserted a series of steel frames into the walls to attach the tower to the main building. These frames were welded outside the building to prevent fire, then bolted together at the corners. The assembled framework was secured by rows of rock anchors driven twenty feet into the ground. The restoration project stabilized the lovely old church building and has preserved it from collapse.

Trinity Church has been restored and will stand for centuries to come. Josiah's renovation program restored the Jerusalem temple and renewed the spiritual vigor of his people. Likewise, each generation of God's people must experience personal reformation.

*City Upon a Hill.* Just before landing in the New World in 1630, John Winthrop, the first governor of Massachusetts, delivered a sermon describing what he and his fellow Puritans intended to build: "a city upon a hill." He enjoined his shipmates to "delight in each other, make others' conditions our own, rejoice together, mourn together, labor and suffer together, always having before our eyes our . . . community . . . as members of the same body."

The agenda of these devout people included securing comfort and safety for themselves, of course. But their primary purpose was to create a community that would be obedient to God in all things. In this way, they knew they could organize themselves to build a society that would support an ethical and spiritual life.

We must make our large, complex urban centers into more than enterprise zones and new housing projects. Such projects only take into account entrepreneurs' personal interests. As Christians, we have an obligation to God and each other to assume personal responsibility for all our institutions.

*Unexpected Outbreak.* A few years ago, medical experts felt certain that tuberculosis had been wiped out in the developed nations. The use of antibiotics had tamed the once-dreaded disease that had killed millions each year. Medical students in the 1960s were advised not to bother majoring in infectious diseases like TB, but to concentrate on cancer and heart disease. Everyone was confident that no new cases of tuberculosis would appear.

Suddenly a startling flare-up of TB occurred in a high school in Westminster, California, in 1993. The case confounded physicians and public health officials, though they eventually traced the disease to a sixteen-year-old Vietnamese immigrant. However, over four hundred young people, thirty percent of the student body, tested positive for the dreaded infection. Twelve suffered a strain of the disease that resisted standard antibiotic treatment, and one student lost part of her lung.

Sin, idolatry, superstition, and immorality, like bacteria, if left unchecked, can spread and infect an entire community. Ancient Israel and Judah learned this lesson as King Josiah took firm steps to eradicate the deadly virus of disobedience to God. Leaders in the Lord's work must be on guard against "idolatry epidemics" that can erupt in any community.

*Questions for Students on the Next Lesson.* 1. How would you describe Jeremiah's background? 2. What excuses did Jeremiah use in trying to evade God's call? 3. What task did the Lord give Jeremiah at the time of his call? 4. What sense of "call" have you received from God in the past? 5. Has He ever called you to stand against public opinion?

## TOPIC FOR YOUTH
### DEMONSTRATING OBEDIENCE

*Re-created the Garden?* In August 1994, Woodstock '94 tried to re-create the first Woodstock event, which had taken place twenty-five years earlier. The ideals of the new Woodstock supposedly included peace on earth, great music, and great family life. The gathering mixed aging fans, high-tech sound systems, cash machines, portable toilets, and corporate sponsors (such as Pepsi, Apple Computer, and Haagen-Dazs ice cream). About a quarter million people, mostly white and middle-class, attended the three-day weekend. Ultimately, commercialism—based on peoples' desire to live off the sixties myth of the past—left many disillusioned. Attenders had trouble producing the ideal love-in experience as they imagined it had been.

Josiah called his people to a new commitment, a renewed faith and loyalty to the living God; to the Truth, not to an old idea or idealized myth. He called for obedience to a person, not a dream.

*Discovery Sparks New Interest.* An accountant going through an old safe at Eastern Baptist Theological Seminary in Philadelphia found a lost manuscript of two famous piano works, "Fantasia in C Minor" and "Sonata in C Minor," by Wolfgang Amadeus Mozart. Music scholars had not known the location of the manuscripts since 1915. Also found were lesser compositions by Joseph Haydn, Giacomo Meyerbeer, Ludwig Spohr, and Johann Strauss the Elder. Scholars were overjoyed to see the original Mozart manuscripts, written in 1784 and 1785 when Mozart was in his late twenties. They sparked a renewed interest in the composer's music.

In similar fashion, discovery of the book of the covenant brought not only renewed interest in God's Word, but new commitment to God Himself. The whole nation rededicated itself to obeying the Lord.

*Made a Promise.* Jack Arment of Crescent, Pennsylvania, has a barn filled with restored automobiles and fire trucks. His interest in antique vehicles has increased since the day he sold a 1937 Buick. He initially kept the old car parked in his back yard, until a fourteen-year-old teenager asked him if he were interested in selling it. "Sure, for $600," Jack said. The teen shook hands with Arment and then left. After a few days, Arment forgot about the conversation.

But the youth returned a few weeks later with his father. The teen had gone home and then, eventually, to the bank to withdraw the $600 from his savings account. He had finally come to pick up his Buick.

With regret, Jack sold his Buick. He had been taught by his father that if you make a promise, it must be kept. He had struck a bargain with the teen, and he had to keep it.

Israel had to relearn obedience. The people had made an agreement with the Lord, but had forgotten it. Josiah reminded them that they had a bargain with the Lord, a bargain that had to be kept.

*Questions for Students on the Next Lesson.* 1. Who was Jeremiah? When and where did he preach? 2. When did God first indicate that Jeremiah was to be His prophet? 3. Describe the content of Jeremiah's message. 4. What excuses did Jeremiah offer to God? 5. Have you ever avoided God's call? If so, when? Why?

# LESSON 3—SEPTEMBER 15

## *HEARING GOD'S CALL*

*Background Scripture:* Jeremiah 1
*Devotional Reading:* Galatians 1:11-17

### KING JAMES VERSION

Jeremiah 1:4 Then the word of the Lord came unto me, saying,

5 Before I formed thee in the belly I knew thee; and before thou camest forth out of the womb I sanctified thee, and I ordained thee a prophet unto the nations.

6 Then said I, Ah, Lord God! behold, I cannot speak: for I am a child.

7 But the Lord said unto me, Say not, I am a child: for thou shalt go to all that I shall send thee, and whatsoever I command thee thou shalt speak.

8 Be not afraid of their faces: for I am with thee to deliver thee, saith the Lord.

9 Then the Lord put forth his hand, and touched my mouth. And the Lord said unto me, Behold, I have put my words in thy mouth.

10 See, I have this day set thee over the nations and over the kingdoms, to root out, and to pull down, and to destroy, and to throw down, to build, and to plant.

14 Then the Lord said unto me, Out of the north an evil shall break forth upon all the inhabitants of the land.

15 For, lo, I will call all the families of the kingdoms of the north, saith the Lord; and they shall come, and they shall set every one his throne at the entering of the gates of Jerusalem, and against all the walls thereof round about, and against all the cities of Judah.

16 And I will utter my judgments against them touching all their wickedness, who have forsaken me, and have burned incense unto other gods, and worshipped the works of their own hands.

17 Thou therefore gird up thy loins, and arise, and speak unto them all that I command thee: be not dismayed at their faces, lest I confound thee before them.

### NEW REVISED STANDARD VERSION

JEREMIAH 1:4 Now the word of the Lord came to me saying, 5 "Before I formed you in the womb I knew you, and before you were born I consecrated you; I appointed you a prophet to the nations." 6 Then I said, "Ah, Lord God! Truly I do not know how to speak, for I am only a boy." 7 But the Lord said to me, "Do not say 'I am only a boy'; for you shall go to all to whom I send you, and you shall speak whatever I command you, 8 Do not be afraid of them, for I am with you to deliver you, says the Lord." 9 Then the Lord put out his hand and touched my mouth; and the Lord said to me, "Now I have put my word in your mouth. 10 See, today I appoint you over nations and over kingdoms, to pluck up and to pull down, to destroy and to overthrow, to build and to plant."

14 Then the Lord said to me: Out of the north disaster shall break out on all the inhabitants of the land. 15 For now I am calling all the tribes of the kingdoms of the north, says the Lord; and they shall come and all of them shall set their thrones at the entrance of the gates of Jerusalem, against all its surrounding walls and against all the cities of Judah. 16 And I will utter my judgments against them, for all their wickedness in forsaking me; they have made offerings to other gods, and worshiped the works of their own hands. 17 But you, gird up your loins; stand up and tell them everything that I command you. Do not break down before them, or I will break you before them.

*KEY VERSE: The word of the Lord came to [Jeremiah] saying, "Before I formed you in the womb I knew you, and before you were born I consecrated you; I appointed you a prophet to the nations." Jeremiah 1:4, 5.*

## HOME BIBLE READINGS

| Sept. | 9 | M. | Psalm 139:13-18 | *God Creates All People* |
|---|---|---|---|---|
| Sept. | 10 | T. | Jeremiah 2:4-13 | *Israel Forsakes God* |
| Sept. | 11 | W. | Jeremiah 1:18—2:3 | *God Promises Jeremiah Strength* |
| Sept. | 12 | T. | Isaiah 50:4-9 | *Response of an Obedient Servant* |
| Sept. | 13 | F. | Jeremiah 15:15-21 | *Jeremiah Encouraged to Persevere* |
| Sept. | 14 | S. | Jeremiah 20:7-12 | *Jeremiah Persecuted* |
| Sept. | 15 | S. | Jeremiah 20:13-18 | *Jeremiah Laments His Birth* |

## BACKGROUND

Perhaps the reform movement in Judah under King Josiah influenced a young man named Jeremiah. During Josiah's reign, Jeremiah received a call from the Lord to serve and speak on God's behalf.

Undoubtedly Jeremiah was also influenced by his family. He was the son of Hilkiah and descended from a long line of priests. Yet his priestly relatives in his home village of Anathoth later turned against him when he denounced the state of religious affairs in Judah. In 627 B.C., Jeremiah heard the summons of the Lord.

Josiah's reign proved to be a temporary halt in the long period of moral and spiritual decline in Judah. Earlier prophets had warned that the nation faced a day of reckoning. The flagrant disobedience of God's commandments would eventually bring disaster. However, except for Hezekiah and Josiah, the rulers and leaders seemed unconcerned. Fertility cults flourished, injustices continued, the poor suffered, and the rich prospered. Horrid worship practices appeared (in which children were sacrificed), and temple worship was neglected. Sensitive, perceptive believers in the Lord suffered criticism and persecution.

Meanwhile, the Chaldean empire in Babylon was launching its conquest of the Middle East. Assyria, for centuries a most feared and hated nation, was rapidly declining as the Babylonians repeatedly invaded and captured Assyrian territories. Little Judah, caught between these superpowers, seethed with plans and plots. Many in Jerusalem assumed a rosy outlook, believing that Judah would always enjoy relative peace and prosperity.

Jeremiah's call came in the lull when Josiah ushered in a period of reform. But the young prophet soon discovered that God's call would require him to speak unpopular words to a people unwilling to listen. Jeremiah's long ministry during the decline and final days of Jerusalem brought him heartache and suffering. But God's call demands a response of faithfulness, regardless of the conditions.

## NOTES ON THE PRINTED TEXT

With the collapse of Assyria, a strong revival of nationalism gripped Judah. Unfortunately, many citizens believed that God would protect and save His chosen people no matter how they acted. During this period—627 B.C., during the thirteenth year of King Josiah's reign—a young man came from Anathoth, a few miles north of Jerusalem. God told Jeremiah that He had chosen him to be a prophet to the nations before he had even been born. *Before I formed you in the womb I knew you, and before you were born I con-*

secrated you; I appointed you a prophet to the nations (1:5). Jeremiah's father was a priest, as were his earlier ancestors. He was already undergoing the training and preparation for his prophetic task, perhaps even officiating in some civil capacity.

However, Jeremiah protested that he was not ready for God's mission. How could a youth in his teens command the respect of the king and his advisors? He insisted that he was too young and inexperienced. *Then I said, "Ah, Lord God! Truly I do not know how to speak, for I am only a boy"* (1:6).

God refused Jeremiah's protests and excuses, but offered the assurance of His presence. God would empower Jeremiah. *But the Lord said to me, "Do not say, 'I am only a boy,' for you shall go to all to whom I send you, and you shall speak whatever I command you. Do not be afraid of them, for I am with you to deliver you, says the Lord"* (1:7, 8).

To emphasize His presence and empowerment, God touched Jeremiah. That touch imparted God's word into the mouth of Jeremiah. *Then the Lord put out his hand and touched my mouth; and the Lord said to me, "Now I have put my words in your mouth. See, today I appoint you over nations and over kingdoms"* (1:9, 10).

God's word was specific. There would be harsh judgment with doom and destruction, implied in the verbs *to pluck up and to pull down, to destroy and to overthrow* (1:10). However, assurance and hope comes through in the words *to build and to plant* (1:10).

God spoke to Jeremiah through a series of visions. First, Jeremiah saw the branch of an almond tree, a sign of spring, hope, and happiness. But God reminded Jeremiah that the vision also demonstrated His eternal watchfulness and vigilance.

The second vision showed a boiling, cooking pot spilling its contents from the north to the south. Judgment would come from the north. *Out of the north disaster shall break out on all the inhabitants of the land. For now I am calling all the tribes of the kingdoms of the north ... and they shall come and all of them shall set their thrones at the entrance of the gates of Jerusalem, against all its surrounding walls and against all the cities of Judah* (1:14, 15). God's judgment would come through a military operation against Judah because the people had abandoned Him. *And I will utter my judgments against them, for all their wickedness in forsaking me; they have made offerings to other gods; and worshiped the works of their own hands* (1:14-16). Numerous sacred pillars and fertility figurines excavated in Israel testify to the people's deep attachment to other deities.

Jeremiah was told to accept his calling without fear. He must stand firm as God's spokesman. *But you, gird up your loins; stand up and tell them everything that I command you. Do not break down before them, or I will break you before them* (1:17).

## SUGGESTIONS TO TEACHERS

Some mistakenly imagine the call of God as a booming bass voice that trumpets its commands from the heavens. Others think God's call means receiving a special dispensation that relieves one from all stress and problems. Both notions are incorrect, as today's lesson shows.

Perhaps the best way to launch your lesson would be to ask for opinions from your group members. How would they describe the nature of God's call? Then compare their responses with the actual experience of Jeremiah.

1. CONSECRATED FROM THE BEGINNING. Jeremiah realized that he belonged to the Lord, was known and claimed by the Lord even at the moment of his conception. Others through the ages have described their relationship to the Lord in similar fashion. Ignatius of Loyola, for example, stated, "I come from God; I belong to God; I return to God."

Every person who has encountered the living Christ must echo such words. Point out to your students that each of them is known, claimed, and loved by the Lord . . . and therefore called into His service.

2. COMMANDED IN SPITE OF YOUTH. Jeremiah acknowledged the Lord's call, but hesitated to respond. He pleaded that he was inexperienced, that he was too young. God brushed aside all such excuses and refused to accept a no from Jeremiah.

Take some time in your session to look at some of the excuses we may use today when we wish to avoid God's call. Inexperience? Impossible task? Uncertainty about the outcome? Remind your students that God stands with those He calls. And He asks only that we be faithful, not successful.

3. CALLED FOR UNPOPULAR TASK. When God calls us, He often calls us to a specific task. And God's call is always to serve. Jeremiah's call to serve led him to speak to a nation that was enjoying a revival of religious nationalism. Popular sentiment held that Assyria was tottering and that the future was bright. Jeremiah, responding to the Lord's question, "What do you see?" (1:11, 13), realized that Babylon would be God's agent for Jerusalem's judgment.

We can learn from Jeremiah's experience. Our own daily call will also be the call to serve, possibly in difficult and thankless ways. We, too, may be misunderstood and criticized. Being a servant of the Lord brings us joy, but not necessarily happy circumstances.

4. CONTROLLED BY GOD. Ask your class members to study Jeremiah 1:17b-19 for a few moments. In spite of hostility that would be directed at Jeremiah, God would be with him. Furthermore, God assured Jeremiah that divine strength overcomes human opposition. "They will fight against you; but they shall not prevail against you, for I am with you, says the Lord, to deliver you" (1:19). Let these mighty words of encouragement inspire your group members to renewed commitment.

## TOPIC FOR ADULTS
### RESPONDING TO GOD'S CALL

*Excuses, Excuses!* An often-used alibi is "I am too young." Yet Alexander the Great conquered the world at thirty-three.

George Washington was appointed an adjutant general at nineteen, was sent at twenty-one as an ambassador to treat with the French, and won his first battle as a colonel at twenty-two.

Lafayette was made general of the whole French army at twenty.

Gladstone was in Parliament before he was twenty-two—and at twenty-four became Lord of the Treasury.

Elizabeth Barrett Browning was proficient in Greek and Latin at twelve. Robert Browning wrote marvelously at twelve.

Luther was but twenty-nine when he nailed his ninety-five theses to the church door.

Nelson was a lieutenant in the British navy before he was twenty and was only forty-seven when he received his death wound at Trefalgar.

Others use old age—the weight of the years—as an excuse. However, Tallyrand was French Ambassador to Britain at eighty.

Tennyson wrote "Crossing the Bar" at eighty.

Benjamin Franklin signed the U.S. Constitution at eighty-one.

Voltaire finished his tragedy *Irene* at eighty-four.

Gladstone was premier of Britain at eighty-five.

Verdi composed his opera *Falstaff* at eighty-five.

Michelangelo designed the dome of St. Peter's in Rome at eighty-seven.

When Oliver Wendell Holmes was ninety, Congress cut his pension. Said he, "I expect I will be able to stand the pay cut, but what worries me is that I will not be able to put aside as much as usual for my old age."

*Called to Save Their Community.* Sarah Hunt Pearson is a retired teacher; Ella Mae Barnes, a homemaker; Betty Holsey, a nurse. They are black women living in a poor area near Devereux, Georgia, that has little industry outside of pulpwood cutting and guarding inmates at a local state prison. Yet these three sensed a call by God to save their church, their land, and their community from becoming the location of the largest garbage dump in Georgia. However, their commitment cost them.

In 1987, an out-of-town developer, Dixie Recycling System, Inc., proposed building an 887-acre landfill around Mitchell Chapel African Methodist Episcopal Church, where the three women had been longtime members. The proposed landfill would receive ten thousand tons of waste per day. Sarah Hunt Pearson, Ella Mae Barnes, Betty Holsey, and others learned that such a dump would mean trash trains rolling into Hancock County day and night, turning it into the dumping ground of the Eastern United States. These women also discovered that the trash would destroy the community's clean water and air.

A protracted court battle followed, but opponents of the landfill were finally able to void its state permit. The whole process, however, produced technical rulings that left only seven of the original opponents eligible to be listed as petitioners in the court case. Three of these were in effect bought off, dropping their appeal "for an agreed-upon sum and other consideration" from Dixie Recycling. That left Ms. Pearson, Ms. Barnes, Ms. Holsey, and one other (Susan Holmes, who moved from the area) as the only persons standing against the developer.

Dixie Recycling offered each woman $50,000, then $75,000 each, to drop her appeal. Each refused. The company offered to air-condition their little church and pave the road leading from the state highway to Mitchell Chapel, hoping to induce church members to bring pressure on the women. But the women and their congregation turned down the money and the enticements. Their attorney, Christopher Coates, could have made $100,000 for himself if the women had gone along with the developer's offers. But Coates, an elder at the Presbyterian Church of Milledgeville, agreed with their commitment to the health and welfare of their community and counted it a privilege to stand with such clients.

Responding to God's call means taking a stand and facing challenges.

*Costly Call.* Bishop Able Muzore of Zimbabwe tells of a critical period in his life when he had been asked by his people to lead the African National Council. He knew that all previous leaders in Rhodesia who criticized government policies (which were unjust to Black Rhodesians) had been either deported from the country, placed in a restricted camp, or killed.

Muzore struggled with his decision and prayed as he had never prayed before. Naturally, he did not want to be killed, deported, or placed in a camp, yet his people were calling him to lead them. As he struggled with his decision, a friend handed him this poem:

> People are unreasonable, illogical, and
>     self-centered—love them anyway.
> If you do good, people will accuse you
>     of selfish, ulterior motives—do good anyway.
> If you are successful, you will win false
>     friends and true enemies—succeed anyway.
> The good you do today will be forgotten
>     tomorrow—do good anyway.
> Honesty and frankness make you vulnerable—
>     be honest and frank anyway.
> The biggest people with the biggest ideas
>     can be shot down by the smallest people
>     with the smallest minds—think big anyway.
> People favor underdogs but follow only top dogs—
>     fight for some underdog anyway.
> What you spend years building may be destroyed
>     overnight—build anyway.
> Give the world the best you've got and you'll get
>     kicked in the teeth—give the world the best
>     you've got anyway.

*Questions for Students on the Next Lesson.* 1. What message comes through in Jeremiah's temple sermon? 2. Why was the worship site at Shiloh destroyed? 3. How did the people respond to Jeremiah's warnings? 4. What is your congregation doing to work for justice and human rights? 5. Does your church understand the relationship between worshiping God and acting justly toward others?

## TOPIC FOR YOUTH
### WHO, ME?

*An Option?* National leaders of the Girl Scouts acknowledge the growing religious and ethnic diversity among the 2.5 million scouts. Believing that such diversity would attract people who might disagree with the Scouts' traditional pledge to serve God, delegates to the national convention voted overwhelmingly to change the official wording in their pledge. Now, in an effort to be more inclusive, the girls may pledge service to the spiritual power of their conscience, or make no such pledge at all.

Some scouts and other citizens are deeply disappointed, noting that a pledge to serve has been divorced from a statement of values or religious ideals. Now a girl has the option to substitute whatever she deems appropriate as the motive for service—simply to be politically correct.

Jeremiah never saw God's call to service as an option. He was appointed a spokesman for God before he was even born. Throughout his ministry, Jeremiah said things that were clearly politically incorrect in his nation. Throughout Jeremiah's ministry, God continued to challenge Jeremiah to stand firm. Never once was it an option to serve.

*Youth's Foe.* Young people must learn to handle anxiety before they are taught anything else. This is the view of Mary MacCracken, a physical education professor at the University of Akron and Robert Stadulis of Kent State University, who completed a fourteen-year study that they hope will help students perform better in the classroom, on the athletic field, or in the concert hall.

The two researchers studied how anxiety affects children's performance and how competitive anxiety changes as children get older. They found that boys were less anxious about competition. They also discovered that spectators increased the anxiety of performers. Their findings also showed that children performed best when partnered with someone else. Their conclusion was that children need to be taught how to deal constructively with their anxiety.

Jeremiah knew all about anxiety. As a mere teen, he felt unworthy to carry out the task God set before him. He felt that he was too young. Yet God reminded Jeremiah that he was not alone. Jeremiah could rely on his Lord. He could be confident that everyone would hear the divine message.

*Concerned about Future Generations.* To some, he is just an "old geezer" in his 90s advocating a return to the good old days. However, the elderly Dr. Benjamin Spock, one of the world's best-known child experts, is concerned about our nation's youth. He says his new mission is based on a need to save our country's children from a society going downhill. He reels off what he labels modern atrocities: instability in marriage and the family, cruel competitiveness (especially in business, sports, and education), racial and ethnic divisiveness, rampant materialism, increasing violence, casual attitudes towards sex, a lack of quality day care and education, and a decline in spiritual and ethical values.

Spock advocates a return to spiritual values, along with a sense of respect for others and recommitment to the ideals of kindness, helpfulness, and service.

Do you agree? Are you concerned enough about your future to join in this senior citizen's commitment? Are you concerned enough with the similar values that spurred Jeremiah to risk even his life?

*Questions for Students on the Next Lesson. 1.* For whom does a prophet speak? 2. Why was Jeremiah in the temple? 3. What message comes through in Jeremiah's sermon? 4. What happened when Jeremiah finished his sermon? 5. Why would it be so difficult to speak against the policies of your own nation?

# LESSON 4—SEPTEMBER 22

## *PROCLAIMING GOD'S WORD*

*Background Scripture:* Jeremiah 7
*Devotional Reading:* Micah 6:1-8

### KING JAMES VERSION

JEREMIAH 7:1 The word that came to Jeremiah from the Lord, saying,

2 Stand in the gate of the Lord's house and proclaim there this word, and say, Hear the word of the Lord, all ye of Judah, that enter in at these gates to worship the Lord.

3 Thus saith the Lord of hosts, the God of Israel, Amend your ways and your doings, and I will cause you to dwell in this place.

4 Trust ye not in lying words, saying, The temple of the Lord, The temple of the Lord, The temple of the Lord, are these.

5 For if ye thoroughly amend your ways and your doings; if ye thoroughly execute judgment between a man and his neighbour;

6 If ye oppress not the stranger, the fatherless, and the widow, and shed not innocent blood in this place, neither walk after other gods to your hurt:

7 Then will I cause you to dwell in this place, in the land that I gave to your fathers, for ever and ever.

8 Behold, ye trust in lying words, that cannot profit.

9 Will ye steal, murder, and commit adultery, and swear falsely, and burn incense unto Baal, and walk after other gods whom ye know not;

10 And come and stand before me in this house, which is called by my name, and say, We are delivered to do all these abominations?

11 Is this house, which is called by my name, become a den of robbers in your eyes? Behold, even I have seen it, saith the Lord.

12 But go ye now unto my place which was in Shiloh, where I set my name at the first, and see what I did to it for the wickedness of my people Israel.

13 And now, because ye have done all these works, saith the Lord, and I spake unto you, rising up early and speaking, but ye heard not; and I called you, but ye answered not;

14 Therefore will I do unto this house, which is called by my name, wherein ye trust, and unto the place which I gave to you and to your fathers, as I have done to Shiloh.

15 And I will cast you out of my sight, as I

### NEW REVISED STANDARD VERSION

JEREMIAH 7:1 The word that came to Jeremiah from the Lord; 2 Stand in the gate of the Lord's house, and proclaim there this word, and say, Hear the word of the Lord, all you people of Judah, you that enter these gates to worship the Lord. 3 Thus says the Lord of hosts, the God of Israel: Amend your ways and your doings, and let me dwell with you in this place. 4 Do not trust in these deceptive words: "This is the temple of the Lord, the temple of the Lord, the temple of the Lord."

5 For if you truly amend your ways and your doings, if you truly act justly one with another, 6 if you do not oppress the alien, the orphan, and the widow, or shed innocent blood in this place, and if you do not go after other gods to your own hurt, 7 then I will dwell with you in this place, in the land that I gave of old to your ancestors forever and ever.

8 Here you are, trusting in deceptive words to no avail. 9 Will you steal, murder, commit adultery, swear falsely, make offerings to Baal, and go after other gods that you have not known, 10 and then come and stand before me in this house, which is called by my name, and say, "We are safe!"—only to go on doing all these abominations? 11 Has this house, which is called by my name, become a den of robbers in your sight? You know, I too am watching, says the Lord. 12 Go now to my place that was in Shiloh, where I made my name dwell at first, and see what I did to it for the wickedness of my people Israel. 13 And now, because you have done all these things, says the Lord, and when I spoke to you persistently, you did not listen, and when I called you, you did not answer, 14 therefore I will do to the house that is called by my name, in which you trust, and to the place that I gave to you and to your ancestors, just what I did to Shiloh. 15 And I will cast you out of my sight, just as I cast out all your kinsfolk, all the offspring of Ephraim.

have cast out all your brethren, even the
whole seed of Ephraim.

*KEY VERSE: Thus says the Lord of hosts, the God of Israel: Amend your
ways and your doings, and let me dwell with you in this place.* Jeremiah
7:3.

## HOME BIBLE READINGS

| | | | |
|---|---|---|---|
| *Sept.* | *16* | *M.* | Jeremiah 7:16-26 | *People Refuse to Obey God* |
| *Sept.* | *17* | *T.* | Jeremiah 7:27-34 | *People Will Not Listen to Jeremiah* |
| *Sept.* | *18* | *W.* | Jeremiah 8:8-17 | *People Are Stubbornly Unrepentant* |
| *Sept.* | *19* | *T.* | Jeremiah 8:18-22 | *Jeremiah Mourns for the People* |
| *Sept.* | *20* | *F.* | Jeremiah 9:12-24 | *True Wisdom Is in Knowing the Lord* |
| *Sept.* | *21* | *S.* | Jeremiah 18:1-11 | *People Called to Amend Their Ways* |
| *Sept.* | *22* | *S.* | Jeremiah 10:1-10 | *The Lord Is the True God* |

## BACKGROUND

Jeremiah encountered a smug sense of superiority and self-righteousness among his people. It was as if they were saying, "We're God's chosen
ones, the holy ones. Therefore, He would never let any catastrophe happen
to His holy people or His holy city."

Jeremiah knew that the people regarded the temple as a kind of good-
luck charm. The prophet also watched with dismay as his fellow citizens
continued to dabble in various cults, indulge in immoral behavior, and permit social injustices. He knew that the ceremonies in the temple were being
celebrated as usual. But many in the nation felt that simply carrying out
these religious rites kept everyone in Judah on good terms with the Lord,
allowing folks to do as they pleased. It had all become mechanical. Faith
was a set of trade-offs with God ensuring divine blessings. The phrase,
"This is the temple of the Lord," had become a hollow slogan. The people
repeated it constantly, as if to say that God would keep them from all harm
as long as the sacred structure stood.

God's call to Jeremiah meant serving as God's spokesman. And serving
as God's spokesman called for delivering tough words to God's people. They
would be words Jerusalem's citizens would not want to hear. Jeremiah realized that the people were not willing to take God's words to heart.
Nevertheless, the prophet obeyed.

One day he stood in the portico at the entrance of the magnificent temple and preached a startling sermon. His hearers seethed at the message.
The report of this sermon in Jeremiah 7 tells us that Jeremiah denounced
his fellow citizens for their hypocrisy and immorality. Worse, he predicted
a dire end to the holy place. Referring to the terrible destruction of the
ancient shrine at Shiloh in the days of Samuel, five centuries earlier (see
I Sam. 4—6), Jeremiah stated that the same fate awaited the temple in
Jerusalem.

## NOTES ON THE PRINTED TEXT

*Stand in the gate of the Lord's house, and proclaim. . . . Hear the word of the Lord, all you people of Judah, you that enter these gates to worship the Lord* (7:2). During one of the great religious festivals (perhaps in 608 or 609 B.C., when Jehoiakim was crowned king), God commanded Jeremiah to stand in the gate of the court area and proclaim God's message to those coming to worship.

Jeremiah preached reform. *Amend your ways and your doings, and let me dwell with you in this place* (7:3). Judah had deteriorated morally and religiously, its moral and spiritual foundation having collapsed. People must change their ways if God was to continue to call the temple His house.

He also challenged the people not to trust in the temple, the symbol of God's presence with them. The people believed that the temple in Jerusalem guaranteed their welfare and protection. This was superstition, Jeremiah bellowed, mouthing their slogan. *Do not trust in these deceptive words: "This is the temple of the Lord, the temple of the Lord, the temple of the Lord"* (7:4).

Jeremiah pointed to certain areas needing reform. Judah's people had victimized the poor, the foreigners, the powerless orphans and widows. They needed to change their ways. If they would begin to act justly toward one another and stay away from false gods, the Lord would dwell with them. *For if you truly amend your ways and your doings, if you truly act justly one with another, if you do not oppress the alien, the orphan, and the widow, or shed innocent blood in this place, and if you do not go after other gods to your own hurt, then I will dwell with you in this place, in the land that I gave of old to your ancestors forever and ever* (7:5-7).

Speaking through Jeremiah, God condemned those who engaged in sinful acts while continuing to worship in the temple. As he watched the crowds of festival-goers enter, he recited their crimes, violations of the first, second, sixth, seventh, eighth, and ninth commandments. The people had disregarded God's covenant. They clung to the absurd notion that God would always remain in His temple and keep it safe. *Here you are, trusting in deceptive words to no avail. Will you steal, murder, commit adultery, swear falsely, make offerings to Baal, and go after other gods that you have not known, and then come and stand before me in this house, which is called by my name, and say, "We are safe!"—only to go on doing all these abominations?* (7:8-10).

Jeremiah compared the worshipers to criminals who commit all sorts of terrible crimes and then flee to a secret hideout. The only difference was that the worshipers fled to the temple for safety, stupidly believing that they were escaping the consequences of their actions. *Has this house, which is called by my name, become a den of robbers in your sight?* (7:11). He reminded the listeners that God was neither blind nor naive. *You know, I too, am watching, says the Lord* (7:11).

If the worshipers needed confirmation of His intent, they need look no further than the ancient sanctuary of Shiloh. *Go now to my place that was in Shiloh, where I made my name dwell at first, and see what I did to it for the wickedness of my people Israel* (7:12). Shiloh had been the center of the tribal league. Located in the territory of Ephraim, twelve miles south of

Shechem and about the same distance north of Gibeah, the site housed the ark of the covenant. The Philistines had overrun the site, carried off the ark, and burned the town to the ground. Total desolation remained. Jeremiah cited this event as an example of God's anger and wrath upon the wickedness of His people.

Jeremiah concluded his temple sermon with a fearful promise. Because the people persisted in their immorality, oppression, and idolatry, they would meet the same fate as those at Shiloh. They and the temple would be destroyed. *And now, because you have done all these things, says the Lord, and when I spoke to you persistently, you did not listen, and when I called you, you did not answer, therefore, I will do to the house that is called by my name, in which you trust, and to the place that I gave to you and to your ancestors, just what I did to Shiloh. And I will cast you out of my sight, just as I cast out all your kinsfolk, all the offspring of Ephraim* (7:13-15).

## SUGGESTIONS TO TEACHERS

Imagine someone interrupting worship at Washington Cathedral on Easter Sunday and delivering a fiery sermon without being invited. Imagine this person criticizing the nation and all the churches for their moral and spiritual failures. Or picture an intruder standing up in Westminister Abbey during a Christmas Eve service attended by royalty and denouncing the worshipers for their hypocrisy. That was Jeremiah when he offered his temple sermon described in today's lesson.

Launch your lesson by describing what Jeremiah might say if he were to appear unannounced during a Sunday service at your church. Ask your students for suggestions: What things might Jeremiah have to say to us? How might he view the spiritual state of our congregation, or the commitment of Christians in our country, in the face of its poverty and violence? What would be our reaction to Jeremiah's pronouncements?

Then turn to Jeremiah 7 and survey a few of the highlights in Jeremiah's temple sermon:

1. INDICATION OF HYPOCRISY. The Jerusalem worshipers assumed they were God's pets. They thought they could never suffer harm. Self-righteously, they chanted, "This is the temple of the Lord!"

Some people in our era, too, imagine they have divine protection from all misfortune because they occasionally attend church. God demands more than a tip of the hat to Him. He does not barter or curry favors. Those who imagine that occasional attendance at worship and a bit of spare cash will butter up the Lord are deluding themselves.

2. INSISTANCE ON REFORM. Just as Jeremiah called his hearers to repent and change their ways, God demands a radical change in attitudes and lifestyles today. Ask your class to think about what kinds of reform the Lord may be calling Christians to undertake in North American churches. Are the stewardship practices in your congregation, for example, consistent with Christ's call for true sacrifice? Is the care for shut-ins delegated only to a few, permitting the rest of the members to ignore those confined to nursing homes? Is Christian education the concern of everyone, or only of the few who are willing to teach Sunday school?

3. IMPLICATIONS OF DISOBEDIENCE. Jeremiah offers hard words

for the disobedient: "I will cast you out of my sight" (7:15). God will not be trifled with. Persons insisting upon putting themselves first are without God in their lives. Some might say this is a definition of hell.

4. INCLINATION TOWARD IDOLATRY. Discuss what forms of "idol worship" flourish in North American society. Although people may not literally bow before a carved image, they may permit other loyalties to displace the Lordship of Christ. Some of these lesser loyalties may not be evil in themselves (such as attention to job or concern for personal security). Others, such as pornography or gambling, are addictive and destructive.

5. INEVITABILITY OF DESTRUCTION. Jeremiah warned Jerusalem of its inevitable doom because of its evil ways. Disobedience destroys fellowship with God. And the broken relationship cuts the offender off from the Lord's sustaining mercy.

## TOPIC FOR ADULTS
### CONFRONTING HYPOCRISY

*Amends for Past Injustices.* Determined to make amends for past injustices to native peoples, the British Columbia Conference of the United Church of Canada has put its money where its apology is. At its 1994 convocation in Vancouver, the conference gave $1 million to a native-run council within the United Church.

The money from the British Columbia Conference will be used by native groups to support land claims, foster self-government, challenge water diversion projects, finance exploratory wilderness programs, develop community programs, and educate whites and natives about one another.

*Promise Keepers.* Bill McCartney, coach of the University of Colorado football team, wondered what it would be like if an entire football stadium could be filled with men to hear the Good News of Jesus Christ. In 1991, over four thousand men showed up in Colorado for what was called a Promise Keepers Conference. In July 1992, attendance swelled to twenty-two thousand. Promise Keepers Conferences of over fifty-thousand men have been packing stadiums each year since. But these gatherings offer more than just back-slapping camaraderie in a religious setting. The Gospel is presented, strongly and effectively evangelical, but the message comes packaged with an insistence on social justice, too: "A Promise Keeper is committed to reaching beyond any racial and denominational barriers to demonstrate the power of biblical unity."

McCartney constantly calls for racial equality and integration, including the acknowledgment and redress of past oppression. In *Seven Promises of a Promise Keeper,* he writes, "Biblical love and unity demand that we . . . share the pain of those who have been hurt by past domination. They oblige us to seek forgiveness for the sins of our fathers and for the same racial oppression that continues to this day."

*Indifference toward Africa.* Each year the industrialized countries send $60 billion in aid to Africa. But these same nations earn $125 billion annually from arms sales to that continent, where one-third of the countries (sixteen of them) are fighting civil wars. Even worse than this disparity between helping and destroying is the industrialized nations' indifference toward Africa in general.

World problems are solvable if we attack them with the sort of vigor we display in war. The director of the World Health Organization has noted that Operation Desert Storm cost twenty times what it costs to design a basic HIV prevention program for developing countries.

Malnutrition among children is a critical problem in Luanda. Massive spending for military hardware limits the funds available for food, which in government-controlled areas must be imported from the West. *The Economist* reported in 1994 that three million of Angola's eleven million people require emergency food assistance. The United Nations predicts that by the year 2000 more than one-third of Africans will be living in absolute poverty. In a country like Angola, paralyzed by war, the number will no doubt be higher.

*Questions for Students on the Next Lesson.* 1. Describe the historical situation when Habakkuk wrote. 2. What were some of Habakkuk's questions for God? 3. How did the Lord answer these questions? 4. How do you respond when prayers seem to go unanswered? 5. When is it most difficult for you to maintain your trust in God?

## TOPIC FOR YOUTH
### SPEAKING OUT

*Sharing Their Lives.* Krystin Granberg, a student at Princeton, traveled to Mexico and Guatemala as part of a cross-cultural missions project. To prepare for the eight-week trip, Krystin had to study Spanish intensively for four weeks. Then she set off for the mountains of Chiapas, Mexico, and the highlands of Guatemala.

In Chiapas, deep in southern Mexico, she worked in a refugee camp for Guatemalans. Krystin heard stories of family members simply "disappearing" at the hands of the army. She saw the Guatemalan army's maiming, burning, and murdering ways. She heard the refugees' stories of fleeing into the jungles, moving across corn fields, trying to eke out a living on the run, then being turned away by the Mexicans. In both places, Krystin wrestled with issues of poverty and oppression while participating in the peoples' life-and-death struggle for existence.

Now she writes and speaks about her experience, calling on people to help Central Americans live with dignity as children of God. Like Jeremiah, this young person challenges people to amend their ways and consider their Christian commitment to others.

*Modern Crusader.* Jason Bostedo's brother, Daniel, was shot and killed during a drug deal in February, 1993. Young Jason immediately became interested in clearing his town (Wilkinsburg, Pennsylvania) of drugs. He sought the help of community and church leaders, politicians, and the police. One of Jason's earliest efforts was to organize marches. The marches continue to grow in number despite troubling incidents.

Bottles and rocks have been thrown at the marchers. As the group marched on August 27, 1994, police officer James F. Carraway was shot in the left thigh after he had responded to a call to help threatened marchers. Bostedo himself received death threats after videotaping bystanders during the parade. Yet he plans to continue crusading.

Jeremiah discovered how hard it is to take a stand and speak out for righteousness. Yet the Lord gave him the courage to speak out, urging those around him to amend their ways and act justly.

*Nailed for His No.* Eight-year-old Terry Snyder knew right from wrong. Three older youths, aged 14, 10, and 9, urged him repeatedly to shoplift a pipe for them from a local drug store in Somerset, Pennsylvania. When Terry refused, the boys grabbed him and dragged him into the woods. There, while two boys held him down, a third used a hammer and drove nails into his feet. Then the attackers pulled the nails from the back of his heels and stuck golf tees into the cuts before they let Snyder go free.

Terry was treated by a physician, and the three boys were eventually arrested by Somerset police. While afraid, Terry spoke out against his attackers—and for what he knew was truthful and correct. Like Terry and Jeremiah, we too are called to speak out for what is right and just.

*Questions for Students on the Next Lesson.* 1. Who was Habakkuk? When and where did he prophesy? 2. Describe the moral and spiritual atmosphere of the times. 3. What popular beliefs did Habakkuk challenge? 4. If God is so active in our world, why does He often seem absent? 5. How can people be faithful to God in difficult times?

# LESSON 5—SEPTEMBER 29

## CONTINUING TO TRUST

*Background Scripture:* Habakkuk
*Devotional Reading:* Psalm 31:1-10

### KING JAMES VERSION

HABAKKUK 2:1 I will stand upon my watch, and set me upon the tower, and will watch to see what he will say unto me, and what I shall answer when I am reproved.

2 And the Lord answered me, and said, Write the vision, and make it plain upon tables, that he may run that readeth it.

3 For the vision is yet for an appointed time, but at the end it shall speak, and not lie: though it tarry, wait for it; because it will surely come, it will not tarry.

4 Behold, his soul which is lifted up is not upright in him: but the just shall live by his faith.

3:17 Although the fig tree shall not blossom, neither shall fruit be in the vines; the labour of the olive shall fail, and the fields shall yield no meat; the flock shall be cut off from the fold, and there shall be no herd in the stalls:

18 Yet I will rejoice in the Lord, I will joy in the God of my salvation.

19 The Lord God is my strength and he will make my feet like hinds' feet, and he will make me to walk upon mine high places. To the chief singer on my stringed instruments.

### NEW REVISED STANDARD VERSION

HABAKKUK 2:1 I will stand at my watchpost, and station myself on the rampart; I will keep watch to see what he will say to me, and what he will answer concerning my complaint. 2 Then the Lord answered me and said: Write the vision; make it plain on tablets, so that a runner may read it. 3 For there is still a vision for the appointed time; it speaks of the end, and does not lie. If it seems to tarry, wait for it; it will surely come, it will not delay. 4 Look at the proud! Their spirit is not right in them, but the righteous live by their faith.

3:17 Though the fig tree does not blossom, and no fruit is on the vines; though the produce of the olive fails, and the fields yield no food; though the flock is cut off from the fold, and there is no herd in the stalls,

18 yet I will rejoice in the Lord; I will exult in the God of my salvation. 19 God, the Lord, is my strength; he makes my feet like the feet of a deer, and makes me tread upon the heights.

*KEY VERSE: Though the fig tree does not blossom, and no fruit is on the vines . . . yet I will rejoice in the Lord; I will exult in the God of my salvation.* Habakkuk 3:17, 18.

## HOME BIBLE READINGS

## BACKGROUND

Habakkuk lived in a dying nation. Although Judah would manage to survive for another thirteen years, by 600 B.C. the death throes had already begun. Judah was a vassal state, having suffered the domination of foreign powers for years. While paying tribute to Assyria, the nation had barely managed to cling to its existence and identity.

When the Assyrian empire finally fell, Judah saw a glimmer of hope for independence. The Chaldeans (Babylonians) began to consolidate the remains of the old Assyrian realm into their empire, and for a brief period of years, Jerusalem did not pay heavy tribute. But the Egyptians moved into the vacuum left by the collapse of Assyria and took control of Judah.

Then the mighty Babylonian ruler Nebuchadnezzar came to power and determined to reclaim the former Assyrian territories in the west, including Judah. By 597 B.C., Nebuchadnezzar had made Judah a captive state with a vassal king named Zedekiah in charge.

Judah seethed with false pride and vain hopes. As long as its leaders paid the heavy annual tribute to Nebuchadnezzar, they could continue as a province with some degree of autonomy. Fired up by nationalistic fervor, however, many of Judah's leaders deluded themselves with heady dreams of freedom. Turmoil, terror, and tragedy followed. Zedekiah was forced to watch the execution of his sons before being blinded and marched to Babylon. In Jerusalem, the temple was burned and the bulk of the citizens deported to Babylon.

As a contemporary of Jeremiah, the prophet Habakkuk tried to make sense of these troubled times. In the face of atrocities by the brutal Babylonians, Habakkuk asked God why He remained silent. How could the righteous Lord allow a cruel, violent people to destroy people more righteous? Why did a just God permit the wicked Babylonians to inflict such barbarities on a less barbarous people? Habakkuk's answer from God constitutes one of the high points of Scripture: "The righteous live by their faith" (2:4).

## NOTES ON THE PRINTED TEXT

Prior to the destruction of Jerusalem, a devout man named Habakkuk prayed. He was perplexed as to why God permitted the nation's sins to go unpunished. If God were holy, then wickedness should be dealt with, not ignored.

Habakkuk learned that God was using the Babylonians as His agents of judgment and punishment. Habakkuk was horrified. How could God utilize a terribly wicked Gentile nation to punish what was apparently a less wicked Jewish one? He did not understand. After raising some perplexing questions, Habakkuk awaited answers from God.

*I will stand at my watch post, and station myself on the rampart; I will keep watch to see what he will say to me, and what he will answer concerning my complaint* (2:1). Habakkuk strolled the massive walls of Jerusalem and stood in its towers awaiting God's answer. Here he resolutely maintained his vigil.

An answer was given in the form of a vision. God instructed Habakkuk to write down the vision so large, perhaps on a billboard, that anyone running by could read it quickly. Then the Lord answered me and said: *Write the vision; make it plain on tablets, so that a runner may read it* (2:2).

God told Habakkuk of His purpose. That purpose, authored by Him and no one else, was being fulfilled in its own time. *For there is still a vision for the appointed time; it speaks of the end, and does not lie. If it seems to tarry, wait for it; it will surely come, it will not delay* (2:3).

In the meantime, Habakkuk was not to be dismayed. Instead, he was to live faithfully. He was not to rely on himself like the proud. His confidence, trust, and dependence were to be in God as he placed his life in God's hands. *Look at the proud! Their spirit is not right in them, but the righteous live by their faith* (2:4).

In answering Habakkuk, God pointed to the difference in attitude between the unrighteous and the righteous. The Babylonians were also guilty and unrighteous, and they, like Israel, would be judged. The prophet could recognize that God was working out His purpose, even through Babylon.

Habakkuk burst into song, proclaiming renewed trust in God. Yet difficult times were at hand. The potential for hunger was real, given crop failures and the scorched-earth policy of the Babylonians. Nevertheless, in the face of all this, Habakkuk could still declare his absolute and joyful trust in God. *Though the fig tree does not blossom, and no fruit is on the vines; though the flock is cut off from the fold and there is no herd in the stalls, yet I will rejoice in the Lord; I will exult in the God of my salvation* (3:17, 18).

Despite the injustice and potential violence around him, plus the threat of an invasion, Habakkuk received strength and support. *God, the Lord, is my strength; he makes my feet like the feet of a deer, and makes me tread upon the heights* (3:19).

## SUGGESTIONS TO TEACHERS

Some of your class members may have read Harold Kushner's *When Bad Things Happen to Good People*. This popular book reexamined the question asked so long ago by Habakkuk. Although not every student will be familiar with Rabbi Kushner's book, all have, at some time in their lives, pondered the seeming silence of God when trouble hits. They will be helped by this lesson. The "problem of pain" faces every sensitive person, and Habakkuk offers significant insights that are still relevant today.

1. PROTEST AND PLEA. Habakkuk maintains a rugged honesty before God. No cheap piety for this prophet! He utters his complaint in the face of all the terrible calamities facing his nation. Evil and injustice flourished within Judah, and the cruel Babylonians threatened from without. Habakkuk pleaded with the Lord to intervene, but the Lord seemed blind and deaf to his cries.

Encourage your students to talk about times when the Lord seemed to ignore their requests for help. Focus on the need for a candid approach to God in prayer, using Habakkuk's example.

2. PROMISE AND POWER. God assured Habakkuk that justice would come in due time, even if the prophet did not live to see it. The Lord then called Habakkuk to continue to trust Him regardless of the circumstances. With this great summons to faith, Habakkuk begin to realize that God

would take action in His own good time. The prophet could rely on the Lord to accomplish His purposes. Focusing on Habakkuk 2:4, remind your class members that justification by faith, the great Pauline doctrine, springs from the Old Testament. We have the same God as Habakkuk had.

3. PREDICTION AND PERDITION. The inevitable result of Judah's wickedness, Habakkuk was convinced, would be the ruin of the nation. The moral decay within Judah posed as great a threat as the menacing demands of Nebuchadnezzar.

What would Habakkuk have to say to our nation today? Ask: What are the greatest moral dangers in our society? How can we keep from accommodating ourselves to the anti-Christian values of our culture?

4. POETRY AND PRESENCE. Focus on the great verses in 3:17-19, Habakkuk's hymn of hope. The prophet promised a joy in the midst of calamity and uncertainty. Anyone can have a "fair weather religion" when life goes smoothly. Faith comes easily when we are healthy, secure, and comfortable. But when disasters threaten to overwhelm, we need help. Habakkuk's message brings us hope. And for us, who remember how God brought life out of death through the Resurrection of our Lord Jesus Christ, Habakkuk 3:17-19 rings true.

## TOPIC FOR ADULTS
### CONTINUING TO TRUST

*Celebration in Spite of Sadness.* Palm Sunday, March 27, 1994: a tornado roared through Piedmont, Alabama. Worshipers in the Palm Sunday service at the Goshen United Methodist Church had no warning. Suddenly the force of the tornado brought the roof crashing onto the congregation. Twenty persons, including six children, were killed, and more than ninety were injured. One of the six children who died in the catastrophe was four-year-old Hannah Clem, daughter of the pastor, Kelly Clem.

One week later, the Goshen congregation gathered to celebrate an Easter sunrise service. Facing the flattened sanctuary as they assembled in the parking lot, the survivors hugged and wept. The Rev. Kelly Clem, her face heavily bruised by the disaster the previous Sunday, read from Romans and gave the children's sermon. Although mourning the loss of her daughter, Kelly led the 200 worshipers in celebrating the Resurrection. Through their tears, the Goshen believers worshiped their living Redeemer.

*Gift of Gospel Music.* Mahalia Jackson, hailed as the world's greatest gospel singer, rose from humble beginnings. Born to poor parents in New Orleans, she lived for a time in a three-room shack between the railroad tracks and the Mississippi levee. Her mother died when Mahalia was five.

Raised by an aunt, the future queen of gospel music regularly attended the Mount Moriah Baptist Church and began singing in the choir as a four year old. Even then, people could hear that her voice was a special gift from God. By the time she reached her fourteenth birthday, Mahalia was known as "the skinny girl with the big voice." But her education ended in the eighth grade, when she begain working as a laundress.

A few years later, moving to Chicago to earn enough money to study nursing, her plans were thwarted when one of her aunts became ill. Mahalia had to forget about school and take odd jobs to help make ends meet. She remained a devout Christian, and sang in the Greater Salem Baptist Church in Chicago in the first gospel-music group in the city.

When Thomas A. Dorsey, composer of hundreds of gospel songs, heard Mahalia's magnificent renditions of such songs as "It's No Secret What God Can Do," and "He's Got the Whole World in His Hands," he encouraged the young lady to sing elsewhere to Christian audiences. Soon Mahalia's talent was noticed outside church circles. Jazz promoters offered her as much as $25,000 per night to perform in Las Vegas nightclubs. But Mahalia spurned all such offers.

Her travels throughout segregated America in the 1930s and 40s also made her conscious of the injustices black people routinely suffered. Her appearances, she noted, were well received by white audiences, but, "When I come down off that stage, they're still likely to treat me as if I had leprosy."

Critics often complained about her clapping and foot-stomping. But Mahalia's recordings of thirty albums earned a dozen gold records. Tunes like "I Will Move On Up A Little Higher" sold nearly two million copies. Her rendition of "We Shall Overcome" at Martin Luther King, Jr.'s march on Washington in 1963 made that song the Civil Rights movement's unofficial anthem.

In spite of the discrimination Mahalia experienced throughout her life, she maintained a deep sense of trust in the Lord. When praised for anything, the queen of gospel music inevitably answered, "My success is the work of the Lord." Mahalia died in 1972, but her legacy lives on in her music.

*Jimmy's Jitters about Jesus.* Little Jimmy was frightened of the dark. When his mother asked him to bring the broom in from the porch one dark evening, Jimmy balked. His mother tried to reassure him, saying, "Jimmy, you know that you don't have to be afraid of anything out there." Jimmy nodded, but still did not move. So his mother tried a theological approach. "Now, Jimmy," she said firmly, "Remember that Jesus is always there. You have nothing to fear."

Jimmy moved hesitantly toward the door. Opening it a crack, he thrust his hand outside and called, "Jesus, would you please hand me the broom?"

Like Jimmy, we often find it difficult to trust the Lord, especially in the dark times.

*Questions for Students on the Next Lesson.* 1. What did God instruct Jeremiah to search for? 2. Why was the Lord so displeased with Jeremiah's people? 3. What did Jeremiah tell them? 4. Is evil always punished in this life? 5. Why should Christians be concerned about truth and justice?

## TOPIC FOR YOUTH
### KEEP ON TRUSTING

*Catalyst for Unity.* On Christmas Eve, 1928, a tiny baby girl was abandoned by her mother in Pittsburgh's Sheridan Square Theater. The theater manager, John Harris, and an employee, Gene Kelly (who would later go on to Hollywood stardom), found the child. A note said the child's name was Catherine and that she had been born on November 29th. Taken to the Roselia Foundling Home, the eleven members of the Variety Club—then a local theatrical social club—informally adopted her and named her Catherine Variety Sheridan. She remained at the Roselia Home until she was five, before being adopted by the Rikers, a childless couple from Long Island. The Rikers renamed their new daughter Joan.

The Variety Club wanted the little girl to have a normal life. Only two members at a time were allowed to know her whereabouts. They continued to nurture the girl.

In the meantime, the group grew into an organization that raised funds for disadvantaged children. Today, the group has fifty chapters in the United States and ten in foreign countries. As for Joan, she also continued to be a catalyst for uniting disadvantaged and disabled children with celebrities and entertainers.

Out of a painful and difficult situation came good. Despite the potential problems around him, Habakkuk, too, became a catalyst for optimism and trust. In a difficult situation, he called for trust.

*Kept on Trusting.* Mike Singletary was regarded by many as the best middle linebacker in professional football. Chicago Bears fans claim Mike was the key to Chicago's great defense when the Bears won the Super Bowl. But the man who once wore the number 50 jersey dismisses any talk of his greatness. Mike Singletary's faith in Jesus Christ is the most important thing in his life.

That faith did not come easily, for Mike Singletary has had more than his share of disappointment and sorrow. When he was younger, he lost two of his brothers. Both boys had been close to Mike. One died accidentally of carbon monoxide poisoning from an unventilated stove. The other brother perished in an accident caused by a drunken driver.

As a child, Mike suffered frequent respiratory illnesses, including hospital stays with severe bronchitis and pneumonia. Growing up with loss and sickness, this fine young man found his faith tested repeatedly. But through the bouts of grief and illness, Mike developed a profound awareness of Jesus Christ's presence. Eventually he excelled as a star athlete on the field and as an outstanding spokesman for Christ off the field.

*Fogged In?* In the earlier days of sea travel, before the advent of radar, heavy fog meant a potential catastrophe. In the vision-blocking and sound-distorting mist, the foghorns of ships and the light of lighthouses were difficult to discern.

How often do we live in a spiritual fog, unable to discern God's purposes? Answers seem hidden at these times. Like Habakkuk, in near blindness we wait.

Habakkuk's experience with God taught him that even when there was no apparent way through a crisis, he must wait patiently. Like this faithful prophet, when we have no vision and no answer, let us wait. The fog will lift and we will move on.

*Questions for Students on the Next Lesson.* 1. What were the people like in Jeremiah's early years? Were they similar to people you know today? 2. What challenge did God offer to Jeremiah? 3. What, specifically, were the crimes of Jerusalem's citizens? 4. What image did Jeremiah use to describe the people's rebellion? 5. Will people today be judged by the same divine standards?

## A VAIN SEARCH

*Background Scripture:* Jeremiah 5
*Devotional Reading:* Jeremiah 5:20, 21

### KING JAMES VERSION

Jeremiah 5:1 Run ye to and fro through the streets of Jerusalem, and see now, and know, and seek in the broad places thereof, if ye can find a man, if there be any that executeth judgment, that seeketh the truth; and I will pardon it.

2 And though they say, The Lord liveth; surely they swear falsely.

3 O Lord, are not thine eyes upon the truth? thou hast stricken them, but they have not grieved; thou hast consumed them, but they have refused to receive correction: they have made their faces harder than a rock; they have refused to return.

4 Therefore I said, Surely these are poor; they are foolish: for they know not the way of the Lord, nor the judgment of their God.

5 I will get me unto the great men, and will speak unto them; for they have known the way of the Lord, and the judgment of their God: but these have altogether broken the yoke, and burst the bonds.

6 Wherefore a lion out of the forest shall slay them, and a wolf of the evenings shall spoil them, a leopard shall watch over their cities: every one that goeth out thence shall be torn in pieces: because their transgressions are many, and their backslidings are increased.

### NEW REVISED STANDARD VERSION

JEREMIAH 5:1 Run to and fro through the streets of Jerusalem, look around and take note! Search its squares and see if you can find one person who acts justly and seeks truth—so that I may pardon Jerusalem. 2 Although they say, "As the Lord lives," yet they swear falsely. 3 O Lord, do your eyes not look for truth? You have struck them, but they felt no anguish; you have consumed them, but they refused to take correction. They have made their faces harder than rock; they have refused to turn back. 4 Then I said, "These are only the poor, they have no sense; for they do not know the way of the Lord, the law of their God. 5 Let me go to the rich and speak to them; surely they know the way of the Lord, the law of their God." But they all alike had broken the yoke, they had burst the bonds. 6 Therefore a lion from the forest shall kill them, a wolf from the desert shall destroy them. A leopard is watching against their cities; everyone who goes out of them shall be torn in pieces—because their transgressions are many, their apostasies are great.

**KEY VERSE:** *Search . . . and see if you can find one person who acts justly and seeks truth. Jeremiah 5:1.*

## HOME DAILY BIBLE READINGS

## BACKGROUND

From the time of his call until Jerusalem's final catastrophe forty years later, Jeremiah had warned his people that their wicked ways would bring destruction. He had been specific: a hostile nation from the north would invade. This basic theme of God's punishment for sins formed the heart of the prophet's message.

Jeremiah's fellow countrymen refused to heed his sermons. The leaders just couldn't believe that disaster would ever befall the holy city. Therefore, few listened to Jeremiah or turned back to the Lord in repentance. Jeremiah was merely another doomsayer, an ungrateful turncoat. It is never patriotic to bad-mouth one's nation and criticize one's society. But Jeremiah persistently proclaimed what he knew to be God's truth. The nation's future depended on obeying and serving God.

The people continued to feel content, since Judah was enjoying a period of relative prosperity after the Assyrian empire fell. Tribute money was no longer going to Nineveh, and comfortable times seemed to stir up vice and encourage corruption in Jerusalem. Many of the country's leaders renounced God's ways, and Jeremiah's warnings were dismissed as the rantings of a crank.

The portions of Jeremiah's sermons in today's lesson were probably delivered before Jerusalem's defeat and surrender in 597 B.C. At that time, Nebuchadnezzar captured the city and hauled off to Babylon the king and many leading citizens. Unfortunately, few in Jerusalem could believe that Jeremiah's words were beginning to come true.

His hearers continued to disregard his warnings. Yet events a few years later vindicated the prophet. His dire prophecies of doom and destruction came true. Revolts against the Babylonian overlord finally brought the Babylonian army back in all its fury. Jerusalem, with its magnificent temple and beautiful palaces, fell in a fiery destruction. The bulk of its population was herded into exile in Babylon for decades to come.

## NOTES ON THE PRINTED TEXT

God offered a challenge. He instructed Jeremiah to comb Jerusalem thoroughly to see if there was just one faithful person. All the streets and the markets were to be carefully searched. The Lord had done this same thing at Sodom when He searched for ten righteous men. He certainly was pessimistic in His challenge to Jeremiah. However, if one just and truthful man could be found, the Lord would forgive the people. *Run to and fro through the streets of Jerusalem, look around and take note! Search its squares and see if you can find one person who acts justly and seeks truth— so that I may pardon Jerusalem* (5:1).

The people professed to be faithful, claiming to acknowledge Yahweh as their Lord. They declared their allegiance to Him. However, in light of their behavior, they were lying and committing perjury. *Although they say, "As the Lord lives," yet they swear falsely* (5:2).

The people refused to be corrected, despite the calamity that struck the nation when young King Josiah died in battle in 609 B.C. The reform movement died. *O Lord, do your eyes not look for truth? You have struck them, but they felt no anguish; you have consumed them, but they refused to take correction. They have made their faces harder than rock; they have refused to turn back* (5:3).

Initially, Jeremiah believed that the fault lay in poverty and ignorance. Perhaps only the poor had broken God's law and failed to seek truth and justice. *Then I said, "These are only the poor, they have no sense; for they do not know the way of the Lord, the law of their God"* (5:4). So Jeremiah decided to examine the lives of the rich and famous. The result was the same. Rich people and poor people alike had turned away from God. All people were like oxen who had escaped their master's yoke and run away from the master's care and protection. *"Let me go to the rich and speak to them; surely they know the way of the Lord, the law of their God." But they all alike had broken the yoke, they had burst the bonds* (5:5).

Jeremiah utilized a picture right out of life on the desert frontier of the Judean wilderness to describe God's judgment. The Lord's anger and judgment for the people's sins and unfaithfulness would be like a wild animal destroying the people. *Therefore a lion from the forest shall kill them, a wolf from the desert shall destroy them. A leopard is watching against their cities; everyone who goes out of them shall be torn in pieces—because their transgressions are many, their apostasies are great* (5:6).

## SUGGESTIONS TO TEACHERS

At God's command, Jeremiah searched throughout Jerusalem for anyone who was just and truthful. The Lord knew that the people claimed allegiance to Him but refused to live accordingly. Sound familiar? Yet Jeremiah sternly warned that continued disregard for truth and justice would eventually destroy society. Will a refusal to heed the Lord's ways have consequences for our nation, too? The Bible emphatically says "Yes!"

Your lesson this Sunday calls believers to practice truth and justice daily, facing the facts about the hurting in our society. With the fifth chapter of Jeremiah in mind, consider the following points.

1. SEARCHING FOR THE FAITHFUL. Just as Jeremiah surveyed Jerusalem for anyone who was just and truthful, so Christ looks through our communities for those who are honest and caring. Emphasize to your group that the Lord is constantly scrutinizing our motives and actions. There is no fooling God. Ever.

2. SINS OF THE FAITHLESS. Jeremiah proclaimed the shortcomings of his fellow countrymen. The list could apply to almost any community today. Note what the prophet mentions: idolatry, immorality, treachery, apostasy, injustice, oppression, and false prophets. Brainstorm together for practical ways to counteract these problems.

3. SENTENCE ON THE FORSAKEN. Jeremiah announced an invasion was imminent. Those who served foreign gods, he said, would serve foreign masters. Trading allegiance to the Lord for commitment to lesser causes means becoming enslaved by these gods. People soon take on the attributes of whom or what they worship.

4. STUBBORNNESS OF THE FOOLISH. Ponder the meaning of the phrase in Jeremiah 5:21 about people "who have eyes, but do not see, who have ears, but do not hear." When some people are challenged to live responsibly, they actually strengthen their resolve to continue in evil. Consider how this can be, but don't let the discussion wander to "those bad folks out there." Stress how our tendency to rationalize can persuade us to have eyes and ears for Christ's ways . . . but not to obey Him in our daily lives.

## TOPIC FOR ADULTS
## *SEARCHING FOR JUSTICE AND TRUTH*

*Internal Decay.* A town in New England was proud of the enormous elm tree gracing the lawn in front of its town hall. The great tree provided a scenic setting on the town green that was often photographed. The towering elm seemed to embody permanence and security. Most of the town's historical events had taken place under its branches.

Yet no one paid much attention to the part-time janitor in the town hall who noticed signs of decay in the elm's trunk. When he warned town authorities to take steps to prevent the loss of the lovely old landmark, he was ignored. The rot grew worse, but the tree continued to stand season after season—until a hurricane in 1991 slammed the tree to the ground. It had been too rotten to withstand the big wind.

Like the janitor, Jeremiah warned Judah of the internal decay threatening its existence. Nations, like trees, can topple from rottenness within.

*Concern for Justice and Truth.* Each summer members of the Hunger Task Force at Edgewood United Church of Christ in East Lansing, Michigan, sponsor a Farmer's Market on Sunday mornings. Edgewood is an urban church close to the campus of Michigan State University. Its membership draws heavily from university faculty and state government personnel. Many of the members grow gardens, and bring extra produce to worship each Sunday. Following worship, members of the congregation help themselves to any produce they can use. Those who can leave a contribution do so, which goes to a shelter for homeless persons.

Receipts have increased each year. Last year, more than $800 was raised, and the money was divided between two shelters supported by the church. In 1994, the Hunger Task Force expanded its outreach, dividing the income between local shelters and a program of aid to South Africa.

*Deadly Residue.* With an earth-shaking roar, a mighty explosion rocked Berlin in September, 1994. Three construction workers were killed and fourteen people injured. Investigations revealed that the blast was triggered by workmen drilling in the area. They had accidentally detonated a bomb left from World War II. The bomb was located in the former East Berlin. Although the communist authorities had known that such unexploded bombs lay under the surface of the ground throughout East Berlin, they made little effort to locate and deactivate them. Their indifference did not seem to make any difference for decades. Finally, fifty years later, their failure to clean up their city resulted in deadly consequences.

The leaders of Judah failed to show responsibility for years with no apparent negative effects. However, like a long-buried explosive device left unattended for years, their refusal to act responsibly had devastating effects when the Babylonians invaded.

*Questions for Students on the Next Lesson.* 1. How did Jeremiah dramatize his prophecy? 2. How did Hananiah react? 3. What did the yoke symbolize? 4. Why do we sometimes prefer fantasies over the truth? 5. How can we tell a false prophet from a genuine one?

TOPIC FOR YOUTH
## A DISAPPOINTING SEARCH

*Injustice and Intolerance Still Alive.* Community leaders like to believe that hate groups are on the decline, but evidence points to the contrary. For example, The Jewish Anti-Defamation League points to new rounds of violence that demonstrate a significant increase in crimes against others.

In October 1992, four young men burned a cross on the front lawn of an interracial couple in Pitcairn, Pennsylvania. Ethnic intimidation charges were filed against the boys, stating that they had conspired to oppress, threaten, and intimidate the couple. Two of them immediately pleaded guilty, admitting that their actions were more than a harmless prank. The youths were sentenced to four months in a halfway house, four months of home confinement, two years of probation, and two hundred hours of community service.

People, young and old, will be punished for their wrongdoing. Make no mistake, wrongdoing will not be tolerated by society, or by God.

*No Breakaway.* Ku Klux Klan leader Thom Robb has been busy trying to clean up the image of the Klan. He has urged his followers to dress respectfully for public rallies, leave their guns at home, and support civic-minded causes (such as opposing drunk driving and dropping out of school).

However, despite the change in image, the group still promotes hatred with its harsh racist language and support of violence. Sadly, a new study shows that the group is making significant inroads in Alabama, Tennessee, Kentucky, Texas, Colorado, and Missouri.

While the KKK tries to shake its old image, the same intolerant behavior exists in its ranks. Members may declare themselves to be God-fearing believers, but their words and actions demonstrate just the opposite. Jeremiah would have declared that words and actions must harmonize. When we claim allegiance to God, our actions must follow.

*What's Hot?* Anyone with a computer modem who logs on to the Internet will soon discover that the most popular items on the bulletin board are pornographic. The most frequently utilized bulletin board deals in sex stories. Over 800,000 readers use it each month. Half a million users logged on to the second most popular category, where viewers scan explicit sex images.

Sadly, all these forms of "hot chat," demonstrate a serious decline in virtue and are an embarrassment to groups trying to introduce computers and the Internet in schools. (At present, it is impossible to censor Internet.) Though it may be easier than ever to involve ourselves in immorality, we are still called to purity. God knows, it is for our own good.

*Questions for Students on the Next Lesson.* 1. What did Jeremiah do to symbolize the nation's bondage to Babylon? 2. Who was Hananiah? What was the theme of his preaching? 3. How can false prophecy be distinguished from the true Word of God? 4. What were the traditional themes of Israel's prophets? 5. Have you ever felt that two preachers seemed to contradict each other? How did you decide which one was right?

# LESSON 7—OCTOBER 13

## *FALSE HOPES FOR PEACE*

*Background Scripture:* Jeremiah 28—29
*Devotional Reading:* Jeremiah 30:13-24

### KING JAMES VERSION

JEREMIAH 28:5 Then the prophet Jeremiah said unto the prophet Hananiah in the presence of the priests, and in the presence of all the people that stood in the house of the Lord,

6 Even the prophet Jeremiah said, Amen: the Lord do so: the Lord perform thy words which thou hast prophesied, to bring again the vessels of the Lord's house, and all that is carried away captive, from Babylon into this place.

7 Nevertheless hear thou now this word that I speak in thine ears, and in the ears of all the people;

8 The prophets that have been before me and before thee of old prophesied both against many countries, and against great kingdoms, of war, and of evil, and of pestilence.

9 The prophet which prophesieth of peace, when the word of the prophet shall come to pass, then shall the prophet be known, that the Lord hath truly sent him.

10 Then Hananiah the prophet took the yoke from off the prophet Jeremiah's neck, and brake it.

11 And Hananiah spake in the presence of all the people, saying, Thus saith the Lord; Even so will I break the yoke of Nebuchadnezzar king of Babylon from the neck of all nations within the space of two full years. And the prophet Jeremiah went his way.

12 Then the word of the Lord came unto Jeremiah the prophet, after that Hananiah the prophet had broken the yoke from off the neck of the prophet Jeremiah, saying,

13 Go and tell Hananiah, saying, Thus saith the Lord; Thou hast broken the yokes of wood; but thou shalt make for them yokes of iron.

14 For thus saith the Lord of hosts, the God of Israel; I have put a yoke of iron upon the neck of all these nations, that they may serve Nebuchadnezzar king of Babylon; and they shall serve him: and I have given him the beasts of the field also.

### NEW REVISED STANDARD VERSION

JEREMIAH 28:5 Then the prophet Jeremiah spoke to the prophet Hananiah in the presence of the priests and all the people who were standing in the house of the Lord; 6 and the prophet Jeremiah said, "Amen! May the Lord do so; may the Lord fulfill the words that you have prophesied, and bring back to this place from Babylon the vessels of the house of the Lord, and all the exiles. 7 But listen now to this word that I speak in your hearing and in the hearing of all the people. 8 The prophets who preceded you and me from ancient times prophesied war, famine, and pestilence against many countries and great kingdoms. 9 As for the prophet who prophesies peace, when the word of that prophet comes true, then it will be known that the Lord has truly sent the prophet."

10 Then the prophet Hananiah took the yoke from the neck of the prophet Jeremiah, and broke it. 11 And Hananiah spoke in the presence of all the people, saying "Thus says the Lord: This is how I will break the yoke of King Nebuchadnezzar of Babylon from the neck of all the nations within two years." At this, the prophet Jeremiah went his way.

12 Sometime after the prophet Hananiah had broken the yoke from the neck of the prophet Jeremiah, the word of the Lord came to Jeremiah: 13 Go, tell Hananiah, Thus says the Lord: You have broken wooden bars only to forge iron bars in place of them! 14 For thus says the Lord of hosts, the God of Israel: I have put an iron yoke on the neck of all these nations so that they may serve King Nebuchadnezzar of Babylon, and they shall indeed serve him; I have even given him the wild animals.

*KEY VERSE: When you call upon me and come and pray to me, I will hear you. When you search for me, you will find me; if you seek me with all your heart.* Jeremiah 29:12, 13.

## HOME BIBLE READINGS

| | | | | |
|---|---|---|---|---|
| Oct. | 7 | M. | Jeremiah 23:16-22 | *Do Not Listen to False Prophets* |
| Oct. | 8 | T. | Deuteronomy 13:1-5 | *False Prophets against God* |
| Oct. | 9 | W. | Deuteronomy 18:15-22 | *Do Not Fear False Prophets* |
| Oct. | 10 | T. | Jeremiah 29:3-9 | *False Prophets Spoke to Exiles* |
| Oct. | 11 | F. | Jeremiah 29:10-14 | *God Promised to Hear Prayers* |
| Oct. | 12 | S. | Jeremiah 29:15-19 | *Prophets Are the Lord's Prophets* |
| Oct. | 13 | S. | Jeremiah 29:20-32 | *God Punishes False Prophets* |

## BACKGROUND

Nebuchadnezzar invaded rebellious Judah, captured Jerusalem, and carried away King Jehoiachin and 10,000 of the leading citizens to Babylon in 597 B.C. Nebuchadnezzar installed Zedekiah as the new king. Judah was expected to send tribute and not stir up trouble against the Babylonian overlord.

But the nationalistic ruling party in Jerusalem persisted in plotting to throw off the yoke of Nebuchadnezzar. Rebellion fermented among other captured provinces in the Middle East, as well. When a revolt broke out in Nebuchadnezzar's army in late 595 B.C., five countries also itching to throw off Babylonian domination met in Jerusalem to conspire against Nebuchadnezzar. Even Jerusalem's religious leaders urged Zedekiah to go along with the rebellious firebrands.

Jeremiah was one of the few cool heads in the nation. Although he knew he was challenging the decision-makers of Jerusalem, he fearlessly opposed the talk of revolt. Jeremiah remembered that he was God's man, first and foremost. To make God's message as vivid as possible, he fashioned an oxen yoke, a heavy wood and leather contrivance, and wore it publicly in Jerusalem. The symbolism was obvious. Judah must endure the yoke of Nebuchadnezzar.

Jeremiah's act infuriated the nation's leaders, including the religious authorities. Other so-called prophets, professional advisors to the royal house, denounced Jeremiah for his lack of patriotism. Many of these false prophets insisted that the booty carried off by Nebuchadnezzar would be returned and that the nation would emerge greater than ever. To many of these nationalist religious leaders, Jeremiah's words and actions seemed treasonous.

Hananiah was the boldest of those despising Jeremiah for his criticisms of the nation. This prophet approached Jeremiah one day in 593 B.C. and smashed Jeremiah's yoke. Hananiah then announced, in the name of the Lord God of Israel, that within two years all the sacred vessels taken from the temple by Nebuchadnezzar would be back in Jerusalem. He also proclaimed that all the captives, along with Jehoiachin, would be home from Babylon and that the yoke of the king of Babylon would be broken.

Jeremiah cooly warned this false prophet that God would not tolerate such insolence. Jeremiah made a new yoke, this one of iron bars, and strapped it to his body to wear in the temple before the people.

## NOTES ON THE PRINTED TEXT

In 595—594 B.C. Babylon was rocked by internal disturbances. Several of the conquered nations began to develop a plan to rebel. These nations' ambassadors gathered in Jerusalem to enlist the support of Zedekiah. Prophets were busy preaching that God would shortly overthrow Babylon and return King Jehoiachin, the other exiles, and all the treasures taken from the temple.

At God's command, Jeremiah made an oxen yoke and put it on his neck. A yoke was a wooden bar that fit around the animal's neck, held together by leather thongs. The prophet appeared before the ambassadors and told them the yoke represented King Nebuchadnezzar's yoke. God had decreed that all would continue to wear this yoke or face total destruction. Jeremiah gave the same message to Zedekiah and to the priests. As a sign to everyone, he continued to wear the yoke.

Shortly thereafter, another prophet appeared in the temple. Hananiah came from Gibeon, not far from Jeremiah's hometown. His message before the priests and the people was just the opposite of Jeremiah's. He assured Zedekiah that Nebuchadnezzar's yoke would be broken within two years. In addition, the temple vessels, King Jehoiachin, and the exiles would be returned.

Jeremiah was respectful. He did not call Hananiah a liar but indicated that he wished that what Hananiah had preached could be true. *Amen! May the Lord do so; may the Lord fulfill the words that you have prophesied, and bring back to this place from Babylon the vessels of the house of the Lord, and all the exiles* (28:6). The listeners must have been puzzled. Two prophets each claimed to have spoken the Lord's word, but each prophet spoke something completely different. There was confusion.

Jeremiah pointed out that Hananiah's prophecy was not in the tradition of the great prophets of the past (such as Isaiah and Micah). He stated that past prophets had warned of wars, famine, and plagues. *The prophets who preceded you and me from ancient times prophesied war, famine, and pestilence against many countries and great kingdoms* (28:8). Jeremiah warned Hananiah that a prophet who foretold peace had to bear the burden of proof that God had really sent him. Only the upcoming events of the future would show which of the two conflicting messages was the true one. *As for the prophet who prophesies peace, when the word of that prophet comes true, then it will be known that the Lord has truly sent the prophet* (28:9).

Jeremiah's message stung and enraged Hananiah. The false prophet snatched the yoke from Jeremiah's neck and broke it. The action signified the end of Judah's exile in Babylon within two years. He reinforced his action by reiterating his message. *Thus says the Lord: This is how I will break the yoke of King Nebuchadnezzar of Babylon from the neck of all the nations within two years* (28:11).

Later, Jeremiah was assured that Hananiah's message was false. He received instructions from God regarding the false prophet, namely that

God had an even stronger yoke for the people. *Go, tell Hananiah, "Thus says the Lord: You have broken wooden bars only to forge iron bars in place of them! For thus says the Lord of hosts, the God of Israel: I have put an iron yoke on the neck of all these nations so that they may serve King Nebuchadnezzar of Babylon, and they shall indeed serve him; I have even given him the wild animals"* (28:13, 14).

Jeremiah delivered God's words. He reminded Hananiah that Nebuchadnezzar ruled only under God's permission. God's true prophet also condemned Hananiah and told him that for his false words he would die within the year.

## SUGGESTIONS TO TEACHERS

A crowd-pleasing preacher will almost always be well received. Perhaps you have seen or heard such popular speakers. Their smooth sermons make few demands, and some of these preachers attract huge audiences. The pastor in your church may sometimes be unfavorably compared to these showmen because he or she is not entertaining folks with pleasant messages.

Jeremiah's encounter with Hananiah (described in today's Scripture) illustrates the way some claiming to speak for God actually make false promises. This material should help you and your class members sort out the genuine prophet from the fake. For both kinds of persons are still around, sometimes using the same type of God-talk.

1. LONGING FOR PEACE. In Jeremiah's tumultuous times, people wanted relief from threats to their way of life, just as we do. Jeremiah was one of the few who realized that the upheaval and uncertainty came from his nation's prolonged turning away from the Lord. Your lesson should examine whether some of the woes currently afflicting our society are due to our refusal to deal with each other with integrity.

2. LURE OF POPULARITY. Spend a few minutes discussing the appeal of speakers who tell church audiences what they like to hear . . . while omitting the Gospel message.

3. LESSONS FOR PATRIOTISM. Jeremiah was denounced for being "unpatriotic." Yet he loved his nation more deeply than the nationalist fanatics in Judah. The genuine patriot cares enough about his country to point out its shortcomings and to work to bring it up to the standards it espouses. Jeremiah's example should inspire us.

4. LIES FROM PROPHETS. Have students look at the characters of Hananiah and Shemaiah in Jeremiah 28 and 29. Consider their ways of deceiving God's people. When two persons claiming to speak for the Lord have opposing messages, how do we distinguish who is truly God's spokesman?

5. LETTER WITH PREDICTIONS. Turning to Jeremiah 29:1-10, mention that Jeremiah advised his readers to settle in for a long period of exile in Babylon. No swift reprieve from problems could be concocted by human wheeler-dealers in Jerusalem. As God's agent, Jeremiah was a realist: he knew that human plots and schemes are always flawed, especially when humans try to take over for God. In effect, Jeremiah advised, get out of God's way and let Him carry out His purposes.

6. LORD WITH PLANS. Throughout the sermons of Jeremiah, we see

the doctrine of God's sovereignty. This is still our Father's world. Jeremiah told his readers in Babylon that a seventy-year exile was a certainty but that God still had plans for His people. God may be trusted to carry out His purposes and to remember us, in spite of what we may suffer.

## TOPIC FOR ADULTS
### REJECTING FALSE PROMISES

*False Promises.* A trucker and his helper were shifting their eighteen-wheeler through a strange city when they approached an underpass. The sign over the bridge stated: CLEARANCE 12 FEET. The two stopped their rig, measured the height of the trailer, and found it was slightly over twelve feet high. Getting back in the cab, the two peered up and down the street. Grinning broadly, the helper said, "Ain't a cop anywhere, Charlie. Put her in gear and go for it!"

Like the trucker's helper, Hananiah and his ilk made false promises and encouraged Judah "to go for it." The phony prophets, like the trucker's helper, forgot that they might be violating reality. They looked for easy ways out and made attractive promises. They all seemed to neglect the fact that there are certain limitations on what we can do.

God's rules cannot be ignored or flaunted. Whether trying to squeeze a too-high rig through a too-low underpass, or trying to proclaim a false hope for peace, we simply are not permitted to get away with it.

*Hot-Tub Religion.* J.I. Packer has come up with a memorable description of what many modern-day church people want: a "hot-tub religion." These folks merely want to soak comfortably in a pleasing worship experience without responding to the call for serious obedience to Jesus Christ. This feel-good spirituality focuses on self, not the Savior. Usually in these congregations, the pews are well-padded for maximum comfort, and the cross is nicely decorated for esthetic effect.

*Eagles in the Chicken Yard.* Alex Haley, the author of *Roots,* related a folktale in which an eagle's nest was jarred and an egg dropped to the ground. Miraculously, the egg was not shattered. However, it landed in a chicken yard. The eagle's egg was taken over by a setting hen, and eventually the egg hatched.

The little eaglet was raised as a chicken, growing up among the hens in the chicken yard. One day, the adolescent eagle met an older, wild eagle. The great eagle tried to convince the barnyard eagle that he was really an eagle and meant to soar. "No," replied the young eagle, "I am a chicken." The great wild bird flew away sadly, and the adopted one lived his entire life in the chicken yard as a chicken.

God means for us to live as eagles, not as chickens. The prophets tried to call our spiritual ancestors in ancient Israel to remember their destiny. But the promise of an chicken-yard existence made them forsake their heritage.

Likewise, we are tempted to forsake our calling as Christ's servants. The chicken-yard world of false prophets and false promises keeps us from soaring like eagles. With the strength of the Spirit, we may reject the lure of chicken existences. We are not meant to be domesticated to the pleasures and comforts of the world—but to soar to the heights of service.

*Questions for Pupils on the Next Lesson.* 1. Describe the historical background of Ezekiel's writings. 2. Why did Ezekiel hesitate to proclaim God's message? 3. Where did Ezekiel live during most of his ministry? 4. How can we keep from becoming discouraged when facing a difficult task? 5. How do you respond when you are not appreciated for what you're doing?

## TOPIC FOR YOUTH
### WISHFUL THINKING

*Unheeded Warnings.* Groups such as the Eileen Stevens Committee to Halt Useless College Killings warn that fraternity hazing has become dangerous and degrading. Her own son Chuck was killed at Alfred University as a result of alcohol poisoning during a fraternity initiation. While such pointless practices are being stopped by some colleges and universities, hazing is still common. It has gone underground and continues to claim new victims.

In February 1993, Kevin Clark, a deaf student at Gallaudet University in Washington, D.C., was ordered to stand in a meeting room without moving for several hours. Eventually he collapsed. He was rushed unconscious to a hospital where he recovered from head injuries sustained by the fall. The university suspended the Kappa Gamma Fraternity for four years.

Dennis Jay, a student at Indiana University, was pledging for the Alpha Tau Omega fraternity. He and nineteen other pledges stripped to their underwear and paraded blindfolded around the fraternity house while sorority girls tugged on their shorts and wrote on their bodies with Magic Markers. They were then forced to drink "beer bongs"—alcohol consumed from a funnel through a plastic tube forced down their throats.

Jay wound up in Bloomington Hospital in a coma. His blood alcohol level was .48 (.50 is normally fatal). His temperature had dropped to ninety-three degrees and he could barely breathe. It took seven hours for him to regain consciousness. The university shut the fraternity down for one year.

While universities, colleges, and independent groups sound warning pleas, all too frequently they are ignored or go unheeded. And foolish behavior continues to bring bad consequences.

*Fallen Role Models.* 1994 was a tough summer for role models. One generation lost a role model, O.J. Simpson, when he was alleged to have murdered his wife and her male friend, Ron Goldman, at the end of June. An All-American and Hall of Fame football player, Simpson had risen from the ghetto and became a celebrity, movie star, spokesperson for various corporations, and endorser of various sports products.

One month earlier, a younger generation watched female tennis star Jennifer Capriati also fall. The eighteen-year-old athlete was touted as one of the greats of women's tennis. Her end came at the Gables Inn in Boca Raton, Florida, when she was arrested for drug possession on May 16, 1994.

Sadly, certain people appear to be good role models but later prove to be negative influences. Hananiah was such a person. Ultimately, Jeremiah was proven to be the true role model. For he himself followed the Lord.

*Life a Game?* Little Christina Johnson, of Pittsburgh, went down into the basement of her house to play. She took her five-year-old sister Keisha, and her six-year-old brother Anthony. The three decided to reenact a scene from a horror film that they had recently watched, "Pet Sematary." Christina wrapped a gray nylon dog leash around her neck, looped it over the hot water pipe, and turned around several times. Anthony rode around on his bicycle several minutes before he became alarmed and rushed upstairs to get his older sister, Chavon. Chavon cut her sister down with a butcher knife. But Christina had accidentally hanged herself.

Christina was like many youth who fail to distinguish reality from make-believe. People in Jeremiah's day had a similar problem. They lived in a make-believe world of wishful thinking, assuming they could do as they pleased without consequence. Their failure to listen to Jeremiah's warnings brought equally fatal results. Life is not a game.

*Questions for Students on the Next Lesson.* 1. Who was Ezekiel? When and where did he preach? 2. What is a "vision," in the biblical sense? 3. Who was Ezekiel's audience? What qualities describe them? 4. Have you ever been afraid to speak for the Lord? 5. How has God prepared you to proclaim His message?

# LESSON 8—OCTOBER 20

## A REBELLIOUS PEOPLE

*Background Scripture:* Ezekiel 2:1—3:21
*Devotional Reading:* Ezekiel 3:16-21

**KING JAMES VERSION**

EZEKIEL 2:3 And he said unto me, Son of man, I send thee to the children of Israel, to a rebellious nation that hath rebelled against me: they and their fathers have transgressed against me, even unto this very day.

4 For they are impudent children and stiffhearted. I do send thee unto them; and thou shalt say unto them, Thus saith the Lord God.

5 And they, whether they will hear, or whether they will forbear, (for they are a rebellious house,) yet shall know that there hath been a prophet among them.

6 And thou, son of man, be not afraid of them, neither be afraid of their words, though briers and thorns be with thee, and thou dost dwell among scorpions: be not afraid of their words, nor be dismayed at their looks, though they be a rebellious house.

7 And thou shalt speak my words unto them, whether they will hear, or whether they will forbear: for they are most rebellious.

3:4 And he said unto me, Son of man, go, get thee unto the house of Israel, and speak with my words unto them.

5 For thou art not sent to a people of a strange speech and of an hard language, but to the house of Israel;

6 Not to many people of a strange speech and of an hard language, whose words thou canst not understand. Surely, had I sent thee to them, they would have hearkened unto thee.

7 But the house of Israel will not hearken unto thee; for they will not hearken unto me: for all the house of Israel are impudent and hardhearted.

8 Behold, I have made thy face strong against their faces, and thy forehead strong against their foreheads.

9 As an adamant harder than flint have I made thy forehead: fear them not, neither be dismayed at their looks, though they be a rebellious house.

10 Moreover he said unto me, Son of man, all my words that I shall speak unto thee receive in thine heart, and hear with thine ears.

**NEW REVISED STANDARD VERSION**

EZEKIEL 2:3 He said to me, Mortal, I am sending you to the people of Israel, to a nation of rebels who have rebelled against me; they and their ancestors have transgressed against me to this very day. 4 The descendants are impudent and stubborn. I am sending you to them, and you shall say to them, "Thus says the Lord God." 5 Whether they hear or refuse to hear (for they are a rebellious house), they shall know that there has been a prophet among them. 6 And you, O mortal, do not be afraid of them, and do not be afraid of their words, though briers and thorns surround you and you live among scorpions; do not be afraid of their words, and do not be dismayed at their looks, for they are a rebellious house. 7 You shall speak my words to them, whether they hear or refuse to hear; for they are a rebellious house.

3:4 He said to me: Mortal, go to the house of Israel and speak my very words to them. 5 For you are not sent to a people of obscure speech and difficult language, but to the house of Israel— 6 not to many people of obscure speech and difficult language, whose words you cannot understand. Surely, if I sent you to them, they would listen to you. 7 But the house of Israel will not listen to you, for they are not willing to listen to me; because all the house of Israel have a hard forehead and a stubborn heart. 8 See, I have made your face hard against their faces, and your forehead hard against their foreheads. 9 Like the hardest stone, harder than flint, I have made your forehead; do not fear them or be dismayed at their looks, for they are a rebellious house. 10 He said to me: Mortal, all my words that I shall speak to you receive in your heart and hear with your ears; 11 then go to the exiles, to your people, and speak to them, Say to them, "Thus says the Lord God"; whether they hear or refuse to hear.

11 And go, get thee to them of the captivity, unto the children of thy people, and speak unto them, and tell them, Thus saith the Lord God; whether they will hear, or whether they will forbear.

*KEY VERSE: You [Ezekiel] shall speak my words to them, whether they hear or refuse to hear; for they are a rebellious house. Ezekiel 2:7.*

## HOME BIBLE READINGS

| | | | | |
|---|---|---|---|---|
| Oct. | 14 | M. | Ezekiel 1:22-28 | *Ezekiel Heard a Voice* |
| Oct. | 15 | T. | Ezekiel 3:12-21 | *Ezekiel to Speak for God* |
| Oct. | 16 | W. | Ezekiel 3:22-27 | *Wait for God's Timing to Speak* |
| Oct. | 17 | T. | Ezekiel 20:1-13a | *God Gave Ordinances in the Wilderness* |
| Oct. | 18 | F. | Ezekiel 20:18-24 | *People Disobeyed Ordinances* |
| Oct. | 19 | S. | Micah 7:1-7 | *Look to the Lord* |
| Oct. | 20 | S. | Matthew 13:53-58 | *Prophets without Honor in Their Own Land* |

## BACKGROUND

With other leading citizens, Ezekiel was marched to Babylon after Nebuchadnezzar captured Jerusalem and took over Judah in 598 B.C. He had descended from a family of priests. At the time of his departure from Jerusalem, his priestly work had focused on carrying out the traditional duties in the temple.

Ezekiel was resettled in Mesopotamia near the ancient city of Nippur, far from the Jerusalem temple and his priestly functions. In 597 B.C., about five years after being deported, Ezekiel underwent a wrenching spiritual experience—his calling by the Lord to be a prophet. From then until about 571 B.C., this spokesman for God offered a series of visionary oracles to fellow exiled Jerusalemites.

Like other biblical characters who received God's call in dramatic fashion, Ezekiel was commissioned to serve in a difficult situation. He knew he was sent to "the people of Israel," meaning both his countrymen in exile and those still in Jerusalem 800 miles away. His message from the Lord was not intended to bring him cheers and appreciation from either group. In today's lesson, Ezekiel addressed those remaining in Judah. He bluntly told them they were "a nation of rebels" against the Lord.

And rebels they were. Seething with conspiracies to throw off the Babylonian yoke, Jerusalem's remaining inhabitants lived under the illusion that God would bless whatever they did and would never permit anything drastic to befall the temple. Ezekiel announced that they were not merely rebels against Nebuchadnezzar, but against the Lord.

Ezekiel's visions may seem strange to us. Yet his ecstatic and dramatic acts, while peculiar by our standards, marked him as a genuine prophet to his hearers. Furthermore, these acts served as symbols, reinforcing his words. Throughout our studies in Ezekiel, we can be inspired by this brave spokesman for God. He remained faithful to his call in spite of extraordinarily difficult circumstances.

## NOTES ON THE PRINTED TEXT

When Jerusalem was beseiged by Nebuchadnezzar's army in 597 B.C., the Babylonians deported ten thousand people. A young priest named Ezekiel was among those individuals resettled in the region of the River Chebar, in the southern part of the Tel Abib plain. While well treated, the exiles did become part of the Babylonian work force.

As Ezekiel walked in the countryside he received his call to be a prophet. During a tremendous thunderstorm he envisioned four creatures in semi-human form. Overwhelmed by the light and flames, Ezekiel fell on his face. God commanded him to stand at attention. Still fearful, he was assisted to his feet by God's Spirit.

*Mortal, I am sending you to the people of Israel, to a nation of rebels who have rebelled against me; they and their ancestors have transgressed against me to this very day* (2:3). God told Ezekiel to go to the rebellious, disobedient people of Israel. Even in exile, they shared in the guilt of the nation. *The descendants are impudent and stubborn. I am sending you to them, and you shall say to them, "Thus says the Lord God"* (2:4). His listeners were to know that they were not separated from God and that God was the source of Ezekiel's message.

Whether the exiles recognized God's closeness was another matter. Like their nation, many were rebellious. *Whether they hear or refuse to hear (for they are a rebellious house), they shall know that there has been a prophet among them* (2:5).

God encouraged Ezekiel not to be discouraged or afraid, even though the people would not listen to him. The Lord indicated that hostility, contempt, even painful physical abuse might result. *And you, O mortal, do not be afraid of them, and do not be afraid of their words, though briers and thorns surround you and you live among scorpions; do not be afraid of their words, and do not be dismayed at their looks for they are a rebellious house* (2:6). He was not to be afraid but to concentrate on his mission, faithfully delivering God's message. *You shall speak my words to them, whether they hear or refuse to hear, for they are a rebellious house* (2:7).

The Lord gave Ezekiel an unusual scroll that had writing on both sides. Normally, writing was done only on the smoothed side of such a scroll. The prophet was commanded to eat the scroll so that God's word would fill his stomach and body. After eating, Ezekiel was ordered to deliver God's message. *He said to me: Mortal, go to the house of Israel and speak my very words to them* (3:4).

The Lord prepared Ezekiel for the people's resistance: they would not listen to the divine message. The reason had nothing to do with language difficulties. In fact, the Lord said that non-Israelites would be more likely to receive God's message than the rebellious Israelites. *For you are not sent to a people of obscure speech and difficult language, but to the house of Israel— not to many peoples with obscure speech and difficult language, whose words you cannot understand. Surely, if I sent you to them, they would listen to you* (3:5, 6). The problem was the people's great stubbornness. They simply possessed hard hearts. *But the house of Israel will not listen to you, for they are not willing to listen to me; because all the house of Israel have a hard forehead and a stubborn heart* (3:7).

In spite of the people's resistance, Ezekiel persevered. With the Lord, he possessed unbreakable strength. *See, I have made your face hard against their faces, and your forehead hard against their foreheads. Like the hardest stone, harder than flint, I have made your forehead; do not fear them or be dismayed at their looks, for they are a rebellious house* (3:8, 9).

God then instructed Ezekiel to meditate on His message before going to proclaim it to the exiles. Ezekiel had to accept the word of the Lord within his own being before he could preach it to others. *Mortal, all my words that I shall speak to you receive in your heart and hear with your ears; then go to the exiles, to your people, and speak to them. Say to them, "Thus says the Lord God"; whether they hear or refuse to hear* (3:10, 11).

## SUGGESTIONS TO TEACHERS

What motivates a person to perform unselfish acts? The hope of recognition and personal glory? The promise of affection? The potential monetary rewards? Yet all these are external incentives. They hardly come into play when we ask: What drives a man or woman to live a life of heroism for God's Kingdom? Here there is no assurance of riches, not even a promise of success (see Heb. 11:39).

Consider the handful of genuine heroes and heroines who have given themselves to Christian service without any thought of the external kinds of motivation. Jesus certainly heads the list, but we must also include Ezekiel. The biblical chapters from this great prophet can provide inspiration to all of us. For we are all called to serve the Lord in our difficult times.

1. DEPLOYING THE MESSENGER. When the Lord calls us, He doesn't necessarily promise success, rewards, or popularity. Ezekiel was sent to impudent fellow countrymen who rebelled against God's plans. Point out that, in some ways, it is easier to be sent to a foreign land to speak for the Lord than to go to our own family and friends in the home community.

Stress that all Christians have been "called" by the Lord to use their spiritual gifts in building up the church. And though the circumstances of our call may be less dramatic than those of Ezekiel, we nevertheless have a commission from the Lord to be His witnesses in all we do and say. (You may wish to refer to Matthew 28:18-20, for instance.)

2. DIGESTING THE MISSION. The words about Ezekiel chewing and swallowing the scroll are strange to modern minds. However, the point is that God's person must internalize God's word. The symbolism here suggests that anyone responding to the Lord's call can serve effectively only after digesting the divine message of Scripture. Let this point lead you into discussing the vital importance of Bible study for each believer.

3. DISCIPLINING THE MAN. Ezekiel realized he would be rejected by his hearers. But this prophet was also aware that his determination to speak must be stronger than the people's refusal to hear.

Gently encourage this kind of resolve in your class members, as opportunities arise. You might view your class as a boot camp for believers. Your students should understand that Sunday mornings with you are, in effect, an equipping and training session. Bible study and fellowship can help them to stand firm in the age-old battle against spiritual indifference and opposition.

TOPIC FOR ADULTS
*LISTENING AND OBEYING*

*Correcting the Report.* Listening is difficult. Even those trained to be experts in this fine art sometimes don't get the message right. Consider, for example, the woman who often tuned in to local police radio frequencies and overheard the following report, "Go to the Tower Apartments and check report on sixty-six year old naked man sitting on curb." She wondered how they knew the man's age. Then came this correction. "Correct first report. Check '66 Olds parked by curb. It's been stripped."

Correctly hearing and interpreting the whispers of the Spirit requires a depth of inner listening that must be cultivated over the years. Ezekiel's hearers did not want to tune in on God's intentions. They had forgotten how to listen to their Lord.

As a Christian, do you take the time to listen to God's voice through Scripture? When you do, you will discover that your understanding of life and its meaning will be continually corrected.

*Called to Obedience.* Consider the following words of archbishop Oscar Romero, spoken before he was shot and killed by terrorists while leading El Salvadorans in worship in September, 1979:

"Let us each endeavor to see what are our own charisms [spiritual gifts] or those of our group. When we look around and see other charisms, perhaps showier and lovelier than what God has given us, let us not feel envious like the disciples of Jesus or Moses: 'Stop them.' Absolutely not. Instead, let us listen to Jesus: 'If they prophesy in my name, they can't be against us. Let them be.' And Moses says: 'Would that all the people might feel themselves flooded with the Spirit.' Indeed, his prophecy is fulfilled in our baptism: by our baptism we all join the church's great charism.

"Among vocations, charisms, and ways of being, what huge differences there are. . . . The point is to be able to bring [our gifts and callings] to bear on the community's welfare. If God gives you a vocation to political activism and you organize the people for their common good, then use that gift of God. It, too, is a vocation. . . . All have to find their own vocation. Let's respect what God says to each man or woman, but let us also, all of us, contribute to the lovely and varied unity of God's kingdom and of the church."

*Expressing Devotion?* Michael Greene, the British evangelist, addressed a large gathering of ministers in the United Church of Christ a few years ago. During his presentation, he asked the clergy, "When was the last time you told your congregation what Jesus means to you?" Afterward, many of the ministers heatedly debated among themselves what Greene's challenge meant. Some rejected the speaker's question, calling it simplistic and revivalistic, representing the kind of piety they had joined the United Church of Christ to get away from.

Later, nearly all of those who heard Greene's challenging question found themselves haunted by it. One minister later said he realized that he talked about Jesus a great deal in his preaching. But he acknowledged that he had not considered how different merely talking about Jesus is from expressing personal devotion to Him. All of us, called by God through Jesus Christ, need to ponder Greene's provocative question.

*Questions for Students on the Next Lesson.* 1. What does it mean that the

children's teeth are set on edge because the fathers have eaten sour grapes?
2. When have you attempted to blame others for things that were actually
your own fault? 3. How does your faith help guide you in making moral
choices? 4. How do you respond to the argument that our upbringing often
causes us to do wrong?

### TOPIC FOR YOUTH
#### *REFUSING TO LISTEN*

*Chose to Ignore Law.* Hayman Ronald Lucas was on vacation with his
parents aboard the Royal Caribbean Cruise Line's ship *Majesty of the Seas*
on July 11, 1994. The trio was sailing from Jamaica to the Bahamas.
Hayman's parents went to bed early, but the fourteen year old joined a
small group of young people gathered on the upper pool deck. While most
of the young people were over eighteen, half a dozen were under that age.

In international waters, the legal drinking age is eighteen. The crew,
therefore, served drinks to the youths. Hayman, who was a hefty five-foot-
four, two-hundred-pound kid, ignored the drinking age rule. He drank a lot
of tequila and rum.

During the hours that he partied, Hayman pushed his blood-alcohol level
to 0.29, more than three times the legal level of intoxication. A crew member found the boy staggering on deck at five o'clock in the morning and
escorted him back to his family's cabin. They all then helped the boy back
into his own cabin.

By eleven o'clock that morning, Hayman was dead. He had stopped
breathing as a result of alcohol poisoning. Despite being aware of the laws
and the potential hazards of alcohol, Hayman had refused to listen.

God reminded Ezekiel that people often ignore His law. Some do it pur-
posely; others do it unintentionally. The result of ignoring any law can have
serious consequences.

*"Dis-ing" God.* Elijah Anderson, a sociology professor at the University of
Pennsylvania, has studied youth gangs for years. He claims that the gang
code centers on respect. Thus, the most dangerous thing an individual can
do is "dis" someone (that is, "dis"respect him or her).

Anderson has found that "decent" youth, who are oriented to family,
church, and school, will typically just walk away when dissed. Street gang
members, though, seldom walk away. Immediately, the one who has been
dissed will strike back with raging vengeance.

In a sense, Israel dissed God over many years. Rebellious and lacking
any authority, the nation asserted its own will. But God calls and pleads for
repentence with great patience. He strikes back only when there is no other
way to redeem the situation. Let us be thankful for God's longsuffering
response to our disrespect.

*Should Refuse to Listen.* Members of the Home Judiciary Committee
hearings, in the early fall of 1994, listened to testimony about youth and
music. The testimony supported or opposed legislation that would prohibit
retailers from selling cassettes or CDs containing parental warning labels
to children under eighteen.

The chairperson of the National Political Congress of Black Women, Dr.
C. Delores Tucker, offered $100 to anyone willing to read aloud lyrics from

gangster rap songs. The lyrics were so obscene that friends, politicians, and even professional athletes were embarrassed to read them. Tucker argued that the music was obscene, sexist, and driven by racism; ultimately it destroys a community's morals and values. According to Tucker, the music motivates youth to commit violence, use drugs, and abuse women.

The daylong hearing brought witness after witness who maintained that gangster rap, rap, and heavy metal music advocated violence and routinely referred to women in derogatory terms. Lawmakers were urged to go beyond the current warning labels and prohibit retailers from selling tapes and CDs to children and underaged kids.

Such lyrics express the rebelliousness and disobedience of the musicians. God's people nurture and care for one another. God's people are committed to one another. Sounding like a modern-day prophet, Tucker urged lawmakers, and all of us, not to listen to this music. Heed her warning. Rather, proclaim God's message of love to everyone.

*Questions for Students on the Next Lesson.* 1. What did the proverb about "sour grapes" mean? 2. Can sin ever be inherited? 3. Is each person responsible for his or her own life? In what way? 4. How does a truly righteous person live? 5. How is sin punished?

# LESSON 9—OCTOBER 27

## PERSONAL RESPONSIBILITY

*Background Scripture:* Ezekiel 18
*Devotional Reading:* Psalm 3:1-12

KING JAMES VERSION
EZEKIEL 18:1 The word of the Lord came unto me again, saying,

2 What mean ye, that ye use this proverb concerning the land of Israel, saying, The fathers have eaten sour grapes, and the children's teeth are set on edge?

3 As I live, saith the Lord God, ye shall not have occasion any more to use this proverb in Israel.

4 Behold, all souls are mine; as the soul of the father, so also the soul of the son is mine: the soul that sinneth, it shall die.

5 But if a man be just, and do that which is lawful and right,

7 And hath not oppressed any, but hath restored to the debtor his pledge, hath spoiled none by violence, hath given his bread to the hungry, and hath covered the naked with a garment;

8 He that hath not given forth upon usury, neither hath taken any increase, that hath withdrawn his hand from iniquity, hath executed true judgment between man and man,

9 Hath walked in my statutes, and hath kept my judgments, to deal truly; he is just, he shall surely live, saith the Lord God.

10 If he beget a son that is a robber, a shedder of blood, and that doeth the like to any one of these things,

11 And that doeth not any of those duties, but even hath eaten upon the mountains, and defiled his neighbour's wife,

12 Hath oppressed the poor and needy, hath spoiled by violence, hath not restored the pledge, and hath lifted up his eyes to the idols, hath committed abomination,

13 Hath given forth upon usury, and hath taken increase: shall he then live? he shall not live: he hath done all these abominations; he shall surely die; his blood shall be upon him.

19 Yet say ye, Why? doth not the son bear the iniquity of the father? When the son hath done that which is lawful and right, and hath kept all my statutes, and hath done them, he shall surely live.

20 The soul that sinneth, it shall die. The son shall not bear the iniquity of the father, neither shall the father bear the iniquity of the son: the righteousness of the righteous shall be upon him, and the wickedness of the wicked shall be upon him.

NEW REVISED STANDARD VERSION
EZEKIEL 18:1 The word of the Lord came to me: 2 What do you mean by repeating this proverb concerning the land of Israel, "The parents have eaten sour grapes, and the children's teeth are set on edge"? 3 As I live, says the Lord God, this proverb shall no more be used by you in Israel. 4 Know that all lives are mine; the life of the parent as well as the life of the child is mine: it is only the person who sins that shall die.

5 If a man is righteous and does what is lawful and right—

7 does not oppress anyone, but restores to the debtor his pledge, commits no robbery, gives his bread to the hungry and covers the naked with a garment, 8 does not take advance or accrued interest, withholds his hand from iniquity, executes true justice between contending parties, 9 follows my statutes, and is careful to observe my ordinances, acting faithfully—such a one is righteous; he shall surely live, says the Lord God.

10 If he has a son who is violent, a shedder of blood, 11 who does any of these things (though his father does none of them), who eats upon the mountains, defiles his neighbor's wife, 12 oppresses the poor and needy, commits robbery, does not restore the pledge, lifts up his eyes to the idols, commits abomination, 13 takes advance or accrued interest; shall he then live? He shall not. He has done all these abominable things; he shall surely die; his blood shall be upon himself.

19 Yet you say, "Why should not the son suffer for the iniquity of the father?" When the son has done what is lawful and right, and has been careful to observe all my statutes, he shall surely live. 20 The person who sins shall die. A child shall not suffer for the iniquity of a parent, nor a parent suffer for the iniquity of a child; the righteousness of the righteous shall be his own, and the wickedness of the wicked shall be his own.

*KEY VERSE: A child shall not suffer for the iniquity of a parent, nor a parent suffer for the iniquity of a child. Ezekiel 18:20.*

## BACKGROUND

For generations, people in Israel had repeated an ancient proverb, "The fathers have eaten sour grapes, and the children's teeth are set on edge." The sins of the fathers are visited on succeeding generations. Exodus 34:7 and Numbers 14:18 emphasize that the iniquities of the Israelites would affect their grandchildren and great-grandchildren. No one can deny that immoral behavior creates a ripple effect, leaving scars on those yet unborn.

In Ezekiel's group of exiled Jerusalemites, however, people were quoting the old proverb as a means of exonerating themselves from any responsibility in the disaster. This community was claiming that Jerusalem in the 6th century B.C. was a guiltless city, suffering for the sins of earlier generations. The citizens of the day were merely innocent victims.

This "no-fault" belief led to self-righteousness and self-pity. Ezekiel knew his people, and he didn't like what he was hearing. His word from the Lord at that point introduced a startling new idea for God's people: personal responsibility.

The Lord instructed Ezekiel not to use the ancient proverb about the sour grapes. It is the one who sins, not the parents or children of that person, who is responsible for sin's consequences. Furthermore, Ezekiel must proclaim that people who obey God will live. Children and grandchildren will not be forced to pay for the sins of the fathers. Each person must accept responsibility for his own wickedness.

This concept of individual responsibility had not been taught in Israel. Previously, everything had been based on the behavior of the community as a whole. From Ezekiel's time on, people of faith have realized that each person must accept responsibility for an upright life before the Lord.

## NOTES ON THE PRINTED TEXT

Eating grapes that aren't quite ripe leaves an unpleasant coating on our teeth. We say our teeth have been set on edge. *The word of the Lord came to me: What do you mean by repeating this proverb concerning the land of Israel, "The parents have eaten sour grapes, and the children's teeth are set on edge?"* (18:1, 2).

The Lord told Ezekiel not to use the proverb about sour grapes because, in reality, it is the one who sins, not the parents or the children of that person, who will die. The proverb should no longer be heard. *As I live, says the Lord God, this proverb shall no more be used by you in Israel. Know that all lives are mine; the life of the parent as well as the life of the child is mine: it is only the person who sins that shall die* (18:3, 4).

The Lord said the righteous would live, and Ezekiel defined a righteous person. First he offered some characteristics that the righteous avoided, such as the worship of idols and adultery. Then he listed the things righteous people do. If a man is righteous and does what is lawful and right—he does not oppress anyone (18:5, 7). Righteous individuals did not exploit others. Rather, they actually gave back the collateral taken from debtors (often in the form of a heavy outer cloak), fed the hungry, clothed the naked, and generally tried not to profit from others' distress. The virtuous person *does not oppress anyone, but restores to the debtor his pledge, commits no robbery, gives his bread to the hungry and covers the naked with a garment, does not take advance or accrued interest, withholds his hand from iniquity, executes true justice between contending parties, follows my statutes, and is careful to observe my ordinances, acting faithfully—such a one is righteous; he shall surely live, says the Lord God* (18:7-9). This individual would be rewarded for obedience to the Lord.

The example continued. The righteous man's son was the complete opposite of his father. *If he has a son who is violent, a shedder of blood, . . . who eats upon the mountains, defiles his neighbor's wife, oppresses the poor and needy, commits robbery, does not restore the pledge, lifts up his eyes to the idols, commits abomination, takes advance or accrued interest, shall he then live? He shall not. He has done all these abominable things; he shall surely die; his blood shall be upon himself* (18:10-13) The evil man who lived only for himself would be duly punished. The wicked man's son, having seen the sins of his father, resolved to live a righteous life similar to his grandfather. Therefore, he was not punished.

Ezekiel summarized the belief of his people. *Yet you say, "Why should not the son suffer for the iniquity of the father?"* (18:19). He then told the people that they were personally responsible for their behavior and its consequences. Children would not suffer for the sins of their parents; nor would parents suffer for the sins of their children. *The person who sins shall die. A child shall not suffer for the iniquity of a parent, nor a parent suffer for the iniquity of a child* (18:20). Righteousness belonged to the righteous person alone; the wicked carried the sole responsibility for their own wickedness. *The righteousness of the righteous shall be his own, and the wickedness of the wicked shall be his own* (18:20).

## SUGGESTIONS TO TEACHERS

In the 1990s in our culture, we have a new phenomenon called victimization, what some call "victimology." Actually, it's the old blame game under a new title: always shift the responsibility to someone else. Arrested for breaking a law? Your attorney argues it's the fault of your poor upbringing. Failing grades in your classes? It's because of your home environment. An addiction you can't handle? Well, it's because of your genes. Slipping in the polls? The press has mistreated you.

These days it seems a person can excuse just about any behavior by claiming victim status. "Nobody understands me," goes the excuse. Sound familiar? Ezekiel confronted the same excuse-making in his own day.

1. OBSOLETE PROVERB. Ezekiel scuttled the notion that all our problems stem from our ancestors' sins. In his generation, the Judean exiles had twisted the old saying about sour grapes to get themselves off the hook after the fall of Jerusalem. "Don't blame us; it's the fault of our fathers and grandfathers," they glibly announced. But invite your students to look at the original meaning of the saying in Exodus 34:7 and Numbers 14:18.

2. UNIVERSAL PRECEPT. Ezekiel would not let his people shift responsibility for the woes of the nation. He insisted that each person must accept responsibility for his or her actions. Discuss some of the ways people today try to duck responsibility for their behaviors.

3. INDIVIDUAL PERSONHOOD. Ezekiel pioneered in the march of human history by reminding his hearers that they were not merely members of a clan, but individuals accountable to God. With your class members, closely examine the words in Ezekiel 18:20, where the prophet so clearly proclaims personal responsibility before God.

4. URGENT PLEA. Ezekiel appealed to his fellow exiles to live personal lives in accord with God's precepts. As Christians, each of us, too, is meant to respond to God's goodness by exhibiting all the qualities we see in Jesus Christ. Out of gratitude for God's grace, our personal behavior must constantly and consistently reflect the personhood of our Lord. In a permissive culture in which lust, greed, and cruelty seem to be increasingly acceptable, we Christians have a deeper responsibility than ever to display holiness in daily living.

5. ULTIMATE PLEASURE. Close with the words in Ezekiel 18:32: "For I have no pleasure in the death of anyone, says the Lord God. Turn, then, and live." Refusal to repent and live responsibly brings death, but God calls us to life. His greatest pleasure resides in our repentance and the resulting renewed relationship with Him.

### TOPIC FOR ADULTS
#### ACCEPTING PERSONAL RESPONSIBILITY

Don't-Blame-Me-itis. An observer of criminal cases in the Van Nuys Municipal Court remarks that a person could spend weeks listening to arrested people (and their lawyers) and never run into a guilty person. Deputy City Attorney Richard Schmidt, supervisor of the Van Nuys office, agrees. "We've had an outbreak of very creative defenses over here and we're not sure why—except that most people have obviously watched too much TV growing up."

In one case, a young man blamed the medication Co-Advil for his act of walking out of a record store with ten compact discs. He claimed the Co-Advil tablets made him "spacey" and he didn't know what he was doing. He tried to persuade Judge Alice Altoon that the cold tablets were at fault, but Judge Altoon was not impressed.

A middle-aged man once tried to convince a jury that the alcohol police officers smelled on his breath was actually the Nyquil he had taken because he was having trouble sleeping. The trial lasted five days, and the jury took one hour to convict him.

A North Hollywood man, when arrested for drunken driving, insisted that he had eaten three bowls of Jell-O laced with vodka and had no way of knowing that he was drunk. The trial dragged on for three days, but the jury found the man guilty.

The "Don't Blame Me" folks preach that nothing is our fault anymore. Personal responsibility? Forget it.

*Accepting Responsibility.* On the night of June 5th, 1944, General Dwight D. Eisenhower visited with the troops preparing to land on Europe's beaches at dawn. As a seasoned military man, Eisenhower knew the risks of the undertaking, the distinct possibility of failure. He also knew that the cost in human lives would be high.

The general moved among his troops in the 101st Airborne that evening, talking to tense young men who would drop into the darkness to battle up rocky cliffs. "Ike" stood as the long line of C-47s took off from Welford, hands in his pockets. A correspondent noticed that there were tears in the General's eyes. Then Eisenhower returned to his quarters to wait.

That same afternoon, he had written a strange note and carefully filed it. The note contained a message that could be handed out in the event that D-Day ended in disaster: "Our landings have failed. . . . The troops, the Air, and Navy did all that bravery and devotion to duty could do. If any blame or fault attaches to the attempt it is mine alone."

*Something I Had to Do.* People give all kinds of reasons for refusing to make the most of their lives. Excuses are many: environment, heredity, fate, bad luck, the stars in the zodiac, supernatural spirits, demons, color of skin, family, school, climate, government, and even Satan or God.

Alison K. Walker, 39, single mother of three, grandmother of five, became a doctor of medicine. Reared in an impoverished neighborhood in Pittsburgh, Dr. Walker, a former welfare recipient, felt that all minorities, especially women, could do more than they are to improve themselves. She determined that becoming a doctor "was something I had to do."

She does not say that God and her brother are responsible for her success. Her brother is also a doctor, who told her she could make it in medicine. But she depended neither upon luck nor anything else except hard work, sacrifice, and borrowed funds of more than $100,000. She could have taken the easy road of least resistance, but something within her caused her to follow the narrower way to a fuller life. It was "something I had to do," said she.

If our life situations need improvement, it is up to us to do something; if we do nothing, we remain responsible for what we are. Henry Adams, the American historian, said that the "ideally free individual is responsible only to himself."

"Sometimes people do what they feel God has influenced them to do. Moses and Abraham, and other biblical characters, were motivated by a lively sense of God's providence. But even then the individual must be responsible for what results, even if it involves pain or death."—Rev. Joseph Mohr.

*Questions for Students on the Next Lesson.* 1. What did the Lord instruct Ezekiel to do in order to portray Jerusalem under siege? 2. What did these strange acts symbolize? 3. Have you ever had to face defeat? If so, how did your faith help you handle it? 4. What can the church do in the face of widespread societal violence? 5. How can Christians give hope to those who see no future for the world or themselves?

## TOPIC FOR YOUTH
### IT'S NOT MY FAULT

*Criticized for Whistle Blowing.* When Rider University student Hagan Scherberger heard his roommate asking to borrow a pair of baggy pants, he was curious as to why. The roommate replied that his fraternity, the Psi Kappa Psi, was having a "Dress Like a Nigger Night" and he needed clothing that would make him look like a rap star. Scherberger, who is white, refused. The idea bothered him so much that he and a friend, Louis Colombo, wrote a letter of complaint to college officials, joining the 200 African Americans protesting the dance as racist and degrading.

As a result of their letter, Scherberger and Colombo were criticized by some of their friends and certain other white students. They even received death threats. They were pushed and spat upon.

However, they felt that they did the right thing. Colombo summed it up by saying that while it was hard to do what was right, it would have been harder to do what was wrong.

The two students, like Ezekiel, stood against popular thinking. Their stand was right, but it cost them friends and comfort. Being responsible as God's people will not always be easy. Still, God's people must act and stand up for their beliefs.

*Destroyed Children.* Attorney and author Andrew Vachss has devoted his life to fighting the scourge of child abuse. One of the most complex and widespread forms of abuse is emotional abuse, the systematic diminishment of another so that the victim feels unworthy of respect, friendship, and love. This form of abuse can be as painful as a physical assault, though it leaves no visible marks.

Emotional abuse scars the heart and soul. Sometimes it is deliberate, as when someone says, "You are fat. You are stupid. You are ugly." It can take the form of belittling, such as "You will never be as good as your brother" or "You're so stupid, I'm ashamed to call you my son." It can even cause a "failure to thrive," a condition similar to children who have not received adequate nutrition. This form of abuse can leave the child full of self-blame and struggling for survival.

Vachss called for a new strategy to combat what might be called a national illness. Parents need to learn how to deal with stress so that their children are not overloaded with that stress. Parents must accept more personal responsibility, or they will destroy their children.

Ezekiel reminded his people of the importance of personal responsibility. The children were not punished for the sins of the parents. No one needs to feel self-blame. God offers nurture to all people, young and old.

*Accepted the Responsibility.* George Leone and some of his friends were driving up Laurel Mountain in Pennsylvania, preparing to celebrate Independence Day. George lit an M-80 firecracker and prepared to throw it out of the open window. Seconds after he lit the fuse, though, it went off in his hand. The explosion blew the outside mirror off the vehicle and sprayed the inside of the truck with glass. Had he not been wearing glasses, George's eyes might have been blinded by the flying glass. The explosion bent his fingers backwards and drilled a hole in the palm of his hand. Around the hole, the skin was black and burned from the gunpowder, and there was much blood. Worse, he had no feeling in his hand.

Thanks to an excellent orthopedic surgeon and his repair work, today George has full use of his right hand. Now he works at an auto body shop. However, he never forgot the night of the M-80 explosion. He realized that he alone was responsible, saying that it was one of the dumbest things he had ever done in his life. No one could be blamed, except himself.

As the holiday approaches each July, George speaks to groups of people, warning about the hazards of fireworks. He joins the chorus of local, state, and national officials who insist that only experts handle fireworks.

*Questions for Students on the Next Lesson.* 1. With what dramatic actions and signs did Ezekiel preach? 2. Why did Ezekiel utilize such signs? 3. Did Ezekiel accept each command of the Lord obediently? 4. Would you like to see Ezekiel's style of preaching utilized by your pastor? 5. Why was God so "tough" on the people of Jerusalem?

# LESSON 10—NOVEMBER 3

## *A PORTRAYAL OF DOOM*

*Background Scripture:* Ezekiel 3:22—5:17
*Devotional Reading:* Acts 10:9-16

KING JAMES VERSION

EZEKIEL 4:1 Thou also, son of man, take thee a tile, and lay it before thee, and portray upon it the city, even Jerusalem:

2 And lay siege against it, and build a fort against it, and cast a mount against it; set the camp also against it, and set battering rams against it round about.

3 Moreover take thou unto thee an iron pan, and set it for a wall of iron between thee and the city: and set thy face against it, and it shall be besieged, and thou shalt lay siege against it. This shall be a sign to the house of Israel

4 Lie thou also upon thy left side, and lay the iniquity of the house of Israel upon it: according to the number of the days that thou shalt lie upon it thou shalt bear their iniquity.

5 For I have laid upon thee the years of their iniquity, according to the number of the days, three hundred and ninety days: so shalt thou bear the iniquity of the house of Israel.

6 And when thou hast accomplished them, lie again on thy right side, and thou shalt bear the iniquity of the house of Judah forty days: I have appointed thee each day for a year.

7 Therefore thou shalt set thy face toward the siege of Jerusalem, and thine arm shall be uncovered, and thou shalt prophesy against it.

8 And, behold, I will lay bands upon thee, and thou shalt not turn thee from one side to another, till thou hast ended the days of thy siege.

9 Take thou also unto thee wheat, and barley, and beans, and lentiles, and millet, and fitches, and put them in one vessel, and make thee bread thereof, according to the number of the days that thou shalt lie upon thy side, three hundred and ninety days shalt thou eat thereof.

10 And thy meat which thou shalt eat shall be by weight, twenty shekels a day: from time to time shalt thou eat it.

11 Thou shalt drink also water by measure, the sixth part of an hin: from time to time shalt thou drink.

12 And thou shalt eat it as barley cakes, and thou shalt bake it with dung that

NEW REVISED STANDARD VERSION

EZEKIEL 4:1 And you, O mortal, take a brick and set it before you. On it portray a city, Jerusalem; 2 and put siegeworks against it, and build a siege-wall against it, and cast up a ramp against it; set camps also against it, and plant battering rams against it all around. 3 Then take an iron plate and place it as an iron wall between you and the city; set your face toward it, and let it be in a state of siege, and press the siege against it. This is a sign for the house of Israel.

4 Then lie on your left side, and place the punishment of the house of Israel upon it; you shall bear their punishment for the number of the days that you lie there. 5 For I assign to you a number of days, three hundred ninety days, equal to the number of the years of their punishment; and so you shall bear the punishment of the house of Israel. 6 When you have completed these, you shall lie down a second time, but on your right side, and bear the punishment of the house of Judah; forty days I assign you, one day for each year. 7 You shall set your face toward the siege of Jerusalem, and with your arm bared you shall prophesy against it. 8 See, I am putting cords on you so that you cannot turn from one side to the other until you have completed the days of your siege.

9 And you, take wheat and barley, beans and lentils, millet and spelt; put them into one vessel, and make bread for yourself. During the number of days that you lie on your side, three hundred ninety days, you shall eat it. 10 The food that you eat shall be twenty shekels a day by weight; at fixed times you shall eat it. 11 And you shall drink water by measure, one-sixth of a hin; at fixed times you shall drink. 12 You shall eat it as a barley-cake, baking it in their sight on human dung. 13 The Lord said, "Thus shall the people of Israel eat their bread, unclean, among the nations to which I will drive them."

cometh out of man, in their sight.
    13 And the Lord said, Even thus shall the
children of Israel eat their defiled bread
among the Gentiles, whither I will drive
them.

KEY VERSE: *You shall set your face toward the siege of Jerusalem, and with your arm bared you shall prophesy against it.* Ezekiel 4:7.

## HOME BIBLE READINGS

| | | | | |
|---|---|---|---|---|
| Oct. | 28 | M. | Ezekiel 5:1-4 | *Ezekiel Ordered to Shave Hair* |
| Oct. | 29 | T. | Ezekiel 5:5-9 | *Jerusalem's Fate for Sinning* |
| Oct. | 30 | W. | Ezekiel 5:13-17 | *The Lord Speaks in Anger* |
| Oct. | 31 | T. | Ezekiel 6:1-10 | *High Places to Be Destroyed* |
| Nov. | 1 | F. | Ezekiel 6:11-14 | *The Lord Known by His Judgments* |
| Nov. | 2 | S. | Hosea 9:1-9 | *Days of Punishment* |
| Nov. | 3 | S. | Hosea 9:10-17 | *God Rejects Israel* |

## BACKGROUND

Symbolic acts have a dramatic effect. The prophets understood this and used the theater of the absurd to reinforce their message from the Lord with power and personal impact. Many of these dramatic acts seem strange to us today. But the contemporary listeners and viewers understood.

We have already seen how Jeremiah strapped on a yoke to demonstrate to his people how the yoke of the Babylonian king would afflict Judah. Three centuries earlier, prophet Ahijah of Shiloh had ripped his robe into twelve strips, giving ten to Jeroboam in order to symbolize the future division of the kingdom (in which the ten northern tribes would be ruled by Jeroboam). The dying Elisha commanded King Joash to shoot arrows out the window, indicating the coming defeat of the Syrians. Isaiah strode naked through Jerusalem to prophesy the fate of Assyria's foes. Jeremiah smashed a clay pot to foretell the destruction of Jerusalem. What might be called "miming the message" was a favorite form of proclamation by the prophets.

Ezekiel's preaching was punctuated by such symbols. Some came in the form of dramatic word-pictures, others were gestures and actions. Yet we must not dismiss Ezekiel as "weird." Remember that he was primarily determined to carry out his calling as God's spokesman. And he was using methods that would punch home that message from the Lord.

Today's Scripture presents a series of such symbolic acts. At the Lord's command, Ezekiel used a brick and an iron plate to portray Jerusalem under siege. The prophet also lay on his left side for 390 days (to indicate the punishment of Israel for three centuries) and on his right side for 40 days (to symbolize the punishment of Judah for 40 years).

Ezekiel also had himself bound with cords to immobilize him until the symbolic siege was over. He ate a meager mixture of grains and water to indicate the coming food shortage in Jerusalem. He identified with his compatriots in Babylonian exile and with those who remained back home in Jerusalem under attack by the Babylonian army. Ezekiel determined to follow the Lord's instructions to the letter. That meant warning his people that they faced defeat at the hands of the Babylonians as a result of their disobedience.

## NOTES ON THE PRINTED TEXT

Ezekiel proclaimed God's message to his people on the Tel-Abib plain. Often using symbolic actions, he spoke of new and greater calamities yet to come. His symbolic acts added dramatic realism and vividly pictured the message.

*Take a brick and set it before you. On it portray a city, Jerusalem; and put siegeworks against it, and build a siege-wall against it, and cast up a ramp against it; set camps also against it, and plant battering rams against it all around* (4:1, 2). The prophet was commanded to take a mud brick and draw a map of Jerusalem upon it. This was unusual in Judah but very common in Babylon. The mud bricks were used not only for building but for writing.

Many inscribed tablets have been excavated in recent years. The bricks were made of soft clay with the sides flattened. Writers would use a stylus to inscribe the tablet, and then the tablet was baked in an oven to harden it. Ezekiel drew the map and then—in what looked like a child's game of war—carried out a miniature siege of a city. He included a besieged wall, the enemy's wall of circumvallation (a wall built for the besiegers' protection and to keep the fleeing occupants captive), siege ramps, camps, and battering rams.

*Then take an iron plate and place it as an iron wall between you and the city; set your face toward it, and let it be in a state of siege, and press the siege against it* (4:3). The prophet was instructed to place a common cooking utensil, an iron plate or griddle, between himself and the brick that represented Jerusalem. This symbolized the Lord's attitude toward the city: no chance for change. The Lord would destroy the city. *Then lie on your left side, and place the punishment of the house of Israel upon it* (4:4).

The Lord commanded a second symbolic action, instructing Ezekiel to lie on his left side for 390 days to indicate the punishment of Israel. In addition, he was to be on his right side 40 days to indicate the punishment of Judah. *When you have completed these, you shall lie down a second time, but on your right side, and bear the punishment of the house of Judah* (4:6).

*You shall set your face toward the siege of Jerusalem, and with your arm bared you shall prophesy against it* (4:7). In another symbolic action, like an attacking warrior lifting his bared arm, Ezekiel was to depict the siege of Jerusalem and denounce its citizens for their wickedness. In still another action, Ezekiel was to be tied with cords to portray the immobilizing siege. *See I am putting cords on you so that you cannot turn from one side to the other until you have completed the days of your siege* (4:8).

Ezekiel vividly portrayed the hardships within the besieged city, depicting famine and the resulting food rations. He ate only a carefully rationed mixture of grains and water. *And you, take wheat and barley, beans and lentils, millet and spelt; put them into one vessel, and make bread for yourself* (4:9). Jewish dietary laws forbade such mixtures of different grains. Yet with this scandalous diet, the prophet typified the shortage of food and how the populace had been reduced to ignoring the law in order to survive. *The food that you eat shall be twenty shekels a day by weight; at fixed times you shall eat it* (4:10). His bread ration was to be roughly eight ounces per day. *And you shall drink water by measures, one-sixth of a hin; at fixed times you shall drink* (4:11). The daily water ration was only two-thirds of a quart. The small amounts of bread and water portrayed the agonizing shortages within a besieged city.

The Lord also told Ezekiel how the Israelites would prepare and consume food and water. *You shall eat it as a barley-cake, baking it in their sight on human dung* (4:12). Ezekiel was ordered to cook his bread in an unclean manner to illustrate the desperate situation. Animal manure mixed with straw was commonly used for fuel in the Middle East where wood was, and still is, scarce. Therefore, cooking over human dung meant that no other fuel was available, that starving people had to resort to disgusting ways to survive. The prepared dough was either laid on a hot stone or placed directly onto the glowing fire. Obviously, the bread would be roughly brushed clean of ashes before it was eaten. Yet this method of cooking certainly made the food ritually unclean.

In this scene, the Lord wished to portray with abject realism the dismal conditions among the exiles. But Ezekiel balked at this command, and the Lord instead allowed him to use cow manure for fuel.

## SUGGESTIONS TO TEACHERS

Nations, like individuals, find it difficult to accept failure and defeat. Even after fifty years, Japan cannot bring itself to accept fully its role in World War II. Memories of being crushed centuries ago by rival ethnic groups have erupted into slaughter in what used to be Yugoslavia. The United States still struggles to come to terms with its defeat in Vietnam. The citizens of Judah, likewise, tried to understand how their nation could be overthrown and destroyed by Nebuchadnezzar.

Today's lesson will help you and your students consider how best to deal with failure and defeat. Each of us has experienced loss and defeat, and will do so again in the future. These things hurt. They also raise questions about life and about our relationship with God. With our culture's emphasis on success, and with the shame connected to failure, this lesson will be timely for everyone in your class.

1. SERMONS IN SYMBOLS. Ezekiel used dramatic actions to illustrate coming defeat and failure. Though stubborn citizens had no desire to hear this message, Ezekiel was sent to make them face up to reality.

God must sometimes deal bluntly with us to keep us from escaping into illusion. Only when we allow Him to show us the truth are we able to deal with our problems and griefs in effective ways.

2. CERTAINTY OF SIEGE. Ezekiel knew that Jerusalem was doomed. As God's spokesman, he could clearly read the signs of the times: the holy city would not survive. Merely having the magnificent temple, with its elaborate daily ceremonies, would not save the city.

People of faith can trace the meaning in the events around them. We have insight from the Spirit. We have a sense of history and of the way God has worked in the past. Let us stay close to the Lord and keep our ears and hearts open to God's message.

3. SIGNIFICANCE OF SUFFERING. Furthermore, as we live obediently before the Lord, we can read significance in the tragedies and failures
that come into our lives. In the final collapse of Jerusalem, Ezekiel and fellow prophets saw the result of Judah's persistent rebellion against God.

Some forms of human suffering follow directly from human disobedience,
just as certain forms of lung cancer, heart disease, and emphysema may
result from smoking. The main question, however, is how believers will
respond to the defeats and failures that befall them.

4. SCATTERING OF SURVIVORS. Ezekiel realized that survivors of
Jerusalem's capture would be deported. Being separated from supportive
families and familiar surroundings, the remnant would be forced to relocate in a hostile foreign area. Ezekiel's harsh picture of being uprooted and
struggling to survive also unintentionally describes the way that some in
our society feel today. Perhaps a few in your class privately think of their
current situation as a survival struggle. God has never given up on His people in any age. Through Christ we may be assured of His caring presence
in all circumstances.

## TOPIC FOR ADULTS
### FACING DEFEAT

*Thanksgiving, 1996.* We have much to be thankful for. Unfortunately, at
the very moment when the United States is continuing to downsize its military force, with consequent savings in the offing, the economy is sputter-
ing and no one seems to know when the next round of major growth will
come. Census statistics reported in the press indicate that the number of
Americans below the poverty line rose to 33.6 million, with nearly one in
seven now living in poverty.

And poverty seems to be on the increase. One-fifth of all children and
one-third of blacks are poor, according to the government's definitions. The
statistics also revealed that 47 percent of the nation's income went to the
20 percent of households with the highest earnings, while the 20 percent of
people earning the least got only 4 percent of income. Such statistics are
appalling. It will be difficult for us to enjoy a sumptuous feast at
Thanksgiving with these kinds of facts on our minds.

Thanksgiving 1996 will be a time for rejoicing that the world seems to be
a little bit safer in most parts than it once was. But it should also be a time
of sadness because so many are still lacking in the basic necessities of life.
Once again we need to be challenged by our political leaders and the
churches to seek a more just order in this land of plenty.

*Prophetic Quote.* "I often wonder whether we do not rest our hopes too
much upon constitutions, upon laws, and upon courts. These are false
hopes; believe me, these are false hopes. Liberty lies in the hearts of men
and women; when it dies there, no constitution, no law, no court can save
it."—Justice Learned Hand

*Triumph in Defeat.* Miami Dolphins receiver Irving Fryar was defeated
by substance abuse, a troubled marriage, and thoughts of suicide. Although
he had been a star at the University of Nebraska, was the number-one pick
in the 1984 draft, and became a successful receiver for the New England
Patriots, his personal life was crumbling. His career appeared to be over.

Then Fryar turned to Jesus Christ. "I was sick and tired of being sick and tired—making the wrong decisions, saying the wrong things, doing the wrong things," he acknowledged. "I decided it was time to stop running and listen to God." Through his relationship with Christ, Fryar began to discover that he was not defeated. The Dolphins provided him with a fresh start in 1993, and he went on to catch 64 passes for 1,010 yards. His new start also took him to the Pro Bowl for the first time.

Now a devout Christian, Irv Fryar kneels briefly in prayer following each of his touchdowns. He explains, "I'm spreading the Gospel. God is using me and football to spread the word." But after his outstanding performances on the field, Fryar shrugs off any praise. He has his focus on greater matters than winning football games. "When I die and go before Christ, He's not going to ask me how many touchdown passes I caught. That's not what's important to Him."

*Questions for Students on the Next Lesson.* 1. What did Zedekiah do to bring Nebuchaddnezzar to Jerusalem? 2. What happened in Jerusalem as a result? 3. Why were these events such a catastrophe to the people of Judah? 4. How does your faith help you in times of chaos and crises?

## TOPIC FOR YOUTH
### FACING DEFEAT

*Dim Forecast.* What will life be like in 2025? Will it continue as we know it? If you have wondered what the next thirty years will bring, then you have a good companion in Joseph F. Coates, president of a futurist consulting firm in Washington, D.C. The staff of Project 2025 prepared their predictions for a meeting of the World Future Society in Cambridge, Massachusetts, in 1994. They predicted continued worldwide stress and border conflicts. They also envisioned widespread contamination by detonation of a nuclear device, either accidentally or as a deliberate act of violence. The Social Security system will collapse.

Does such a portrayal of doom concern you? Is it defeatist? Remember that these are human predictions, not God's statements. Ezekiel was enacting God's sure word, not a futurist's guess.

*Apocalypse Maybe?* In the late summer of 1994, the prospect of comets crashing on the planet Jupiter produced a number of "end of the world" predictions. Some speculated that this event would flood planetariums with phone calls from fearful people. Radio commentator Harold Campbell went so far as to predict that the dreadful end of the earth would come on September 6th or 7th, based on his interpretation of signs in the sun, moon, and stars. Ultra-orthodox Lubavitch Jews interpreted the Zohar, an ancient Jewish mystical text, as predicting the comet's impact on Jupiter; they prepared for the Messiah's coming.

Perhaps you were like the 65 percent of Americans who wondered if life would continue as we know it. Certainly there were those in Ezekiel's audience who felt the same way.

*Prophets of Doom.* The high school class of the year 2000 faces some major problems, according to educators and pollsters. One expert, Joe Yavorka, states that the greatest challenge will be simply for those students to get to junior high, given the freedoms and concepts they are faced with everyday.

Others are even more pessimistic. The Carnegie Task Force on Meeting the Needs of Young Children reports that twelve million children under the age of three confront major risk factors. High infant mortality rates, low rates of child immunizations, poverty, substandard child care, and the increase in single-parent families will lead to serious educational and health problems. These problems will be expensive to tackle and hard to reverse. The task force concluded that some six million young people are not receiving the essential building blocks of good health and a nurturing home environment. This will lead to delinquency and high dropout rates. The report called for better health care protection, a quality child care program, and more support for the American family.

Ezekiel portrayed an even more devastating future for his people. Existence would become a life-or-death struggle as a result of the nation's sinfulness.

*Questions for Students on the Next Lesson.* 1. Who was Zedekiah? 2. Was he a good leader? 3. What happened to Jerusalem and Zedekiah? 4. Who was Nebuzaradan? 5. Which people were not taken into exile? Why?

# LESSON 11—NOVEMBER 10

## JERUSALEM FALLS

*Background Scripture:* II Kings 24—25
*Devotional Reading:* Psalm 74:1-12

### KING JAMES VERSION

II KINGS 24:20b Zedekiah rebelled against the king of Babylon.

25:1 And it came to pass in the ninth year of his reign, in the tenth month, in the tenth day of the month, that Nebuchadnezzar king of Babylon came, he, and all his host, against Jerusalem, and pitched against it; and they built forts against it round about.

2 And the city was besieged unto the eleventh year of king Zedekiah.

3 And on the ninth day of the fourth month the famine prevailed in the city, and there was no bread for the people of the land.

4 And the city was broken up, and all the men of war fled by night by the way of the gate between two walls, which is by the king's garden: (now the Chaldees were against the city round about:) and the king went the way toward the plain.

5 And the army of the Chaldees pursued after the king, and overtook him in the plains of Jericho: and all his army were scattered from him.

6 So they took the king, and brought him up to the king of Babylon to Riblah; and they gave judgment upon him.

7 And they slew the sons of Zedekiah before his eyes, and put out the eyes of Zedekiah, and bound him with fetters of brass, and carried him to Babylon.

8 And in the fifth month, on the seventh day of the month, which is the nineteenth year of king Nebuchadnezzar king of Babylon, came Nebuzaradan, captain of the guard, a servant of the king of Babylon, unto Jerusalem:

9 And he burnt the house of the Lord, and the king's house, and all the houses of Jerusalem, and every great man's house burnt he with fire.

10 And all the army of the Chaldees, that were with the captain of the guard, brake down the walls of Jerusalem round about.

11 Now the rest of the people that were left in the city, and the fugitives that fell away to the king of Babylon, with the remnant of the multitude, did Nebuzaradan the captain of the guard carry away.

12 But the captain of the guard left of the

### NEW REVISED STANDARD VERSION

II KINGS 24:20b Zedekiah rebelled against the king of Babylon.

25:1 And in the ninth year of his reign, in the tenth month, on the tenth day of the month, King Nebuchadnezzar of Babylon came with all his army against Jerusalem, and laid siege to it; they built siegeworks against it all around. 2 So the city was besieged until the eleventh year of King Zedekiah. 3 On the ninth day of the fourth month the famine became so severe in the city that there was no food for the people of the land. 4 Then a breach was made in the city wall; the king with all the soldiers fled by night by the way of the gate between the two walls, by the king's garden, though the Chaldeans were all around the city. They went in the direction of the Arabah. 5 But the army of the Chaldeans pursued the king, and overtook him in the plains of Jericho; all his army was scattered, deserting him. 6 Then they captured the king and brought him up to the king of Babylon at Riblah, who passed sentence on him. 7 They slaughtered the sons of Zedekiah before his eyes, then put out the eyes of Zedekiah; they bound him in fetters and took him to Babylon.

8 In the fifth month, on the seventh day of the month—which was the nineteenth year of King Nebuchadnezzar, king of Babylon—Nebuzaradan, the captain of the bodyguard, a servant of the king of Babylon, came to Jerusalem. 9 He burned the house of the Lord, the king's house, and all the houses of Jerusalem; every great house he burned down. 10 All the army of the Chaldeans who were with the captain of the guard broke down the walls around Jerusalem. 11 Nebuzaradan the captain of the guard carried into exile the rest of the people who were left in the city and the deserters who had defected to the king of Babylon—all the rest of the population. 12 But the captain of the guard left some of the poorest people of the land to be vinedressers and tillers of the soil.

poor of the land to be vinedressers and hus-
bandmen.

*KEY VERSE: If you will not listen, my soul will weep in secret for your
pride; my eyes will weep bitterly and run down with tears, because the
Lord's flock has been taken captive.* Jeremiah 13:17.

## HOME BIBLE READINGS

| Nov. | 4 | M. | II Kings 24:1-7 | *The Reign of Jehoiakim* |
|------|---|----|-----------------|--------------------------|
| Nov. | 5 | T. | II Kings 24:8-19 | *Second Capture of Jerusalem* |
| Nov. | 6 | W. | II Kings 25:13-17 | *The Destruction of the Temple* |
| Nov. | 7 | T. | II Kings 25:18-24 | *The Leaders Taken to Babylon* |
| Nov. | 8 | F. | II Kings 25:25-30 | *King Jehoiakim Set Free* |
| Nov. | 9 | S. | Psalm 74:1-11 | *Appeal to God for Help* |
| Nov. | 10 | S. | Psalm 74:12-17 | *God's Sovereign Power* |

## BACKGROUND

"O Lord, what a century you caused me to live in," the great church
father Polycarp once prayed, referring to the tumultuous days in which he
lived (about A. D. 69—156). Those who survived the calamitous final days of
Jerusalem could have echoed his words.

For years, the prophets had foretold a day of reckoning. The nation, the
temple, and all the institutions of the great kingdom inaugurated by David
and Solomon had gradually decayed. Like dry rot slowly destroying the
supporting timbers of a great structure, moral and spiritual decay had been
eating away at God's community. The process had been slow, taking centuries. But in the final century of its existence, Judah displayed disturbing
symptoms of spiritual disease. Hezekiah and Josiah tried to shore up the
collapsing nation with their reform movements. But after their deaths, the
ominous signs of collapse appeared again.

When one of history's decisive battles took place at Carchemish in 605
B.C., the Chaldeans of Babylon defeated the Assyrians. The international
chessboard changed drastically. The new world superpower, Babylon,
quickly captured the Middle East.

In Judah, King Jehoiachin foolishly allowed himself to support a revolt
against the sovereign Babylonians, who had demanded tribute. King
Nebuchadnezzar swiftly quashed the uprising in 597 B.C. The best of the
temple articles and the cream of Judah's leaders, including Jehoiachin,
were packed off to Babylon.

The vassal king installed in Jerusalem, Zedekiah, should have been content to preserve the vestiges of freedom and national identity left to Judah
under the Babylonian overlords. Yet like his predecessor, Jehoiachin, he
was poorly advised by hotheaded nationalists. Another rebellion flared in
Judah. This time the Babylonians were pitiless, and Jerusalem suffered
horribly under a terrible siege. The Hebrew army fled and was wiped out.

The victorious Babylonian troops ruthlessly slaughtered many of the citizens and brutally herded the survivors along an 800-mile death march to
camps in Babylon. The last valuable treasures in the temple were seized,
the magnificent structure itself burned and razed. The rest of Jerusalem

was also torched, reducing the once-beautiful capital to smoking rubble. The unbelievable had happened. Jerusalem had fallen.

## NOTES ON THE PRINTED TEXT

*Zedekiah rebelled against the king of Babylon* (24:20). Nebuchadnezzar besieged Jerusalem in 597, and Jehoiachin surrendered the city. The leaders of the anti-Babylonian government, including the king, were deported. (Many nonbiblical references detail these times: The Babylonian Chronicle and hundreds of receipts unearthed in the archives of Babylonia.)

Nebuchadnezzar appointed Jehoiachin's twenty-one-year-old uncle, Zedekiah, to rule. Unfortunately, anti-Babylonian feelings still ran high, and Zedekiah began to plot with Egypt. Supported by Egyptian promises, Zedekiah rebelled against Babylon in 589 B.C. As a result, Nebuchadnezzar came to Palestine bent on destruction. Within a year he was again at the walls of Jerusalem. *And in the ninth year of his reign, in the tenth month, on the tenth day of the month, King Nebuchadnezzar of Babylon came with his army against Jerusalem, and laid siege to it* (25:1).

Quickly Nebuchadnezzar sealed off the city with siegeworks while he devastated the rest of the country. *They built siegeworks against it all around* (25:1). He constructed earthen-work walls, tunnels, and towers. Battering rams were hauled in to destroy the gates and break down the thick walls of the city. Jeremiah urged the fearful Zedekiah to surrender the city.

In the summer of 587 B.C., the city's food supply ran out, and some of the starving inhabitants resorted to cannibalism. *On the ninth day of the fourth month the famine became so severe in the city that there was no food for the people of the land* (25:3).

The battering rams continued to hammer the city's walls. *Then a breach was made in the city wall* (25:4). In the late 1960s, Dr. Kathleen Kenyon excavated along the southern wall of the temple, searching for the ancient walls of the city. Along the hillside, well down the slope, she found a wall. Evidently Nebuchadnezzar's battering rams hammered the wall with such force that they loosened the terraces, causing homes built on them to slide down the hillside.

*The king with all the soldiers fled by night by way of the gate between the two walls, by the king's garden, though the Chaldeans were all around the city. They went in the direction of the Arabah* (25:4). Under the cover of darkness, Zedekiah and his men slipped through the city's southeastern gate near Ophel and hurried toward the Jordan River. Apparently they were hoping to reach Ammon, whose citizens had loyally supported the rebellion.

However, the pursuing Babylonians captured Zedekiah on the plains of Jericho and transported him northward to Riblah in Syria, where Nebuchadnezzar awaited. *But the army of the Chaldeans pursued the king, and overtook him in the plains of Jericho; all his army was scattered, deserting him. Then they captured the king and brought him up to the king of Babylon at Riblah, who passed sentence on him* (25:5, 6).

Nebuchadnezzar had had enough of Judean intrigue and rebellion. Zedekiah's sons were murdered before his eyes. Then he was blinded, placed in chains, and deported to Babylon.

About a month later, Nebuzaradan, the captain of Nebuchadnezzar's personal bodyguard, arrived in Jerusalem. With ruthless precision he destroyed the city. First his men looted the temple, stripping it of everything of value. Then they burned it. The king's palace and all the homes were then destroyed.

Recent excavations reveal the terrible destruction. Charred wood, ashes, and soot are mixed with the triple-winged Babylonian arrowheads. The fire caused the upper stories of homes to collapse, thereby preserving bits of furniture, pottery, and pieces of ivory intact. Finally, the city walls were pulled down. *He burned the house of the Lord, the king's house, and all the houses of Jerusalem; every great house he burned down. All the army of the Chaldeans who were with the captain of the guard broke down the walls around Jerusalem* (25:9, 10).

While the elite of the land, along with the military and governmental leaders, were executed, much of the populace was deported to Babylon. Only the poorest remained behind. *But the captain of the guard left some of the poorest people of the land to be vinedressers and tillers of the soil* (25:12).

## SUGGESTIONS TO TEACHERS

Immediately after the disastrous 1993 earthquake in Los Angeles, a man who survived the loss of his wife and destruction of his home tearfully told a reporter, "I just don't know how I can pick up the pieces and go on."

We've all suffered loss and despair. But the scene described in our Scripture for this lesson is truly devastating. Jerusalem's sixth-century citizens experienced the kind of trauma we would have if Washington or Ottawa or London were bombed and burned into total ruin, and all leading citizens executed or imprisoned. The great holy city was demolished. All the promises begun with King David were seemingly dismantled. Hope had been extinguished, the catastrophe complete.

Hardest to understand, however, was the assertion by the prophets that God had allowed all of this to happen. How could the survivors pick up the pieces of life and go on? Is God truly involved in human affairs?

1. RESULT OF SINS. The Bible plainly states that God is indeed involved in human affairs. In fact, God continues to hold humans accountable. Their actions must be in accord with His will . . . or disorder in society results. In the case of ancient Judah, the fall of Jerusalem followed years of disregard for God's divine commandments.

2. REFUSAL OF SOVEREIGN. Jehoiachin, Judah's ruler, persisted in evil ways. He thereby led his country deeper into difficulty. Leaders have the duty to lead their people in right living. Whether leading a congregation, a class, a club, or a family, we are accountable to the Lord to set the moral tone and provide godly guidance.

3. REBELLION OF SURVIVORS. Before the final collapse of Jerusalem, many people refused to accept the prophets' proclamations and started another uprising against the Babylonians. Their foolish decision resulted in the fiery end of Jerusalem.

God's people know they must accept responsibility for their sins and also suffer for the sins of those in the wider community. Along with individual guilt, we all share in a corporate guilt. Even innocent persons suffer from the wrongdoing of others.

4. REIGN OF SUFFERING. The Scripture readings in this lesson describe the terrors of Jerusalem's final days. The catalog of horrors includes cowardly desertion, assassination, torture, murder, looting, and other crimes.

You need not dwell on all the details of II Kings 25. But stress that God fulfills His purposes for His people even in the midst of crisis and chaos. Encourage your class members to reflect on God's sovereignty in all circumstances. Help them develop the kind of faith they'll need to navigate life's deepest waters.

## TOPIC FOR ADULTS
### EXPERIENCING THE UNBELIEVABLE

*Lost Brilliance and Promise.* No baseball season started with more promise than the season of 1994. Baseball's owners planned playoffs featuring wild-card entries, and an exciting World Series would follow.

As the season advanced, everyone thought the change would be one of baseball's shining moments. Attendance figures soared.

Old performance records were being challenged, too. Ken Griffey, Jr., Matt Williams, and Frank Thomas chased Roger Maris's home-run record. Tony Gwynn threatened Ted Williams's hallowed .406 batting average. Jeff Bagwell closed in on a triple crown; Cal Ripken came closer to Lou Gehrig's string of consecutive games; the Cleveland Indians edged toward a pennant race. The century-old American pastime thrived.

Then came the strike. Even during World War II, when the game's greatest stars served in the military, the October Classic went on. When the great Bay Area earthquake struck California in 1989, baseball continued. Yet the 1994 season collapsed in a wrangle of whining, greed, and anger. The year that had opened with such grand possibilities concluded in loss and failure for everyone. In addition to disappointing their fans, major league players lost $230 million in salaries—an average of almost $300,000 per player. And owners failed to collect around $600 million in revenues. Each major-league city lost an average of $1.6 million for each canceled home game, and 1,200 full-time or part-time employees lost their jobs at each ball park. Local businesses lost over $640,000 per canceled game.

Great countries, like great national pastimes, can be ruined by moral decline on the part of leaders and participants. The nation of Israel began with brilliance and promise. The temple and the holy city embodied the greatness of the community of God's people. Through the centuries, though, the ways of the Lord lost their appeal for the people. Jerusalem began to live under the illusion that God would never allow the institution of the temple to end. But the unthinkable occurred in 586 B.C.

*Banished.* Two seventeen-year-old Tlinget Indian boys, Simon Roberts and Adrian Guthrie, pleaded guilty to attacking an Everett, Washington, man with a baseball bat in May, 1994. The victim's hearing and eyesight were permanently damaged. Rather than sending them to prison, a Washington state judge agreed to send the boys north to Alaska to face the Tlinget tribal court. The tribal court held a hearing in Klawock, Alaska, to determine the sentence to hand the two youths and to decide what amount of restitution to give the victim.

This was the first time a criminal case had been referred by a state court to a tribal panel for sentencing. The tribal court finally decided on banishment to two unpopulated islands for a year to eighteen months. In its opinion, this would be preferable to a prison term in a state penitentiary. Each boy was sent to a separate isolated island in Alaska's vast Alexander Archipelago. Each was given materials to construct a simple, one-room cabin along with supplies to survive during the harsh winters.

God decreed that the most suitable punishment for Jerusalem's sin was also banishment. In spite of repeated warnings by His prophets, Judah persisted in flouting the divine will. Finally, the Lord called the nation to accountability and meted out the sentence: banishment of the leaders to Babylon.

*God's Verdict on Nations Today?* The *London Guardian* estimates that the cost of building 23 Patriot missiles would "buy twelve months of clothes, seeds, and pots—and pay for their storage—for two million people in Mozambique." The cost of building 216 Tomahawk cruise missiles would "buy food needed in Ethiopia for six months." One bomb on a B-52 would "run a clinic for 4,060 patients in Bangladesh for one month, or set up a self-running medical supply system for a rural population of 100,000." The cost of training one Tornado jet pilot would "provide 25,000 Eritrean families with enough seeds and tools to recover from drought."—World Press Review.

What is the verdict of the Lord on the world's powers today, we who spend this disproportionate amount on armaments while neglecting the needy?

*Questions for Students on the Next Lesson.* 1. What happened to Jerusalem's citizens after the fall of the city? 2. Whom did some of the people blame for their troubles? 3. How do you think it feels to be forsaken by God? 4. What kinds of people often feel forgotten and rejected in our society today? 5. How has God sustained you during life's trials?

## TOPIC FOR YOUTH
### JUDGMENT COMES

*Returned.* Sarah Thompson, then thirteen, vanished on Saturday morning, August 20, 1994. She, along with her mother and her ten-year-old sister, were staying with her brother for the weekend in Pittsburgh. They had stopped for a visit as they moved from Charlotte, North Carolina, to Newport, Rhode Island. Sarah arose early Saturday and left a note saying she was going for a walk. She never returned.

A massive police hunt ensued. Special dogs sniffed through the parks. Officers interviewed people and checked buildings and garbage cans, looking for Sarah. All-points bulletins were issued. Family members around the nation were alerted.

Thirty-eight hours later, Sarah was found in Charlotte by her friends. The teen had simply decided to return to her home city. She had approached elderly people and asked for rides, fearful of any young person.

While Sarah's crisis had a happy ending, Israel's did not. The nation and its people could not escape and return to their home. God's foretold judgment had come to pass.

*Accepted the Court's Judgment.* A teen-age girl from Kittanning, Pennsylvania, apologized to the court and to the parents of three-year-old Ashley Cunningham and her five-year-old sister, Tashina. The teen was baby-sitting the two girls when she became upset that the two youngsters would not go to sleep. She decided to discipline the two. She took Ashley and placed her in the family's dryer and then turned it on for several minutes. Fortunately, the little girl was only bruised. Her sister was not so lucky. Forced into the now hot dryer, the five-year-old received second degree burns and bruises over her ears, arms, thighs, hands, and buttocks. When removed from the dryer, she was bright red.

Charged with aggravated assault, reckless endangerment, and child endangerment, the baby-sitter faced a hearing and trial. Instead, the young woman agreed to the judgment of psychiatric counseling and probation.

The baby-sitter had to understand that these two children suffered because of her decisions and actions. Israel had to make a similar discovery. The people's actions brought repercussions they never dreamed of, in the form of judgment.

*Food for Thought.* Eleven-year-old Heather Saunders and her four younger siblings know hunger and deprivation. When Heather's father left and divorced her mother, Terri, the family discovered how life-styles can drastically change. The father pays the family $50 dollars a month. Terri receives $294 in cash from the state every two weeks and $350 a month in food stamps. Her rent is $335 a month, leaving little money for other things.

Terri and Heather have turned to a local food bank for help. There they receive some butter and canned goods. Occasionally, they receive a turkey. On these days of the month, the refrigerator and pantry are as full as they will get. In months that have a fifth week, the pantry is bare. Terri and her five children survive on what little is left over.

This family quickly discovered what hunger, deprivation, and poverty mean. Many youth who have full stomachs and warm clothing and comfortable homes will never know what it is to be poor and hungry. Jeremiah proclaimed judgment to such people; they would suffer poverty and hunger because of their own sins.

*Questions for Students on the Next Lesson.* 1. What is the theme of Lamentations? 2. Is the author pessimistic, optimistic, or realistic? 3. How were those not taken into exile treated? 4. Is it permissible to complain to God? Explain. 5. On what note does Lamentations end? Why?

# LESSON 12—NOVEMBER 17

## A CRY OF ANGUISH

*Background Scripture:* Lamentations
*Devotional Reading:* Psalm 13:1-6

### KING JAMES VERSION

LAMENTATIONS 5:1 Remember, O Lord, what is come upon us: consider, and behold our reproach.

2 Our inheritance is turned to strangers, our houses to aliens.

3 We are orphans and fatherless, our mothers are as widows.

4 We have drunken our water for money; our wood is sold unto us.

5 Our necks are under persecution: we labour, and have no rest.

6 We have given the hand to the Egyptians, and to the Assyrians, to be satisfied with bread.

7 Our fathers have sinned, and are not; and we have borne their iniquities.

8 Servants have ruled over us: there is none that doth deliver us out of their hand.

9 We gat our bread with the peril of our lives because of the sword of the wilderness.

10 Our skin was black like an oven because of the terrible famine.

19 Thou, O Lord, remainest for ever; thy throne from generation to generation.

20 Wherefore dost thou forget us for ever, and forsake us so long time?

21 Turn thou us unto thee, O Lord, and we shall be turned; renew our days as of old.

22 But thou hast utterly rejected us; thou art very wroth against us.

### NEW REVISED STANDARD VERSION

LAMENTATIONS 5:1 Remember, O Lord, what has befallen us; look, and see our disgrace! 2 Our inheritance has been turned over to strangers, our homes to aliens. 3 We have become orphans, fatherless; our mothers are like widows. 4 We must pay for the water we drink; the wood we get must be bought. 5 With a yoke on our necks we are hard driven; we are weary, we are given no rest. 6 We have made a pact with Egypt and Assyria, to get enough bread. 7 Our ancestors sinned; they are no more, and we bear their iniquities. 8 Slaves rule over us; there is no one to deliver us from their hand. 9 We get our bread at the peril of our lives, because of the sword in the wilderness. 10 Our skin is black as an oven from the scorching heat of famine.

19 But you, O Lord, reign forever; your throne endures to all generations. 20 Why have you forgotten us completely? Why have you forsaken us these many days? 21 Restore us to yourself, O Lord, that we may be restored; renew our days as of old— 22 unless you have utterly rejected us, and are angry with us beyond measure.

**KEY VERSE:** *Restore us to yourself, O Lord, that we may be restored; renew our days as of old. Lamentations 5:21.*

## HOME BIBLE READINGS

| | | | | |
|---|---|---|---|---|
| Nov. | 11 | M. | Lamentations 3:1-9 | *Prophet's Lament* |
| Nov. | 12 | T. | Lamentations 3:10-20 | *Prophet Bitter Over Conditions* |
| Nov. | 13 | W. | Lamentations 3:21-30 | *Prophet Recalls God's Mercies* |
| Nov. | 14 | T. | Lamentations 3:31-39 | *Prophet Acknowledges Need for Punishment* |
| Nov. | 15 | F. | Lamentations 3:40-48 | *Prophet Examines the Situation* |
| Nov. | 16 | S. | Lamentations 3:55-66 | *Prophet Urges Vengeance on Enemies* |
| Nov. | 17 | S. | Psalm 13 | *Assurance of God's Deliverance* |

## BACKGROUND

Long before Elizabeth Kubler-Ross and others began to describe the various aspects of grieving, the Hebrew poet described them in Lamentations. The writer poured out his feelings of anger, guilt, and despair, questioning the meaning of his sufferings in a series of five poems.

Hebrew scholars point out that each of these poems is a literary masterpiece. The first four start with the first letter of the Hebrew alphabet in the first verse. These poems then continue with the successive letters at the start of each of the succeeding verses, going through the entire alphabet of twenty-two letters. In the third poem or chapter, the process is repeated three times for a total of sixty-six verses. This literary device is called an acrostic. Some think this carefully-devised scheme of arranging the verses was meant to help people memorize them as prayers.

The five poems sob with a sense of utter tragedy. The horrors of the siege and its aftermath are told with stark frankness. The poet plaintively cries out that Jerusalem's destruction does not make any sense. He and his people feel wronged and tormented by God. Is there any meaning in the midst of this soul-searing experience?

Significantly, Jews to this day use portions of Lamentations each August 9th to commemorate the destruction of Solomon's Temple in 586 B.C. Some churches' liturgies incorporate selections from Lamentations in their services during the last three days of Holy Week.

Although these five laments over the terrible ruin of Jerusalem show the candle of faith flickering, they also reveal that faith had not been snuffed out. Throughout these verses, we notice that God's people, though crying out in anguish, continue to have some sense that the Lord has a future in store for them.

Through the Good News of the risen Christ, we Christians realize that God insists on bringing new beginnings to tragic endings. We are the "Easter people." We know that tears and tragedy are not God's final word. Rather, He bestows new life through the triumphant living Lord.

## NOTES ON THE PRINTED TEXT

Jerusalem lay devastated; the temple was in ruins. Judah's most prominent citizens had been deported to Babylon. Out of this experience arose poetic dirges expressing profound grief.

*Remember, O Lord, what has befallen us; look, and see our disgrace!* (5:1). The writer asked God to remember the devastation that had befallen the covenant people. The author went on to describe the nation's plight. *Our inheritance has been turned over to strangers, our homes to aliens. We have become orphans; fatherless; our mothers are like widows* (5:2, 3). The land, which was the nation's inheritance, had been occupied by strangers. Even their homes had been taken over by foreigners. The people sensed no heavenly support, feeling like helpless orphans. Many of the fathers, in fact, had died in the battle for Jerusalem or had been carried into exile.

Forced to labor, they now had to pay for what had once been free. *We must pay for the water we drink; the wood we get must be bought* (5:4). The people had been enslaved, laboring like animals without rest. *With a yoke on our necks we are hard driven; we are weary, we are given no rest* (5:5).

The land that once flowed with milk and honey was originally able to produce more than enough food for everyone. Now the nation had to look to other parts of the world to buy food. The nation literally had to make deals with its traditional enemies in order to purchase food. *We have made a pact with Egypt and Assyria, to get enough bread* (5:6).

The writer, like the people, blamed the nation's problems on his ancestors. While many had died or were exiled, the children now were paying for the parents' sins. *Our ancestors sinned; they are no more, and we bear their iniquities* (5:7).

Puppet rulers, those who had been given power by the Babylonians, now ruled the people. Quite likely, these were slaves of the Babylonians who were now given power to serve in responsible positions for their masters. *Slaves rule over us; there is no one to deliver us from their hand* (5:8). So weak were the people that they had no defense against desert raiders. Even their food was in jeopardy. *We get our bread at the peril of our lives, because of the sword in the wilderness* (5:9).

Forced to labor long and hard in the hot sun, the people experienced only hunger and famine. *Our skin is black as an oven from the scorching heat of famine* (5:10). The writer continued his lament, describing the appalling suffering and torture of women, rulers, and old and young men. The people's spirits had collapsed; depression reigned.

In spite of the terrible catastrophe, people still had confidence in the Lord. Even though the people felt forsaken, they affirmed that God was still in charge. *But you, O Lord, reign forever; your throne endures to all generations. Why have you forgotten us completely? Why have you forsaken us these many days?* (5:19, 20).

The poem closed on a prayerful note of restoration. Hope, faith, and trust still existed. *Restore us to yourself, O Lord, that we may be restored; renew our days as of old—unless you have utterly rejected us, and are angry with us beyond measure* (5:21, 22).

## SUGGESTIONS TO TEACHERS

In the past few decades, a specialty known as "grief therapy" has come into existence within the counseling profession. Professional counselors, ministers, nurses, and others who work with people in mourning know that "keep a stiff upper lip" is poor advice. Grief must be addressed and expressed.

Sensibly, the Hebrew Scriptures have dealt with grieving in a helpful way, allowing people avenues to express their anguish. God does bring healing as we come to Him in all candidness about our deepest hurts.

1. WOUNDED PEOPLE LIKE A WIDOWED PRINCESS. The five laments can be read in one sitting. Pick out some of the details that describe the suffering and heartache of those who survived destruction and deportation.

The Bible faces death head-on. No pretense in Lamentations! Let some of the vivid images in these verses open the way for students to share about how they deal with death and loss in their own lives. Before healing takes place, the pain and loss must be acknowledged and consciously grieved. And the Scriptures allow God's people to express exactly how they feel.

After all, God knows how they feel. He is no doubt pleased to have us come before Him in all honesty—even when we passionately express our hurt and anger.

2. WEEPING PROPHET AND A WOEFUL PETITION. Look at chapters 3 and 5, in which the writer pours out a torrent of tears mingled with anger, guilt, and questioning. Trying to find meaning in the terrible tragedy, he pleads with the Lord to give him answers. The entire range of grief pours forth. Let these chapters encourage discussion on the ways in which Christians may appropriately deal with death and tragedy. This might also be a good time to discuss what constitutes a proper Christian funeral.

3. WORTHY PRAISE TO THE WATCHFUL POWER. Don't overlook the ways that the poet continually brings up the Lord in his musings. He cannot shake the certainty that God continues to remember His people and will eventually restore them. Spend plenty of lesson time focusing on Lamentations 3:21-36; 4:22; and 5:19-22.

God has assured us through Christ that He stays with us through all circumstances. Throughout the anguishing times that His people may suffer, His promise abides: "Although he causes grief, he will have compassion according to the abundance of his steadfast love; for he does not willingly afflict or grieve anyone" (3:32, 33). With such a promise, believers may face every kind of trial and terror.

## TOPIC FOR ADULTS
### LONGING FOR RESTORATION

*Lament at Sunrise.* One of the earliest European travelers to Tierra del Fuego, the barren, windswept area on the extreme southern part of South America, reported a curious practice among the hostile natives. Each morning at sunrise they howled with anguish. Their piercing wails bewildered the visitor. He finally learned that the inhabitants were so miserable with hunger and afflictions in their inhospitable land that they dreaded the arrival of each new day. Each sunrise meant more trouble, another round of unhappiness. Their response was to break into shrieks of despair.

Although most of us don't howl with anguish at sunrise, we may often dread the dawn of a new day. All of our problems come rushing back at us as soon as the mindless bliss of sleep departs.

The people of Jerusalem plunged to the depths of despair after the Babylonians captured and destroyed their city. Had God indeed forsaken them? Lamentations reflected their sense of rejection. Only a few of the faithful were able to affirm that God was still in charge and would bring restoration.

*Pass It On.* George and Laurie Navin experienced crushing heartache when their newborn daughter Lindsey was diagnosed with cerebral palsy. In addition, they learned that their little infant was mentally retarded, blind, and afflicted with a severe seizure disorder. Their problems were made worse by the extremely expensive medical equipment required to care for Lindsey, much of it not covered by insurance.

But George and Laurie Navin refused to whimper with disappointment. It occurred to them that other couples might face the same struggles in securing expensive medical equipment. As Lindsey grew, they began passing on the things she had outgrown. Since 1992, the Navins have been collecting and donating used medical equipment to people with little or no health insurance. George and Laurie call their enterprise "Pass It On."

Headquartered in their home in Hatchville, Massachusetts, Pass It On has helped more than 600 families. In addition to walkers, crutches, and commodes, they have provided hundreds of hospital beds, nearly a hundred manual wheelchairs, dozens of pediatric wheelchairs, porch lifts, and intravenous pumps throughout Massachusetts. Pass It On is one family's answer to a cry of anguish.

*Remembering the Forgotten.* As most of us sit down to sumptuous turkey dinners in comfortable surroundings on Thanksgiving Day, we must recall the biblical injunction to remember the poor and oppressed. Although many agencies will be providing a hot Thanksgiving meal to needy persons, more than twenty million fellow Americans depend on soup kitchens or food banks for meals each day throughout the year.

Consider some of the other startling statistics. One-fifth of the world's people are too poor to feed themselves. More than 900 children a day go blind in developing countries due to the lack of vitamin A in their diets. And over 500,000 rural homes here in the U.S., affecting at least 1.2 million Americans, do not have clean, running water. Many of these folks feel forsaken by society and by the Lord.

*Questions for Students on the Next Lesson.* 1. Describe Ezekiel's vision in the valley of the dry bones. 2. What did this vision symbolize? 3. What was Ezekiel's message (as a result of his vision) to those in exile? 4. In what ways has God given you a new beginning? 5. How might your congregation help bring hope to those in desperate circumstances in your community?

## TOPIC FOR YOUTH
### WHY ME?

*Pitcher's Answer.* "Why me?" Judah was asking when the Book of Lamentations was written. And the same question continues to be asked by persons today. Perhaps you throw that "Why me, Lord?" to God when things aren't going well in your own life.

Ralph Branca did. Ralph was a young star pitcher in the National League. His skill brought him awards and a good salary. In the National League play-offs in 1951, Ralph threw the famous pitch that Bobby Thomson hit for a home run to win the National League pennant. And Branca was not allowed to forget that he was the pitcher who lost the game and the pennant race. He received hate mail and abusive telephone calls. Extremely troubled, he went to his minister.

"Why did this have to happen to me?" he asked his pastor.

The clergyman replied, "God gave you this cross to bear because he knew you'd be strong enough to carry it."

Branca has lived with the awareness that people still identify him with only that one pitch. But his faith enables him to live with it. Unlike other sports stars who have been driven to alcoholism or suicide in trying to deal with the "Why me?" question, Branca has enjoyed a successful business career. He attributes his ability to handle that episode to this: knowing that God has given him enough strength to carry any failure or setback.

*Anguished Cry.* A Chinese family had settled in Hawaii in the 1860s. The family members were put to work clearing the land to plant sugar cane. It was hard work, but they were willing to do the backbreaking labor in the hot sun. What they resented was the rule that forbade talking on the job. Overwhelmed by the natural beauty—and the loneliness—they wished to converse.

A young Chinese girl watched her great-grandfather go through a ritual. Lonely, overworked, and far from home and family, he would go out and dig a large hole in the rich Hawaiian cane field. Then he would kneel at it's side and chant, "I want my home. I want my home. Home. Home." Then, he would cover the soil, trusting that the cane, when it had grown, would seed the air with his lament.

Centuries earlier, Hebrew exiles voiced a similar lament and prayed to God to remember them.

*Ignored by the System.* Katie Beers was abandoned by her mother when she was two months old. She was taken in by her godmother, Linda Inghilleri, and her husband, Sal. Even then, life was not good. As early as age seven, Katie was often seen hauling dirty clothes to the laundry. Poorly dressed and dirty, she was nicknamed "Roach Girl" by other children. As a result, she skipped school and wandered the streets alone at night. At age eight, she was abused by Sal. County social workers in Bay Shore, New York, reported the squalid conditions they found in the Inghilleri home, but the pathetic little girl was ignored by the system.

Katie became a national symbol of child abuse when she was kidnapped by John Esposito and imprisoned in a six-foot-square concrete bunker under his converted garage. For sixteen days, Katie sat chained in the underground cage before being rescued by police.

Now she has begun a new life. She lives with a family that has three children. She has made the school honor roll and has won awards in chorus and softball. Despite the times when she hides her face in a pillow, recalling her past abuse and rejection, her life is beginning again. Her abusive past is behind her; a new life has opened for her.

*Questions for Students on the Next Lesson.* 1. Describe the historical background of Ezekiel's preaching. 2. How was the imagery of Ezekiel's vision appropriate? 3. What promise did Ezekiel offer to his people? 4. Does God still breathe renewal into people, congregations, and nations? If so, how? 5. Does God always forgive and renew? What is your personal experience with this?

# LESSON 13—NOVEMBER 24

## GOD'S POWER TO RESTORE

*Background Scripture:* Ezekiel 37
*Devotional Reading:* Hosea 14:1-9

### KING JAMES VERSION

EZEKIEL 37:1 The hand of the Lord was upon me, and carried me out in the spirit of the Lord, and set me down in the midst of the valley which was full of bones,

2 And caused me to pass by them round about: and, behold, there were very many in the open valley; and, lo, they were very dry.

3 And he said unto me, Son of man, can these bones live? And I answered, O Lord God, thou knowest.

4 Again he said unto me, Prophesy upon these bones, and say unto them, O ye dry bones, hear the word of the Lord.

5 Thus saith the Lord God unto these bones; Behold, I will cause breath to enter into you, and ye shall live:

6 And I will lay sinews upon you, and will bring up flesh upon you, and cover you with skin, and put breath in you, and ye shall live; and ye shall know that I am the Lord.

7 So I prophesied as I was commanded: and as I prophesied, there was a noise, and behold a shaking, and the bones came together, bone to his bone.

8 And when I beheld, lo, the sinews and the flesh came up upon them, and the skin covered them above: but there was no breath in them.

9 Then said he unto me, Prophesy unto the wind, prophesy, son of man, and say to the wind, Thus saith the Lord God; Come from the four winds, O breath, and breathe upon these slain, that they may live.

10 So I prophesied as he commanded me, and the breath came into them, and they lived, and stood up upon their feet, an exceeding great army.

11 Then he said unto me, Son of man, these bones are the whole house of Israel: behold, they say, Our bones are dried, and our hope is lost: we are cut off for our parts.

12 Therefore prophesy and say unto them, Thus saith the Lord God; Behold, O my people, I will open your graves, and cause you to come up out of your graves, and bring you into the land of Israel.

14 And shall put my spirit in you, and ye shall live, and I shall place you in your own land: then shall ye know that I the Lord have spoken it, and performed it, saith the Lord.

### NEW REVISED STANDARD VERSION

EZEKIEL 37:1 The hand of the Lord came upon me, and he brought me out by the spirit of the Lord and set me down in the middle of a valley; it was full of bones. 2 He led me all around them; there were very many lying in the valley, and they were very dry. 3 He said to me, "Mortal, can these bones live?" I answered, "O Lord God, you know." 4 Then he said to me, "Prophesy to these bones, and say to them: O dry bones, hear the word of the Lord. 5 Thus says the Lord God to these bones: I will cause breath to enter you, and you shall live. 6 I will lay sinews on you, and will cause flesh to come upon you, and cover you with skin, and put breath in you, and you shall live; and you shall know that I am the Lord."

7 So I prophesied as I had been commanded; and as I prophesied, suddenly there was a noise, a rattling, and the bones came together, bone to its bone. 8 I looked, and there were sinews on them, and flesh had come upon them, and skin had covered them; but there was no breath in them. 9 Then he said to me, "Prophesy to the breath, prophesy, mortal, and say to the breath: Thus says the Lord God: Come from the four winds, O breath, and breathe upon these slain, that they may live." 10 I prophesied as he commanded me, and the breath came into them, and they lived, and stood on their feet, a vast multitude.

11 Then he said to me, "Mortal, these bones are the whole house of Israel. They say, 'Our bones are dried up, and our hope is lost; we are cut off completely.' 12 Therefore prophesy, and say to them, Thus says the Lord God: I am going to open your graves, and bring you up from your graves, O my people; and I will bring you back to the land of Israel. 14 I will put my spirit within you, and you shall live, and I will place you on your own soil; then you shall know that I, the Lord, have spoken and will act," says the Lord.

*KEY VERSE: I will put my spirit within you, and you shall live, and I will place you on your own soil; then you shall know that I, the Lord, have spoken and will act.* Ezekiel 37:14.

## HOME BIBLE READINGS

| Nov. | 18 | M. | Ezekiel 37:15-22 | *Israel and Judah Reunited* |
|------|----|----|------------------|------------------------------|
| Nov. | 19 | T. | Ezekiel 37:23-28 | *They Will Worship One God* |
| Nov. | 20 | W. | Zechariah 9:11-17 | *Israel Delivered from Captivity* |
| Nov. | 21 | T. | Amos 9:11-15 | *Restoration of Davidic Kingdom* |
| Nov. | 22 | F. | Zechariah 10:11-15 | *God Redeemed His People* |
| Nov. | 23 | S. | Isaiah 49:8-15 | *God Comforted His People* |
| Nov. | 24 | S. | Psalm 98 | *Sing Praise to the Righteous Lord* |

## BACKGROUND

More than a few readers of Ezekiel's words have concluded that the man was not only strange but emotionally unbalanced. His peculiar behavior and weird visions have kept some folks from taking him seriously. But God used this eccentric prophet in a wondrous way. His sermons, regardless of their odd imagery, were the means by which God communicated clearly to His people in the sixth century B.C. The valley of the bones vision—the focus of today's lesson—is a case in point.

Sometimes people in situations that echo biblical situations can help us understand difficult passages. African Americans who lived in slavery, for example, knew what Ezekiel meant in the sermon we are examining today. Those exiles, far from their African homes in a hostile land, could identify with Ezekiel's people. Many must have held on to Ezekiel's word from the Lord promising new life in the midst of death. The powerful Negro Spiritual "Dry Bones" put to music Ezekiel's magnificent message.

Ezekiel had brooded over the desolate state of God's people in exile. In his mind's eye, he was transported to an enormous valley strewn with bleached bones. These bones were not even complete skeletons, but had been picked apart and spread helter-skelter by the jackals, hyenas, and vultures. The ghastly sight conveyed a picture of complete hopelessness.

But Ezekiel's God, our God, is the giver of new life. Under the prophetic words Ezekiel was commanded to speak, a dramatic power was released. An impossible rehabilitation took place. The dissassembled bones were knit together into complete skeletons, then enfleshed again, life breathed into them, and finally enabled to rise up on their feet as a great army. This dramatic miracle that Ezekiel "saw" in his vision was then interpreted as the Lord's message of hope and comfort for His people in Babylon. Ezekiel's great vision assured them that God brought new life and new beginnings.

## NOTES ON THE PRINTED TEXT

*The hand of the Lord came upon me, and he brought me out by the spirit of the Lord and set me down in the middle of a valley; it was full of bones* (37:1). In his vision, Ezekiel was seized by God's hand and led to the sandy Tel Abib Valley plain. This was the plain where God had called him to speak judgment to the nation. It was a place where judgment had taken place because it was full of lifeless, sun-bleached bones. Apparently a great army had been slaughtered, in light of the huge amount of skeletal remains. *He led me all around them; there were very many lying in the valley, and they were very dry* (37:2).

The Lord asked Ezekiel a surprising question: *Mortal, can these bones live?* (37:3). Knowing God's capability, Ezekiel answered, *O Lord God, you know* (37:3). Then God told Ezekiel to preach to the dry, lifeless bones. The most lifeless congregation in history was to hear God's word! *Prophesy to these bones, hear the word of the Lord* (37:4). Ezekiel was to prophesy a miraculous event, to promise that these bones would live again. *Thus says the Lord God to these bones: I will cause breath to enter you, and you shall live. I will lay sinews on you, and will cause flesh to come upon you, and cover you with skin, and put breath in you, and you shall live; and you shall know that I am the Lord* (37:5, 6).

As Ezekiel preached, the bones came together with a rattling noise. The bones came together, arranging themselves in proper order. Finally flesh covered the bones as God's Word bound them together into bodies. But these bodies lacked God's life-giving breath.

The wind moaned over the floor of the plain entering nostrils and reinflating the bodies' lungs. Then the dead army stood up. *I prophesied as he commanded me, and the breath came into them, and they lived, and stood on their feet, a vast multitude* (37:10). God explained his action to the prophet. The bones symbolized the hopelessness and despair of the exiles.

Here in Babylon, the graveyard of nations, the deported exiles heard words of promise and renewal. Their nation would be revived and restored. *Thus says the Lord God: I am going to open your graves, and bring you up from your graves, O my people; and I will bring you back to the land of Israel* (37:12).

The Lord promised the exiles they would return to Israel. God's power would restore the nation. *I will put my spirit within you, and you shall live, and I will place you on your own soil; then you shall know that I, the Lord, have spoken and will act* (37:14).

## SUGGESTIONS TO TEACHERS

Photojournalist Kevin Carter's career took him to places where death seemed overpowering. He snapped memorable pictures of the violence in South Africa's townships, where murderous gangs were shooting up buses, hacking men to death on the streets, and setting fire to inhabited houses. In 1993, Carter was sent north to photograph the rebel movement in famine-stricken Sudan.

One day, Carter came across a tiny girl trying to make her way to a feeding center as a huge vulture crouched nearby. Carter's picture of the child and vulture won him the Pulitzer Prize for feature photography in 1994. He was famous, looking at a promising future. Two months after receiving his Pulitzer, however, Carter killed himself. A line in his suicide note reflected his overwhelming sense of hopelessness: "The pain of life overrides the joy to the point where joy does not exist."

Many resonate with Kevin Carter's final words, sensing that death and despair reign triumphant in the world. Yet your lesson from Ezekiel proclaims God's eternal message of hope. In this season of Thanksgiving, you and your students can offer gratitude to God for His unbreakable promises of new life.

1. VALLEY OF BONES. The hopelessness of exile seemed so over-whelming that Ezekiel's fellow countrymen despaired of the future. The pain of their lives overrode all joy so that joy did not exist. What kinds of "valleys of bones" do people find themselves in today? Ask for personal sharing along these lines.

2. VITALITY OF THE SPIRIT. The bones were enfleshed and revived in order to stand as a great army of living humans. Imagine it! You may even want to play a tape or have students sing the old Spiritual, "Dry Bones."

3. VISION OF HOPE. The main thrust of this lesson is the new sense of hope that our God brings His despairing people. Let the words in Ezekiel 37 speak for themselves, but also be sure to refer to the greatest vision of hope in human history, namely the resurrection of Jesus Christ. Our God is stronger even than death.

4. VISION OF A FUTURE. Ezekiel's people heard the message that God had dreams and plans for them. Life had not ended for His community. Likewise, in spite of the problems besetting the Christian church, God will instill new vitality and open new vistas of service for His faithful people.

## TOPIC FOR ADULTS
### FINDING HOPE BEYOND DESPAIR

*Ezekiel's Vision Continues to Inspire.* "An unforgettable evening in Jerusalem in 1946, or was it 1947? During this time, shattered remnants of the Jewish people were breaking out of the European post-Holocaust graveyard, trying to make their way to the land of Israel and being cruelly shipped back from its shores as 'illegals.' Jewish underground activists of Hagana, the Irgun, and the Stern group were bitterly suppressed by the authorities. The city was besieged, the country at its lowest mood.

"A young boy from the Orthodox Mea Shearim quarter found himself on that evening in the midst of so-called 'secular Jews' gathered in a home in the fashionable Rehavia quarter. They gathered to discuss the *matzav*, the gloomy situation and its even gloomier prospects. Many hard, painful questions were asked that evening by some learned, well-informed speakers. There were doubts and deep sighs. Tears rolled down some cheeks. Towards the end of the meeting, instead of listening to another informative speech, a short and stout man (I later discovered that it was the famed Habima actor Yehoshua Bertonov), stood up in the middle of the dimly-lit, crowded living room and read aloud in a resounding voice, word by word, the 37th chapter of Ezekiel.

"As he finished, the meeting dispersed in total silence. Not a syllable was uttered. All questions were answered. Each person knew, or thought that he knew, what he or she was supposed to do now. Hope again filled their hearts.

"The young boy who happened to be there on that evening would never forget the meeting, its conclusion with the words of Ezekiel, and the total silence that followed them."—Pinhas Peli, *The Jerusalem Post,* April 28, 1986.

*Vision for the Future.* President Thomas Jefferson dispatched the famous Lewis and Clark expedition in 1804 to explore the newly acquired Oregon country. Under these two officers of the U.S. Army, the small force of men left St. Louis, went up the Missouri River to the Bitter Root Mountains, then made their way across the Rockies. They continued until they came upon one of the tributaries of the Columbia River and followed it to that great river's mouth. After mapping the area, the weary party returned to St. Louis two years later.

One disgusted member of the group reported that the Oregon country was a useless wasteland, totally unfit for human habitation. Like the people of Judah, he had no expectations for the future for this part of his nation. But what humans write off as hopeless, God sees as opportunity. Fortunately, President Jefferson realized the Northwest held great promise for the young nation.

*Symbol of Hope.* Reuel Howe, the noted counselor, once recalled an experience from his boyhood that left a lasting impression on him. When he was in his early teens, the family's rural home caught fire one night. Miraculously, the members of the Howe family managed to escape safely. But all their belongings were destroyed in the blaze. Reuel and his father disconsolately began walking the many miles to town to obtain clothing and household supplies.

When they trudged back to the charred ruins of their home, they saw something that remained in the memory of Reuel Howe throughout his life. There sat his mother on a log, with a simple lunch prepared from some bread and jam she'd found in the charred shell of her burned-out kitchen. But what caught Reuel's eye was a tin can she had carefully filled with wild flowers and placed on the log. His mother's actions filled him with hope in the midst of despair.

*Questions for Students on the Next Lesson.* 1. Who were Elizabeth and Zechariah? 2. Why was Zechariah in the temple? 3. What happened to him one day in the temple? 4. How have you handled unexpected disappointments in your life? 5. In what ways has God surprised you with His unexpected goodness and blessings?

## TOPIC FOR YOUTH
### HOPE BEYOND DESPAIR

*New Hope for Eric.* Eric Wallace, defensive back for Ohio's Wheelersburg High School Pirates made a tackle during the third quarter of a crucial game at the end of his team's undefeated string of nine games. If the Pirates won, they would advance to the state play-offs. But Eric Wallace collapsed in convulsions after that tackle.

The medics determined that severe bleeding inside his skull was crushing his brain. Although Eric underwent emergency surgery, his prognosis was not good. Eric Wallace, honor student, letterman athlete in football and track, was not expected to survive. He had hoped to receive an appointment to West Point and become an astronaut, but now he lay in a coma.

On the Sunday following the game, Eric's teammates and coaches met to pray for him. They also debated whether to go on with the play-offs. The consensus was that Eric would want them to participate in the state play-offs. Most importantly, they agreed to continue to pray for their friend.

Each day, teammates and coaches drove the 200-mile round trip to the hospital to stand and pray beside Eric's bed. To everyone's amazement, exactly a week after the accident, Eric opened his right eye—though the doctors continued to be skeptical of any recovery. (Meanwhile, the members of the Wheelersburg football team pledged themselves not only to continue to pray for their paralyzed teammate, but to win every game for him. Although behind at halftime in each game, they managed to come back in the second half to win.)

To the amazement of the medical experts, Eric regained consciousness and showed that he would survive. His doctors transferred Eric to a rehab center nearer Wheelersburg.

As the Wheelersburg team advanced in the state play-offs, his schoolmates carried a large banner inscribed, "This One's for You, Eric!" The team moved to the final game for the championship, and once again fought back to win. This time, Eric was able to watch the game in a wheelchair.

Eric Wallace's condition continued to improve, and he can now walk and talk. His astounding comeback from the valley of lifeless existence echoes the promise of Ezekiel to the exiled people of Judah. New life will spring from apparent death.

*Happy Birthday.* Jack Hutchinson's kids decided to do something different for their father's birthday. They remembered how he had taught them the Ten Commandments and the Golden Rule. They also had seen his example of helping others and recalled his motto, "If you see something that needs doing, Do It!" So, for a birthday present that year, Jack's children planned a novel gift. They contacted Habitat for Humanity, the nonprofit organization that repairs and builds homes for those in need. All of Jack Hutchinson's children had worked with him to remodel their house, and they had helped fix up others' homes. The Hutchinson children pledged themselves to give up one week during the summer to serve with Habitat for Humanity in Jack's name.

The children were assigned an empty dilapidated house in Donora, Pennsylvania. All nine children gathered on Memorial Day, 1994, and presented a poster-size birthday card to their dad. Then they plunged in, stripping the roof, the chipped plaster, and the rotten wood. They tore out broken fixtures, replaced wiring and plumbing, and repainted the exterior, making the place livable. Each member of Jack's family proudly wore a T-shirt emblazoned, "Our Father's Love in Action."

A week later, a family that had suffered severe financial setbacks moved into their new home. Jack Hutchinson's children brought hope and new life through their love in action.

*Questions for Students on the Next Lesson.* 1. Who were Zechariah and Elizabeth? 2. What happened to Zechariah when the angel announced John's birth? 3. Does God still make promises? 4. How do you typically handle life's disappointments? 5. Are there always "rewards" for faith?

# DECEMBER, 1996, JANUARY, FEBRUARY 1997

## NEW TESTAMENT PERSONALITIES

### LESSON 1—DECEMBER 1

#### ELIZABETH AND ZECHARIAH

*Background Scripture:* Luke 1:5-25, 57-80
*Devotional Reading:* Luke 1:18-24

KING JAMES VERSION

LUKE 1:5 There was in the days of Herod, the king of Judea, a certain priest named Zacharias, of the course of Abia: and his wife was of the daughters of Aaron, and her name was Elisabeth.

6 And they were both righteous before God, walking in all the commandments and ordinances of the Lord blameless.

7 And they had no child, because that Elisabeth was barren, and they both were now well stricken in years.

8 And it came to pass, that while he executed the priest's office before God in the order of his course,

9 According to the custom of the priest's office, his lot was to burn incense when he went into the temple of the Lord.

10 And the whole multitude of the people were praying without at the time of incense.

11 And there appeared unto him an angel of the Lord standing on the right side of the altar of incense.

12 And when Zacharias saw him, he was troubled, and fear fell upon him.

13 But the angel said unto him, Fear not, Zacharias: for thy prayer is heard; and thy wife Elisabeth shall bear thee a son, and thou shalt call his name John. . . .

24 And after those days his wife Elisabeth conceived, and hid herself five months, saying,

25 Thus hath the Lord dealt with me in the days wherein he looked on me, to take away my reproach among men.

59 And it came to pass, that on the eighth day they came to circumcise the child; and they called him Zacharias, after the name of his father.

NEW REVISED STANDARD VERSION

LUKE 1:5 In the days of King Herod of Judea, there was a priest named Zechariah, who belonged to the priestly order of Abijah. His wife was a descendant of Aaron, and her name was Elizabeth. 6 Both of them were righteous before God, living blamelessly according to all the commandments and regulations of the Lord. 7 But they had no children, because Elizabeth was barren, and both were getting on in years.

8 Once when he was serving as priest before God and his section was on duty, 9 he was chosen by lot, according to the custom of the priesthood, to enter the sanctuary of the Lord and offer incense. 10 Now at the time of the incense offering, the whole assembly of the people was praying outside. 11 Then there appeared to him an angel of the Lord, standing at the right side of the altar of incense. 12 When Zechariah saw him, he was terrified; and fear overwhelmed him. 13 But the angel said to him, "Do not be afraid, Zechariah, for your prayer has been heard. Your wife Elizabeth will bear you a son, and you will name him John. . . .

24 After those days his wife Elizabeth conceived, and for five months she remained in seclusion. She said, 25 "This is what the Lord has done for me when he looked favorably on me and took away the disgrace I have endured among my people." . . .

59 On the eighth day they came to circumcise the child, and they were going to name him Zechariah after his father. 60 But his mother said, "No; he is to be called John." 61 They said to her, "None of your relatives has this name." 62 Then they began motioning to his father to find out what name he

60 And his mother answered and said, Not so; but he shall be called John.

61 And they said unto her, There is none of thy kindred that is called by this name.

62 And they made signs to his father, how he would have him called.

63 And he asked for a writing table, and wrote, saying, His name is John. And they marvelled all.

64 And his mouth was opened immediately, and his tongue loosed, and he spake, and praised God.

wanted to give him. 63 He asked for a writing tablet and wrote, "His name is John." And all of them were amazed. 64 Immediately his mouth was opened and his tongue freed, and he began to speak, praising God.

KEY VERSE: *Both of them [Zechariah and Elizabeth] were righteous before God.* Luke 1:6a.

## HOME BIBLE READINGS

| Nov. | 25 | M. | I Samuel 1:9-20 | Hannah Prays for a Child |
| Nov. | 26 | T. | I Samuel 2:1-7 | Hannah's Joy Completed |
| Nov. | 27 | W. | I Chronicles 28:28-32 | Priestly Duties |
| Nov. | 28 | T. | Luke 1:14-18 | Angel Promised Great Joy |
| Nov. | 29 | F. | Luke 1:19-23 | Zechariah Struck Dumb |
| Nov. | 30 | S. | Psalm 111:1-9 | Praise God for His Works |
| Dec. | 1 | S. | Luke 1:76-80 | John Grew Strong in the Spirit |

## BACKGROUND

New Testament persons had the fears and flaws, foibles and failures that characterize every human being. We sometimes dismiss these folks as super-pious, too holy for us to emulate. Yet our next series of lessons will examine them as flesh-and-blood followers of Jesus, just like us.

The common thread through these thirteen weeks will be the impact of Christ's life on the lives of these followers. His life, His teachings, His death and resurrection—these events cause us to remember the biblical personalities. Had it not been for Jesus, their lives would not have been recorded in history. The effect of Christ's coming, however, radically changed each of them and thrust them into a mission that would change the world.

Although we do not know if Elizabeth and Zechariah personally had a relationship with Jesus during His ministry, we know they were deeply affected by Him. Luke, the Gospel writer, took pains to show their connection to the story of Jesus. This devout couple raised the famous preacher John the Baptist, forerunner of Jesus.

Zechariah and Elizabeth suffered the disappointment of childlessness. They longed for and prayed for a baby. Zechariah, as a priest serving in the Jerusalem temple, faithfully carried out his responsibilities and lived an exemplary life. Elizabeth, descended from a family of priests, was also devoted to the Lord and to serving others. But both felt a sense of reproach from God because they had not been given a child. As old age advanced, and the possibility of conceiving seemed to pass, they resigned themselves to living with apparent divine disfavor.

One afternoon while Zechariah was leading worship in the temple, God's

messenger Gabriel confronted him with the astonishing news that he would
have a son. When Zechariah disbelieved the message, the angel told the
priest that he would be unable to speak until the prophecy was fulfilled.
Luke related this account to tie John the Baptist in to the story of Jesus.
But he also wanted to set the stage for the experience of joy that God brings
through knowing Jesus. God confers jubilation! The elderly couple's delight
was a foretaste of the joy that God brought to the world through the birth
of Jesus.

## NOTES ON THE PRINTED TEXT

*In the days of King Herod of Judea, there was a priest named Zechariah,
who belonged to the priestly order of Abijah* (1:5). Zechariah lived during
the reign of Herod the Great, who ruled from 40 to 4 B.C. Zechariah was an
aged priest whose name meant "God remembered." He belonged to Abijah,
the eighth division of the twenty-four priestly orders. *His wife was a
descendant of Aaron, and her name was Elizabeth* (1:5). As priests were
expected to marry the daughter of another priest, Zechariah had married
Elizabeth, whose name meant "God is my oath." She came from a priestly
family whose ancestors went all the way back to Aaron, the brother of
Moses. Both individuals were devout and scrupulous in their observance of
the Jewish law. *Both of them were righteous before God, living blamelessly
according to all the commandments and regulations of the Lord* (1:6).
However, they were elderly and had never had children.

*Once when he was serving as priest before God and his section was on
duty, he was chosen by lot, according to the custom of the priesthood, to enter
the sanctuary of the Lord and offer incense* (1:8, 9). The twenty-four families of the sons of Aaron were responsible, in rotation, for the temple service at Jerusalem. Each division performed duties for two separate weeks,
offering the morning's burnt offering and the evening's sacrifices. As the
sacrificed animal was burned outside, the officiating priest would enter the
temple and place incense on the red-hot coals of the altar of incense. Then,
as the smoke rose inside the room, the priest prayed for Israel's Messiah.
Following this duty, the priest emerged and blessed the gathered worshipers. Since there were over 18,000 eligible priests, some were never chosen for this rare honor, and no one could serve more than once. Lots were
cast to determine which priest would enter the sanctuary. Having traveled
from his village near Jerusalem to take his turn serving as priest,
Zechariah was chosen to tend the brazier on the altar of incense, in front of
the Most Holy Place.

While the worshipers prayed outside, Zechariah burned incense and
prayed. At the conclusion of his prayer he was startled by an angel standing at the right side of the altar. Zechariah was terrified, but the angel
calmed the old priest. *Do not be afraid, Zechariah, for your prayer has been
heard. Your wife Elizabeth will bear you a son, and you will name him John*
(1:13). The child was an answer to their personal and priestly prayers. The
boy, John, had been given by God to prepare Israel for God's salvation. He
would be the second Elijah, preparing Israel for the Messiah. The boy's
name, which meant "God is gracious," was to be a proclamation of God's
great goodness.

Zechariah could hardly believe the announcement. He told the angel that he and his wife were simply too old to have children. Because of his disbelief, the angel declared that he would be silent and unable to speak. Meanwhile, the people outside wondered at Zechariah's delay. When he finally emerged, they concluded that he had received a vision. Mute, he tried to communicate with sign language, but that did not work. With his term of service completed, he returned home with Elizabeth.

*After those days Elizabeth conceived, and for five months she remained in seclusion* (1:24). Elizabeth concealed her pregnancy for five months, rejoicing because the disgrace of childlessness had now been removed. She faithfully credited God's gracious goodness for her blessing. *This is what the Lord has done for me when he looked favorably on me and took away the disgrace I have endured among my people* (1:25).

Finally, the long-anticipated child was born. The neighbors and relatives gathered and, as was the custom, on the eighth day the child was circumcised. The officiating priest wished to name the child after his father, Zechariah (though normally the child would be named for his grandfather.) Elizabeth protested. *No, he is to be called John* (1:60). The priest and others argued that there was no one among their relatives by that name. Doubting her authority to give the name, they made signs to Zechariah to find out what he would like to name the child. Zechariah took a small wooden board coated in wax and wrote, *His name is John* (1:63). Immediately, Zechariah regained his speech and praised God. The baby's name confirmed what they knew: God's graciousness to His people.

## SUGGESTIONS TO TEACHERS

The word *advent* means "coming" in Latin. This lesson begins the season of God's coming to earth in the person of Jesus Christ. The keynote is joy. What better way to show the joy of Advent than to explore the reactions and feelings of those associated with Jesus' nativity and early life? The birth of John the Baptist brought inexpressible joy to his parents, Elizabeth and Zechariah, who had been childless for years.

To launch your lesson, you may wish to focus on the joy and excitement a birth brings to a couple wanting a family. If you are a parent, tell about how you felt when your baby arrived.

1. SACRED VOCATION. Elizabeth and Zechariah lived blameless lives. Sadly, however, they were not blessed with children. Discuss the fact that even believers must live with disappointment; Christians do not always have their wishes fulfilled. About 1 out of 8 couples, for instance, cannot conceive a child, and many of these couples are devout believers. Lift up the example of Zechariah, who continued to pursue his priestly calling, though God had not given him offspring for many years.

2. STARTLING VISITATION. The angel's message came to Zechariah at a time when he was directing his attention to God's presence in the temple. He was worshiping and serving the Lord, focused on the Lord's work—and the joyful message came.

3. SILENCED VOICE. Zechariah was so awestruck by the announcement of the angel that he could not speak. Sometimes the deepest experiences cannot be put into words, and sometimes "divine interruptions" ren-

der us speechless. Perhaps some of your students have been similarly over-powered by an awareness of God's nearness and goodness. Ask if any would like to tell about that experience.

4. SPECIAL VISIONARY. The baby was named John. The name in Hebrew means "God is gracious." The joy and gratitude felt by this couple were so profound that they broke with tradition by not naming their baby after the father or grandfather. Instead, "John" expressed their experience of God's great goodness toward them. A special name for a special son!

## TOPIC FOR ADULTS
### EXPERIENCE GOD'S JOY

*Season of Joy?* The scene: a shopping mall at Christmas time. The walk-way was crowded with shoppers. Strains of "Good Christian Men, Rejoice!" wafted over the loudspeakers. But the carol was almost drowned out by the sound of a shrieking child. The little one was obviously tired, but the equal-ly tired and frustrated mother was apparently determined to keep going. With an angry tone, she told the small child to shut up. The wailing con-tinued. Cuffing the youngster, the woman hissed loudly, "Shut up, I said! I brought you here to enjoy yourself!" Meanwhile, the syrupy rendition of "Good Christian Men, Rejoice!" warbled on.

Rejoicing? Not on the faces of the shoppers. Instead, boredom, weariness, distraction, perhaps frustration, seemed to be the moods.

Rejoicing? I think of the single parent with too many pressures and too little money. And I remember those who have lost loved ones this past year facing the first Christmas without that beloved familiar face. I also think of those trying to endure the pressure cooker of a thankless job with little sense of joy or fulfillment.

In the season of Advent we celebrate God's coming to us. Elizabeth and Zechariah learned to experience God's joy, and they provide a model for us, who need to learn as well. This godly couple discovered that God brings new beginnings, that all who wait for God will experience joy.

*More than Fun.* Pleasant circumstances don't guarantee happiness.True joy comes from being aware that God has come to us in the person of Jesus. Merely acquiring the toys and trinkets in our advertising pages can hardly bring lasting fulfillment. Joy stems from something deeper than just hav-ing fun.

Ironically, our society has multiplied the opportunities for pleasure more than ever before. Yet we seem to have even more difficulty rejoicing. I know a couple that says they rejoiced more when they were barely making ends meet during the Depression than when they acquired a million-dollar man-sion. Many of our young people, with all they have, now "rejoice" only when they get high on drugs, booze, or casual sex.

We rejoice not because of what we buy, what we have, or where we are. We rejoice because the Lord is at hand!

*Wesley's Wise Words.* Yes, we will have times of tears. Yes, we will know trials. Yes, we will experience loneliness. Yes, we may have times of confu-sion. We will have pain.

As frail, vulnerable humans, we will discover that life can be cruel and harsh. But the Lord of grace lives among us. He carries us through the times when we believe that joy and singing are gone forever. This gracious God assures us that nothing—not even death—can separate us from His loving presence. Therefore, rejoice!

Elderly John Wesley knew all of this. Just before the feeble preacher lapsed into the coma that preceded his death, Wesley smiled with radiance and wheezed his last words: "And the best of all, God is with us!"

*Questions for Students on the Next Lesson.* 1. Why was Mary troubled by the angel's message? 2. What is the meaning of the name "Jesus"? 3. How have you sensed God's guidance in a time of stress? 4. How did Elizabeth help Mary? 5. Have you ever struggled over whether to surrender to God's will? What happened?

## TOPIC FOR YOUTH
### *SOMETHING TO SHOUT ABOUT!*

*Impossible Ideal.* In 1994 the most popular toy ever created celebrated its thirty-fifth birthday. Every second, two Barbie dolls are sold in the world. She now has over a billion pairs of shoes and has had 500 makeovers. However, she also sets an impossible standard and creates a terrible role model for women, proving that Barbie is more than a toy.

A recent study by the University of Arizona investigated the attitudes of teenage girls toward their bodies. Ninety percent of white girls were dissatisfied with their bodies. To them, the perfect girl was 5 feet 7 inches, weighing just over 100 pounds, having long legs, flowing hair, and a distinctly curvy figure. Researchers concluded that the ideal girl was a living manifestation of the Barbie doll.

Black girls tended to be more realistic, complaining that they lack role models in advertisements, commercials, movies, and dolls. These African-American teens tended to be satisfied with their weight, focusing on style, attitude, and personality instead of thinness and shapeliness.

The biblical Elizabeth frees teens from a ridiculous standard of appearance. The ideal virtues that the Lord and Luke recognized had nothing to do with outward beauty or youthfulness. Goodness, righteousness, and morality were more important.

*His Favorite Role.* He seemed out of place dressed in his gray sweater, navy trousers, and black boots. He was sitting in the gym at the Boys and Girls Club of America in Wilkinsburg, Pennsylvania (a poor area of Pittsburgh), but Denzel Washington, the award-winning actor, was quite comfortable. He sat with the forty teens, telling them that the lessons he learned at the club had been a great character-building experience in his life. He joined as a six-year-old and loved it so much that he became a counselor until his junior year at Fordham University.

His mentors' reassurance, help, and enthusiasm taught him the fundamental disciplines of life. Washington continues to share that message, saying today's street gangs are simply young men looking for love, friendship, companionship, and a sense of belonging. These are things that Boys and Girls Clubs of America offer, he maintains.

Washington also reminded his listeners that he was not the role model, but that they themselves were the role models in their neighborhoods. They must share the message of acceptance with others.

We, too, are called to be role models. Like Zechariah, we have received instructions on how to live and share God's story. Like him, we have something to tell through our words and style of living.

*Sky-High Ambition.* Vicki Van Meter wants to be an astronaut. While most children her age are playing with the controls of an electronic game, the twelve-year-old Meadville, Pennsylvania, youth has done all she can to accomplish her goal.

On June 5, 1994, she took off from Augusta State Airport in Maine to follow the 2,000-mile flight path of Amelia Earhart (the first woman to fly solo across the Atlantic in 1932). On June 7, 1994, Vicki landed her red-white-and-blue, two-seater Cessna 150, named "Harmony," in Glasgow, Scotland, before completing her flight to Frankfurt, Germany.

The trip was watched by many, and Vicki was extended an invitation to the Johnson Space Center in Houston. There she sat in a simulator and successfully repaired a satellite in the manned maneuvering unit. She also landed the space shuttle. In addition, Vicki received a scholarship to the U.S. Space and Rocket Camp in Huntsville, Alabama.

Why did Vicki fly across the ocean? She answered that she always likes to complete the goals that she sets for herself.

Zechariah had a simple desire to serve in the temple. While he achieved this ambition, God gave him a greater one. However, the goal seemed beyond his ability or understanding. With God's help, however, all was accomplished. God still helps his people achieve their goals and ambitions . . . and gives them work to do in His kingdom, as well..

*Questions for Students on the Next Lesson.* 1. Why is Mary important to the message of salvation? 2. Why had Mary found favor with God? 3. How did Mary know that she was going to give birth to the Messiah? 4. Why is Mary "blessed" among women? 5. Was it hard for Mary to accept the angel's message? Would you be able to accept such an announcement?

# LESSON 2—DECEMBER 8

## MARY, MOTHER OF JESUS

### Background Scripture: Luke 1:26-56
### Devotional Reading: Luke 1:4-56

**KING JAMES VERSION**

LUKE 1:26 And in the sixth month the angel Gabriel was sent from God unto a city of Galilee, named Nazareth,

27 To a virgin espoused to a man whose name was Joseph, of the house of David; and the virgin's name was Mary.

28 And the angel came in unto her, and said, Hail, thou that art highly favoured, the Lord is with thee: blessed art thou among women.

29 And when she saw him, she was troubled at his saying, and cast in her mind what manner of salutation this should be.

30 And the angel said unto her, Fear not, Mary: for thou hast found favour with God.

31 And, behold, thou shalt conceive in thy womb, and bring forth a son, and shalt call his name JESUS.

32 He shall be great, and shall be called the Son of the Highest: and the Lord God shall give unto him the throne of his father David:

33 And he shall reign over the house of Jacob for ever; and of his kingdom there shall be no end.

34 Then said Mary unto the angel, How shall this be, seeing I know not a man?

35 And the angel answered and said unto her, The Holy Ghost shall come upon thee, and the power of the Highest shall overshadow thee: therefore also that holy thing which shall be born of thee shall be called the Son of God.

36 And, behold, thy cousin Elisabeth, she hath also conceived a son in her old age: and this is the sixth month with her, who was called barren.

37 For with God nothing shall be impossible.

38 And Mary said, Behold the handmaid of the Lord; be it unto me according to thy word. And the angel departed from her.

39 And Mary arose in those days, and went into the hill country with haste, into a city of Juda;

40 And entered into the house of Zacharias, and saluted Elisabeth.

41 And it came to pass, that, when Elisabeth heard the salutation of Mary, the babe leaped in her womb; and Elisabeth was filled with the Holy Ghost:

**NEW REVISED STANDARD VERSION**

LUKE 1:26 In the sixth month the angel Gabriel was sent by God to a town in Galilee called Nazareth, 27 to a virgin engaged to a man whose name was Joseph, of the house of David. The virgin's name was Mary. 28 And he came to her and said, "Greetings, favored one! The Lord is with you." 29 But she was much perplexed by his words and pondered what sort of greeting this might be. 30 The angel said to her, "Do not be afraid, Mary, for you have found favor with God. 31 And now, you will conceive in your womb and bear a son, and you will name him Jesus. 32 He will be great, and will be called the Son of the Most High, and the Lord God will give to him the throne of his ancestor David. 33 He will reign over the house of Jacob forever, and of his kingdom there will be no end." 34 Mary said to the angel, "How can this be, since I am a virgin?" 35 The angel said to her, "The Holy Spirit will come upon you, and the power of the Most High will overshadow you; therefore the child to be born will be holy; he will be called Son of God. 36 And now, your relative Elizabeth in her old age has also conceived a son; and this is the sixth month for her who was said to be barren. 37 For nothing will be impossible with God. 38 Then Mary said, "Here am I, the servant of the Lord; let it be with me according to your word." Then the angel departed from her.

39 In those days Mary set out and went with haste to a Judean town in the hill country, 40 where she entered the house of Zechariah and greeted Elizabeth. 41 When Elizabeth heard Mary's greeting, the child leaped in her womb. And Elizabeth was filled with the Holy Spirit 42 and exclaimed with a loud cry, "Blessed are you among women, and blessed is the fruit of your womb."

42 And she spake out with a loud voice,
and said, Blessed art thou among women,
and blessed is the fruit of thy womb.

*KEY VERSE: Mary said, "Here am I, the servant of the Lord; let it be with me according to your word." Luke 1:38.*

## HOME BIBLE READINGS

| Dec. | 2 | M. | Psalm 138:1-8 | *Accepting God's Plan* |
|------|---|----|---------------|------------------------|
| Dec. | 3 | T. | Matthew 1:18-25 | *Joseph Accepted Mary* |
| Dec. | 4 | W. | Luke 1:46-56 | *Mary's Song of Praise* |
| Dec. | 5 | T. | Luke 2:1-7 | *Mary and Joseph Go to Bethlehem* |
| Dec. | 6 | F. | Matthew 2:13-18 | *Mary and Joseph Go to Egypt* |
| Dec. | 7 | S. | Matthew 2:19-23 | *Mary and Joseph Go to Nazareth* |
| Dec. | 8 | S. | John 19:23-27 | *Jesus Provides for Mary's Care* |

## BACKGROUND

Mary was a young peasant girl from a small town in the back country of Galilee. She evidently was in her early teens, to be married to a dedicated man named Joseph. Raised a strict Jew, she had never slept with a man, and wouldn't until her wedding night.

In the midst of all this ordinariness, an angel messenger entered. Mary would receive God's grace in a special way. Mary reacted with fear and questioning, wrestling with the meaning of the divine presence in her life.

One of the reasons Mary is called "blessed" in the New Testament is that she was willing to trust the announcement. Mary is a model of costly discipleship because she took the risk of faith. She believed—in spite of all the evidence to the contrary and in spite of all the risk to herself. Even Jesus' disciples had more on which to base their faith.

Mary believed that God had plans for her, an ordinary peasant girl from an obscure village. In spite of there being no precedent for her, she trusted God. Yes, she struggled with her faith, but finally stated, "I am your servant."

Mary had a sense of unworthiness, but she agreed to partnership with the Lord. As Augustine once wrote, "God created us without our consent, but He cannot save us without our cooperation." Christmas, our remembrance of the birthday of Jesus, happened because of the courageous cooperation of a girl named Mary.

## NOTES ON THE PRINTED TEXT

*In the sixth month the angel Gabriel was sent by God to a town in Galilee called Nazareth* (1:26). We don't know very much about Mary's background. A second-century apocryphal narrative, called the The First Gospel of James, stated that Mary was the child of elderly parents, Joachim and Anna, who lived in Jerusalem and had priestly connections. Other sources give Mary's birthplace as Sepphoris in Galilee. Church tradition and the Bible state that Mary lived in Nazareth, a small Galilean village about eighty-eight miles from Jerusalem. Here, when Mary's cousin Elizabeth was six months' pregnant with John the Baptist, the angel Gabriel came to her.

*Mary was a virgin engaged to a man whose name was Joseph, of the house of David* (1:27). Engagement was preliminary to marriage, but considered a commitment as binding as marriage. While the two individuals did not live together, any violation of the pledge was considered adultery. Joseph, a carpenter and descendant of David, had made the verbal commitment with Mary before witnesses, along with financial pledges.

*Greetings, favored one. The Lord is with you* (1:28). When the messenger announced that Mary had found particular favor with God, Mary was unnerved and frightened. The angel reassured her; the Lord was helping her. *Do not be afraid, Mary, for you have found favor with God* (1:30). *And now, you will conceive in your womb and bear a son, and you will name him Jesus* (1:31). The angel announced that Mary was to become pregnant. The unborn child was to be named Jesus, which meant "the Lord saves." She was to be the human mother of God's salvation, for her son would be Israel's deliverer. *He will be great, and will be called the Son of the Most High, and the Lord God will give him the throne of his ancestor David. He will reign over the house of Jacob forever, and of his kingdom there will be no end* (1:32, 33).

Still grappling with the God-sent intermediary's announcement, Mary asked, *How can this be, since I am a virgin?* (1:34). She was genuinely stunned and confused, since she had not consummated her relationship with Joseph.

The God-sent visitor answered, *The Holy Spirit will come upon you, and the power of the Most High will overshadow you; therefore the child to be born will be holy; he will be called Son of God* (1:35). God Himself would be the agent.

The angel offered a sign to Mary to confirm that nothing was impossible for God. Her elderly relative Elizabeth, who had been barren, was also pregnant. *And now, your relative Elizabeth in her old age has also conceived a son; and this is the sixth month for her who was said to be barren. For nothing will be impossible with God* (1:36, 37).

With humility and faith, Mary accepted her responsibility, agreeing to submit and fulfill God's will. *Then Mary said, "Here am I, the servant of the Lord; let it be with me according to your word"* (1:38).

Knowing what her life would be like as a pregnant, unwed teenager, Mary knew it would be helpful to visit Elizabeth. This cousin lived miles away in the hills of Judea. There she would find the necessary support and comfort. *In those days Mary set out and went with haste to a Judean town in the hill country* (1:39).

When Mary arrived at the home of Zechariah and Elizabeth, Elizabeth sensed the excited movement of her child within her own womb. Elizabeth, filled with the Holy Spirit, blessed Mary's expected child. With a loud voice she declared, *"Blessed are you among women, and blessed is the fruit of your womb"* (1:42).

## SUGGESTIONS TO TEACHERS

Today, although there has been considerable dialogue between Roman Catholics and Protestants on the subjects of baptism, holy communion, ordination, and ministry, there is little dialogue on the topic of Mary, the mother of Jesus. Yet, in the New Testament, only John the Baptist is praised as highly as Mary.

We Protestants extol Old Testament heroines like Miriam, Hannah, Deborah, and Huldah. And we frequently speak favorably and gratefully of New Testament heroines of the faith: Mary and Martha, the sister of Lazarus, Dorcas, Phoebe, Lois, Priscilla, Lydia and Eunice. But Mary, the Lord's mother?

What does the New Testament say? If the Bible is the standard for our faith and worship as Christians, let us listen closely to the Scripture passages today and grow in respect for Mary.

1. ANGEL. Look at the messenger's message: "Hail, O favored one, the Lord is with you" (1:28). Gabriel, sent from God, startled Mary with this greeting. The Lord had special plans for this young woman. She was given an extraordinary role in God's cosmic plan to save us from sin.

2. ANNOUNCEMENT. The words spoken by Gabriel are known as the Annunciation (meaning "announcement"). Let his statement in verses 30 through 33 soak in. Gabriel informed Mary that she would conceive a child. Have your students examine the significance of Gabriel's words about the role that Mary's baby would have, as described in verses 32 and 33. Jesus would be the anointed deliverer, the long-promised Messiah. Furthermore, Gabriel announced that Mary's child would inaugurate God's new realm, which would continue throughout human history. How do these phrases from Gabriel give new insights into who Jesus is meant to be in our lives?

3. ASTONISHMENT. Mary's reaction to Gabriel's greeting shows us that she is a human being like us. The figures populating Scripture were real flesh-and-blood persons.

Help your students identify with Mary. Her difficulty in comprehending the announcement is understandable. Yet she accepted her divinely appointed mission.

4. AFFIRMATION. Take a few minutes to think together about Mary's visit to her cousin Elizabeth. Sometimes we need to be with an understanding friend. And sometimes we ourselves must be an affirming friend. Elizabeth, pregnant with the one who became known as John the Baptist, helped Mary understand and accept her role as mother of the Savior. Perhaps Elizabeth also helped alleviate young Mary's anxieties about her relationship with Joseph.

5. ACCEPTANCE. Devote lesson time to Mary's song of acceptance of God's will, known as the Magnificat (from the opening word in the Latin text). This beautiful hymn of praise reflects Mary's trust and obedience.

Note that the words emphasize God's identification with the suffering and oppressed. The "officially unimportant" (Robert Frost's term) may be ignored and the rich and successful may seem to have all the power and rewards. But Mary's song reveals God's promises to the poor and forgotten.

## TOPIC FOR ADULTS
### SURRENDER TO GOD'S WILL

*Place of Mary.* A few years ago, a deranged man attacked Michaelangelo's beautiful Pieta, the statue of Mary holding the limp form of her crucified son. The vandal furiously smashed the face and arm of Mary with a large hammer. Experts have restored the masterpiece and now keep it under tight security in its display in Rome.

The vandal's attack on Mary is a kind of parable, calling to mind the damage done to Mary by the church over the centuries. Both the Catholic and Protestant churches have participated.

The Roman Catholic community has seemed to idolize Mary at times, elevating her to a "Queen of Heaven" status. Yet she has been largely ignored in most Protestant teaching. Protestants have neglected Mary, reducing her to a mere prop in the Christmas story—along with the donkey, sheep, and innkeeper. Thus, Mary has become either a stiff statue in pale blue in musty cathedrals . . . or a cardboard accessory to the coffee-table manger set.

*The Blessed Ones.* Three times in this portion of Scripture Luke uses the word "Blessed!" to describe Mary. It's a strong word in Greek, conveying God's gracious goodwill toward a person.

God uses those whom He blesses—often the weak and powerless—to carry out his plans. Through the most insignificant person imaginable, a teenage girl from a backwater village, God made possible His personal contact with us. He chose to ignore the Who's Who in the Roman World, and passed by the Social Register of Palestine. This is the God who "scatters the proud in the plans of their hearts" and "casts down the mighty and exalts the humble," who turns the old order upside down.

The blessed ones are those who trust God and serve Him. Yet His blessing is what He does for us, not what we have done for Him. Allow yourself to give hospitable space to God in your life.

*Questions for Students on the Next Lesson.* 1. What do you learn from the fact that Jesus was born into poverty? 2. What was God's purpose in announcing Jesus' birth to shepherds? 3. What has been your personal response to the Incarnation? 4. How did Mary react to the shepherds' story? How might you have reacted? 5. Why is there such an interest in angels today? In your opinion, is this healthy?

## TOPIC FOR YOUTH
### LET IT BE!

*Lack of Belief.* A 1994 Harris Poll reported that significant numbers of American Christians do not believe in such religious doctrines as the miracle of the Virgin Birth. Humphrey Taylor, chairman of Louis Harris and Associates, noted that while 95 percent of Americans say they believe in God, only 85 percent believe in the Virgin Birth, while 49 percent of non-Christians believe in the Virgin Birth.

If the Virgin Birth seems confusing and difficult to accept today, how must its announcement have sounded to Mary? Yet she accepted the message in faith. She believed with a simple "Let it be."

*Ultimate Leap of Faith?* One of the sports crazes among young people is bungee jumping. Enthusiasts leap headfirst from bridges, cranes, and hot-air balloons, diving hundreds of feet with only a nylon-cased rubber cord to halt their fall. Attached to the ankles, the thin cord allows a few seconds of free-fall before it stretches. It stops the jumper a few feet from the ground, before rebounding him or her skyward like a yo-yo.

Devotees claim that jumping is like facing death—and surviving. Life literally hangs by a thread, and the survival experience issues in ecstasy and profound relief. Bungee jumping is billed as the ultimate leap of faith.

Long before bungee jumping, a teenage girl made the ultimate leap of faith by accepting the call of God to do something seemingly impossible. She had no rubber cord, only a verbal promise. But she trusted God and accepted her job . . . and was thrilled to do it.

*Social Problem.* Some of our social statistics are truly shocking. Consider: One in ten American teenage girls becomes pregnant every year in the thirteen- to nineteen-year-old age range. Expanding the ages down to ten year olds adds another 300,000 girls. In fact, according to federal figures, one out of six babies is born out of wedlock. For girls age fourteen today, four in ten will become pregnant by age twenty.

Chances are, you know youth who have conceived or have friends who have conceived outside of marriage. Perhaps you will understand better the feelings and fears of Mary and the difficult choice she made to be the Lord's handmaiden. Remember that this was no case of irresponsible pregnancy. It was a willingness to do God's bidding in spite of social disapproval. May all of our actions be so purposefully pleasing to our Lord.

*Questions for Students on the Next Lesson.* 1. Why was Jesus born in such a humble manner? 2. Why do you think God sent an announcement of Jesus' birth to shepherds? 3. Is your response to the birth of Jesus like that of the shepherds? How? 4. What was Mary's reaction to the shepherds' story? Why? 5. Do you believe God still uses angels today?

# LESSON 3—DECEMBER 15

## THE SHEPHERDS

*Background Scripture:* Luke 2:1-20
*Devotional Reading:* Micah 5:2-9

### KING JAMES VERSION

LUKE 2:8 And there were in the same country shepherds abiding in the field, keeping watch over their flock by night.

9 And, lo, the angel of the Lord came upon them, and the glory of the Lord shone round about them: and they were sore afraid.

10 And the angel said unto them, Fear not: for, behold, I bring you good tidings of great joy, which shall be to all people.

11 For unto you is born this day in the city of David a Saviour, which is Christ the Lord.

12 And this shall be a sign unto you; Ye shall find the babe wrapped in swaddling clothes, lying in a manger.

13 And suddenly there was with the angel a multitude of the heavenly host praising God, and saying,

14 Glory to God in the highest, and on earth peace, good will toward men.

15 And it came to pass, as the angels were gone away from them into heaven, the shepherds said one to another, Let us now go even unto Bethlehem, and see this thing which is come to pass, which the Lord hath made known unto us.

16 And they came with haste, and found Mary, and Joseph, and the babe lying in a manger.

17 And when they had seen it, they made known abroad the saying which was told them concerning this child.

18 And all they that heard it wondered at those things which were told them by the shepherds.

19 But Mary kept all these things, and pondered them in her heart.

20 And the shepherds returned, glorifying and praising God for all the things that they had heard and seen, as it was told unto them.

### NEW REVISED STANDARD VERSION

LUKE 2:8 In that region there were shepherds living in the fields, keeping watch over their flock by night. 9 Then an angel of the Lord stood before them, and the glory of the Lord shone around them, and they were terrified. 10 But the angel said to them, "Do not be afraid; for see—I am bringing you good news of great joy for all the people: 11 to you is born this day in the city of David a Savior, who is the Messiah, the Lord. 12 This will be a sign for you: you will find a child wrapped in bands of cloth and lying in a manger." 13 And suddenly there was with the angel a multitude of the heavenly host, praising God and saying,

14 "Glory to God in the highest heaven, and on earth peace among those whom he favors!"

15 When the angels had left them and gone into heaven, the shepherds said to one another, "Let us go now to Bethlehem and see this thing that has taken place, which the Lord has made known to us." 16 So they went with haste and found Mary and Joseph, and the child lying in the manger. 17 When they saw this, they made known what had been told them about this child; 18 and all who heard it were amazed at what the shepherds told them. 19 But Mary treasured all these words and pondered them in her heart. 20 The shepherds returned, glorifying and praising God for all they had heard and seen, as it had been told them.

KEY VERSE: *The shepherds returned, glorifying and praising God for all they had heard and seen.* Luke 2:20.

## HOME BIBLE READINGS

| | | | | |
|---|---|---|---|---|
| Dec. | 9 | M. | Isaiah 41:11-16 | *Don't Be Afraid of Adversaries* |
| Dec. | 10 | T. | Isaiah 51:4-8 | *Don't Be Afraid of Criticism* |

| Dec. | 11 | W. | Isaiah 54:4-8 | *Don't Be Afraid of Changes* |
| Dec. | 12 | T. | Haggai 2:4-9 | *Don't Be Afraid of Adversities* |
| Dec. | 13 | F. | Luke 12:22-32 | *God Can Free Us from Fear* |
| Dec. | 14 | S. | Genesis 15:1-6 | *God Is Our Shield* |
| Dec. | 15 | S. | Psalm 150:1-6 | *Everything Praise the Lord!* |

## BACKGROUND

Shepherds in the first-century Middle East were not held in high esteem. In spite of Jesus' words about being the Good Shepherd (see John 10), a shepherd stood at the bottom of the social scale. Pious rabbis placed shepherds in the same category as innkeepers and camel drivers—people whose reputations were far from respectable.

The duties of shepherds kept them from scrupulously observing the requirements of the Jewish law. Living in the hills meant that shepherds couldn't keep the rules about cooking and washing and often couldn't make it to the temple for holy days. Shunned by the religious authorities as being "unclean," shepherds were outcasts, rejected by the community and—supposedly—by God. Yet Luke's account shows that Christ came to the forgotten and rejected in society.

Life was hazardous and lonely for shepherds. Daily they lived with life-threatening danger. Occasionally, wild animals preyed on straying sheep, and bands of thugs roamed the outlying grazing areas. The shepherds who heard the news of Jesus' birth had probably resigned themselves to their lowly social status and their daily deprivations. Yet, astonishingly, they became the first to hear the news of Jesus' birth on the cold hillsides near Bethlehem. God's good news of the Savior was first given not to the rich, famous, and powerful . . . but to a few shepherds.

## NOTES ON THE PRINTED TEXT

Common people populate the story of Christ's birth. *In that region there were shepherds living in the fields, keeping watch over their flock by night* (2:8). Shepherds were social outcasts. These poor and powerless individuals were despised by orthodox Jews because they could not observe all the ceremonial laws of cleanliness and food preparation while in the wilderness. However, they were a necessary part of a society that depended on them to care for the sheep.

Normally, a single shepherd cared for his flock. Since there were several shepherds here, perhaps it was lambing season. Or, perhaps several shepherds had merged their flocks for protection against thieves and wild animals, or for the ease of care at night. They could easily separate their own flocks in the daylight, with each shepherd playing his distinctive tune on a flute, which would call their sheep to follow. Sheep also recognize the shepherd's voice. As the shepherds sat and conversed around the flickering light of a campfire, that light was dwarfed by another light.

*Then an angel of the Lord stood before them, and the glory of the Lord shone around them, and they were terrified* (2:9). Blazing glory marked the presence of God's messenger. The shining brightness terrified the men, young and old. But the angel calmed their fears, reassuring them of his peaceful purpose. He then made a staggering announcement. *But the angel* said to them, "Do not be afraid; for see—I am bringing you good news of great joy for all the people: to you is born this day in the city of David a Savior, who is the Messiah, the Lord" (2:10, 11). Instead of being afraid, the shepherds should rejoice, the angel stated. Israel's long-awaited and expected deliverer had been born in Bethlehem. Israel's hope and salvation had at last arrived.

As proof of the truthfulness of the message, God's messenger provided a sign. This will be a sign for you; you will find a child wrapped in bands of cloth and lying in a manger (2:12). When the shepherds arrived in Bethlehem, they would find a newborn child. The young child would have already been washed in olive oil and rubbed with some salt, as all newborns were, and then wrapped tightly with strips of cloth. The child was then laid in clean straw in a feed box for warmth.

Whenever a child was born, it was customary for local musicians to congregate at the child's home to offer praises to God in song. When Jesus was born, all heaven sang. And suddenly there was with the angel a multitude of the heavenly host, praising God and saying, "Glory to God in the highest heaven, and on earth peace among those whom he favors!" (2:13, 14).

So they went with haste and found Mary and Joseph, and the child lying in the manger (2:16). In front of well-wishers, the shepherds blurted out their astonishing story. Their tale created a variety of reactions. When they saw this, they made known what had been told them about this child; and all who heard it were amazed at what the shepherds told them (2:17, 18). Mary's reaction was deeper. Along with the flush of excitement came faith. Mary had seen the fulfillment of God's promise to her, and she contemplated this tiny boy and His destiny. But Mary treasured all these words and pondered them in her heart (2:19).

The shepherds hurried back to their flocks, singing songs of praise to God. They had been privileged to see the advent of a new chapter in Israel's history. The shepherds returned, glorifying and praising God for all they had heard and seen, as it had been told them (2:20).

## SUGGESTIONS TO TEACHERS

Most Christmas cards portray the shepherds as cherubic boys among a couple of cuddly lambs. The scene is cute, but looks as if the shepherds and sheep were lifted from the stuffed-animal shelf of a toy store. Your task in this lesson is to rescue the story of the Bethlehem shepherds from greeting card artists. Present the account as Luke intended it.

1. REQUIREMENT BY SOCIETY'S MOVERS. Before getting to the shepherds, we must understand why the birth of Jesus took place in Bethlehem. Point out that Mary and Joseph were displaced from Nazareth for a time, forced by government edict to journey far from home. Manipulated by authorities, and suffering expense and inconvenience, Mary and Joseph were pushed around by forces beyond their control. Some in your class who have been laid off from jobs or were forced to take early retirement or had to relocate will sympathize with this couple's plight.

2. REJECTION OF THE MIGHTY. When Jesus' birth took place in the stable area beneath the Bethlehem inn, the first to hear the news of Messiah's coming was not the Roman emperor and his mighty court, not

King Herod and his powerful henchmen, not even the wealthy aristocracy of the empire's great cities . . . but some ragged shepherds. God chose the least "important" for His announcement of the greatest news of history. Discuss how the Lord continues to select the seemingly insignificant for His grace and service.

3. REJOICING BY MENIALS. Shepherds—at the bottom of the social scale—were forgotten by most in that society. But they learned to rejoice at the message. "Good news for all people,"—including shepherds! Many in our society see no cause for joy or hope. The angels' message to the shepherds needs to be taken to heart by many in our communities. Discuss how that might be done in your own neighborhoods.

4. RESPONSE TO THE MANGER. The shepherds heard the glad tidings of Jesus' birth—then responded. The news of Jesus, when it is taken seriously, compels a response. We today cannot remain neutral, either. Ask your students how they are reacting to the message of God's great gift.

5. RETURN TO THE MUNDANE. God will not permit us to enjoy the "high" of angelic choruses or moving manger scenes constantly. He sends us back to the everyday world. Why? To praise Him and share the news of His goodness with our neighbors.

For some people, the days following Christmas are a let-down. But those who have truly understood the meaning of the manger message go back to the world of the mundane with a new outlook on life.

## TOPIC FOR ADULTS
### RECEIVE GOD'S MESSAGE

*Still in the Drawer?* I like the cartoon I once read in the "Family Circus" comic strip. A little girl, about five years old, is depicted standing on a chair and looking down into an open drawer. Behind her is a lovely creche set. It's obviously Christmas. But in the caption the little girl calls out, "We forgot to put the baby Jesus in the manger on Christmas Eve, Mommy. He's still in the drawer."

Don't we sometimes forget to put Christ in our Christmas? There was no room for Him in the inn. And sometimes we don't make a place for Him in our busy days. We sing "God Rest You Merry, Gentlemen," but there is no rest in us. Or "Silent Night, Holy Night . . . sleep in heavenly peace," but there is little peace in our hearts. Sometimes we get so busy that we forget about Jesus, and the Holy Child of Bethlehem ends up, figuratively speaking, in some back drawer.—Alex Gondola, *The Steeple Bell,* Dec., 1994.

*Watching for the King?* About twenty miles northwest of Edinburgh, Scotland, on the Firth of Forth, is the village of Linlithgow, where the Stuarts maintained a palace. Mary, Queen of Scots, was born there. Some time around A.D. 1500 one of the Stuart kings, James IV, established a tradition. He and his royal entourage would leave London in time to arrive at Linlithgow by December 6th. Then the king and his court would enjoy themselves hunting, fishing, and partying, every single day from December 6 till Christmas Eve. After a brief break for worship on Christmas morning, and again on Christmas afternoon, they would return to the business of feasting, which would continue without a break until Epiphany on January 6th. It was a solid month of celebration. Only then would the king return to London and the business of state.

Commenting on this custom, George Bass writes, "[This has] been the popular nature of Advent ever since . . . Christians in America have been able, through opportunity and prosperity, to keep Advent as kings and queens once did, instead of keeping watch for the King of Kings."—*The Gift, the Glitter and the Glory.*

*Gospel into Gullah.* After fifteen years of painstaking work, the Gospel of Luke has been published in Gullah, the language spoken by slaves and their descendants for centuries along the Southeast coast.

"De Good Nyews Bout Jedus Christ Wa Luke Write" is the first complete book of the Bible translated into a language that is a mixture of English and West African tongues. Gullah survived in its purest form in isolated communities of former African slaves and their descendants on coastal islands. Those islands once held massive cotton plantations. Now dotted with rural fishing communities, they are separated from the mainland by wide expanses of marsh.

Linguists estimate that 250,000 people, from North Carolina to northern Florida, can speak Gullah. And for about 20,000 of them—Gullah, a purely oral language—is the primary language. "We are trying to let people hear the Word of God in our own tongue," said the Rev. Ervin Green, the lead translator. "It's our language. It's just wonderful to come to this."

God has introduced His promise in the person of the baby of Bethlehem to all people, including the poorest and humblest. The first to hear this good news were the lowly shepherds, people similar to the Gullah speakers in our time. The news of the divine visitation continues to be told to each in his or her own tongue today.

*Questions for Students on the Next Lesson.* 1. Who were the "Magi" in New Testament times? 2. Why did they travel to Jerusalem? 3. What was Herod like? 4. What was the significance of the Magi's gifts to the Christ child? 5. What are you searching for in life?

## TOPIC FOR YOUTH
### TELL IT ALL

*Rejected Life.* Willie Nelson and Waylon Jennings, two of country music's superstars, soared to the top of the charts with a song whose refrain intoned, "Mama, don't let your babies grow up to be cowboys." The plea of the song was for mothers to encourage their children to be doctors or lawyers.

That refrain reflects the world's view of vocations. Most youth grow up desiring a white-collar job. Most reject the life of a common laborer. What friend of yours has grown up announcing that he or she intends to be a shepherd?

Interestingly enough, these common laborers were the first to hear and tell of the news that a Savior was born. Common laborers and world leaders alike were all the same to that baby in the manger.

*Classic Switch.* Samuel Langhorne Clemens, better known as Mark Twain, wrote *The Prince and the Pauper* in 1882. It is the story of two boys born on the same day in London. The first, Tom Canty, was the unwanted son of John Canty. The child grew up in the rags and filth of Offal Court.

Tom was forced by his father to beg during the day and was beaten by his father at night. He grew up dreaming of being a prince and gathered other street urchins into his ragtag court as a game. The second boy was Edward Tudor, the son of King Henry VIII, who was wrapped in silks, raised in a palace, and protected from the terrible life of those beyond the palace grounds.

One day, Tom sneaked into the royal grounds, hoping to see Prince Edward of England. As he approached the young prince, he was struck down by a guard and ordered out. Edward intervened and took Tom into his private chamber. There, Tom confessed his longing to be a prince. The two decided to exchange places. As they exchanged clothing, they discovered that they were identical in appearance.

Later in the day, the real prince was mistaken for the dirty beggar seen earlier and was thrown into the streets. His protests that he was Prince Edward went unheeded. Tom, now in the palace, was suspected of having gone mad since he could remember no one, none of the royal business, or the location of the Great Seal.

The book follows the two boys' adventures until they reestablish their true identities and eventually right some of the many social wrongs that existed in England. The plot is universally appealing because many youth in contemporary society have little or no contact with their counterparts in other levels of society. As Twain demonstrated, there is a nobility and kingliness in the poor just as there is understanding and compassion in the rich—when the two are allowed to experience one another's lives.

The lowly shepherds were the first to come and praise the Lord. Ironically, the poorest and lowliest were the first to pay homage to the King of creation.

*Willing to Tell It.* A *Time Magazine* poll indicated that 69 percent of Americans believe in angels. In fact, interest in angels has never been greater. A bimonthly newsletter, *Angel Watch*, published in Mountainside, New Jersey, keeps people posted on angels' activities. Boston College and Yale also have courses on angels for students. But many who claim to have encountered angels (only 32 percent say they have experienced an angel's presence) are strangely reluctant to discuss their experiences.

The shepherds, though, were not reluctant to share their story. They hurried to Bethlehem to proclaim what they had seen and heard.

*Questions for Students on the Next Lesson.* 1. Who were the wise men? 2. How many were there? 3. What was the significance of their trip and gifts? 4. What gifts can you give to Jesus today? 5. What kind of man was King Herod, and why did the Magi not return to him?

# LESSON 4—DECEMBER 22

## THE WISE MEN AND HEROD

*Background Scripture:* Matthew 2:1-23
*Devotional Reading:* Matthew 2:13-23

### KING JAMES VERSION

MATTHEW 2:1 Now when Jesus was born in Bethlehem of Judea in the days of Herod the king, behold, there came wise men from the east to Jerusalem,

2 Saying, Where is he that is born King of the Jews? for we have seen his star in the east, and are come to worship him.

3 When Herod the king had heard these things, he was troubled, and all Jerusalem with him.

4 And when he had gathered all the chief priests and scribes of the people together, he demanded of them where Christ should be born.

5 And they said unto him, In Bethlehem of Judea: for thus it is written by the prophet,

6 And thou Bethlehem, in the land of Juda, art not the least among the princes of Juda: for out of thee shall come a Governor, that shall rule my people Israel.

7 Then Herod, when he had privily called the wise men, enquired of them diligently what time the star appeared.

8 And he sent them to Bethlehem, and said, Go and search diligently for the young child; and when ye have found him, bring me word again, that I may come and worship him also.

9 When they had heard the king, they departed; and lo, the star, which they saw in the east, went before them, till it came and stood over where the young child was.

10 When they saw the star, they rejoiced with exceeding great joy.

11 And when they were come into the house, they saw the young child with Mary his mother, and fell down, and worshipped him: and when they had opened their treasures, they presented unto him gifts; gold, and frankincense, and myrrh.

12 And being warned of God in a dream that they should not return to Herod, they departed into their own country another way. . . .

16 Then Herod, when he saw that he was mocked of the wise men, was exceeding wroth, and sent forth, and slew all the children that were in Bethlehem, and in all the coasts thereof, from two years old and under, according to the time which he had diligently enquired of the wise men.

### NEW REVISED STANDARD VERSION

MATTHEW 2:1 In the time of King Herod, after Jesus was born in Bethlehem of Judea, wise men from the East came to Jerusalem, 2 asking, 'Where is the child who has been born king of the Jews? For we observed his star at its rising, and have come to pay him homage." 3 When King Herod heard this, he was frightened, and all Jerusalem with him; 4 and calling together all the chief priests and scribes of the people, he inquired of them where the Messiah was to be born. 5 They told him, "In Bethlehem of Judea; for so it has been written by the prophet: 6 'And you, Bethlehem, in the land of Judah, are by no means least among the rulers of Judah; for from you shall come a ruler who is to shepherd my people Israel.' "

7 Then Herod secretly called for the wise men and learned from them the exact time when the star had appeared. 8 Then he sent them to Bethlehem, saying, "Go and search diligently for the child; and when you have found him, bring me word so that I may also go and pay him homage." 9 When they had heard the king, they set out; and there, ahead of them, went the star that they had seen at its rising, until it stopped over the place where the child was. 10 When they saw that the star had stopped, they were overwhelmed with joy. 11 On entering the house, they saw the child with Mary his mother; and they knelt down and paid him homage. Then, opening their treasure chests, they offered him gifts of gold, frankincense, and myrrh. 12 And having been warned in a dream not to return to Herod, they left for their own country by another road. . . .

16 When Herod saw that he had been tricked by the wise men, he was infuriated, and he sent and killed all the children in and around Bethlehem who were two years old or under, according to the time that he had learned from the wise men.

*KEY VERSE: They knelt down and paid him homage. Then opening their treasure chests, they offered him gifts.* Matthew 2:11.

## HOME BIBLE READINGS

| Dec. | 16 | M. | Jeremiah 23:1-8 | *Prophecy of a Savior* |
|------|----|----|-----------------|-------------------------|
| Dec. | 17 | T. | Zechariah 9:9-11 | *Prophecy of a Victorious King* |
| Dec. | 18 | W. | Psalm 72:1-11 | *All Kings Will Worship Him* |
| Dec. | 19 | T. | Psalm 72:12-20 | *The Lord Has Done Great Things* |
| Dec. | 20 | F. | Isaiah 9:2-7 | *The Messiah Is Born* |
| Dec. | 21 | S. | Isaiah 60:10-16 | *Unbelievers Will Bow to Christ* |
| Dec. | 22 | S. | Ephesians 4:9-16 | *Present Our Talents to God* |

## BACKGROUND

The Gospel of Matthew makes no mention of the manger scene of the babe surrounded by adoring onlookers and heralded by angelic choirs. Matthew, the most Jewish of the Gospel writers, records the visit of some non-Jewish strangers from afar, while omitting all the details that we cherish in Luke's account of the Christmas story.

Who were these non-Jewish travelers? An enormous collection of traditions and legends have now attached to them:

• that there were three of them (but the Scripture doesn't say, meaning there may have been two, three, four, or a dozen);

• that they were kings (but the Bible says nothing about their royalty);

• that their names were Caspar, Melchior, and Balthasar (but no names are given in Matthew);

• that they were kings from India, Persia, and Arabia (though no such record exists in Scripture);

• that they were of three different races, representing the three sons of Noah, supposedly the progenitors of the three human races (again, silence in the Bible about this).

Matthew states simply that the strangers coming to the infant Jesus were Magi. The Magi in ancient Persia were originally a caste of priests. Eventually, they came to be respected as the learned scholars in society. They delved deeply into the knowledge of that time, especially studying astronomy, mathematics, medicine, and philosophy. The learning of these ancients was amazingly accurate, revealing what perceptive and dedicated researchers they were in that pre-scientific era. We could call the Magi the "think tank" intellectuals of the first-century world.

Above all, they were constant observers of the skies. They accurately plotted the constellations and the movements of the planets. When an exceptionally unusual point of light appeared in the sky, the Magi were convinced that an event of cosmic importance was about to happen. Astronomers today speculate that what the Magi saw could have been either a supernova (a stellar explosion of exceptional brilliance such as the one that flared for seventy days in 5 B.C.), or the conjunction of Saturn and Jupiter (which took place in 7 or 8 B.C.).

If the "star" leading the Magi was actually a conjunction of Saturn and Jupiter, it would have had profound meaning for them. Jupiter was believed to be the royal star, and Saturn was thought to influence the destiny of the Jews. And the conjunction took place originally in Pisces' constellation, where the Magi thought celestial events of great importance to Israel were foretold. In May, September, and again in December of 7 B.C. Jupiter closed in on Saturn, perhaps influencing these Magi to leave the safety of their homes and depart.

This great star trek required traveling hundreds of miles across forbidding landscapes and through bandit-infested wastelands. The Magi traveled in a time of political unrest and dangerous conditions. At times, the star was not visible, but they pressed on. Finally, they reached Jerusalem, where they thought they would find the answer to their quest.

The men asked the local ruler, King Herod—a maniac who had already murdered his wife and two of his sons—about the new king of the Jews that had been born. Herod called the Jewish scholars and learned that Bethlehem was to be the Messiah's birthplace. Then he cunningly plotted to snuff out the life of any rival to his throne.

The Magi went to Bethlehem and located the baby they had come so far to see. Their quest came to fruition. Their immense investment of time, money, and energy proved worthwhile. They presented their gifts and acknowledged the baby of Bethlehem as the God-sent Savior. The brainiest persons of that time bowed at the manger.

## NOTES ON THE PRINTED TEXT

Although there is no biblical evidence as to how long Joseph and Mary remained in Bethlehem, it would appear to have been about six weeks. In that intervening time, according to Matthew, a remarkable visit took place in Bethlehem. *In the time of King Herod, after Jesus was born in Bethlehem of Judea, wise men from the East came to Jerusalem, asking, "Where is the child who has been born king of the Jews? For we observed his star at its rising, and have come to pay him homage"* (2:1, 2).

The wise men were probably members of a priestly class from Media, Persia, or Arabia. Perhaps they had come from Ubar. For Matthew, the East was simply anything east of the Jordan River. These men were astronomer-astrologers who had witnessed a celestial phenomenon unlike anything they had seen before. Some speculate that the star was an angel that led the Magi. Others suggest a glowing nebula, a comet, a fireball, a meteor, a nova, or a conjunction of the planets Mars, Jupiter, and Saturn. Many of these events occurred in the skies about the time Jesus was born and would not have gone unnoticed by men trained to study the skies.

Leaving home with gifts of gold, frankincense, and myrrh, they may have followed the traditional frankincense trade route. This ran from southern Arabia to Gaza, a distance of almost 1,500 miles that was divided into sixty-five camel stations. Lacking full understanding of Jewish Scriptures, they went to Jerusalem, the capital, to ask the political leaders and scholars for directions to the new Jewish king.

*When King Herod heard this, he was frightened, and all Jerusalem with him* (2:3). Herod and the Jewish leaders were unaware of a new king's birth. Weakening under the onset of illness and old age, and paranoid about possible threats to his throne, Herod was suspicious. He assembled all the religious experts and asked them where Israel's Messiah was to be born. *Calling together all the chief priests and scribes of the people, he inquired of them where the Messiah was to be born* (2:4).

Herod needed more information. He discovered the place, but did not know the age of the child. In a secret meeting, he questioned the wise men as to when the star had first appeared. *Then Herod secretly called for the wise men and learned from them the exact time when the star had appeared* (2:7).

Herod also had a plan. Hiding his real motive, he pretended to be interested in worshiping the child. He ordered the wise men to go, search, and find the child. Then they were to send word to him as to the child's location. *Then he sent them to Bethlehem, saying, "Go and search diligently for the child; and when you have found him, bring me word so that I may also go and pay him homage"* (2:8).

Matthew recorded that the star led the wise men to Bethlehem. *When they had heard the king they set out, and there ahead of them, went the star that they had seen at its rising, until it stopped over the place where the child was* (2:9).

Overwhelmed with joy, the wise men entered the house. Their posture (they knelt) expressed their submission and allegiance. Their costly gifts represented what was usually presented to a monarch in the ancient Middle East. Gold was, and still is, very precious. Frankincense was a symbol of holiness. A pound of frankincense was worth six denarii, a full six days' wages for a common day laborer. Myrrh was a gum resin used in the making of incense. It was even more expensive, a pound being sold for fifty denarii. *On entering the house, they saw the child with Mary his mother; and they knelt down and paid him homage. Then, opening their treasure chests they offered him gifts of gold, frankincense, and myrrh* (2:11).

The wise men bypassed Jerusalem and returned home by a different route. They had been warned in a dream to avoid King Herod. Perhaps the shepherds guided them over some little-used trails to Jericho. *And having been warned in a dream not to return to Herod, they left for their own country by another road* (2:12).

Failing to receive any report from the wise men, Herod ordered the deaths of all the male children in the area under the age of two. For cruel Herod, murder was merely an extension of political rule. The slaughter of the innocents in little Bethlehem probably took the lives of ten to twenty young boys. But the child and His family had fled to Egypt, the traditional asylum for Jews on the run.

## SUGGESTIONS TO TEACHERS

Is it time to declare a moratorium on children's Christmas pageants in church? Have we seen too many tableaus of giggling kids, with oversized bathrobes on tiny frames, tea towels on heads, pasted-on cotton beards—all parading in front of apple-crate mangers? Before we dismiss this idea as the latest killjoy ploy of grinches out to spoil Christmas fun, we may well pause to ponder to what extent we have smothered the meaning of Christ's birth in seasonal sentiment. The visit of the wise men is a case in point. Let's look carefully at the Matthew account today.

1. WONDER. Give your students some information on the identity of the Magi. Make the point that they were the learned scholars of that day. Made aware of the cosmic importance of an impending birth, they wondered where this great event would take place. These brainy people, the equivalent of the most brilliant research scientists in our day, headed toward Jerusalem in search of answers. Today, wise men and women will make their life quest a journey to the manger.

2. WANDERING. The search for answers cost the men time, money, and energy. At great expense and inconvenience, they may have traveled from central Mesopotamia across hundreds of miles to Jerusalem. Their journey ended when they bowed before the Christ child.

Do your class members know their life journeys also must be directed toward Christ; that the purposes of their lives are disclosed only in the light of their relationship to Him?

3. WORRY. The report of the Magi to Herod and his court proved threatening. Herod couldn't tolerate the possibility of a rival king. Worried that the report of a royal birth could mean his displacement, Herod was deeply upset.

Like Herod, each of us wants to be sole ruler in our little realm. We resist the possibility that the Lord might make claims on our time and energy. However, Jesus Christ is absolute monarch in the believer's life.

4. WORSHIP. Ultimately, the wise men bowed before the infant Jesus. The beginning of true wisdom begins when we kneel before the Christ. Worship precedes everything significant in our lives. Discuss how we can make worship the keystone of our lives today. What would that mean, in practical terms?

5. WICKEDNESS. Herod's insane jealousy drove him to the horrible crime of murder. Evil is present and pervasive, the Bible reminds us. The powers of destruction unleashed by the Herods of our age are terrible, and Christians must never minimize the reality of sin. But Christians also know that God is still in control of the universe. Christ triumphs over all Herods. The power of the Lord surpasses the powers of petty kings.

## TOPIC FOR ADULTS
### RESPOND TO GOD'S SON

*End of Your Quest.* An ancient legend tells how the conqueror Marco Polo once passed through Persia and took great pains to find the home of the biblical Magi. He learned that there were three Magi named Caspar, Melchior, and Balthasar. Caspar was young and beardless. Melchior was supposedly old and white-haired. Balthasar was a swarthy middle-aged man.

According to the legend, the trio carried various gifts to whatever kind of new being they were to encounter. They carried gold in case the person turned out to be royalty. They brought frankincense in case he would have any divinity about him. And they had myrrh to offer in the event the person were a physician. Upon arriving in Bethlehem, the Magi entered the small cave where the manger was, one at a time. First Melchior the eldest went in and visited the child. Then Balthasar entered. Finally Caspar, the youngest, found himself before the Christ child. Afterwards, comparing their observations, they agreed that all three of their gifts should be left, because the promised one was a king, possessed with divinity, and able to bring healing to the world.

Pious legend, yes. But the truth behind the tale is that Jesus Christ fulfills every man and woman's quest. The search is over! Yet He will be the end of your quest for meaning in life and direction in the future only when you kneel before Him.

*Bow at the Manger.* Wise men and women from the West also must recognize the glory of that event in Bethlehem. Unless we kneel before Christ, we will think of ourselves as gods. Only when we bow at the manger can we temper our learning with humility, our knowledge with compassion. For learning without humility leads to arrogance, and knowledge without compassion leads to destruction.

Many of the leaders of the Third Reich, such as Josef Goebels, held Ph.D.'s from prestigious German universities. During the war they considered themselves intelligent, even cultured persons, attending symphony concerts and patronizing the arts. Their scientists produced an array of the world's deadliest weapons and most sophisticated equipment. Yet these men and women of such intellectual abilities systematically exterminated six million Jews. These wise men and women from the West refused to bow at the manger.

Some of the most gifted persons in Washington during the 1960s and early 1970s were brainy, brilliant men and women who wrote and read serious books and thought they knew all the answers from their charts and computers. Their brash pride made them unwilling to acknowledge mistakes, smug and insensitive in their dealings with others. Impressed with their own sense of power, these wise men and women, who couldn't acknowledge the reign of Christ, thrust us into difficult times.

The folly of human pride and the arrogance of human power can be offset only by bowing at the manger. When we kneel before Christ, we gain a proper perspective about our goals and achievements. When we acknowledge that Christ is King, we gain a set of values in which humans count. Beginning this new year, we wise men and women from the West must bow in obedience before Christ as we have not done before. Let us worship him, and no other.

*Questions for Students on the Next Lesson.* 1. Who was Simeon? Why was he in the temple? 2. Who was Anna? Why was she in the temple? 3. Why did Mary and Joseph take the infant Jesus to the temple? 4. What were the predictions of Simeon and Anna regarding Jesus? 5. What rituals are important to you and your church. Why?

## TOPIC FOR YOUTH
### SEARCH UNTIL YOU FIND!

*A Thousand Questions.* "Daddy, what's that?" the four year old asked. "It's a screwdriver, honey," the father replied. "What's it for?" she continued. "Well dear, we're going to replace this switch here," Dad patiently explained. "What's a switch?" Blair persisted. "It turns the light on and off," Dad answered. "How's it work?" the daughter continued. Five more minutes of conversation had the harried father finally asking, "Is this all that you can do, stand and ask a thousand questions?"

Most young people ask lots of questions about things they don't understand. The Magi asked about Israel's Savior in an effort to learn about Him.
You, too, will ask questions and receive answers that will nurture your
faith. Never be afraid to ask even a thousand questions. That is how you
will find answers to the problems that have brought about your search.

*Dreams.* We moderns may smile at the mention of dreams, especially the
idea of God speaking through dreams. However, a study by the National
Opinion Research Center found that 40 percent of the population had
admitted to a supernatural experience through a dream. This finding was
echoed in a 1986 Gallop poll, in which roughly 30 percent claimed a spiritual experience in a dream.

The Magi also dreamed. They knew God was communicating to them in
a special way.

*Completed Search.* Senior Holly Harris at Thomas Jefferson High School
in Pleasant Hills, Pennsylvania, spent five weeks at the prestigious
Governor's School at Penn State University. She studied agricultural sci-
ences along with sixty-four other students. Her study project brought her
honor when she wrote "The Effect of Birdsfoot Trefoil on Corn
Development."

Holly was only one of many students capable of accepting responsibility
for searching out information. Her quest for knowledge eventually brought
her honors. She was like the wise men who searched out information and
completed their quest. Eventually, their search was rewarded. And they
bestowed honor on the Christ child.

*Questions for Students on the Next Lesson.* 1. Why was baby Jesus taken
to the temple by His parents? 2. Who were Simeon and Anna? 3. What
prophecies were made about Jesus? 4. What does "redemption" mean?
5. How have older adults helped you to grow in your understanding of God?

# LESSON 5—DECEMBER 29

## *SIMEON AND ANNA*

*Background Scripture:* Luke 2:21-40
*Devotional Reading:* Psalm 42:1-13

### KING JAMES VERSION

LUKE 2:22 And when the days of her purification according to the law of Moses were accomplished, they brought him to Jerusalem, to present him to the Lord; . . .

25 And, behold, there was a man in Jerusalem, whose name was Simeon; and the same man was just and devout, waiting for the consolation of Israel: and the Holy Ghost was upon him.

26 And it was revealed unto him by the Holy Ghost, that he should not see death, before he had seen the Lord's Christ.

27 And he came by the Spirit into the temple: and when the parents brought in the child Jesus, to do for him after the custom of the law,

28 Then took he him up in his arms, and blessed God, and said,

29 Lord, now lettest thou thy servant depart in peace, according to thy word:

30 For mine eyes have seen thy salvation,

31 Which thou has prepared before the face of all people;

32 A light to lighten the Gentiles, and the glory of thy people Israel.

33 And Joseph and his mother marvelled at those things which were spoken of him.

34 And Simeon blessed them, and said unto Mary his mother, Behold, this child is set for the fall and rising again of many in Israel; and for a sign which shall be spoken against;

35 (Yea, a sword shall pierce through thy own soul also,) that the thoughts of many hearts may be revealed.

36 And there was one Anna, a prophetess, the daughter of Phanuel, of the tribe of Aser: she was of a great age, and had lived with an husband seven years from her virginity;

37 And she was a widow of about fourscore and four years, which departed not from the temple, but served God with fastings and prayers night and day.

38 And she coming in that instant gave thanks likewise unto the Lord, and spake of him to all them that looked for redemption in Jerusalem.

### NEW REVISED STANDARD VERSION

LUKE 2:22 When the time came for their purification according to the law of Moses, they brought him up to Jerusalem to present him to the Lord . . .

25 Now there was a man in Jerusalem whose name was Simeon; this man was righteous and devout, looking forward to the consolation of Israel, and the Holy Spirit rested on him. 26 It had been revealed to him by the Holy Spirit that he would not see death before he had seen the Lord's Messiah. 27 Guided by the Spirit, Simeon came into the temple; and when the parents brought in the child Jesus, to do for him what was customary under the law,

28 Simeon took him in his arms and praised God, saying, 29 "Master, now you are dismissing your servant in peace, according to your word; 30 for my eyes have seen your salvation, 31 which you have prepared in the presence of all peoples, 32 a light for revelation to the Gentiles and for glory to your people Israel."

33 And the child's father and mother were amazed at what was being said about him. 34 Then Simeon blessed them and said to his mother Mary, "This child is destined for the falling and the rising of many in Israel, and to be a sign that will be opposed 35 so that the inner thoughts of many will be revealed—and a sword will pierce your own soul too."

36 There was also a prophet, Anna the daughter of Phanuel, of the tribe of Asher. She was of a great age, having lived with her husband seven years after her marriage, 37 then as a widow to the age of eighty-four. She never left the temple but worshiped there with fasting and prayer night and day. 38 At that moment she came, and began to praise God and to speak about the child to all who were looking for the redemption of Jerusalem.

*KEY VERSES: It had been revealed to him [Simeon] by the Holy Spirit
that he would not see death before he had seen the Lord's Messiah. . . .
[Anna] came, and began to praise God and to speak about the child to all
who were looking for the redemption of Jerusalem. Luke 2:26, 38.*

## HOME BIBLE READINGS

| Dec. | 23 | M. | Psalm 42:1-11 | *Simeon's Wait Rewarded* |
|------|----|----|----|----|
| Dec. | 24 | T. | I Timothy 5:3-10 | *Honor Older Widows* |
| Dec. | 25 | W. | Exodus 13:11-16 | *First-born Son Redeemed* |
| Dec. | 26 | T. | Isaiah 42:1-9 | *The Mission of Servant-Christ* |
| Dec. | 27 | F. | I Thessalonians 5:1-11 | *God Destined People for Salvation* |
| Dec. | 28 | S. | Acts 4:5-12 | *Salvation Through Jesus Christ* |
| Dec. | 29 | S. | Romans 8:31-39 | *A Sure Salvation* |

## BACKGROUND

All of the Gospel writers viewed Jesus in terms of fulfillment. According
to Matthew, Jesus' coming fulfilled all the messianic prophecies of Judaism.
John put forth a picture of Jesus as the cosmic Lord, answering all the
expectations of the ages. Mark's picture of Jesus shows Him satisfying all
the messianic expectations of Peter and the early followers.

But Luke wanted to present a somewhat different viewpoint. As a well-
educated, sophisticated medical man who never met Jesus, Luke had probably searched for clues to help him with his questions. Perhaps Theophilus
(Luke 1:3) was like him—one who wanted to know more.

For Luke, the coming of Jesus meant that God had finally revealed
Himself in no uncertain terms. After years of waiting patiently for some
disclosure of God's intentions, Luke joyfully realized that Jesus' birth fulfilled all that anyone could expect from the Almighty. The wait was worth
it; the Messiah had come.

Luke related the stories of two elderly people who had been living with
great expectations. Luke, who liked to balance his reporting with accounts
of both men and women, no doubt delighted in telling how an old man and
an old woman had each discovered that their waiting was over when they
encountered the infant Jesus in the temple. Anna had endured years of
loneliness and poverty, but had not stopped believing that she would see
the God-sent deliverer. Through the joyous experience of these elderly worshipers, Luke illustrated that Jesus truly fulfills all we could hope for from
the Lord.

## NOTES ON THE PRINTED TEXT

*When the time came for their purification according to the law of Moses,
they brought him up to Jerusalem to present him to the Lord* (2:22). Jewish
law stated that the firstborn son in a Jewish family had to be presented in
Jerusalem forty days after birth (see Lev. 12:2-8; Exod. 13:2, 12). The law
declared that the child should be brought by his parents in order that an
offering of five shekels be made.

Mary and Joseph were also prepared to make the purification offering demanded in Leviticus. Since they could not afford the required lamb, they bought a pair of birds. Perhaps they bought these at the numerous shops near the southern wall of the temple mount excavated by archaeologists. Their ceremony took place near this area. Recently, an ancient stone vessel has been unearthed. On it the Hebrew word "sacrifice" is inscribed, along with a picture of two doves or pigeons. Such a vessel might have been used in celebrating the birth of a son.

*Now there was a man in Jerusalem whose name was Simeon; this man was righteous and devout, looking forward to the consolation of Israel, and the Holy Spirit rested on him* (2:25). The couple was approached by an old priest in the temple. Simeon was known for his righteousness, devotion, and hope. People knew he had seen visions and had the gift of prophecy. For years he had labored in the temple looking forward to the deliverance of Israel. He had also been promised by God that he would see the Messiah before his death. *It had been revealed to him by the Holy Spirit that he would not see death before he had seen the Lord's Messiah* (2:26).

The Spirit led this devout man to Mary and Joseph. *Guided by the Spirit, Simeon came into the temple; and when the parents brought in the child, Jesus, to do for him what was customary under the law, Simeon took him in his arms and praised God* (2:27, 28). Describing himself as a slave of the Lord, he was now ready to die because he had seen the fulfillment of God's promise. He was a witness to God's life and light in this child, a life and a light that would be revealed to all people, including the Gentiles. *Master, now you are dismissing your servant in peace, according to your word; for my eyes have seen your salvation, which you have prepared in the presence of all peoples, a light for revelation to the Gentiles and for glory to your people Israel* (2:29-32).

Concluding his prayer, Simeon handed the child back to his startled parents. He looked at Mary and warned that this little child would someday be opposed and rejected and made to suffer. The child, though, would force people to make a decision. They would admit their sins to God or try and hide them. Simeon predicted that Mary also would suffer and experience anguish. *This child is destined for the falling and the rising of many in Israel, and to be a sign that will be opposed so that the inner thoughts of many will be revealed—and a sword will pierce your own soul too* (2:34, 35).

Another person, led by the Holy Spirit, came up to the three. Anna was a prophetess, daughter of Phanuel of the tribe of Asher. Her tribal roots were in Galilee although she was living in Jerusalem. She, too, was very old, having been widowed after only seven years of marriage. She was exceptionally devout and worshiped constantly in the temple with fasting and prayer, night and day. It was said she never departed from the temple.

She had patiently waited for Israel's redemption through the Messiah. Now that day of deliverance had arrived. Coming over to Simeon, Joseph, and Mary, she could not stop praising God and prophesying about the child who would be Israel's liberator.

## SUGGESTIONS TO TEACHERS

Everyone is waiting for something. For some, it is to get a driver's license; for others, to get away from home. Some are waiting for a phone call or letter with eagerly expected news. Maybe some are waiting for word of a promotion. Or the results of a test. Others wait to retire. Some are merely waiting to die. Everyone is playing some form of the waiting game.

What are your students waiting for in their lives? You may wish to launch your lesson with that question. Then point out that the theme of this lesson is that God has answered our often misdirected longing through the wondrous birth of His Son. Jesus Christ fulfills the longings of the human heart for joy, purpose, acceptance, and peace as nothing else can. Help your students to trust more deeply in that promise.

1. ACKNOWLEDGEMENT. Mary and Joseph acknowledged God's promise by presenting their infant at the temple. Jesus' earthly parents are an example of a devout couple. They recognized that the birth of a child into their family was a special gift from God.

2. FULFILLMENT. Focus attention on Simeon for a while. This godly man had waited for years for the Lord to keep His promise about seeing the Messiah. Others perhaps teased him or chided him for what seemed to be a pointless vigil. But Simeon believed that God would keep His word, in spite of everything. Finally, his wait was rewarded. True faith often requires patient waiting.

3. ACCOMPLISHMENT. Simeon reacted with gratitude upon seeing the baby Jesus. He knew what God had accomplished and indicated to the parents that the child had a great part to play in God's plan for the world. Are your class members truly aware of the significance of Christ's coming for our world? Do they appreciate what God has accomplished for them and all people?

4. DISCERNMENT. Imagine the scene in the temple that day when old Anna approached the couple carrying young Jesus. Consider how Anna must have felt, having been a widow for many years. Think of the struggle against poverty and loneliness. Yet Anna, too, persevered in her confidence that God would keep His promises.

Ask your students: When is it hardest to believe in God's promises today? Help your class recognize that Christ's coming, after all the centuries of promise, confirms God's essential trustworthiness.

## TOPIC FOR ADULTS
### BELIEVE GOD'S PROMISES

*New Year's Promise.* A new year is a reminder to us that our time on this earth is limited. As the people of God, we know that every segment of time is a gift from God. Each day is a fresh opportunity presented to us from the Timeless One. We also celebrate that the God who stands above all our measurements of time, the Eternal One, has entered our human scene of clocks and calendars. When God came among us in the person of Jesus, the eternal entered earthly time.

Our universe is not an icy emptiness. We are not alone, and we will never be forgotten. Simeon and Anna, who had seen many years pass, saw the timeless God come into the world of human time. A new era had come, ushered in by a child. God had kept his word! New Years Day, January 1, 1997, is our opportunity to start a new segment of our allotted time on earth by worshiping that Child, renewing the bond with Him and acknowledging

His covenant with us.

*Message from Beyond?* One evening in December, 1977, television viewers in an area around Southampton, England, were startled when bleeps overtook the normal sound on their sets. A few seconds later a voice mysteriously interrupted the programming, saying, "This is the voice of Asteron. I am an authorized representative of the intergallactic mission, and I have a message for the planet earth." The message warned that earth people must make many corrections, destroy weapons of evil, and learn to live together in peace—or be expelled from the galaxy.

After the three-minute message, hundreds of telephone calls flooded police and television stations. It was a fake, of course, created by some practical jokers with access to sophisticated electronic equipment. However, it touched a nerve; many people wanted to believe that it really was a message from outer space.

People do crave a message from beyond. A desire for the supernatural is deeply ingrained in us. But to gain some sense of the sacred, millions have taken up eastern cults, embraced pyramid power, dabbled with crystals and New Age magic. None of these can fulfill a human's deepest longing.

Simeon and Anna had searched and waited for God's revelation. They understood the "message from beyond" for them and all persons. It was embodied in the baby whom Mary and Joseph presented in the temple.

*No More Waiting.* Samuel Beckett's play *Waiting for Godot* portrays two penniless, smelly tramps waiting in a barren countryside for a third party named Godot, who never shows up. Periodically, there are announcements that Godot will soon make an appearance, but he never comes into view. Meanwhile, the two characters on stage become intolerably bored and cranky. They try to work up a sense of companionship, but find little likeable in each other. They cannot even entertain each other, but weary each other with their poses.

The play's dialogue meanders pointlessly, reflecting the longing of the two tramps for a glimpse of Godot, the one who never comes to them. The central noncharacter in the play, of course, is Godot (who seems to represent God). Our absurd plight, according to Beckett, is that we persist in waiting for God, the God who never comes and never will.

However, the waiting game was over centuries ago. God has indeed put in an appearance—a very personal appearance—in the form of Mary's baby. God has come on to the stage of time and space, at a specific date and place. When have you met Him?

*Questions for Students on the Next Lesson.* 1. Summarize the message of John the Baptist. 2. Why did the people flock to hear him and to be baptized? 3. Why did John the Baptist send his message to Jesus from prison? What was Jesus' reply? 4. What did John mean when he said that Jesus would baptize with the Holy Spirit? 5. What was the meaning of the dove at Jesus' baptism?

### TOPIC FOR YOUTH
### *TELL TO ALL!*

*The Past Unlocked.* How can an eight year old of today picture horse-drawn carriages on cobblestone streets or a blacksmith's forge? Hope

Wasburn, a youngster from Lafayette, Indiana, wanted to know what life was like in the past. As part of a school assignment she wrote her grandmother, Hilda Abramson Hurwitz, asking what life was like in the past. From that first letter of June 10, 1987, and other letters sent during the next four years, Hilda guided her granddaughter through life in old St. Louis.

Mara Wasburn, Hope's mother, read the letters and realized what wonderful pieces of the family's history they were. She collected each letter so that she could gather the family stories and publish them in a book, *Dear Hope . . . Love, Grandma.*

When Hilda died she left Hope a brass candlestick and a beautiful piece of lace that her mother had made. The most precious possession for Hope Wasburn was the packet of letters unlocking her family's past.

Hilda gave Hope a sense of the past, revealing the things that had gone before her. Simeon and Anna gave a sense of the past to those gathered around the Christ child. They reminded those listeners of the hopes for a Messiah that had been cherished for so long. The Child unlocked their past and was the key to their future—and ours.

*From Each Generation.* One of the fastest growing hobbies in America is the ancient art of bonsai. It's the practice of pruning and guiding tree branches into a miniature growth pattern that mimics natural growth. It originated in Japan, where grandfathers taught their grandsons the lessons they learned from their own grandfathers. In the process, generations drew together. The discipline was passed on to each generation, from old to young.

Simeon and Anna drew all the generations together by introducing them to God's true unifier. They passed on the nation's hopes and joy in the fulfillment of God's promises.

*High Ratings.* Despite constant news stories to the contrary, most young people do show deep respect for elderly citizens. In fact, young people give their grandparents the highest ratings, says Chicago psychologist Helen Kivnick, who has been studying grandparenting for fifteen years. She maintains that the bond between children and their grandparents is so strong that parents should do everything possible to foster it, even at the expense of their own needs. Children give their grandparents a sense of immortality while receiving unconditional love in return. The grandparent feels valuable and wise. They sense the continuity among the generations and offer patient, emotional support.

Simeon and Anna sensed the continuity that Jesus brought to all succeeding generations. They saw in Him love and support that His parents never dreamed possible.

*Questions for Students on the Next Lesson.* 1. Who was John the Baptist? 2. What message did he preach? 3. How was John's baptism different from yours? 4. Why was Jesus baptized? 5. Why did John question whether Jesus was the Messiah? How did Jesus respond to that question?

# LESSON 6—JANUARY 5

## *JOHN THE BAPTIZER*

*Background Scripture:* Mark 1:1-15; Luke 7:18-30
*Devotional Reading:* Matthew 11:7-17

KING JAMES VERSION

MARK 1:4 John did baptize in the wilderness, and preach the baptism of repentance for the remission of sins.

5 And there went out unto him all the land of Judea, and they of Jerusalem, and were all baptized of him in the river of Jordan, confessing their sins.

6 And John was clothed with camel's hair, and with a girdle of a skin about his loins; and he did eat locusts and wild honey;

7 And preached saying, There cometh one mightier than I after me, the latchet of whose shoes I am not worthy to stoop down and unloose.

8 I indeed have baptized you with water: but he shall baptize you with the Holy Ghost.

9 And it came to pass in those days, that Jesus came from Nazareth of Galilee, and was baptized of John in Jordan.

10 And straightway coming up out of the water, he saw the heavens opened, and the Spirit like a dove descending upon him:

11 And there came a voice from heaven, saying, Thou art my beloved son, in whom I am well pleased. . . .

14 Now after that John was put in prison, Jesus came into Galilee, preaching the gospel of the kingdom of God,

15 And saying, The time is fulfilled, and the kingdom of God is at hand: repent ye, and believe the gospel.

LUKE 7:18 And the disciples of John shewed him of all these things.

19 And John calling unto him two of his disciples sent them to Jesus, saying, Art thou he that should come? or look we for another?

20 When the men were come unto him, they said, John Baptist hath sent us unto thee, saying, Art thou he that should come? or look we for another?

21 And in that same hour he cured many of their infirmities and plagues, and of evil spirits; and unto many that were blind he gave sight.

22 Then Jesus answering said unto them, Go your way, and tell John what things ye have seen and heard; how that the blind see, the lame walk, the lepers are cleansed, the deaf hear, the dead are raised, to the

NEW REVISED STANDARD VERSION

MARK 1:4 John the baptizer appeared in the wilderness, proclaiming a baptism of repentance for the forgiveness of sins. 5 And people from the whole Judean countryside and all the people of Jerusalem were going out to him, and were baptized by him in the river Jordan, confessing their sins. 6 Now John was clothed with camel's hair, with a leather belt around his waist, and he ate locusts and wild honey. 7 He proclaimed, "The one who is more powerful than I is coming after me; I am not worthy to stoop down and untie the thong of his sandals. 8 I have baptized you with water; but he will baptize you with the Holy Spirit."

9 In those days Jesus came from Nazareth of Galilee and was baptized by John in the Jordan. 10 And just as he was coming up out of the water, he saw the heavens torn apart and the Spirit descending like a dove on him. 11 And a voice came from heaven, "You are my Son, the Beloved; with you I am well pleased." . . .

14 Now after John was arrested, Jesus came to Galilee, proclaiming the good news of God, 15 and saying, "The time is fulfilled, and the kingdom of God has come near, repent, and believe in the good news."

LUKE 7:18 The disciples of John reported all these things to him. So John summoned two of his disciples 19 and sent them to the Lord to ask, "Are you the one who is to come, or are we to wait for another?" 20 When the men had come to him, they said, "John the Baptist has sent us to you to ask, 'Are you the one who is to come, or are we to wait for another?'" 21 Jesus had just then cured many people of diseases, plagues, and evil spirits, and had given sight to many who were blind. 22 And he answered them, "Go and tell John what you have seen and heard: the blind receive their sight, the lame walk, the lepers are cleansed, the deaf hear, the dead are raised, the poor have good news brought to them. 23 And blessed is anyone who takes no offense at me."

poor the gospel is preached.
23 And blessed is he, whosoever shall not
be offended in me.

*KEY VERSE: I have baptized you with water, but he will baptize you with*
*the Holy Spirit. Mark 1:8.*

### HOME BIBLE READINGS

| Dec. | 30 | M. | Luke 3:1-9 | The Ministry of John the Baptist |
|------|----|----|-----------|-----------------------------------|
| Dec. | 31 | T. | Luke 3:10-18 | People Ask for Directions |
| Jan. | 1 | W. | John 1:29-34 | John's Witness to Jesus Christ |
| Jan. | 2 | T. | Matthew 3:13-17 | John Baptizes Jesus Christ |
| Jan. | 3 | F. | Matthew 11:7-19 | Jesus Affirms John's Ministry |
| Jan. | 4 | S. | Luke 20:1-6 | People Believe John Was a Prophet |
| Jan. | 5 | S. | Matthew 14:1-12 | The Death of John the Baptist |

### BACKGROUND

Sometimes a great person is so overshadowed by an even greater personality that we overlook the greatness in the lesser figure. Such is the case with John the Baptist. Next to Jesus, John fades into relative insignificance. However, if John had lived at another time, we would remember him as one of history's most outstanding religious leaders.

John the Baptist is mentioned in the New Testament and in the Jewish historian Josephus's *Antiquities*. As an ascetic preacher, he reminds us of the earlier prophets, especially Elijah and Amos, in his message and temper. John's was a fresh voice at a time when the scribes' sermons seemed to be secondhand talk about religion.

This no-nonsense, unsophisticated preacher lived in the desert area near the Dead Sea. Some think he was influenced by the Essene community because he emphasized repentance and baptism, and like the Essenes, practiced a strict asceticism. Both John and the Essenes stressed holiness and the law's ethical demands.

But the differences between the Essenes and John should be noted. John the Baptist was concerned about the people of his nation. The Essene community members were interested only in preparing the way for themselves, separating themselves from others. Furthermore, John called the nation to repent by demanding that Jews be baptized for forgiveness. This shocked respectable Jewish leaders. Formerly, only converts from the Gentile world—never Jews—were baptized. No one could imagine that Jews might need baptism.

John preached like a prophet, predicting impending judgment by the coming Messiah. His radical message called for repentance because God's kingdom was at hand. His revival meetings in the Jordan Valley attracted enormous numbers. The smug Jerusalem temple authorities seethed as he blasted them for imagining that their status or ancestry made them superior before God. Disregarding his personal safety, John even stood up to Herod Antipas to denounce this petty ruler for his scandalous marriage. For that John was executed.

John had made such an impact that nearly thirty years later groups of his followers were still active, some as far away as Ephesus. Great as he was, though, he willingly stepped aside before Jesus. John saw his role only as introducing the one whose sandal thongs he was unworthy to untie, the Son of God who would baptize with fire. John was a "pointer"; Jesus was the Person.

## NOTES ON THE PRINTED TEXT

*John the baptizer appeared in the wilderness, proclaiming a baptism of repentance for the forgiveness of sins* (1:4). John lived in the Judean wilderness just north of the Dead Sea. Here, in an area of barren, sunbaked limestone hills and deep, twisted ravines, the Jordan River flows into the Dead Sea.

John was known as "the baptizer" because he practiced baptism while preaching repentance. To repent means to turn around, to change direction and return to God. Baptism was a sign of such change, denoting cleansing and purification. Some scholars have long noted the similarities between John's practice and those of the Qumran community, which authored the Dead Sea Scrolls. Its Manual of Discipline discussed baptism, with which the community sanctified individuals by purification baths. Yet while this community lived nearby, there is no firm link to indicate John was ever one of its members.

*And people from the whole Judean countryside and all the people of Jerusalem were going out to him, and were baptized by him in the river Jordan, confessing their sins* (1:5). People responded to John's call for a change in their spiritual lives. Jews came from Judea and Jerusalem, as well as from the neighboring areas of Perea—and from as far away as Galilee. They heard his message of promise and judgment, and confessed their sins. Then they were baptized in the Jordan.

*Now John was clothed with camel's hair, with a leather belt around his waist, and he ate locusts and wild honey* (1:6). John dressed in rough garments of woven camel's hair held in place with a leather belt. His diet was quite simple, perhaps stemming from a Nazarite vow. While locusts were permissible as food in the Levitical law (eaten roasted and salted), they were normally only eaten in times of famine. Locusts were difficult to catch and not very filling. Perhaps the "locusts" that John ate were actually wild carob pods. These were high in glucose and were an excellent energy food. John's honey would have been mixed with farina and rolled into a wafer-thin sheet. Pieces could be torn off and eaten as needed.

John preached that God was about to act for Israel. The Messiah's coming was imminent. However, John was only the forerunner preparing the people. Israel's deliverer was mightier than he. John confessed that he was not even worthy to be this liberator's slave or perform even the most minimal duties for Him. *He proclaimed, "The one who is more powerful than I is coming after me; I am not worthy to stoop down and untie the thong of his sandals"* (1:7). There was also one huge contrast between him and God's anointed. The Messiah would share God's own Spirit with those who believe. *I have baptized you with water; but he will baptize you with the Holy Spirit* (1:8).

*In those days Jesus came from Nazareth of Galilee and was baptized by John in the Jordan* (1:9). Among those who came to John was Jesus. Journeying down the Jordan River Valley to the mouth of the river, Jesus came to be baptized. Afterwards, He was identified by a voice from heaven and by the Holy Spirit as God's beloved Son. *And just as he was coming up out of the water, he saw the heavens torn apart and the Spirit descending like a dove on him. And a voice came from heaven, "You are my Son, the Beloved; with you I am well pleased"* (1:10, 11).

Following His baptism, temptation, and John's arrest, Jesus returned to Galilee. There, in His homeland, the most populous area of the land, He began to preach. Jesus preached that God's new era was at hand. He called the people to respond, repent, and believe in the Good News. *Now after John was arrested, Jesus came to Galilee, proclaiming the good news of God, and saying, "The time is fulfilled, and the kingdom of God has come near; repent, and believe in the good news"* (1:14, 15).

Jesus' teachings, and especially His healings, led people to conclude that He was a great prophet. But was He the Messiah? Even John, a man of deep belief in Jesus, pondered this question. Finally he sent two of his disciples to ask Jesus the crucial question, *Are you the one who is to come, or are we to wait for another?* (Luke 7:19).

Since John's disciples had arrived in the midst of healings, Jesus instructed them to tell John what they had witnessed. Jesus also quoted Isaiah's prophesy about the Messiah. *Go and tell John what you have seen and heard: the blind receive their sight, the lame walk, the lepers are cleansed, the deaf hear, the dead are raised, the poor have good news brought to them* (7:22). Then Jesus added that John was not to lose his faith in Him. *And blessed is anyone who takes no offense at me* (7:23).

## SUGGESTIONS TO TEACHERS

When we speak about being a witness to Jesus Christ, we are using an expression laden with meaning. In the Greek New Testament, the word we translate as "witness" is also the word from which our word "martyr" comes. Whether we realize it or not, we are saying that as "witnesses" to the Lord we have knowledge to share and a testimony to give . . . and also a willingness to be martyred for that knowledge and testimony. Strong stuff!

Are we aware of the implications of being "witnesses" for Christ? John the Baptist serves as an excellent model of a witness. Keep his excellent qualities before your students as your lesson unfolds.

1. PREPARER. John claimed to prepare the way for Jesus' coming. This is the task of every believer today. The words from Isaiah, quoted in all four Gospels, state that John's mission was to open avenues to the Lord. Witnessing means providing ways that Christ's rule may be revealed and honored. This is the Monday-through-Saturday daily task of each of us. Discuss how it can be a very practical task in our world.

2. PREACHER. "Don't preach at me!" should not keep us from sharing the good news of Christ's coming. The word "preacher" may sound stuffy and pretentious, but the fact still remains that every Christian must proclaim the Gospel message. Few mount a pulpit and deliver sermons, but

everyone knowing anything of God's wondrous news is expected to communicate what it means. Talk about how we may "preach" Christ among our neighbors today.

3. PREDECESSOR. John the Baptist steadfastly maintained that he merely preceded the one who was coming. Then John willingly stepped aside for Jesus, giving Him all the glory. It was important to him to pass on the news, not to seize the spotlight. Witnesses today, likewise, are to pass on the news, not presume they are the news. In what ways do churches sometimes put the spotlight on their programs—rather than shining light on the Person who gives the programs meaning?

4. PERPLEXED. In his prison cell, John knew moments of doubt. He was perplexed that Jesus had not brought about the messianic kingdom as expected. He smuggled out a message, asking if Jesus was truly the promised one. Devote some lesson time to Luke 7:18-30, encouraging class members to express their questions and confusion about Jesus' person and mission. Particularly call attention to Jesus' response to John's query.

5. PROPHET. Luke commented on John the Baptist's ascetic ways (7:24-30). Discuss with your students what kind of life-style a Christian should follow today. The prophets like John lived simply. How can we do that in our luxury-loving, consumer-oriented society?

## TOPIC FOR ADULTS
### WITNESS ABOUT CHRIST

*Witnessing as Road-building.* I gained a healthy respect for road builders years ago in western Pennsylvania. My son took on a project for Boy Scouts that had to do with the first road built into western Pennsylvania in 1758. At that time, the juncture of the Monongehela and Allegheny Rivers was in the hands of the French. Fort Duquesne and a string of French forts farther west controlled the area. The British were confined mostly to the eastern seaboard.

The series of mountain ridges across what is now Pennsylvania were popularly known as "the endless mountains." A few paths crisscrossed this wilderness, but no true road. Eventually General John Forbes, with a detachment of Native American troops and a few companies of the Black Watch Highlanders, hacked out a road, beginning at Fort Carlisle. The road proceeded on to Fort Bedford, and subsequently to Fort Ligonier.

Building the road was backbreaking work, sometimes taking several days to advance only a few yards. Forbes himself was going through a painful terminal illness, so weakened by loss of fluids that he often could not walk. The weather was rainy and cold. Wagons and equipment often had to be manhandled up slippery slopes. But Forbes finally completed his mission. He followed up with a brilliant attack on the French at Fort Duquesne and renamed the place Fort Pitt.

According to military strategists and historians, Forbes' road-building effort and successful campaign changed the future of North America. That area of the frontier became English-speaking instead of French-speaking, and as a result became part of the colonies instead of part of the empire of the Versailles Court.

All of us believers in Jesus are summoned to road-building through the wilderness, to make a passage for the entrance of the Lord's reign in this world. It starts within the circle of our friends, neighbors, and relatives. We must build pathways of peace and caring, grading out the rough and bumpy places of resentment and anger that inhibit the Kingdom values from infusing our society.

*Prophet's Message Today.* John's message of repentance was explained in Luke 3:10-14 in terms of doing justice and showing concern for the hurting. Repentance, in other words, meant more than feeling sorry for one's sins. Repentance meant acting as the Lord intended toward the less fortunate.

Boston physician Tom Durant left his busy schedule at Massachusetts General Hospital to go to Somalia for several weeks to treat civilian refugees in that war-torn African country. Ordinarily, Dr. Durant is able to preserve a carefully controlled demeanor, what he calls "detached involvement," in the face of human suffering. But this ability was sorely tested one day in Somalia. Ordinarily, he reports, he and fellow workers tried not to eat in the camps because the people had so little. But one afternoon, Durant was sitting in the cab of a truck with two small bananas. He stripped one and threw the peel out the window. A small child picked it up and wolfed it down. Obviously, the youngster got the other banana, Durant reported. "It blew me away for the rest of the day," he said.

John the Baptist's call for repentance, amplified by Jesus, means sharing the other banana with the hungry neighbor.

*Leadership Model.* John the Baptist is considered to be one of the great leaders in Scripture. But what is leadership?

*Time* magazine, in its December 5, 1994, issue chose fifty men and women under age forty as prime examples of leadership. These people were said to display the vision, ambition, and community spirit needed to guide the United States into the new millennium. Among those selected was a black law professor at Yale University named Stephen Carter. Carter's book *The Culture of Disbelief* criticized our courts and the academic world for treating "God as a hobby." The book became the talk of Washington after President Clinton praised it.

Carter is a devout Christian. He states, "Each of us is a complex of our ideas and experiences. I am shaped by being an African American. But I am also shaped by being a Christian." This man acknowledges that true leadership comes from being molded by commitment to Christ. What kind of leadership are you offering your world?

*Questions for Students on the Next Lesson.* 1. How would you characterize Martha? Mary? 2. With which of these two sisters do you most identify? Why? 3. What do Jesus' words to Martha mean to you? 4. When have you been task-oriented at the expense of people's needs? 5. When is it hardest to get your priorities straight in your daily life?

TOPIC FOR YOUTH
*PASS ON THE LEADERSHIP*

*Real Person.* You may think that Uncle Sam is a fictional character created by artists as a symbol of America's government. Perhaps you are skeptical of his historicity or that of other famous people.

Actually, Uncle Sam was Samuel Wilson of Arlington, Massachusetts. At age fourteen, he fought in the American Revolution. When the war was over, he moved to Troy, New York, and at age twenty-three opened a meat-packing company. He was affectionately called "Uncle Sam" because of his jovial manner and fair business practices.

During the War of 1812, Sam won a military contract from the government to provide beef and pork to the soldiers. His warehouse stamped the initials "U.S." on its crates to designate that they were intended for military use. On October 1, 1812, a government inspector asked a meat packer at the plant what the letters represented. The worker, uncertain himself, joked that the letters stood for his employer, Uncle Sam.

The idea stuck. Soldiers soon referred to their rations as bounty from Uncle Sam. From that time on, all governmental-issued supplies were considered the property of Uncle Sam.

Some may doubt the historicity of John the Baptist, or even Jesus. Never doubt that they existed! Mark and Luke tell the story of two real people. As you learn the story and accept it, you are to pass their Good News message along to others.

*Potential Golden Boy.* When Ron Powlus arrived at Notre Dame in 1993, he had been predicted as an All-American, even though he had not yet played a game. As a three-year starter for Berwick High School, Powlus set records in Pennsylvania for completed passes, touchdowns, and total yards.

The freshman phenomenon, though, was hit by two huge linemen in a pre-season scrimmage and broke his right collarbone. He was unable to play that season and lost the starting quarterback job.

As a sophomore with no experience, some on the team questioned if he had the ability to lead the team. But their doubts were unfounded. Powlus led his team quite well, picking up where he left off in 1992. The Fighting Irish football tradition was intact under the field leadership of Ron Powlus.

John's doubts about Jesus were likewise unfounded. From the reports of his disciples he heard that Israel's Messiah had indeed come. His original conviction was validated.

*Leads by Example.* Heather Whitestone, a twenty-one-year-old junior from Jacksonville State University, was crowned Miss America in September, 1994. During the subsequent photo session, she asked the photographers to stop shooting pictures. The flashes made it hard for her to read the reporters' lips as they asked their questions.

Whitestone is deaf as a result of a DPT shot she received when she was one year old. This Miss America saw herself as a leader, demonstrating what the hearing impaired can achieve. She refused to be a negative thinker, stating that everything is possible to those who work hard. Her position provided her a great platform to demonstrate that deaf people can accomplish great things.

Many young people found a wonderful role model in Heather because she led by example. Leading by example is the best form of leadership. Jesus demonstrated such an example and gained the commitment of devoted followers. That same leader now calls on you to follow His example.

*Questions for Students on the Next Lesson.* 1. Who were Mary and Martha? 2. Why was Martha upset? 3. How did Jesus respond to Martha's criticism? 4. Why was Judas upset when Mary poured the perfume on Jesus? 5. How did Jesus respond to Judas's criticism of Mary?

# LESSON 7—JANUARY 12

## MARY AND MARTHA

*Background Scripture:* Luke 10:38-42; John 12:1-8
*Devotional Reading:* Psalm 27:1-6

### KING JAMES VERSION

LUKE 10:38 Now it came to pass, as they went, that he entered into a certain village: and a certain woman named Martha received him into her house.

39 And she had a sister called Mary, which also sat at Jesus' feet, and heard his word.

40 But Martha was cumbered about much serving, and came to him, and said, Lord, dost thou not care that my sister hath left me to serve alone? bid her therefore that she help me.

41 And Jesus answered and said unto her, Martha, Martha, thou art careful and troubled about many things:

42 But one thing is needful: and Mary hath chosen that good part, which shall not be taken away from her.

JOHN 12:1 Then Jesus six days before the passover came to Bethany, where Lazarus was which had been dead, whom he raised from the dead.

2 There they made him a supper; and Martha served: but Lazarus was one of them that sat at the table with him.

3 Then took Mary a pound of ointment of spikenard, very costly, and anointed the feet of Jesus, and wiped his feet with her hair: and the house was filled with the odour of the ointment.

4 Then saith one of his disciples, Judas Iscariot, Simon's son, which should betray him,

5 Why was not this ointment sold for three hundred pence, and given to the poor?

6 This he said, not that he cared for the poor; but because he was a thief, and had the bag, and bare what was put therein.

7 Then said Jesus, Let her alone: against the day of my burying hath she kept this.

8 For the poor always ye have with you; but me ye have not always.

### NEW REVISED STANDARD VERSION

LUKE 10:38 Now as they went on their way, he entered a certain village, where a woman named Martha welcomed him into her home. 39 She had a sister named Mary, who sat at the Lord's feet and listened to what he was saying. 40 But Martha was distracted by her many tasks; so she came to him and asked, "Lord, do you not care that my sister has left me to do all the work by myself? Tell her then to help me." 41 But the Lord answered her, "Martha, Martha, you are worried and distracted by many things; 42 there is need of only one thing. Mary has chosen the better part, which will not be taken away from her."

JOHN 12:1 Six days before the Passover Jesus came to Bethany, the home of Lazarus, whom he had raised from the dead. 2 There they gave a dinner for him. Martha served, and Lazarus was one of those at the table with him. 3 Mary took a pound of costly perfume made of pure nard, anointed Jesus' feet, and wiped them with her hair. The house was filled with the fragrance of the perfume. 4 But Judas Iscariot, one of his disciples (the one who was about to betray him), said, 5 "Why was this perfume not sold for three hundred denarii and the money given to the poor?" 6 (He said this not because he cared about the poor, but because he was a thief; he kept the common purse and used to steal what was put into it.) 7 Jesus said, "Leave her alone. She bought it so that she might keep it for the day of my burial. 8 You always have the poor with you, but you do not always have me."

**KEY VERSES:** *Martha, Martha, you are worried and distracted by many things; there is need of only one thing. Mary has chosen the better part, which will not be taken away from her. Luke 10:41, 42.*

## HOME BIBLE READINGS

| Jan. | 6 | M. | John 11:1-15 | *Mary and Martha Send for Jesus* |
|---|---|---|---|---|
| Jan. | 7 | T. | John 11:17-27 | *Martha Believed in the Resurrection* |
| Jan. | 8 | W. | John 11:28-36 | *Mary Believed in Jesus' Power* |
| Jan. | 9 | T. | John 11:38-44 | *Jesus Raised Lazarus from the Dead* |
| Jan. | 10 | F. | Mark 14:3-9 | *Jesus Anointed by Mary of Bethany* |
| Jan. | 11 | S. | Matthew 27:51-56 | *Women Minister to Jesus' Body* |
| Jan. | 12 | S. | Psalm 27:1-6 | *Be Confident in the Lord* |

### BACKGROUND

Although Jesus' home had been in Nazareth, He spent little time there during His ministry. His townsfolk had rejected Him and tried to lynch Him after His initial sermon in the local synagogue. And His own family, feeling uneasy with His notoriety, tried to get Him out of the public spotlight. But Jesus was apparently a welcome guest elsewhere. He enjoyed the company of others.

The Gospels mention that Jesus was entertained at the home of sisters named Mary and Martha, and their brother, Lazarus. Their village, Bethany, lay just over the Mount of Olives outside of Jerusalem. Jesus would have passed through Bethany each time He traveled to Jerusalem.

We read in John 12:1-8 that Martha served Jesus at a dinner party in Bethany, and that Mary anointed His feet. We also read in Mark 14:3-9 that Jesus enjoyed a meal in Bethany at the home of Simon the leper, at which time He was anointed by a woman. Some think these accounts are reports of the same incident. This could imply that Simon, who had been healed by Jesus, might have been the father or the husband of Martha, and might have been the one who first brought Jesus to the house to dine. In any case, Martha and Mary and Lazarus became beloved friends of Jesus. Their hospitality provided the nearest thing to what Jesus could call "home" during His earthly ministry. On His several visits to Jerusalem, these sisters welcomed Him as one of the family as well as an honored guest.

The two sisters had markedly different personalities. Mary was contemplative; Martha was practical. Martha was obviously the take-charge type. Whether she was the elder, or perhaps the mistress of the house, Martha showed great concern for the down-to-earth household matters. On one occasion, Martha's preoccupation with the details of the meal made her complain to Jesus that Mary was not doing enough to help. Jesus gently reminded Martha that a concern for God's realm was the most important thing, and that Mary should not be scolded for her interest in learning the meaning of His kingdom.

### NOTES ON THE PRINTED TEXT

Jesus was readily welcomed into Mary and Martha's home in Bethany, near Jerusalem. Martha, probably the eldest sister, may have been a widow. *Now as they went on their way, he entered a certain village, where a woman named Martha welcomed him into her home* (10:38). Her hospitality included a large meal that she was busily preparing.

Mary, the younger sister, was very different from Martha. She sat listening to Jesus, unworried about the entertainment responsibilities. Listening to Jesus was more important to her. *She had a sister named Mary, who sat at the Lord's feet and listened to what he was saying* (10:39).

Martha became more and more irritated as she bustled about, while Mary sat at Jesus' feet listening to His words. Finally, Martha had had enough. Ignoring common courtesy, she strode up to Jesus and demanded that He order Mary to help her. Martha was so angry she did not even use Mary's name. *But Martha was distracted by her many tasks; so she came to him and asked, "Lord, do you not care that my sister has left me to do all the work by myself? Tell her then to help me"* (10:40).

Jesus addressed Martha affectionately by name. He reminded her that she had been too burdened with elaborate meal preparations; He would have been content with a simple meal, along with her company. *But the Lord answered her, "Martha, Martha, you are worried and distracted by many things; there is need of only one thing. Mary has chosen the better part, which will not be taken away from her"* (10:41, 42).

*Six days before the Passover Jesus came to Bethany, the home of Lazarus, whom he had raised from the dead* (12:1). Another visit brought Jesus to His friends' home. On a previous visit He had raised Lazarus from the dead (see John 11). The Passover was nearing, as was Jesus' hour. But though the atmosphere was full of threats against Jesus' life, the family welcomed Jesus again. As always, Martha was busy serving the meal, while her brother Lazarus reclined with Jesus and the disciples. *Martha served, and Lazarus was one of those at the table with him* (12:2).

Sensing Jesus' impending death, Mary wanted to express her love for Jesus. *Mary took a pound of costly perfume made of pure nard, anointed Jesus' feet, and wiped them with her hair* (12:3). The fragrant perfume was made from the roots and hairy stems of an aromatic Indian herb. Because the syrupy essence was so expensive, it was frequently diluted with oil. Packed in small, narrow-necked clay juglets, it was used for anointing at burial.

Mary's perfume was pure, undiluted nard, worth about a year's wages. In front of all the men, she lovingly poured the perfume on Jesus' feet. *The house was filled with the fragrance of the perfume* (12:3). Then she wiped His feet with her hair. Even today, Middle Eastern women cover their hair. A respectable woman undid her tresses only before her husband. Mary's action was an uncalculated, spontaneous demonstration of her love.

Judas was indignant. In his mind, all propriety had been cast aside. *"Why was this perfume not sold for three hundred denarii and the money given to the poor?"* (12:5). John pointed out that Judas was not motivated by genuine concern for the poor, but merely by greed. In charge of the disciples' treasury, he stole from their common money bag. *He said this not because he cared about the poor, but because he was a thief; he kept the common purse and used to steal what was put into it* (12:6).

Jesus defended Mary and told Judas not to harass her. Jesus sensed Mary's love and commitment and He accepted her gift, and He added to it a deeper meaning. *Jesus said, "Leave her alone. She bought it so that she might keep it for the day of my burial"* (12:7).

Jesus reminded the disciples that the poor would always be present, but His time with them was very short. *You always have the poor with you, but you do not always have me* (12:8).

## SUGGESTIONS TO TEACHERS

With which sister do you identify more—Mary or Martha? Most people seem to feel that they are closer to Martha. And many think that Martha was unappreciated, treated unfairly. Launch your lesson by asking your class members how they react to the account in Luke 10. You probably will find most are "Marthas."

1. DISTRACTED SERVER. When you draw attention to Martha, remind everyone that Jesus was not chastising this woman for preparing a meal. After all, Jesus enjoyed her cooking and appreciated her hospitality. Martha's problem was that she became so absorbed with minor matters that she overlooked the major one. Her busyness in the kitchen led her to forget the Guest.

Discuss how Christians can establish a proper balance between "secular work" and "sacred work." Our culture, which stresses productivity but scorns contemplation, tries to make us into successful super-Marthas. Focus on what Jesus meant when He said, "One thing is needful" (10:42).

2. DEVOTED STUDENT. Mary "sat at the Lord's feet" (Luke 10:39), an expression signifying that Mary was a student. Mary took seriously her commitment to Jesus by studying and listening. The account never implies that she was a lazybones. While Martha became "distracted with much serving" (10:40), Mary recognized the place of simplicity and set her priorities. Mary also realized that taking time to enjoy Jesus' company was just as important as preparing a lavish feast in His honor.

3. DISCERNING SAVIOR. Jesus did not condemn those who do necessary chores. Nor did He praise Mary as being a better person than her sister. His words reflect a gentleness; He addressed her by name, "Martha, Martha," and with kindness tried to help her overcome her being "anxious and troubled about many things" (10:41). Jesus sensitively calms and corrects us when we are upset with worries and pressures. What daily problems do you and your class members worry about? How can Jesus' words here help you?

4. DRAMATIC SACRIFICE. Turn to the passage in John 12:1-3, where Mary anointed Jesus. Set the scene: Jesus knows that His time is running out and that He will soon be arrested and called to complete His mission by giving up His life on the cross. His closest companions have heard His predictions of sacrificial death but have failed to comprehend them. At the familiar house of Martha and Mary during a meal, Mary anointed Jesus. Mary understood what no one else had. She sacrificed a jar of expensive nard probably saved for her own burial, as her way of acknowledging Jesus' impending sacrifice and His messiahship.

5. DULLED SENSIBILITIES. As time permits, discuss Judas' case. This traitorous disciple thought only in "practical" terms of dollars and common sense, power and privilege. How often do we do the same?

TOPIC FOR ADULTS
*CHOOSE RIGHT PRIORITIES*

*Contemplation over Service?* Jesus spoke to Martha, repeating her
name, "Martha, Martha," signifying affection and concern. Jesus didn't
scold Martha. He knows that meals aren't prepared without work. He does
not put down housework and glorify piety. He never praises contemplation
over service. Both are important. Both are needed.

There is always a tension between prayer and action, worship and service, piety and picketing. But don't ever think that getting the baptism
water ready is somehow more "religious" than cleaning the mixing bowl in
the kitchen. Or that distributing bread at Communion is more sacred than
dividing hamburger buns at a kids' cookout.

Both the candles and flowers on Sunday morning and the committees
and the finances on Monday night are "holy." Don't elevate one above the
other. Both have their place in God's plans. Both are needed.

To be devout is not to be indolent. Devotion is never dreaminess. Loving
God is not a license for loafing. Peeling the potatoes and pushing the mop
are forms of servanthood and are worthy of praise. But there must also be
a time to listen to the Lord. Martha was allowing the work to take over.
Instead of holding a dinner party, the dinner party was holding her. Martha
thought she was keeping house, but the house was keeping her. Poor
Martha allowed herself to be enslaved by busyness, just as we so often do.

*Warped Priorities.* A Labrador retriever named Smokey hated uniforms
and snarled whenever the mailman approached. One day Smokey threatened to bite a representative of the U.S. Postal Service. The dog was condemned to die by a judge in Danville, Virginia.

A photograph of Smokey with a look both reproachful and loving
appeared in many newspapers. The accompanying article reported that the
Lab with the "How could you condemn me to die?" and "I still love you" gaze
was on death row for dogs. Hundreds of letters and telephone calls poured
in, pleading for clemency. Even Henry Kissinger, who as secretary of state
ordered the Christmas bombing of Hanoi without turning a hair, rallied to
Smokey's cause. The judge who had sentenced Smokey to death relented.

People can become concerned over the plight of a pup while ignoring the
needs of human beings. People in prison often receive no pity. Dogs that
growl at postmen seem more important.

We often misplace our priorities. Jesus Christ enables us to reestablish
the proper order of our concerns when we take time to sit at His feet and
listen to His words.

*Time for Listening.* Perhaps you are feeling tense and tired, anxious and
irritable, restless and critical. Like Martha, you may have been too busy
with serving and doing. You have not permitted yourself to listen to the
Lord. You have neglected the Mary aspect of your life.

Remember that Mary is not accused of shirking her responsibilities.
Undoubtedly Mary had already helped her sister. Furthermore, Mary
might have felt that Martha's bossy ways and determination to do everything herself made it sensible to get out of the way. In any case, Mary was
liberated from busyness. She knew that there was a time to listen to Jesus
as well as to serve Him. She realized that both serving and listening are

important.

We will find release from busyness only when we learn to listen to the Lord.

*Questions for Students on the Next Lesson.* 1. Many people call Peter their favorite disciple. Why might that be? 2. How did Peter react to Jesus' questions on the road to Caesarea Philippi? 3. What did Peter want to do on the Mount of Transfiguration? 4. What did Jesus mean by "the keys of the kingdom"? 5. Why did Jesus rebuke Peter, saying "Get behind me, Satan"?

## TOPIC FOR YOUTH
### CHOOSE THE BETTER PART

*Similar Complaint.* As more women join the work force, roles in the home are changing. A poll cited in the *FDA Consumer* noted that 93 percent of female teenagers shop for the food and prepare the family's meals. Results were equally similar in a Teenage Research Unlimited poll, which found that 90 percent of teenage boys and 94 percent of teenage girls do the grocery shopping and cooking. The simple fact is that parents have made their children the meal managers.

For some, this situation causes resentment. Young people are learning how much work goes into meal preparation and often complain about the time and effort required to make a meal.

Martha fully realized what went into the preparation of the meal. She, too, wanted help. Jesus explained to her that there was a time to work and a time to listen. She needed to realize that He was more important than the dinner. A hospitable heart, not a lavish spread, was what He desired.

*Chess Was My Life.* If someone had asked me four years ago what I was living for, there could have been little doubt. I had buried myself in the only thing I was good at—playing chess.

At first it was fun—winning and losing were just by-products. Then it got serious. Winning became an aim. Losing was unthinkable.

In the midst of this I started to find a faith. My upbringing was Christian, but to me God was simply someone you apologized to if you did something wrong. I went to a conference and met people who had something more. Their warmth was genuine, and it was difficult not to respond. I began to open up the little hurts I had locked away inside me.

People at the conference talked of "absolute love." But surely I was a loving person; I did care for others. Only a few months earlier I had sat up night after night with a friend who was going through a difficult time.

Then I thought of my father. I knew something in my heart was not right. The space for him was empty. It hung like a stone. I knew that if I wanted to be like these new friends, I had to look closely at what "absolute love" meant for me. I wrote to my father telling him of all the times I had "killed him off" when it was inconvenient to explain our relationship—like in French oral exams at school. I said I was sorry and asked him to forgive me. And I meant it. It was still some time before we met.

Before that, however, other things happened. God started to become real. My friends told me that God could speak to me if I was silent, wrote down my thoughts and checked them with the teachings of my faith. It seemed crazy, but I tried it. I found myself breaking out of my introverted shell. Then came a thought I did not expect, "Could you give up chess for God?" This was the limit. Chess was my life; it filled my mind as well as all my free time. Could I give up living? The early stages of looking for God's guidance had been so exciting that I felt I could obey this thought too. A great empty void stretched out before me.

At this stage Dad and I met up again. My newfound love for him threatened to burst my heart, and we grew closer each time we met. My attitude toward my job changed, and I became a generally more confident person. It seems strange to surrender the deepest things in one's heart, but I have found a purpose for living that I had never known.

As I have given to God, He has given me more in return. Some months later I felt I should take up chess again—and all the friendships and teamwork that went with it. I played with a new spirit and joy—a peace that comes from playing for the game's sake. The results were even better than before, capped by my team winning the British Intermediate Championship.

I am on the road to a faith. Though it is long and rocky I know it is the right road, and I plan to follow it to the end.—Ian Healey, *For a Change*, February, 1989.

*Responsibilities versus Appreciation.* Raising good children is a lifelong task, according to child psychologists. One suggestion they make is to assign children chores. These chores are important. Chores challenge a child to carry out a responsible role in the family. They assume responsibility and experience appreciation for what they have done.

Martha and Mary obviously each had responsibilities, but Martha felt unappreciated for what she did. Jesus reminded Martha that He loved and appreciated her for all that she did. While He undoubtedly enjoyed her meals, her friendship and conversation were equally appreciated. Therefore, Martha needed to relax a bit more so that she might have time with Him.

*Questions for Students on the Next Lesson.* 1. What kinds of people were called to be disciples? 2. Are you prone to commiting yourself quickly to a group or a person—as Peter did? 3. What did Peter confess about Jesus at Caesarea Philippi? 4. What did most people believe about the Messiah? 5. Who do you say that Jesus is?

# LESSON 8—JANUARY 19

## *PETER*

*Background Scripture:* Matthew 4:18-20; 16:13-23
*Devotional Reading:* Luke 22:54-62

### KING JAMES VERSION

MATTHEW 4:18 And Jesus, walking by the sea of Galilee, saw two brethren, Simon called Peter, and Andrew his brother, casting a net into the sea: for they were fishers.

19 And he saith unto them, Follow me, and I will make you fishers of men.

20 And they straightway left their nets, and followed him.

16:13 When Jesus came into the coasts of Caesarea Philippi, he asked his disciples, saying, Whom do men say that I the Son of man am?

14 And they said, Some say that thou art John the Baptist: some, Elias; and others, Jeremias, or one of the prophets.

15 He saith unto them, But whom say ye that I am?

16 And Simon Peter answered and said, Thou art the Christ, the Son of the living God.

17 And Jesus answered and said unto him, Blessed art thou, Simon Bar-jona: for flesh and blood hath not revealed it unto thee, but my Father which is in heaven.

18 And I say also unto thee, That thou art Peter, and upon this rock I will build my church; and the gates of hell shall not prevail against it.

19 And I will give unto thee the keys of the kingdom of heaven: and whatsoever thou shalt bind on earth shall be bound in heaven: and whatsoever thou shalt loose on earth shall be loosed in heaven.

20 Then charged he his disciples that they should tell no man that he was Jesus the Christ.

21 From that time forth began Jesus to shew unto his disciples, how that he must go unto Jerusalem, and suffer many things of the elders and chief priests and scribes, and be killed, and be raised again the third day.

22 Then Peter took him, and began to rebuke him, saying, Be it far from thee, Lord: this shall not be unto thee.

23 But he turned, and said unto Peter, Get thee behind me, Satan: thou art an offence unto me: for thou savourest not the things that be of God, but those that be of men.

### NEW REVISED STANDARD VERSION

MATTHEW 4:18 As he walked by the Sea of Galilee, he saw two brothers, Simon, who is called Peter, and Andrew his brother, casting a net into the sea—for they were fishermen. 19 And he said to them, "Follow me, and I will make you fish for people." 20 Immediately they left their nets and followed him.

16:13 Now when Jesus came into the district of Caesarea Philippi, he asked his disciples, "Who do people say that the Son of Man is?" 14 And they said, "Some say John the Baptist, but others Elijah, and still others Jeremiah or one of the prophets." 15 He said to them, "But who do you say that I am?" 16 Simon Peter answered, "You are the Messiah, the Son of the living God." 17 And Jesus answered him, "Blessed are you, Simon son of Jonah! For flesh and blood has not revealed this to you, but my Father in heaven. 18 And I tell you, you are Peter, and on this rock I will build my church, and the gates of Hades will not prevail against it. 19 I will give you the keys of the kingdom of heaven, and whatever you bind on earth will be bound in heaven, and whatever you loose on earth will be loosed in heaven." 20 Then he sternly ordered the disciples not to tell anyone that he was the Messiah.

21 From that time on, Jesus began to show his disciples that he must go to Jerusalem and undergo great suffering at the hands of the elders and chief priests and scribes, and be killed, and on the third day be raised. 22 And Peter took him aside and began to rebuke him, saying, "God forbid it, Lord! This must never happen to you." 23 But he turned and said to Peter, "Get behind me, Satan! You are a stumbling block to me; for you are setting your mind not on divine things but on human things."

*KEY VERSE: Simon Peter answered, "You are the Messiah, the Son of the living God." Matthew 16:16.*

## HOME BIBLE READINGS

| Jan. | 13 | M. | Mark 1:14-20 | *The Calling of Simon Peter* |
|------|----|----|--------------|------------------------------|
| Jan. | 14 | T. | Acts 2:14-20 | *Peter's Pentecost Sermon* |
| Jan. | 15 | W. | Acts 2:22-36 | *Peter Confirms Jesus' Resurrection* |
| Jan. | 16 | T. | Acts 9:32-42 | *Peter Raises Two Persons from the Dead* |
| Jan. | 17 | F. | Acts 10:9-16 | *Peter's Vision of Food* |
| Jan. | 18 | S. | Acts 10:17-23 | *Peter Visits Cornelius* |
| Jan. | 19 | S. | Acts 10:34-43 | *Peter's Sermon to Cornelius* |

## BACKGROUND

His given name was Simon, but we know him by his nickname, Peter, or Cephas. Both Peter and Cephas mean "rock" in the biblical Greek. "Cephas" is the Greek transliteration of the Aramaic *kepha,* and "Peter" translates the Greek word *petros.* Unlike other New Testament characters, we have several tidbits about Peter's personal life. His father was named Jonah. Peter was a married man with at least one brother, Andrew. He came from Bethsaida and lived in Capernaum, where like others, he was a fisherman.

Peter's encounter with Jesus changed his life dramatically. An enthusiastic follower, Peter emerged as one of Jesus' three closest associates. The names "Peter, James, and John," in that order, repeatedly appear in the Gospel narratives.

Peter was sometimes an impetuous man. On the way to Caesarea Philippi, when Jesus asked His disciples who they thought He was, Peter blurted, "You are the Messiah, the Son of the living God!" (Matt. 16:16). Shortly afterward at the Transfiguration, Peter reacted by suggesting three booths be built to commemorate Moses, Elijah, and Jesus (Matt. 17:4). At the Last Supper, Peter made grandiose promises that he'd never forsake Jesus, then fell asleep in Gethsemane. When Jesus was arrested, Peter foolishly swung a sword, thinking he'd save Jesus. But when a servant girl asked if he knew Jesus, Peter hotly denied any association with his Master.

Peter the impetuous loudmouth was changed by the Resurrection. He took charge of the frightened group of early believers, preached the news of the risen Christ on the Jerusalem streets, and suffered imprisonment. He emerged as one of the key leaders of the early church, visiting congregations in outlying areas of Judea as the apostles' representative. Although initially in disagreement with Paul over welcoming Gentiles into the Christian fellowship, Peter's Jewish scruples were overcome by a heavenly vision (Acts 10). He and Paul reached a friendly accord before, as tradition holds, Peter was martyred in Rome during Nero's persecution.

## NOTES ON THE PRINTED TEXT

Towns like Capernaum, along the coast of the Sea of Galilee, were filled with fishermen. Capernaum still has the remains of fish pens along the water's edge. Simon and Andrew, with their tunics tucked into their leather belts, wading in the water, cast out a circular net, about nine feet across, with small lead pellets for weight and a draw rope on its edge. The net was repeatedly cast in a semi-circular pattern, then drawn back to trap the fish. Jesus called to the two fishermen. *"Follow me, and I will make you fish for people"* (4:19). They responded to His summons. *Immediately they left their nets and followed him* (4:20).

Caesarea Philippi was built by Herod Philip at the site of ancient Panias. Nearby, on the southern slopes of Mt. Hermon, were steep cliffs and narrow ravines within a woodland. Here, in the beautiful woods, the ancients worshiped Baal and Pan, eventually giving the place its name, Panias. Worshipers had carved niches into the sides of the cliff to hold statues of Pan. Over them were various carvings and inscriptions. Perhaps these motivated Jesus to question His disciples about His identity. *And they said, "Some say John the Baptist, but others Elijah, and still others Jeremiah or one of the prophets"* (16:14). People anticipated the return of John the Baptist. But his murderer, King Herod Antipas, lived in fear of his return.

The prophet Malachi had promised that Elijah would return to usher in the anticipated day of the Lord. There was also a tradition that Jeremiah had removed the ark of the covenant from the temple and hidden it before Jerusalem fell. Many expected Elijah to return before the Messiah's coming and bring the ark out of hiding. None of these answers, though, were what Jesus desired to hear. For almost three years these men had been with Him. They should have had some better insight into His true identity. Pointedly and directly, He asked them a personal question." *But who do you say that I am?* (16:15).

Peter had a thought. All that he had seen and heard made him suspect that Jesus was Israel's Messiah. With God's prompting, he confessed his belief. *You are the Messiah, the Son of the living God* (13:16).

Indicating that the conviction Peter had spoken had been revealed by God, Jesus blessed Peter. Perhaps staring at the towering rock cliffs around Him, Jesus added, *And I tell you, you are Peter, and on this rock I will build my church, and the gates of Hades will not prevail against it* (16:18). Peter received the name that we have called him throughout this lesson. The name Peter and the noun for "rock" are the same word in the biblical Greek. Jesus conveyed to Peter that much would be expected from his solid faith and firm leadership.

In addition, Peter received responsibility for the continuing ministry. *I will give you the keys of the kingdom of heaven, and whatever you bind on earth will be bound in heaven, and whatever you loose on earth will be loosed in heaven* (16:19). Pharisees and scribes carried keys as a symbol of their authority and responsibility to unlock the Law's secrets. Peter was to unlock and interpret the story of Jesus for the world.

*Then he sternly ordered the disciples not to tell anyone that he was the Messiah* (16:20). The Messiah, in the average person's understanding, was a glorious military leader who would lead a great war of independence against the Romans and reestablish David's kingdom. Jesus was a different Messiah, however, so the disciples were to say nothing.

Jesus defined His Messiahship for the disciples. *From that time on, Jesus began to show his disciples that he must go to Jerusalem and undergo great*

*suffering at the hands of the elders and chief priests and scribes, and be
killed, and on the third day be raised* (16:21). Peter, reflecting the common
viewpoint about the Messiah, was shocked. Surely Messiahship did not
include rejection, suffering, or death! Peter decided he would set Jesus
straight. *And Peter took him aside and began to rebuke him, saying, "God
forbid it, Lord! This must never happen to you"* (16:22).

No one else in the Gospels earned a rebuke from Jesus such as Peter
received. Sternly Jesus told Peter that he was opposing God's plan. *But he
turned and said to Peter, "Get behind me, Satan! You are a stumbling block
to me; for you are setting your mind not on divine things but on human
things"* (16:23).

## SUGGESTIONS TO TEACHERS

Peter is such a fascinating personality study that we could spend many
lessons discussing him as a case study in Christian growth. Part of his
appeal is his humanness. Peter strikes a responsive chord in all of us.
Today's material looks at his call and his confession at Caesarea Philippi.
In each episode, Peter's unique character comes through. Everything about
this disciple's response to Jesus seemed to be etched in primary colors,
never in pale pastels.

1. CALL. Jesus approached Peter and his brother Andrew while they
were busy with everyday chores. Christ's call comes to people in a variety
of ways and situations, but the summons is always "Follow me!"

Some Christians feel they have not had a "call" because there has been
no dramatic spiritual experience. Remind such folks in your class that
they've been called by Christ through these verses in Matthew 4. The words
here may be understood as their call as well as Peter's.

2. COMMITMENT. Whatever form Christ's call may take in the life of
each believer, the result must be obedience to Him. Peter, Andrew, and millions since their day have understood that Jesus' call compels a response.
And that response ultimately means commitment.

Commitment is what we mean by "following Christ." We follow the leadership of a living, loving Lord—not simply a set of principles, nor a rule
book, nor mere traditions. Talk with your students about the practical
implications of Christ's call in our society today. What about our use of free
time, or money, or talents? What does following Christ mean when choosing a career, nurturing a marriage, or raising children?

3. CONFESSION. Move on to a study of Peter's confession at Caesarea
Philippi. Note his concise statement of faith. Comment on the significance
of his words, especially the meaning of "the Christ," and "the Son of the living God." What do these words mean today?

Invite your class members to write a two-sentence confession of faith,
then read the statements aloud. Is Jesus central in each? What, exactly, is
each person saying about the place of Jesus Christ in his or her life? How
do your students express Jesus' importance?

4. CONFUSION. Peter was human. He had his moments of illumination
but he also misunderstood the nature of Jesus' messiahship. Since he conceived Jesus' rule as that of a worldly conqueror, Peter failed to grasp the
words about sacrificial love, suffering, and dying on a cross. Thus Peter

scolded Jesus for talking about laying down His life for others.

Peter's confusion and misunderstanding should warn each of us of the temptation to categorize the Lord to our liking. He will not conform to our ideas; we must conform to His way and example.

## TOPIC FOR ADULTS
### CONFESS CHRIST

*Cafeteria-Style Religion. Newsweek* magazine (November 28, 1994) carried an article on religion in which a woman named Rita McClain described what she called her spiritual journey. After trying several Protestant denominations, Ms. McClain devoted eighteen years to finding inner peace through rock climbing and desert hiking. She attended a metaphysical gathering in Marin County, California, near her home for a time, then switched to examining Native American spiritual practices. Next, she looked into Buddhism.

The article mentioned that McClain, a fifty-year-old nurse, was currently celebrating at a self-designed altar in her home. The altar consisted of an angel statue, a bowl of "sacred water" blessed at a women's vigil, a crystal ball, a pyramid, a brass image of Buddha sitting on a brass leaf, a votive candle, a Hebrew prayer, a Native American basket dating to the 1850s, and a picture of herself.

This cafeteria approach to religion has become popular with many seekers, especially among baby boomers reaching middle age. The search for the sacred, however, has already been answered. God has come in the person of Jesus. Through this Jesus, God presents the way, the truth, the life.

The quest ends when we confess Jesus as the Christ, the Son of the living God, just as Simon Peter did.

*The Real Chairman.* Several years ago I heard of a company that practiced an unusual ritual at board meetings. As the corporate officers met, an empty chair was placed at the head of the table. The chairman of the board sat on one side of the empty chair; the president sat on the other side of the chair; directors sat around the table. But the chair at the head of the table always remained empty. If someone asked about the empty chair, the president responded, "The empty chair is to remind us that the real chairman of the board . . . is the Lord."

*Claims of the Messiah.* Here is a wonderful statement of faith from ancient times. It was written by Bishop Melito of Sardis, between A.D. 169 and 180, when Christians were persecuted by the Roman intelligentsia:

I, he says, am the Christ.
I am the one who destroyed death,
    and triumphed over the enemy,
    and trampled Hades underfoot,
    and bound the strong one,
    and carried off man
    to the heights of heaven,
    I, he says, am the Christ.
Therefore, come, all families of men,
you who have been befouled with sins,

and receive forgiveness for your sins.
> I am your forgiveness,
> I am the passover of your salvation,
> I am the Lamb which was sacrificed for you,
> I am your ransom,
> I am your light,
> I am your savior,
> I am your resurrection,
> I am your king,
> I am leading you up to the heights of heaven,
> I will show you the eternal Father,
> I will raise you up by my right hand.

This is the Alpha and the Omega.
This is the beginning and the end—
> an indescribable beginning
> and an incomprehensible end.
>> This is the Christ.
>> This is the king.
>> This is Jesus.
>> This is the general.
>> This is the Lord.

*Questions for Students on the Next Lesson.* 1. What are some of the popular explanations as to why Judas betrayed Jesus? 2. How did Jesus react toward Judas at the Last Supper? 3. What did Jesus say to Judas at the Garden of Gethsemane when Judas approached with the police to arrest Jesus? 4. Why do you think Judas finally took his own life?

## TOPIC FOR YOUTH
### FOLLOW THE LEADER

*Reign Ended in Fire.* Luc Jouret was a forty-six-year-old quack physician and so-called spiritual leader who expounded New Age theories of nutrition and child rearing. Jouret saw himself as the Messiah coming in a reign of fire. His Order of the Solar Temple was an odd mix of mysticism, yoga, alchemy, anticommunism, and Roman Catholicism. Urging his followers to stockpile weapons for the end of the world, he charged would-be followers steep initiation fees and required them to sign over their assets to him. The leader and fifty-two members of his community ended their lives in mass suicide in a chapel with mirrored walls and red satin draperies . . . under a portrait of Jouret.

Why did people join this man? One follower, who joined young and then eventually departed, said it was because Jouret made the individual feel chosen and part of a privileged congregation.

Peter made a decision to follow as well. Jesus led him to realize that He was Israel's Messiah and chosen by God to carry out the means of redemption for humankind. Although this plan went against Peter's idea of a messianic reformer, he continued to follow and saw the fulfillment of God's plan through the Cross. His Messiah's reign brought life and joy eternal—not a sad, suicidal obsession.

*Tiny Cracks.* When the Greater Pittsburgh International Airport opened in 1992, it was hailed as one of a new generation of airports. However, one problem surfaced even before the opening ceremonies began. Tiny cracks were discovered in some of the precast concrete beams. These cracks still pose problems for the entire structure.

Our temptations are like tiny moral cracks within us. They weaken us and threaten moral collapse. We must focus on God to help us resist.

Peter had to learn this lesson too. He had to resist the temptation to force Jesus into his messianic mold.

*Seek the Living.* In 1940, Pope Pius XII gave permission to a group of archaeologists to excavate under the high altar of St. Peter's Church on the Vatican Hill. The work was to be done in private, without public notice, and was not to harm the church or interfere with its worship. Interest was generated in 1939 when Vatican workmen discovered a Roman mausoleum under the grotto of St. Peter's Basilica. That discovery, coupled with the knowledge that Emperor Constantine had buried a cemetery, seemed to confirm earlier stories that the apostle Peter had been buried at this spot after his martyrdom.

Excavators believe that after Peter's execution around A.D. 65, his body was recovered either by stealth or bribery. The Christian community then secretly buried the body. The site was remembered by the community, which finally erected a shrine over the site in the mid-second century. Since the shrine was in a pagan cemetery, no one took notice of it. When persecution threatened the Christians over the years, Peter's bones were moved to a nearby repository in a wall. Even when Constantine built the Basilica, the Christians kept the location a secret, fearing that a pagan emperor would soon reign again. The bones lay there until 1942, when they were apparently uncovered. There is, of course, no way of knowing whose bones these are.

This makes for a marvelous tale, but sadly points out that too many people, even scholarly people who should know better, are more interested in searching for a dead figure than following the living Lord.

Peter proclaimed Jesus as Lord. His interest was in the one who rose from the dead and demanded his faith. Follow the same Lord and Him alone. Declare Him to be the Christ, the Son of the living God for your life.

*Questions for Students on the Next Lesson.* 1. Who was Judas? Why did he agree to betray Jesus? 2. What were the disciples' reactions when they learned that Judas would betray Jesus? 3. How did Judas betray Jesus? 4. What were Judas' feelings after the betrayal? How did he handle those feelings? 5. How do you handle your remorse?

# LESSON 9—JANUARY 26

## *JUDAS ISCARIOT*

*Background Scripture:* Matthew 26:14-16, 20-25, 47-50; 27:1-5
*Devotional Reading:* Matthew 27:1-10

### KING JAMES VERSION
MATTHEW 26:14 Then one of the twelve, called Judas Iscariot, went unto the chief priests,

15 And said unto them, What will ye give me, and I will deliver him unto you? And they covenanted with him for thirty pieces of silver.

16 And from that time he sought opportunity to betray him. . . .

20 Now when the even was come, he sat down with the twelve.

21 And as they did eat, he said, Verily I say unto you, that one of you shall betray me.

22 And they were exceeding sorrowful, and began every one of them to say unto him, Lord, is it I?

23 And he answered and said, He that dippeth his hand with me in the dish, the same shall betray me.

24 The Son of man goeth as it is written of him: but woe unto that man by whom the Son of man is betrayed! it had been good for that man if he had not been born.

25 Then Judas, which betrayed him, answered and said, Master, is it I? He said unto him, Thou hast said. . . .

47 And while he yet spake, lo, Judas, one of the twelve, came, and with him a great multitude with swords and staves, from the chief priests and elders of the people.

48 Now he that betrayed him gave them a sign, saying, Whomsoever I shall kiss, that same is he: hold him fast.

49 And forthwith he came to Jesus, and said, Hail, master; and kissed him.

50 And Jesus said unto him, Friend, wherefore art thou come? Then came they, and laid hands on Jesus, and took him.

27:1 When the morning was come, all the chief priests and elders of the people took counsel against Jesus to put him to death:

2 And when they had bound him, they led him away, and delivered him to Pontius Pilate the governor.

3 Then Judas, which had betrayed him, when he saw that he was condemned, repented himself, and brought again the thirty pieces of silver to the chief priests and elders,

4 Saying, I have sinned in that I have

### NEW REVISED STANDARD VERSION
MATTHEW 26:14 Then one of the twelve, who was called Judas Iscariot, went to the chief priests 15 and said, "What will you give me if I betray him to you?" They paid him thirty pieces of silver. 16 And from that moment he began to look for an opportunity to betray him. . . .

20 When it was evening, he took his place with the twelve; 21 and while they were eating, he said, "Truly I tell you, one of you will betray me." 22 And they became greatly distressed and began to say to him one after another, "Surely not I, Lord?" 23 He answered, "The one who has dipped his hand into the bowl with me will betray me. 24 The Son of Man goes as it is written of him, but woe to that one by whom the Son of Man is betrayed! It would have been better for that one not to have been born." 25 Judas, who betrayed him, said, "Surely not I, Rabbi?" He replied, "You have said so." . . .

47 While he was still speaking, Judas, one of the twelve, arrived; with him was a large crowd with swords and clubs, from the chief priests and the elders of the people. 48 Now the betrayer had given them a sign, saying, "The one I will kiss is the man; arrest him." 49 At once he came up to Jesus and said, "Greetings, Rabbi!" and kissed him. 50 Jesus said to him, "Friend, do what you are here to do." Then they came and laid hands on Jesus and arrested him.

27:1 When morning came, all the chief priests and the elders of the people conferred together against Jesus in order to bring about his death. 2 They bound him, led him away, and handed him over to Pilate the governor.

3 When Judas, his betrayer, saw that Jesus was condemned, he repented and brought back the thirty pieces of silver to the chief priests and the elders. 4 He said, "I have sinned by betraying innocent blood." But they said, "What is that to us? See to it yourself." 5 Throwing down the pieces of silver in the temple, he departed; and he went and hanged himself.

betrayed the innocent blood. And they said,
What is that to us? see thou to that.
 5 And he cast down the pieces of silver in
the temple, and departed, and went and
hanged himself.

*KEY VERSE: Judas, who betrayed him, said, "Surely not I, Rabbi?" He replied, "You have said so." Matthew 26:25.*

## HOME BIBLE READINGS

| | | | | |
|---|---|---|---|---|
| Jan. | 20 | M. | Matthew 10:1-6 | *Judas Named One of the Disciples* |
| Jan. | 21 | T. | John 6:60-65 | *Jesus Knows His Betrayer* |
| Jan. | 22 | W. | John 6:66-71 | *One Disciple Acknowledged to be Devil* |
| Jan. | 23 | T. | Luke 22:1-6 | *Judas Contacted the Chief Priests* |
| Jan. | 24 | F. | John 13:21-30 | *Jesus Dismisses Judas from Supper* |
| Jan. | 25 | S. | Luke 22:47-53 | *Jesus' Betrayal and Arrest* |
| Jan. | 26 | S. | Acts 1:15-26 | *Judas' Replacement* |

## BACKGROUND

Perhaps no person in human history is more despised than Judas. Even the name, once honorable and proudly bestowed on male babies (even one of Jesus' brothers was named Judas), now carries a stigma. The Judas goat, for example, was used to lead sheep to the butcher in a slaughterhouse.

The man who betrayed Jesus was once so respected that he was named treasurer of the twelve apostles. As an important member of the disciple band, he enjoyed the trust and companionship of Jesus and the others. A tradition in the Eastern Orthodox Church maintains that Judas's name was at one time not at the bottom of the list of the twelve, but third or sixth.

What went wrong? Why did Judas defect? No one really knows what drove this disciple to his treacherous actions. Perhaps he was a fanatic adherent to tradition and came to resent Jesus' casual approach to the Law. After all, scrupulous Jews never ate with sinners and tax collectors. Judas may have become disillusioned with Jesus' behavior. Some say his enthusiasm for Jesus gradually cooled. Others think that Judas became disappointed when Jesus did not strike out forcefully at those opposing him. Still others think Judas's motive was to force Jesus' hand.

The New Testament writers do not give us a full explanation for Judas's treacherous sellout. Perhaps he was consumed by greed and could not resist an opportunity to get his hands on easy money (see John 12:4-6 as well as Matt. 26:14-16). But the payment was relatively small for such an evil deed.

The Gospels state that the betrayer told the temple authorities where they could seize Jesus without causing a public uproar. Jerusalem was jammed with thousands of Passover pilgrims, who seethed with unrest. The religious leaders were pleased to have Judas's cooperation in snatching Jesus under the cover of darkness and away from the crowds.

## NOTES ON THE PRINTED TEXT

The name "Judas" was a proud and honorable name. "Iscariot" may have meant "dagger bearer." Others, though, suggest it referred to Judas's hometown, Kerioth, in southern Palestine.

*Then one of the twelve, who was called Judas Iscariot, went to the chief priests and said, "What will you give me if I betray him to you?"* (26:14, 15). What motivated Judas remains unknown. About two days before the Passover, he went to the Sanhedrin and declared himself a follower of Jesus who was willing to bargain. He knew they wanted to kill Jesus. He also knew Jesus' prayer habits and where He would be at certain times. This information was worth money. *They paid him thirty pieces of silver* (26:15). Some scholars estimate that thirty pieces of silver would be worth about 120 days of wages.

*"Truly I tell you, one of you will betray me"* (26:21). During the Passover seder [SAY-durr] meal, Jesus made a distressing announcement. Despite their three years together, one in their midst was a traitor who would betray Him. The shock wore off quickly. Suspicious glances followed, and confused questions were put to Jesus. *And they became greatly distressed and began to say to him one after another, "Surely not I, Lord?"* (26:22).

It was customary for the honored guest to sit near the host. Often the host would take a piece of bread, dip it into the wine, and present it to the honored guest. Jesus apparently sat next to Judas (who was possibly in the position of honor), knowing that Judas was about to betray Him. *He answered, "The one who has dipped his hand into the bowl with me will betray me."* (26:23)

Judas, acting innocent, asked if he were the one about whom Jesus spoke. Jesus did not hedge. *He replied, "You have said so"* (26:25). Since a door had earlier been opened for the prophet Elijah (as part of the Passover meal ritual), Judas likely slipped out of the supper at this point. The two would shortly meet again.

That meeting came in Gethsemane, a garden in which Jesus had planned to pray that evening. Judas and the squad of temple police arrived as Jesus spoke with Peter, James, and John. The Sanhedrin was taking no chances. The police were well armed in the event of any show of resistance.

Judas likely kissed Jesus' wrist, since in that culture only equals kissed on the cheek. Judas was a disciple, while Jesus was the teacher; therefore, Judas may have offered the traditional show of respect. The kiss was the signal identifying Jesus to the police. *Now the betrayer had given them a sign, saying, "The one I will kiss is the man; arrest him." At once he came up to Jesus and said, "Greetings, Rabbi!" and kissed him (26:48, 49).*

*Jesus said to him, "Friend, do what you are here to do." Then they came and laid hands on Jesus and arrested him* (26:50). Jesus called Judas "Friend." Was it one last attempt to reach out to Judas? Jesus then surrendered Himself to the police.

The final act of Judas the betrayer took place after the religious leaders had conferred about Jesus' death and had then sent Him bound to Pilate. Judas came to his senses and felt remorse. He stood before the Sanhedrin and confessed his sin to the ones who would not, and could not, provide true forgiveness. They refused to accept his plea or his money. Judas threw the money down and rushed out in suicidal despair. *Throwing down the pieces of silver in the temple, he departed; and went and hanged himself* (27:5).

## SUGGESTIONS TO TEACHERS

This is one of those lessons that can veer off into pointless conjecture. Discussions about why Judas betrayed Jesus may be interesting, but rarely prove helpful. No one, of course, knows exactly what was in Judas's mind. So avoid being diverted by amateur psychoanalyses of his motives. Stick with the Scripture account. Most important, use this material to illumine the tendencies all of us have—to forsake and betray our commitments.

1. FINAL GRAB. Matthew insisted that Judas was an opportunist who sold out to salvage whatever he could from a doomed cause. "What will you give me if I betray him to you?" (26:15), this devious disciple demanded. Whether Judas was trying to save his own skin, or just grab what he could, will never be known. But focus on the words he spoke to the authorities, and the attitude the words reveal.

2. FOOLISH GUILE. Part of the drama of the Judas saga appears in the Last Supper scene. Some commentators think Judas was seated beside Jesus at a place of honor, since Jesus was able to hand him a morsel of food. In any case, Jesus realized that he was going to be betrayed. Judas, who had already arranged his deal with the authorities and received his thirty pieces of silver, had the guile to false innocence and ask, "Is it I?"

We, like Judas, may think we can con the Lord in some way. The streak of Judas lurking in us leads us to imagine we can get away with deceit. But the Lord knows us better than we know ourselves.

3. FALSE GREETING. Judas tried to keep up the pretense even in Gethsemane, when he led the police to arrest Jesus. Judas identified the man to seize by bestowing a disciple's kiss on his rabbi, the traditional mark of respect for a beloved teacher. The hypocrisy of this gesture was not lost on Jesus, but Jesus nevertheless responded by calling Judas "Friend."

Even at this point, Jesus cared about the turncoat follower. Some think that this word "Friend" was Jesus' final attempt to salvage Judas. Impress on your students that Jesus regards all persons as worthy of His friendship.

4. FATAL GUILT. Judas's feelings of guilt so overwhelmed him that he took his own life. The final act of self-loathing and refusal to accept grace is self-destruction.

The reality of guilt is frequently brushed aside in our culture. Discuss the reality of guilt and its effects, and lead the discussion to the significance of the Cross. Through Jesus Christ's death and resurrection, God has handled our guilt. At terrible cost, Jesus bought mercy for us.

### TOPIC FOR ADULTS
#### BE TRUE TO CHRIST

*Evaders. Forbes* magazine featured a report about wealthy folks who have given up their American citizenship and moved to Caribbean countries in order to evade paying federal taxes. According to the 1993 article, over 300 Americans renounced their loyalty to the United States by taking up citizenship in island pseudo-countries like St. Kitts, Turks, Nevis, and Caicos.

These well-to-do former Americans wanted to keep more of their money. They have shed the normal responsibilities of citizenship and do little to alleviate the poverty in these Third-World island countries. Ironically, these rich ex-Americans, who fled for purely selfish reasons, are not barred from our shores. Under U.S. law, they are allowed to spend 120 days a year in the country they have deserted and decline to support. And most of them still do spend considerable time in the U.S.

Greed and rampant self-interest drove Judas to renounce his loyalty to Jesus. The same unbridled selfishness has persuaded hundreds of Americans to turn their backs on their country. Avarice and ambition will eventually lead to the grossest forms of disloyalty.

*Amazing Choice.* The preacher Joseph Parker of London Temple was once asked by an unbeliever, "How, sir, do you account for the fact that Jesus chose Judas to be a disciple?" Dr. Parker answered, "I have a greater problem than this. I do not know why Jesus chose Judas. But a bigger problem to me is why did Jesus choose Joseph Parker?"

It is incredible that God should choose any one of us, but it is only when the choice is His that people become His children. It is an admired thing, I suppose, to be a man's man or a woman's woman. But it is a greater thing to be God's man or woman.

*Questions for Students on the Next Lesson.* 1. Who was Barnabas, and what is the meaning of his name? 2. How did he help Paul? 3. What role did Barnabas have in the church in Antioch? 4. Who has encouraged you in your growth as a Christian? What form did the encouragement take?

## TOPIC FOR YOUTH
### PUT FIRST THINGS FIRST

*Murdered by Friends.* Parents lined up with their children in the bright sun on Chicago's South Side in September, 1994. They were letting their children file by a casket containing a scrawny eleven-year-old boy. He was dressed in a tan suit, lying amid stuffed animals. His face was stitched where the bullets fired into the back of his head had torn through.

Robert "Yummy" Sandifer, so called because of his love of cookies and Snickers bars, had been in trouble with the law most of his brief life. He stole from local grocers and young children. He joined a street gang, the Black Disciples, and was told to fire on some rival gang members in a revenge shooting sparked by a drug feud.

On August 28, Yummy accidentally but fatally shot fourteen-year-old Shavon Dean, bringing the police down hard on the gang. Gang members kept Yummy on the run for three days, moving him from one abandoned building to another as police swept the area. As pressure mounted, gang leaders began seeing Yummy as a liability. He had even begun talking of turning himself in to police.

Gang members Derrick Hardaway and his brother Craig took Yummy in their car, promising to take him out of town. They drove him to a railroad underpass and there, in the dark, muddy tunnel, they shot him twice in the back of his head. Yummy had been betrayed and murdered by two boys he thought were his friends.

Yummy's story is a familiar story of betrayal by friends. His friends, like

Judas, never realized that commitment to God and others must be first. Money and other considerations must be secondary. Resist the temptation to repeat Yummy's story in any way.

*Stats Show Despair.* There has been a 15 percent increase in suicides over the past fifteen years. Sadly, the greatest increase is among children. This rate has doubled in fifteen years, while the rate over the last thirty years has nearly tripled among teenagers. While the rate is very small compared with other age groups, this dramatic increase is alarming. The unmistakable conclusion is that teens are at greater risk than ever before when it comes to taking their own lives.

Tragically, many youth consider suicide as an answer to despair. Judas never sought Jesus' forgiveness, but you, through Jesus Christ, have been forgiven. Realize that God has accepted you just as you are. He sees great possibilities in you and will bring them to pass by His indwelling Spirit. Because of that, you need not despair.

*In His Hands.* In a display in New York's Museum of Jewish Heritage are casts of some leather gloves. They are the gloves that Israeli agent Peter Malkin wore when he grabbed Nazi Adolf Eichmann as he walked home from his bus stop in Buenos Aires on May 11, 1960. Eichmann was the man who organized the transport and death of six million Jews in the death camps of World War II. He was the one who first coined the phrase "final solution."

Malkin wore gloves because he could not bear to touch the man. He admits he had no second thoughts about the righteousness of his mission or about Eichmann's death. He saw this mission as one of justice, and thus felt no guilt.

Judas had unquestionable guilt. The guilt of Jesus' death could not be removed from his hands. He had no pair of gloves to take off, and the stain of his betrayal remained. He could not undo the wrong because it was too late.

It is not too late for you and me, though. God acted to wash sin from our hands through the Cross. Let us place our lives in His hands today.

*Questions for Students on the Next Lesson.* 1. Who was Barnabas? 2. Do you find it easy or hard to share your money? 3. Is it hard to trust others like Barnabas? 4. What are you doing to help your church? 5. Have you ever been God's instrument for good?

# LESSON 10—FEBRUARY 2

## *BARNABAS*

*Background Scripture:* Acts 4:32-37; 9:23-31; 11:19-30
*Devotional Reading:* Acts 15:1-11

### KING JAMES VERSION

ACTS 4:32 And the multitude of them that believed were of one heart and of one soul: neither said any of them that ought of the things which he possessed was his own; but they had all things common. . . .

36 And Joses, who by the apostles was surnamed Barnabas, (which is, being interpreted, The son of consolation,) a Levite, and of the country of Cyprus,

37 Having land, sold it, and brought the money, and laid it at the apostles' feet.

9:26 And when Saul was come to Jerusalem, he assayed to join himself to the disciples: but they were all afraid of him, and believed not that he was a disciple.

27 But Barnabas took him, and brought him to the apostles, and declared unto them how he had seen the Lord in the way, and that he had spoken to him, and how he had preached boldly at Damascus in the name of Jesus.

11:22 Then tidings of these things came unto the ears of the church which was in Jerusalem: and they sent forth Barnabas, that he should go as far as Antioch.

23 Who, when he came, and had seen the grace of God, was glad, and exhorted them all, that with purpose of heart they would cleave unto the Lord.

24 For he was a good man, and full of the Holy Ghost and of faith: and much people was added unto the Lord.

25 Then departed Barnabas to Tarsus, for to seek Saul:

26 And when he had found him, he brought him unto Antioch. And it came to pass, that a whole year they assembled themselves with the church, and taught much people. And the disciples were called Christians first in Antioch.

27 And in these days came prophets from Jerusalem unto Antioch.

28 And there stood up one of them named Agabus, and signified by the Spirit that there should be great dearth throughout all the world: which came to pass in the days of Claudius Caesar.

29 Then the disciples, every man according to his ability, determined to send relief unto the brethren which dwelt in Judea:

### NEW REVISED STANDARD VERSION

ACTS 4:32 Now the whole group of those who believed were of one heart and soul, and no one claimed private ownership of any possessions, but everything they owned was held in common. . . .

36 There was a Levite, a native of Cyprus, Joseph, to whom the apostles gave the name Barnabas (which means "son of encouragement"). 37 He sold a field that belonged to him, then brought the money, and laid it at the apostles' feet.

9:26 When he had come to Jerusalem, he attempted to join the disciples; and they were all afraid of him, for they did not believe that he was a disciple. 27 But Barnabas took him, brought him to the apostles, and described for them how on the road he had seen the Lord, who had spoken to him, and how in Damascus he had spoken boldly in the name of Jesus.

11:22 News of this came to the ears of the church in Jerusalem, and they sent Barnabas to Antioch. 23 When he came and saw the grace of God, he rejoiced, and he exhorted them all to remain faithful to the Lord with steadfast devotion; 24 for he was a good man, full of the Holy Spirit and of faith. And a great many people were brought to the Lord. 25 Then Barnabas went to Tarsus to look for Saul, 26 and when he had found him, he brought him to Antioch. So it was that for an entire year they met with the church and taught a great many people, and it was in Antioch that the disciples were first called "Christians."

27 At that time prophets came down from Jerusalem to Antioch. 28 One of them named Agabus stood up and predicted by the Spirit that there would be a severe famine over all the world; and this took place during the reign of Claudius. 29 The disciples determined that according to their ability, each would send relief to the believers living in Judea; 30 this they did, sending it to the elders by Barnabas and Saul.

30 Which also they did, and sent it to the
elders by the hands of Barnabas and Saul.

*KEY VERSES: When he [Barnabas] came and saw the grace of God, he
rejoiced, and he exhorted them all to remain faithful to the Lord with
steadfast devotion; for he was a good man, full of the Holy Spirit and of
faith. Acts 11:23, 24.*

## DAILY BIBLE READINGS

| | | | | |
|---|---|---|---|---|
| *Jan.* | *27* | *M.* | Acts 13:1-5 | *Barnabas and Paul Called to Ministry* |
| *Jan.* | *28* | *T.* | Acts 14:1-7 | *Ministering in Iconium* |
| *Jan.* | *29* | *W.* | Acts 14:11-18 | *Ministering in Lystra* |
| *Jan.* | *30* | *T.* | Acts 15:1-11 | *Sent to Jerusalem* |
| *Jan.* | *31* | *F.* | Acts 15:22-29 | *Sent to Antioch* |
| *Feb.* | *1* | *S.* | Acts 15:36-41 | *Separated* |
| *Feb.* | *2* | *S.* | Galatians 2:1-10 | *Reunited* |

## BACKGROUND

Many Jewish artisans, merchants, and traders traveled throughout the
Roman world on business. And many eventually settled in towns distant
from Jerusalem. Although these businessmen and workers had emigrated,
they kept their Jewish identity. Large Jewish communities flourished in
most of the major cities, including Alexandria and Rome. Although they
and their children spoke Greek, they remembered their Hebrew roots and
kept their ties to the homeland of Judea. Most tried to make pilgrimages to
Jerusalem for the major festivals (such as Passover) as often as possible.
Consequently, Jerusalem had several synagogues whose congregations
were comprised of Greek-speaking Jews. The synagogues in Roman cities
often produced a fervor for the faith that could come only from a minority
enduring suspicion and discrimination.

The island of Cyprus lies only sixty miles off the coast of Syria. From
ancient times, Cyprus had a close tie with what we call the Holy Land.
Trade was brisk between Cyprus and Palestine. Cyprus' copper mines made
it a prize for a series of conquerors. In the time of the New Testament, the
island's exports also included timber for shipbuilding, fine textiles, grain,
and copper. Its inhabitants were known for their wealth.

Jewish businessmen and entrepreneurs had established homes on the
rich island. One of those families had descended from the priestly Levites.
A son who carried the name Barnabas was born and raised on Cyprus. This
Greek-speaking Jew, known as a "Hellenist" by the native-born, Hebrew-
speaking in Judea, visited the mother country on occasion. Like many
Diaspora Jews, Barnabas had relatives still living in the Jerusalem area.

How did Barnabas become a Christian? Did he hear Stephen preaching
in Jerusalem? Did some unknown believer or missionary come to Cyprus to
spread the Good News of Christ? Did Barnabas meet Peter in one of his
trips to Jerusalem? Was Barnabas a witness to the outpouring of the Spirit
at Pentecost? We pick up no clues in the New Testament about the source
of his conversion, but this great-hearted Christian became a stalwart of the
early church. He lived up to his name, "Son of Encouragement.".

## NOTES ON THE PRINTED TEXT

*Now the whole group of those who believed were of one heart and soul, and no one claimed private ownership of any possessions, but everything they owned was held in common* (4:32). One of the admirable qualities of the early church was its spirit of sharing. Empowered by the Holy Spirit, the members realized that they were only stewards of their possessions, which were owned by Jesus Christ. All of their land, money, and property had to be used to feed the hungry, clothe the naked, heal the sick, and care for the widows and the orphans. Luke provided an example of such generosity by introducing Barnabas.

*There was a Levite, a native of Cyprus, Joseph, to whom the apostles gave the name Barnabas (which means "son of encouragement"). He sold a field that belonged to him then brought the money, and laid it at the apostles' feet* (4:36, 37). Barnabas was a Jew from Cyprus. He was a Levite from a distinguished priestly family. Evidently, he was one of those touched by the Spirit at Pentecost. As a man of some means, he sold a piece of ground and donated the proceeds to the disciples. So committed to Christ and so generous was he that he was nicknamed "son of encouragement."

Barnabas was also the only individual who recognized the great potential within Saul after his conversion. When Saul returned to Jerusalem, everyone was wary and highly suspicious of the new convert. The Christians refused to accept Saul. He was thought to be an imposter, an undercover agent, or simply a flighty enthusiast. *When he had come to Jerusalem, he attempted to join the disciples; and they were afraid of him, for they did not believe that he was a disciple* (9:26).

Barnabas took a risk and welcomed Saul. With compassion and understanding he listened to Saul's story and laid his own reputation on the line by bringing Saul into the fellowship of Christian believers. In front of the apostles, Saul recounted his experience on the road to Damascus. *But Barnabas took him, brought him to the apostles, and described for them how on the road he had seen the Lord, who had spoken to him, and how in Damascus he had spoken boldly in the name of Jesus* (9:27).

Saul immediately preached in Jerusalem. But soon the situation became too hot for Saul, and he sneaked out of the city to Caesarea. From there he was sent to his hometown of Tarsus, where he labored for several years.

In the meantime, many believers fled from Jerusalem to Antioch to escape persecution. Because the church needed workers, Barnabas was sent to join the working staff at Antioch. He was to preach and encourage the believers to remain steadfast in the faith. *News of this came to the ears of the church in Jerusalem, and they sent Barnabas to Antioch. When he came and saw the grace of God, he rejoiced, and he exhorted them all to remain faithful to the Lord with steadfast devotion; for he was a good man, full of the Holy Spirit and of faith* (11:22-24).

The need for workers continued to grow as the church expanded. Barnabas remembered Saul and went to Tarsus to search for him. *Then Barnabas went to Tarsus to look for Saul, and when he found him, he brought him to Antioch* (11:25, 26).

Together in Antioch, Barnabas and Saul preached. Led by the Spirit they testified and witnessed to huge numbers. *So it was that for an entire year they met with the church and taught a great many people* (11:26).

A terrible famine had struck, and believers in Jerusalem were suffering great need. Barnabas again lived up to his name as a son of encouragement. *At that time prophets came down from Jerusalem to Antioch. One of them named Agabus stood up and predicted by the Spirit that there would be a severe famine over all the world* (11:27, 28).

Barnabas organized a relief effort. Teaching that everyone was a brother or sister in Christ's family, he broke down the geographical barriers and provincial feelings among the believers. He and Saul gathered an offering of money, and the two carried the relief fund from Antioch to famine-stricken Jerusalem. *The disciples determined that according to their ability, each would send relief to the believers living in Judea; this they did, sending it to the elders by Barnabas and Saul* (11:29, 30).

## SUGGESTIONS TO TEACHERS

Beginning this Sunday, we will look at five persons who participated in the life and ministry of the first-century church. This lesson's subject is Barnabas. This outstanding leader radiated the qualities of Christ so strongly that he was respected by all parties in the often-divergent early Christian movement. Every congregation needs some Barnabases, and our lesson today is meant to bring out his laudable characteristics in each of us.

1. SELFLESS GIVER. We first note that Barnabas made a generous gift to the Christian community. The fact that Barnabas sold land—a valuable commodity in that part of the world, which no one parted with easily—indicates the depth of this believer's commitment. He placed Jesus Christ and the needs of others ahead of his own interests.

One of the marks of a genuine Christian is the way he or she views personal possessions. Discuss how we can become better stewards of our possessions today.

2. SENSITIVE GO-BETWEEN. Barnabas graciously welcomed Saul of Tarsus when the former persecutor of the church appeared in Jerusalem after his conversion. Others feared Saul or were suspicious of him. Suppose Barnabas had not intervened at that point in Saul's life, introducing him to the apostles. Would Saul have become a great missionary without Barnabas' encouragement and intercession?

Barnabas trusted Saul when no one was willing to take seriously Saul's claim of conversion. Help your students realize that they are called to welcome others to the faith. Remind them also to encourage those who may be newer Christians or fledgling believers, like the young people in your congregation.

3. STALWART GOVERNOR. Barnabas's balanced judgment and positive disposition won him respect as a mature leader. Notice the description of Barnabas: "a good man, full of the holy Spirit, and of faith" (11:24). Dwell on each of these words for a moment with your class, extracting the meaning of each. Are your students remembered primarily for being "good" people (not goody-goodies, but those respected for doing good works)? Are they known as being empowered by the Spirit, and showing steadfast trust in Christ? What would all of this mean, in practical terms today?

4. SKILLFUL GUIDE. Barnabas was the one who "found" Saul. What if

Barnabas had not gone to Tarsus to recruit him for active service? Barnabas for the second time took Saul under his wing. Later, he and his protégé were sent as relief emissaries to Jerusalem by the Antioch congregation. Barnabas had the gifts of humility and perseverance, putting aside thoughts of personal glory to bring the more gifted Saul into a prominent role in the early church.

## TOPIC FOR ADULTS
### BE A COMMITTED ENCOURAGER

*Wrangler or Strangler?* Barnabas's name means "son of encouragement," and he lived up to his name. He seemed always to be encouraging others, including Paul, John, and Mark. Being an encourager brings out the creativity in others.

Years ago, two groups of aspiring writers met at the University of Wisconsin in Madison. Both groups had talented young undergraduates in them. Both were literary clubs. In each, the members met together to read their work to one another. The purpose of each club was to allow members to critique their own writings. One of the literary clubs, an all-male group, was known as "The Stranglers" because of the way they brutally attacked each other's material, finding all the fault possible in each word of every line.

The other gathering happened to be an all-female literary society of would-be writers. This club also met regularly to hear and discuss the efforts of the various members. They dubbed themselves "The Wranglers," and offered helpful criticism and encouragement to one another.

Many years later, a researcher looked into what had become of the people in these two societies of budding authors. The researcher discovered that not one of the men in The Stranglers had ever amounted to anything as a writer, whereas at least six of the women in The Wranglers had gone on to win recognition as literary artists. What was the deciding factor? In the one club, the members deliberately chopped each other down with negative comments. In the other, members strengthened each other with encouragement. The Stranglers effectively strangled their creativity. The women fostered and encouraged the God-given gifts for writing.

*Magnifying-glass Lives.* Our lives are a magnifying glass through which people see either Christ or something else. The only way many people will experience the Gospel is through Christians. If our words proclaim our faith, and our whole life is exemplary, but we fail to illustrate an effective stewardship of the gifts God has entrusted to us, will that witness stand up to scrutiny?

*Encouragement in Solitary.* Olin Stockwell, a missionary to China, spent two years in Communist prisons. He was facing his second Christmas in solitary confinement when his loneliness was broken by music floating out from another cell. A rich, baritone voice, possessed by some unknown Chinese prisoner, was singing Christmas carols. The next day, a homemade card was furtively pushed under Stockwell's cell door.

Some days later, as Stockwell was about to be moved to another prison, he began to whistle "God Be with You Till We Meet Again," and back came the verses sung in Chinese, "God be with you . . . guide, uphold you . . . till we meet at Jesus' feet."

The support of Christian fellowship gave these men the courage they needed to witness under pressure. Like Barnabas, they encouraged each other to hold to the faith in spite of torture and loneliness.

*Questions for Students on the Next Lesson.* 1. Who was Stephen? 2. Why was he brought before the authorities and sentenced? 3. What was the people's reaction to Stephen's steadfastness? 4. What similarities do you see in Stephen's last words and Jesus' words on the cross? 5. When have you made a significant sacrifice because you were a Christian?

## TOPIC FOR YOUTH
### BE AN ENCOURAGER

*Lost Interest.* A study released by the research organization Child Trends concluded that about half of all parents of teens are uninvolved in their children's high school activities. While three-quarters of elementary school children's parents are involved in their children's school activities, the number of parents involved drops off quickly at junior high and once again at high school. Over half of high-school-age children's parents do not attend PTA meetings, open houses at schools, parent-teacher conferences, class plays, sports events, science fairs, or any other school function. The end result of low involvement is that these parents relinquish great influence to their children's peers. The study, entitled "Running in Place," concluded that all the lofty goals held by parents, such as academic success, were opposed to the values of peer culture. The study called for more parental involvement and encouragement.

Barnabas was involved in the lives of those around him, particularly the life of Paul. Specifically, he encouraged Paul. His interest and nurture of Paul and his involvement in Paul's life, produced one of the great leaders of the church.

*Encouraged with God's Word.* Have you eaten a Cadbury chocolate bar? They have been produced in Birmingham, England, for over 100 years. But are you aware of the unusual story of Helen Cadbury, the founder's daughter?

Helen became a Christian at age twelve and soon became interested in witnessing to her faith. She began carrying a large Bible to school. Because of its size, her father eventually gave her a smaller New Testament that she could carry in her pocket. Helen's friends, with whom she read and studied the Bible each day, admired the small Bible, and asked for one. They began to call themselves the Pocket Testament League. They also began to give New Testaments to anyone who agreed to read them.

The Pocket Testament League has now grown into a worldwide ministry with millions of members. The original concept, though, remains the same: carry God's Word, share it, and encourage others with your witness.

Helen is an example of a person seriously willing to encourage her friends. You, too, can do the same.

*Truly Enriched the Community.* In September, 1994, sixty-nine-year-old Sheela Ryan died. Everyone in Winter Springs, Florida, knew her and knew her work.

Ryan made headlines in 1988 when she won fifty-five million dollars.

She made a pledge to use the money to help others, saying that now she had the ability to encourage others. Preferring to live modestly in a trailer park with her retired friends, the former real-estate broker established a trust to fund shelter programs for women and children, provide medical and food assistance, and repair poor people's homes.

While this sounds wonderful, Ryan was helping people even before her big win. She once helped pay for a teenager's kidney transplant, funded animal rights projects, and bought flagpoles for Oviedo High School.

Sheela Ryan understood stewardship. She was willing to share her material possessions with others, enriching the community and encouraging her fellow citizens. She did that quite well.

*Questions for Students on the Next Lesson.* 1. Who was Stephen? 2. What office did he hold in the early church? 3. What was it about his preaching that got him into trouble with the Sanhedrin? 4. Should he have been more careful about what he said? Why, or why not? 5. Has your faith ever gotten you into trouble? What happened?

# LESSON 11—FEBRUARY 9

## STEPHEN

*Background Scripture:* Acts 6:1—8:3
*Devotional Reading:* Matthew 5:43-48

KING JAMES VERSION

ACTS 6:8 And Stephen, full of faith and power, did great wonders and miracles among the people.

9 Then there arose certain of the synagogue, which is called the synagogue of the Libertines, and Cyrenians, and Alexandrians, and of them of Cilicia and of Asia, disputing with Stephen.

10 And they were not able to resist the wisdom and the spirit by which he spake.

11 Then they suborned men, which said, We have heard him speak blasphemous words against Moses, and against God.

12 And they stirred up the people, and the elders, and the scribes, and came upon him, and caught him, and brought him to the council,

13 And set up false witnesses, which said, This man ceaseth not to speak blasphemous words against this holy place, and the law:

14 For we have heard him say, that this Jesus of Nazareth shall destroy this place, and shall change the customs which Moses delivered us.

15 And all that sat in the council, looking stedfastly on him, saw his face as it had been the face of an angel.

7:54 When they heard these things, they were cut to the heart, and they gnashed on him with their teeth.

55 But he, being full of the Holy Ghost, looked up stedfastly into heaven, and saw the glory of God, and Jesus standing on the right hand of God,

56 And said, Behold, I see the heavens opened, and the Son of man standing on the right hand of God.

57 Then they cried out with a loud voice, and stopped their ears, and ran upon him with one accord,

58 And cast him out of the city, and stoned him: and the witnesses laid down their clothes at a young man's feet, whose name was Saul.

59 And they stoned Stephen, calling upon God, and saying, Lord Jesus, receive my spirit.

60 And he kneeled down, and cried with a loud voice, Lord, lay not this sin to their charge. And when he had said this, he fell asleep.

NEW REVISED STANDARD VERSION

ACTS 6:8 Stephen, full of grace and power, did great wonders and signs among the people. 9 Then some of those who belonged to the synagogue of the Freedmen (as it was called), Cyrenians, Alexandrians, and others of those from Cilicia and Asia, stood up and argued with Stephen. 10 But they could not withstand the wisdom and the Spirit with which he spoke. 11 Then they secretly instigated some men to say, "We have heard him speak blasphemous words against Moses and God." 12 They stirred up the people as well as the elders and the scribes; then they suddenly confronted him, seized him, and brought him before the council. 13 They set up false witnesses who said, "This man never stops saying things against this holy place and the law; 14 for we have heard him say that this Jesus of Nazareth will destroy this place and will change the customs that Moses handed on to us." 15 And all who sat in the council looked intently at him, and they saw that his face was like the face of an angel.

7:54 When they heard these things, they became enraged and ground their teeth at Stephen. 55 But filled with the Holy Spirit, he gazed into heaven and saw the glory of God and Jesus standing at the right hand of God. 56 "Look," he said, "I see the heavens opened and the Son of Man standing at the right hand of God!" 57 But they covered their ears, and with a loud shout all rushed together against him. 58 Then they dragged him out of the city and began to stone him; and the witnesses laid their coats at the feet of a young man named Saul. 59 While they were stoning Stephen, he prayed, "Lord Jesus, receive my spirit." 60 Then he knelt down and cried out in a loud voice, "Lord, do not hold this sin against them." When he had said this, he died.

KEY VERSE: *Stephen, full of grace and power, did great wonders and signs among the people. Acts 6:8.*

## HOME BIBLE READINGS

| | | | | |
|------|---|----|---------------|---------------------------------------------|
| *Feb.* | *3* | *M.* | Acts 6:1-7 | *Stephen Chosen to be Deacon* |
| *Feb.* | *4* | *T.* | Acts 7:1-10 | *Stephen's Testimony before the High Priest* |
| *Feb.* | *5* | *W.* | Acts 7:44-53 | *Stiff-necked People Resist the Holy Spirit* |
| *Feb.* | *6* | *T.* | Luke 21:10-19 | *Gain True Life by Enduring Persecution* |
| *Feb.* | *7* | *F.* | Psalm 57:1-11 | *Take Refuge in God* |
| *Feb.* | *8* | *S.* | Matthew 5:43-46 | *Pray for Those Who Persecute You* |
| *Feb.* | *9* | *S.* | Luke 12:4-12 | *Acknowledge God before People* |

## BACKGROUND

The original followers of the risen Christ were Jews born and raised in the "homeland" of Jerusalem and Galilee. Their mother tongue was Aramaic, but they regarded themselves as "Hebrews." These believers in Jesus Christ continued to observe their Jewish practices, including circumcision, certain dietary laws, and regular temple worship.

The Good News of Jesus quickly won followers among Jews who lived elsewhere. These Diaspora (or scattered) Jews lived in the great cities of the Roman Empire and spoke Greek as their mother tongue. When they returned to Jerusalem on pilgrimages for the great festivals, as most tried to do as often as possible, they were inclined to feel more at home in a synagogue where other Greek-speaking Jews gathered. Inevitably, however, differences arose between the early Christians who were Jews from Palestine and Jews from elsewhere. The stay-at-home Jewish converts became known as "Hebrews," whereas the Greek-speaking Jews were called "Hellenists."

As the church grew in numbers, it became more difficult to maintain the sense of close fellowship that had marked the earliest Jerusalem congregation. The original followers, steadfastly holding to their ancient traditions as Jews, looked with some suspicion upon the "foreign" Jewish Christians, the Hellenists. These believers were not as scrupulous in keeping all the Jewish requirements as they, the Hebrews, did.

During a time of high prices and food shortages, it was discovered that the poor and widows from among the Hellenists were not being looked after as well as those from the Hebrews. This matter was resolved with the appointment of "the seven" to supervise a daily food distribution to needy Hellenists. Each of the seven was highly respected for his piety and wisdom.

One of the seven, Stephen, also became respected for his preaching. His sermons in the synagogues where Greek-speaking Jews congregated began to win so many converts that the fanatic synagogue leaders and temple authorities became alarmed. More than any other early Christian, Stephen recognized that following Christ meant sharing the Good News everywhere. The Gospel fulfilled the ancient Hebrew Scriptures, and Stephen boldly and effectively told his fellow Greek-background Jews to welcome the Jesus as Messiah.

The opposition could not best him in debate and resorted to false accusations of blasphemy, which carried the death penalty. Stephen became the first Christian martyr.

## NOTES ON THE PRINTED TEXT

*Stephen, full of grace and power, did great wonders and signs among the people* (6:8). As the church grew, so did the problems within the fellowship. One problem was a complaint by the Greek-speaking, non-native-born Jewish Christians that some of the poor within their group were being neglected. The disciples suggested that certain individuals be elected and designated to serve the needy. Seven men were elected and ordained, including Stephen. However, Stephen viewed his task as more than simply caring for the needy. He was an excellent orator, a persuasive speaker, and able to heal. Soon he was evangelizing in the synagogues.

*Then some of those who belonged to the synagogue of the Freedmen (as it was called), Cyrenians, Alexandrians, and others of those from Cilicia and Asia, stood up and argued with Stephen* (6:9). Within Jerusalem were several synagogues for Greek-speaking Jews. Many of the members were former captives of Rome or children of former captives who had been freed and who had returned to Jerusalem. The church inevitably found their views clashing with these people. Stephen was the church's chief spokesperson and did an excellent job with God's help. *But they could not withstand the wisdom and the Spirit with which he spoke* (6:10).

Antagonism against Stephen grew because of his success. The authorities, looking for a way of removing him, devised a plot. He would be arrested on a trumped-up charge of blasphemy. *Then they secretly instigated some men to say, "We have heard him speak blasphemous words against Moses and God." They stirred up the elders and the scribes; then they suddenly confronted him, seized him, and brought him before the council* (6:11, 12).

Stephen was brought before the high priest and the council, where the charges were raised. Several witnesses had to offer testimony that agreed; all lied perfectly. *They set up false witnesses who said, "This man never stops saying things against this holy place and the law; for we have heard him say that the Jesus of Nazareth will destroy this place and will change the customs that Moses handed to us"* (6:13, 14).

Stephen's defense was a long, well-reasoned exposition of the Gospel, beginning with Abraham and moving through the patriarchs and Moses. He culminated with Jesus Christ, the righteous one. He accused the council of murdering Jesus and opposing the Holy Spirit, just as their predecessors had opposed every prophet and God-sent messenger. Although they were the law's guardians, they were not keeping that law, Stephen charged.

*When they heard these things, they became enraged and ground their teeth at Stephen* (7:54). The members of the Sanhedrin were infuriated. The Greek language in this passage gives the vivid impression that they became like wild, snarling and snapping dogs.

In stark contrast to these learned men stood Stephen. He seemed unperturbed and stood his ground. *But filled with the Holy Spirit, he gazed into heaven and saw the glory of God and Jesus standing at the right hand of God* (7:55). The growing cries of anger nearly drowned out the concluding sentence in his defense. *"Look," he said. "I see the heavens opened and the Son of Man standing at the right hand of God!"* (7:56). For Stephen, Jesus came as the world's Messiah, not simply the Savior for the Jews.

The law and protocol demanded that the high priest take an individual voice vote, starting with the youngest member and moving toward the eldest. Law demanded a twenty-four-hour waiting period (if the expected punishment was to be death) before that vote could be taken. All these laws were disregarded. Mob justice took over without a vote or a verdict. Stephen was seized and brutally dragged through the streets of Jerusalem. Outside the city he was stoned to death. *But they covered their ears, and with a loud shout all rushed together against him. Then they dragged him out of the city and began to stone him* (7:57, 58). Luke noted that a young man named Saul witnessed Stephen's death. He watched over the executioners' garments.

While he was dying, Stephen knelt and prayed, committing his spirit to Jesus. *"Lord Jesus, receive my spirit"* (7:59). He also asked God to forgive his executioners and murderers. *Then he knelt down and cried out in a loud voice, "Lord, do not hold this sin against them." When he had said this, he died* (7:60).

## SUGGESTIONS TO TEACHERS

Stephen died for the faith. We may be under the impression that the days of martyrdom ended centuries ago, that Stephen's type of sacrifice no longer takes place. Yet the roll call of martyrs in the church grows longer each year. Brothers and sisters in Christ have recently laid down their lives in faithful witness in Haiti, Rwanda, Sudan, Iraq, Iran, El Salvador, Guatamala, and elsewhere.

There is little likelihood that we will be put to death for our faith. Remind your students, however, that every follower of Christ must be prepared to accept forms of suffering for the sake of the Gospel. This lesson is intended to prepare your class members to be faithful witnesses for Christ no matter what the cost.

1. SERVANT. Stephen preached powerfully and effectively. But he had been appointed as one of the seven to serve at the tables. His form of serving in that capacity undoubtedly meant carrying food baskets to the needy. A Christian may witness in humble kitchen tasks as well as in the more dramatic forms of ministry.

2. SERMON. Examine Stephen's homily before the authorities after his arrest. In it, he recapitulated the saga of the Hebrew people and showed how Jesus' death and resurrection tied in with the great story that began with Abraham. Note how Stephen made no effort to soft-pedal the message of Christ to save his own neck. He fearlessly reminded his hearers that they were guilty of murder. Ask your students about times when they have had to stand up and speak out as Christians.

3. SENTENCE. Stephen suffered the gruesome form of execution known as stoning. Undoubtedly, this first man to be martyred for Christ knew the

price he would pay for his commitment. But Stephen did not flinch. Talk with your students about the kinds of pain that may be forced on them as a result of their Christianity. For some it may mean losing a friend or being passed over for promotion. All of us will sacrifice in some ways when we clearly identify with Christ among our neighbors and relatives.

4. SEQUEL. The Book of Acts mentions that Saul of Tarsus held the cloaks of those who stoned Stephen. Obviously, Stephen's witness in dying so nobly made an impression on Saul. Hearing Stephen's final words addressed to Jesus, must have shaken Saul so deeply that he became a prime candidate for conversion.

Our sacrifices may seem pointless, and some perhaps thought Stephen's martyrdom was meaningless. But God uses each form of faithful witness for His glory.

## TOPIC FOR ADULTS
### BE A FAITHFUL WITNESS

*Death Brings Conversions.* The gruesome martyrdom of a pastor in central India led to several hundred conversions to Christianity in 1994. A former Hindu who had changed his name to Paul James was murdered by extremists as he preached in a field in the Phulabani district.

Eyewitnesses said James called out "Jesus, forgive them," as his assailants cut off his hands and legs, and severed his torso. The attackers also decapitated James, an outspoken believer who had planted twenty-seven churches.

The murder drew heavy media attention in the area, which is charged with Hindu-Muslim tensions. Some, but not all, of James' assailants reportedly have been caught.

*Faithful Witness.* Three-quarters of a century after Massachusetts closed its leper hospital on desolate Penikese Island, lawmakers finally honored Dr. Frank H. Parker by placing a plaque at the Statehouse to celebrate his courageous work. Dr. Parker left a lucrative private practice in 1907 and volunteered to work as the state's physician on Penikese Island. At that time, Massachusetts deported lepers to the remote island located fourteen miles off the coast of New Bedford. Leprosy in those days was still believed to be highly contagious and always fatal, though research has now proven all of these notions to be false. Dr. Parker believed that treatment could be found for leprosy and that it was not as infectious as everyone thought. This compassionate doctor also wanted to find a cure for the unfortunate victims. He dedicated fourteen years of his life to serving the people sent to Penikese Island.

Paid only $2,000 a year by the state, Dr. Parker and his wife, Marion, spent their own money to provide food, medical supplies, and other necessities for his patients. He served as more than a doctor, organizing a farm with vegetable crops and dairy cows, and working as a carpenter and electrician. When a fire destroyed their separate living quarters, the Parkers moved in with their patients.

When politicians decided to close the colony in 1921, Dr. Frank Parker knew that the island-dwellers would not be welcomed in any community on the mainland. He tried to have the state delay the closure, but over his objections, the colony was closed down.

Parker then tried to raise funds to look after his patients and spent his own money to care for them. The state retaliated by denying him his final month's pay and refusing to grant him a pension. Without funds, this Christian physician tried to return to private practice, but found himself shunned because the public still believed leprosy was contagious. He finally moved to Montana, where he died penniless. His brave witness as a compassionate healer for Christ touched the lives of all who came under his care on Penikese.

*Witness of an Early Martyr.* Polycarp was a personal disciple of the apostle John. As an old man, he was the bishop of the church at Smyrna in Asia Minor (present-day Turkey). Persecution against the Christians broke out there, and believers were being fed to the wild animals in the arena. One day in A.D. 155, the crowd began to call for the Christians' leader, Polycarp.

Despite the cries of the crowd, the Roman authorities saw the senselessness of making this aged man a martyr. So when Polycarp was brought into the arena, the proconsul pled with him: "Curse Christ and I will release you."

Polycarp replied, "Eighty-six years I have served Him. He has never done me wrong. How then can I blaspheme my King who has saved me?"

The proconsul reached for an acceptable way out: "Then do this, old man. Just swear by the genius of the emperor and that will be sufficient." The "genius" was sort of the "spirit" of the emperor. To do this would be a recognition of the polytheistic religion.

The old bishop answered, "If you imagine for a moment that I would do that, then I think you pretend that you don't know who I am. Hear it plainly. I am a Christian. Bring [the beasts] forth. I would change my mind if it meant going from the worse to the better, but not to change from the right to the wrong."

The proconsul's patience came to an end, and he proclaimed, "I will have you burned alive."

Replied Polycarp, "You threaten fire that burns for an hour and is over. But the judgment on the ungodly is forever."

The fire was prepared, and Polycarp lifted his eyes to heaven and prayed: "Father, I bless you that you have deemed me worthy of this day and hour, that I might take a portion of the martyrs in the cup of Christ. . . . Among these may I today be welcome before thy face as a rich and acceptable sacrifice."

*Questions for Students on the Next Lesson.* 1. Who were Aquila and Priscilla? 2. How did the apostle Paul meet them? 3. How did this couple help Apollos? 4. How do you typically respond to a change in residence or occupation? 5. Who are some of the more experienced believers who have helped you in your life as a Christian? How did these persons help you?

## TOPIC FOR YOUTH
### TAKE A STAND

*Most Influential.* The Siena Research Institution, in cooperation with the National Women's Hall of Fame in Seneca Falls, New York, surveyed 300 historians and academics in American studies and women's studies to discover who were the most influential American women of the twentieth century. The ten most influential women were: Eleanor Roosevelt (defender of the rights of women, minorities, and the poor), Jane Addams (labor organizer and founder of Chicago's Hull House), Rosa Parks (the major impetus behind the civil rights movement), Margaret Sanger (organizer of Industrial Workers of the World and Planned Parenthood), Margaret Mead (writer of studies on family structure and social organization), Charlotte Perkins Gilman (pioneer feminist), Betty Friedan (founder of the National Organization of Women), Barbara Jordan (lawyer-educator), Helen Keller (blind and deaf woman who called attention to the needs of the physically handicapped), and Alice Paul (founder of the Union for Women's Suffrage, the movement for women's right to vote). All these women were recognized for taking stands or having the courage to face society's opposition.

Stephen provides an excellent role model as well . . . but for an eternal cause. He took a stand for his Lord and his faith. Even in the pressure-packed situation of a trial he stood strong. We are all called to do the same.

*Today's Heroes.* Sports and entertainment stars are often the role models for American youth. That may not be a good thing, in the opinion of a Teen Forum in Pittsburgh. This group of church youth point to the scandals associated with various celebrities who have "fallen from grace." For example, singing superstar Michael Jackson has been plagued by child molestation allegations. Baseball legend Pete Rose spent time in jail for tax evasion after gambling. Boxing champ Mike Tyson was jailed for raping a teenage beauty pageant contestant. O.J. Simpson was tried for the grisly murder of his wife and her friend.

Teen Forum panelists said that although they might influence some people, they did not consider themselves role models, even to younger siblings. A junior in high school, Bill Stoops, said he knew few people to whom he would be a role model. No one, he felt, would look up to him. Stacy Omecene from Springdale High School said she was just average. Even her sister would not look up to her. In fact, she felt no one would. All saw themselves as having little influence on others.

However, the story of Stephen demonstrates that individuals are capable of being role models for those who are younger than themselves. A young man named Saul, who watched the trial and stoning of Stephen, was greatly influenced. He went on to try and crush the Christian movement. Then, after encountering the risen Christ, he himself became a worker for Christ. His influence and encouragement touched thousands. Never underestimate the influence you can exert—or the power of the Spirit.

*Questions for Students on the Next Lesson.* 1. Who were Priscilla and Aquila? 2. Do all church leaders have to be seminary trained and ordained? Why or why not? 3. How do you show your commitment to Jesus? 4. How are potential church leaders advised and nurtured in your congregation and denomination?

# LESSON 12—FEBRUARY 16

## PRISCILLA AND AQUILA

*Background Scripture:* Acts 18:1-4, 18, 19, 24-26; Romans 16:3-5a
*Devotional Reading:* I Thessalonians 5:12-22

### KING JAMES VERSION

ACTS 18:1 After these things Paul departed from Athens, and came to Corinth;

2 And found a certain Jew named Aquila, born in Pontus, lately come from Italy, with his wife Priscilla; (because that Claudius had commanded all Jews to depart from Rome:) and came unto them.

3 And because he was of the same craft, he abode with them, and wrought: for by their occupation they were tentmakers.

4 And he reasoned in the synagogue every sabbath, and persuaded the Jews and the Greeks. . . .

18 And Paul after this tarried there yet a good while, and then took his leave of the brethren, and sailed thence into Syria, and with him Priscilla and Aquila; having shorn his head in Cenchrea: for he had a vow.

19 And he came to Ephesus, and left them there: but he himself entered into the synagogue, and reasoned with the Jews. . . .

24 And a certain Jew named Apollos, born at Alexandria, an eloquent man, and mighty in the scriptures, came to Ephesus.

25 This man was instructed in the way of the Lord; and being fervent in the spirit, he spake and taught diligently the things of the Lord, knowing only the baptism of John.

26 And he began to speak boldly in the synagogue: whom when Aquila and Priscilla had heard, they took him unto them, and expounded unto him the way of God more perfectly.

ROMANS 16:3 Greet Priscilla and Aquila my helpers in Christ Jesus:

4 Who have for my life laid down their own necks: unto whom not only I give thanks, but also all the churches of the Gentiles.

5z Likewise greet the church that is in their house.

### NEW REVISED STANDARD VERSION

ACTS 18:1 After this Paul left Athens and went to Corinth. 2 There he found a Jew named Aquila, a native of Pontus, who had recently come from Italy with his wife Priscilla, because Claudius had ordered all Jews to leave Rome. Paul went to see them, 3 and, because he was of the same trade, he stayed with them, and they worked together—by trade they were tentmakers. 4 Every sabbath he would argue in the synagogue and would try to convince Jews and Greeks. . . .

18 After staying there for a considerable time, Paul said farewell to the believers and sailed for Syria, accompanied by Priscilla and Aquila. At Cenchreae he had his hair cut, for he was under a vow. 19 When they reached Ephesus, he left them there, but first he himself went into the synagogue and had a discussion with the Jews. . . .

24 Now there came to Ephesus a Jew named Apollos, a native of Alexandria. He was an eloquent man, well-versed in the scriptures. 25 He had been instructed in the Way of the Lord; and he spoke with burning enthusiasm and taught accurately the things concerning Jesus, though he knew only the baptism of John. 26 He began to speak boldly in the synagogue; but when Priscilla and Aquila heard him, they took him aside and explained the Way of God to him more accurately.

ROMANS 16:3 Greet Prisca and Aquila, who work with me in Christ Jesus, 4 and who risked their necks for my life, to whom not only I give thanks, but also all the churches of the Gentiles. 5a Greet also the church in their house.

**KEY VERSES:** *Greet Prisca and Aquila, who work with me in Christ Jesus, and who risked their necks for my life, to whom not only I give thanks, but also all the churches of the Gentiles.* Romans 16:3, 4.

## HOME BIBLE READINGS

| | | | | |
|---|---|---|---|---|
| Feb. | 10 | M. | I Corinthians 16:15-24 | *They Acknowledged Other Churches* |
| Feb. | 11 | T. | Acts 18:5-11 | *They Supported Paul's Teachings* |
| Feb. | 12 | W. | I Corinthians 3:5-11 | *Each Person Has a Special Day* |
| Feb. | 13 | T. | Romans 12:1-8 | *Support Others' Christian Work* |
| Feb. | 14 | F. | Romans 12:9-21 | *Share Christian Life-Styles* |
| Feb. | 15 | S. | Romans 13:8-14 | *Fulfill the Law of Love* |
| Feb. | 16 | S. | I Thessalonians 5:12-22 | *Respect Your Leaders* |

## BACKGROUND

Jews in the first-century world inhabited every large city. Often they took on Latin names to do business in the Roman Empire. Aquila was such a person. Originally from Pontus (in what is now Asia Minor), he settled in Rome. We don't know his Hebrew name; we read only that he was known by his Roman name, "Aquila." (His name doesn't rhyme wiht Priscilla, but is actually pronounced ACK-wih-luh.)

Every Jewish boy was taught a trade, usually by his father. Just as Jesus learned from Joseph the craft of carpentry, Aquila learned tentmaking, probably from his family. "Tentmaking" could refer to the art of weaving course black threads into the heavy cloth used for awnings and tents. Or it could also mean sewing strips of leather together to make large tarp-like pieces used in tents.

Priscilla, Aquila's wife, worked with him at tentmaking in Rome. Both were devout people. Perhaps they were won to Christ in Rome. Or perhaps they became Christian believers in Corinth after hearing Paul testify; the records do not say. At any rate, their lives abruptly changed around A.D. 50, when the Emperor Claudius expelled Jews from Rome. Since the Roman authorities could not differentiate between Jews and Christians, many Christians were rounded up and forced to leave as well. If Aquila and Priscilla were Christians at the time, they were forced to relocate for the first time—but not the last—because of their faith.

They came to Corinth, one of the great mercantile and shipping centers in the ancient world, and reestablished their business. When the apostle Paul arrived in Corinth, he joined their household as a fellow tentmaker. The three quickly became close friends and trusted companions. Paul earned his living in Corinth in the employ of Aquila and Priscilla, but the strength of the relationship came from their common commitment to Jesus Christ.

Aquila and Priscilla were apparently a successful business couple. When Paul left Corinth to go to Ephesus, they both accompanied him. Some think business took them to Ephesus, but the account in Acts 18 implies that their faith caused them to uproot once again. In Ephesus they became effective, trusted leaders. Paul left them in charge of the house-church there when he moved on.

In the New Testament, the name of Priscilla (or "Prisca," as Paul usually called her in his letters) often precedes Aquila's. This suggests that she was one of the wisest leaders in the early Christian church, as well as a woman of some means and social standing. A devoted wife to Aquila, a loyal friend to Paul, a mature Christian in every circumstance, this outstanding woman ranks as one of the great persons of the faith.

## NOTES ON THE PRINTED TEXT

*After this Paul left Athens and went to Corinth* (18:1). Paul's effort to evangelize Athens was a disappointing failure. Yet instead of despairing, he pushed on to Corinth, which lay on a narrow isthmus between the Gulf of Corinth on the west and the Saronic Gulf on the east. Rather than sail around the treacherous tip of Greece, most ships put into one of these gulfs and off-loaded their cargos to have them transported across the isthmus. Or sometimes the whole ship was dragged across the narrow piece of land on rollers. Largely due to the shipping trade, Corinth became rich and powerful. It was also notoriously immoral, an unlikely place for a Christian congregation.

*There he found a Jew named Aquila, a native of Pontus, who had recently come from Italy with his wife Priscilla, because Claudius had ordered all Jews to leave Rome* (18:2). Paul found a cloth-weaving couple, a husband-wife team who had recently been expelled from Rome by an anti-Semitic edict of Emperor Claudius. Aquila was originally from Pontus, an area along the Black Sea in modern northern Turkey. The two wove tents, sails, and awnings. These items were in great demand in Corinth because of the Isthmian games every two years and because of the shipping industry. Since Paul was a tentmaker skilled in making cloth from goat hair, he worked with this couple. The three developed a strong relationship as they labored together. *Because he was of the same trade, he stayed with them, and they worked together—by trade they were tentmakers* (18:3).

After about a year and a half of work in Corinth, Paul established a church there. Then, with his fellow workers, Paul sailed for Syria. *After staying there for a considerable time, Paul said farewell to the believers and sailed for Syria, accompanied by Priscilla and Aquila* (18:18). Before sailing from Cenchreae, Paul voluntarily took a Nazarite vow expressing his thanks to God for his recent experience in Corinth. *At Cenchreae he had his hair cut, for he was under a vow* (18:18).

Arriving in Ephesus Paul went to the synagogue to share the Gospel and debate with the Jews. He stayed only a few days before sailing for Caesarea and then continuing his trip to Jerusalem. He promised, though, to return. He did leave Priscilla and Aquila in Ephesus, confident they would continue the missionary work there. *When they reached Ephesus, he left them there, but first he himself went into the synagogue and had a discussion with the Jews* (18:19).

As Priscilla and Aquila continued to nurture the tiny Ephesian church, a young man arrived. He had been raised and educated in Alexandria, Egypt, a center of learning. He was a skilled debater and a forceful orator who made a powerful impression as he spoke about Jesus. *Now there came to Ephesus a Jew named Apollos, a native of Alexandria. He was an eloquent man, well versed in the scriptures* (18:24).

Apollos did have one deficiency. *He had been instructed in the Way of the*

*Lord; and he spoke with burning enthusiasm and taught accurately the things concerning Jesus, though he knew only the baptism of John* (18:25). "Instructed" in Greek meant "catechized." He had become well-versed on the life of Jesus and had learned all the facts about Him. He had read many writings and agreed that Jesus was the Messiah, but he did not know Jesus. His baptism was John the Baptist's baptism of repentance.

Apollos lacked the Holy Spirit,and without the Spirit, he was incomplete. *He began to speak boldly in the synagogue; but when Priscilla and Aquila heard him, they took him aside and explained the Way of God to him more accurately* (18:26). As the two listened to this promising man speak, they saw his potential but also his inadequacies. The two cloth weavers carefully instructed Apollos in the ways of the Lord. When his education was complete, the two likely supplied letters of introduction for him when he sailed for Corinth.

How long the two stayed in Ephesus is unknown. Their home was a meeting place for the Ephesian congregation, though later the couple returned to Rome for eight years. When Paul was preparing to visit the church he acknowledged the significant contributions the two had made to his ministry and to other churches. *Greet Prisca and Aquila, who work with me in Christ Jesus, and who risked their necks for my life, to whom not only I give thanks, but also all the churches of the Gentiles* (16:3, 4).

## SUGGESTIONS TO TEACHERS

We all need supportive friends. Even Jesus enjoyed the hospitality of Mary and Martha and chose twelve close associates. Likewise, Paul gathered a circle of close friends. Among these supportive companions were the wife and husband we are studying today. Priscilla and Aquila serve as models of the kind of caring we are called to offer one another in the church.

1. DEPORTED BY CLAUDIUS. Driven from Rome during the turbulent reign of the inept Claudius, Aquila and Priscilla were forced to flee to Corinth. Commitment to the faith, this couple learned, sometimes brings hardship and unexpected changes in personal plans.

With a commitment to God, however, are given stability and spiritual stamina. This support from God's Spirit helps us, in turn, to maintain our loving relationships with brothers and sisters in Christ.

2. DEVOTED AS COMPANIONS. Priscilla and Aquila welcomed Paul as a fellow tentmaker and believer. Trace their willingness to pack up and move on with Paul to Ephesus, and note the subsequent references to these two in the New Testament. Throughout, they were loyal and helpful co-workers in the faith.

3. DISTINGUISHED AS CAREGIVERS. Devote some lesson time to examining the way Aquila and Priscilla helped Apollos grow in the faith. This good-hearted couple didn't tear apart Apollos for his defective understanding of the Gospel; instead, they graciously helped him mature. They pointed out his mistaken interpretation of baptism and his flawed theology of the Holy Spirit, but did it in a way that enabled young Apollos to know he was supported by their care and prayers. This example should open a discussion about how we in the church can correct one another without being hurtful.

4. DARING IN COMMITMENT. Paul commended Aquila and Priscilla for having "risked their necks for my life" (Rom. 16:3, 4). True friendship means sacrificing for the other. Love means placing the interests of others ahead of one's own. Whether the "other" is a spouse, a child, a sibling, another family member, or a fellow church member, being a supportive companion demands some risk-taking for Christ's sake. Caring is always risky; we can be hurt. But risky, caring companionship is the kind Jesus Himself modeled.

## TOPIC FOR ADULTS
### BE A SUPPORTIVE COMPANION

*Supportive Coach.* One of baseball's greatest heroes, Branch Rickey, took his Christian faith as seriously as his sport. In his early career, he coached baseball at Ohio Wesleyan. He later told of a turning point in his career when his team went to South Bend, Indiana, to play Notre Dame.

At that time, Indiana, like many other states, permitted segregation to be practiced in restaurants and hotels. One of the pitchers on Ohio Wesleyan's team was black. This African-American found himself denied hotel service because of his color. Rickey immediately told the member of his team, "There are two beds in my room," and invited him to stay with him. When Rickey entered the room, he found the young man sitting in a chair, crying. Between sobs, the young black athlete said that he wished he could tear off his skin in order to avoid the humiliations he was forced to endure on account of his color.

Branch Rickey never forgot that young man's suffering. He resolved to be a companion to all black athletes and support them in their claims for equal treatment. In 1947, Rickey was instrumental in breaking the color barrier in Big League Baseball. In spite of the "gentlemen's agreements" among owners and managers in both leagues, barring African-American players from team rosters, Rickey determined to support black ball players. He was vilified, but Branch Rickey brought the great Jackie Robinson to the Brooklyn Dodgers. The rest is history. Rickey, the Christian, proved to be a truly supportive companion.

*A Missionary's Perspective.* "Why go? Why not just send the missionaries the money?"

We arrived in the village of El Tunal to find a small piece of property with only the foundation of what would later be a church. As the work group labored each day, people gathered to watch . . . and talk . . . and help . . . and sometimes laugh with this hardworking bunch of people. Children learned English phrases and songs about Jesus. Group members learned Spanish phrases and songs about Jesus. And while all this was going on, one solitary figure, with an expressionless face, stood across the road and watched all the activity.

I asked one of the church leaders who this man was. "He is an atheist!" was the reply. "He isn't Catholic or anything else. He doesn't believe in anything. He's just a bitter old man set in his ways." Later in the day I walked across the rough street to where this man was standing. As I approached, I smiled and greeted him. He barely acknowledged me. He just kept watching the young people work on the church.

Days passed. The block walls reached eight feet into the air. The project site that started as a pile of building materials was now tidy—and most notable for the clean structure that took its position on the front of the lot.

The last day, we were finishing the floor. The team members were excitedly pouring the last wheelbarrow loads of concrete. And still the old man watched from across the street.

I shared with him briefly why these people had come to work and to show God's love to others. He didn't accept Jesus that day, but the seed was planted by young people from Minnesota, Ohio, Japan, Bolivia, Iowa, the West Coast.

Why not just send money? El Tunal now has a church. I can go nearly anywhere in the village and people know me. This work team, through their selfless, enthusiastic labor, paved the way for me as a missionary to have a fuller ministry. They opened doors that otherwise wouldn't have been opened.

They came to build a church—they did. They came to share God's love—they did. They came to help a missionary—they did. Thank you!—*Traveler*, Fall-Winter 1994 (Marion, IN: World Gospel Mission).

*Dedicated Support.* On the evening of October 3, 1993, an MH-60 Black Hawk helicopter from the Army's 160th Special Operations Aviation Regiment was brought down from the skies over Mogadishu, Somalia. It had succumbed to rockets fired by clan leader Mohammed Aidid's troops. The chopper was part of the Ranger operations sent to capture the fugitive general's top deputies. It contained four members of one of the most elite combat units, the U.S. Army Rangers. When it crashed, two Rangers were killed and two were badly wounded.

Within minutes, a band of Rangers fought their way to the wreckage. They quickly picked up their two wounded buddies and the body of one of the dead. But the body of the other was caught in the twisted frame of the downed copter and could not be extricated without special equipment. Yet the Rangers would not leave their dead comrade. Taking up defensive positions, the team fought off a series of attacks by Somali soldiers. Finally, twelve hours later, at 5:30 a.m., other Rangers arrived. Using a Humvee, they managed to pry apart the wreckage and retrieve the body.

This episode was typical of the Rangers' commitment to one another. This elite band of specially trained warriors are bonded by an extraordinary loyalty. The name for this code of mutual support and responsibility is known as The Ranger Creed. Written in 1974 by Command Sergeant Neil R. Gentry, the Army Rangers refer to this code simply as "the creed."

Among other things, the creed states: "Never shall I fail my comrades. I will always keep myself mentally alert, physically strong, and morally straight. I will shoulder more than my share of the task, whatever it may be. One hundred percent and then some . . . I will never leave a fallen comrade to fall into the hands of the enemy, and under no circumstances will I ever embarrass my country."

This is the kind of supportive companionship that Christians are expected to display toward one another. Priscilla and Aquila exemplified such qualities. How well are we doing today?

*Questions for Students on the Next Lesson.* 1. Who was Timothy? 2. What was his background? 3. Why did Paul refer to Timothy as his "son"? 4. Why

did Paul encourage Timothy to rekindle God's gift within him? (see
II Tim.1:6, 7). 5. How did Timothy's family background affect him?

## TOPIC FOR YOUTH
### BE A FRIEND

*Paid Friendships?* A few years ago, the Los Angeles Times ran a feature
in its business section about a California businessman who left his million-
dollar computer operation to start a new corporation, Interpersonal
Support Network. It was designed to help people experience caring relationships with an ongoing group of people. To put it briefly, the purpose of
the organization was to help people make friends.

This man believed that people do not take time to learn the social skills
required in forming friendships. For a fee, the customer enters a family-
style group and learns how to make friends with the help of a trained facil-
itator.

Paul, Priscilla, and Aquila recognized that God had called people together to be the church. God provided an example of friendship in Jesus Christ
and empowered His people to befriend others and share the plan of salvation. The three became friends through the power of the Spirit and drew in
others as well. There was no need for fees or payments here!

*Choices.* High school counselors normally place students into one of two
tracks. One track involves students in a vocational program for those not
intending to go on to college. These students study electrical work, plumbing, meat cutting, baking, or other trades. The second group follows the
academic track designed to prepare them for college. Colleges, though,
often ask at an interview what career the student wishes to follow at a time
when many students are struggling with vocational choices.

Ask yourself: Do you have a sense of calling to a profession? If so, is this
career the one that God wants you to follow? Are you following this career
to honor Him, or are you in it simply for the money?

Priscilla and Aquila sensed a call to serve God. They glorified Him
through all of their labors and found happiness. Hopefully, you too will find
the same satisfaction as you serve God, no matter what your career choice.

*Each One Teach One.* Can a young person teach another young person at
school? Some educators answer yes. An innovative program at Pleasant
Hills Middle School in Pennsylvania places young people in pairs. One student, an eighth grader, is a mentor to a younger sixth- or seventh-grade student. The older student teaches, tutors, and helps the younger one in a program called "Study Buddies."

You are never too young to maintain a positive influence on others
around you. The two tentmakers became mentors to Apollos. You can do the
same for your friends.

*Questions for Students on the Next Lesson.* 1. Who was Timothy? 2. Does
your church actively cultivate and nurture youth? 3. Do you have a spiritual mentor or advisor? If so, whom? 4. Do you imitate anyone? 5. What is
the foundation of your faith?

# LESSON 13—FEBRUARY 23

## *TIMOTHY*

*Background Scripture:* Acts 16:1-5; I Corinthians 4:14-17;
Philippians 2:19-24; II Timothy 1:3-7; 3:14, 15
*Devotional Reading:* I Timothy 4:6-19

### KING JAMES VERSION

ACTS 16:1 Then came he to Derbe and Lystra: and, behold, a certain disciple was there, named Timotheus, the son of a certain woman, which was a Jewess, and believed; but his father was a Greek:

2 Which was well reported of by the brethren that were at Lystra and Iconium.

3 Him would Paul have to go forth with him; and took and circumcised him because of the Jews which were in those quarters: for they knew all that his father was a Greek.

4 And as they went through the cities, they delivered them the decrees for to keep, that were ordained of the apostles and elders which were at Jerusalem.

5 And so were the churches established in the faith, and increased in number daily.

I CORINTHIANS 4:14 I write not these things to shame you, but as my beloved sons I warn you.

15 For though ye have ten thousand instructers in Christ, yet have ye not many fathers: for in Christ Jesus I have begotten you through the gospel.

16 Wherefore I beseech you, be ye followers of me.

17 For this cause have I sent unto you Timotheus, who is my beloved son, and faithful in the Lord, who shall bring you into remembrance of my ways which be in Christ, as I teach every where in every church.

PHILIPPIANS 2:19 But I trust in the Lord Jesus to send Timotheus shortly unto you, that I also may be of good comfort, when I know your state.

20 For I have no man likeminded, who will naturally care for your state.

21 For all seek their own, not the things which are Jesus Christ's.

22 But ye know the proof of him, that, as a son with the father, he hath served with me in the gospel.

II TIMOTHY 1:4 Greatly desiring to see thee, being mindful of thy tears, that I may be filled with joy;

5 When I call to remembrance the unfeigned faith that is in thee, which dwelt first in thy grandmother Lois, and thy

### NEW REVISED STANDARD VERSION

ACTS 16:1 Paul went on also to Derbe and to Lystra, where there was a disciple named Timothy, the son of a Jewish woman who was a believer; but his father was a Greek. 2 He was well spoken of by the believers in Lystra and Iconium. 3 Paul wanted Timothy to accompany him; and he took him and had him circumcised because of the Jews who were in those places, for they all knew that his father was a Greek. 4 As they went from town to town, they delivered to them for observance the decisions that had been reached by the apostles and elders who were in Jerusalem. 5 So the churches were strengthened in the faith and increased in numbers daily.

I CORINTHIANS 4:14 I am not writing this to make you ashamed, but to admonish you as my beloved children. 15 For though you might have ten thousand guardians in Christ, you do not have many fathers. Indeed, in Christ Jesus I became your father through the gospel. 16 I appeal to you, then, be imitators of me. 17 For this reason I sent you Timothy, who is my beloved and faithful child in the Lord, to remind you of my ways in Christ Jesus, as I teach them everywhere in every church.

PHILIPPIANS 2:19 I hope in the Lord Jesus to send Timothy to you soon, so that I may be cheered by news of you. 20 I have no one like him who will be genuinely concerned for your welfare. 21 All of them are seeking their own interests, not those of Jesus Christ. 22 But Timothy's worth you know, how like a son with a father he has served with me in the work of the gospel.

II TIMOTHY 1:4 Recalling your tears, I long to see you so that I may be filled with joy. 5 I am reminded of your sincere faith, a faith that lived first in your grandmother Lois and your mother Eunice and now, I am sure, lives in you. 6 For this reason I remind you to rekindle the gift of God that is within you through the laying on of my hands; 7 for God did not give us a spirit of cowardice, but rather a spirit of power and of love and of self-discipline.

mother Eunice; and I am persuaded that in
thee also.

6 Wherefore I put thee in remembrance
that thou stir up the gift of God, which is in
thee by the putting on of my hands.

7 For God hath not given us the spirit of
fear; but of power, and of love, and of a
sound mind.

*KEY VERSE: I [Paul] sent you Timothy, who is my beloved and faithful
child in the Lord, to remind you of my ways in Christ Jesus, as I teach
them everywhere in every church.* I Corinthians 4:17.

## HOME BIBLE READINGS

| Feb. | 17 | M. | *I Corinthians 16:3-12* | *Timothy Worked in Corinth* |
| Feb. | 18 | T. | *I Timothy 1:3-11* | *Timothy to Teach Sound Doctrine* |
| Feb. | 19 | W. | *II Timothy 1:8-14* | *Speak Out for the Lord* |
| Feb. | 20 | T. | *Ephesians 6:10-20* | *Be Strong for the Lord* |
| Feb. | 21 | F. | *I Corinthians 1:26-31* | *Be True to God's Call* |
| Feb. | 22 | S. | *II Timothy 3:1-10* | *Timothy's Mission* |
| Feb. | 23 | S. | *II Timothy 3:10-17* | *Defend the Faith* |

## BACKGROUND

Apart from a brief mention of a nephew and sister in Jerusalem (Acts
23:16), Paul tells us nothing of his family in his writings. The famous apostle apparently did not have a wife or children. Yet he felt very close to a
young man who did not have a blood tie, the young convert named Timothy.
Paul referred to Timothy variously as his "child" (I Cor. 4:17 and I Tim. 1:2)
and "brother" (II Cor. 1:1), demonstrating a special tie between the old missionary and the younger colleague.

Timothy grew up in Lystra, a city in the rough backcountry of Asia
Minor. His father was not a believer. His mother, Eunice, although married
to a Gentile, came from a Jewish background. Perhaps Timothy's mother
and his grandmother Lois had heard something of the Gospel before Paul
arrived in Lystra. Many scholars think Lois was already a Christian. But
the young Timothy had not been inducted into Judaism and had not even
been circumcised as a Jew. He committed himself wholeheartedly to Christ
after hearing Paul preach.

Paul invited the young convert to accompany him on an evangelistic tour
through Asia Minor to establish new congregations. Knowing that he would
be preaching primarily to synagogue attenders, and realizing the suspicions these worshipers from Jewish backgrounds held toward Gentile converts, Paul decided to have Timothy circumcised. Paul was not surrender-
ing his principles; rather, he was intent on receiving a hearing as quickly
as possible in order to present Christ. After all, the issue had already been
settled in Jerusalem; circumcision was not required for Christians.

Timothy became a trusted companion and coworker. Reading Paul's letters gives us a fairly good portrait of Timothy as a person. Apparently, at
least in his younger days, he appeared to be timid and inexperienced.
Portions of the Corinthian correspondence indicate that Timothy felt intim-

idated by the belligerent Corinthian church troublemakers. But the somewhat ineffectual young preacher developed into a strong leader and faithful friend to Paul. He faithfully represented his spiritual mentor in various troubled churches.

## NOTES ON THE PRINTED TEXT

*Paul went on also to Derbe and to Lystra, where there was a disciple named Timothy, the son of a Jewish woman who was a believer, but his father was a* Greek (16:1). Timothy's mother was a Jewish Christian, but his father was a Greek. Still, he was held in high regard and respected by believers as far north (some twenty miles) as Iconium. *He was well spoken of by the believers in Lystra and Iconium* (16:2).

*Paul wanted Timothy to accompany him; and he took him and had him circumcised because of the Jews who were in those places, for they all knew that his father was a Greek* (16:3). Before Paul departed, he had Timothy circumcised. This may seem surprising because it seemed to go against Paul's beliefs and teachings as well as the verdict of the Jerusalem Council. Even though Timothy was considered a Jew under Jewish law, Paul understood that if Timothy were to evangelize the Jews he would have to be circumcised. This outward sign of the covenant would enable Timothy to preach in the synagogues.

Paul, Silas, and Timothy traveled through the cities in which Paul had founded congregations on his first missionary journey. In the churches they preached, taught, and told the believers of the Jerusalem Council's decisions. *As they went from town to town, they delivered to them for observance the decisions that had been reached by the apostles and elders who were in Jerusalem. So the churches were strengthened in the faith and increased in numbers daily* (16:4, 5).

Preparing for the third journey, Paul and Timothy went to Ephesus. From there Timothy was sent on ahead of Paul to Corinth to prepare the church for a special relief offering. Later the two would rejoin for more evangelism in Greece.

Corinth was a tough first assignment for young Timothy. The Corinthian congregation was plagued with corruption, immorality, and division. In his first letter to the church, Paul reminded readers of their problems. *I am not writing this to make you ashamed, but to admonish you as my beloved children* (4:14). Paul spoke as a spiritual parent, emphasizing that his role and intent was not to shame but to correct in a positive manner. Although they had countless tutors and missionaries, he was their spiritual father. His work had made them Christians. *For though you might have ten thousand guardians in Christ, you do not have many fathers. Indeed, in Christ Jesus I became your father through the gospel* (4:15). For that reason, they should imitate his style of life and his patterns of behavior. *I appeal to you, then, be imitators of me* (4:16).

To help them in this task, Paul wrote the Corinthians that he had sent Timothy to remind them of his ways and teachings. Paul spoke affectionately of Timothy. *For this reason I sent you Timothy, who is my beloved and faithful child in the Lord, to remind you of my ways in Christ Jesus, as I teach them everywhere in every church* (4:17).

While in prison, Paul wrote another Greek congregation, one at Philippi. The members of that congregation had grown careless in their faith. Paul appealed for unity and a concern for others. They were to show themselves as God's children and beware of false teachers. For those reasons, he was planning to send Timothy to help them. *I hope in the Lord Jesus to send Timothy to you soon, so that I may be cheered by news of you* (2:19).

Again Paul spoke of Timothy with genuine affection and admiration. *I have no one like him who will be genuinely concerned for your welfare* (2:20). Others were only concerned for their own ambitions and goals. Many of these goals were not in keeping with a Christian world view. *All of them are seeking their own interests, not those of Jesus Christ* (2:21).

Timothy had been with Paul when the church was founded. He was like Paul's son, not a simple spokesperson or poor substitute for Paul. *But Timothy's worth you know, how like a son with a father he has served with me in the work of the gospel. I hope therefore to send him as soon as I see how things go with me; and I trust in the Lord that I will also come soon* (2:22-24). Paul also expressed his hope to follow if he were freed from prison. However, Paul realized that liberation from jail was only a remote possibility. He wrote several letters to Timothy while Timothy was serving in Ephesus. It was a particularly difficult assignment and Paul knew that Timothy would need much encouragement. *Recalling your tears, I long to see you so that I may be filled with joy* (1:4).

Paul remembered Timothy's confident faith, a faith that was nurtured by his believing family members. *I am reminded of your sincere faith, a faith that lived first in your grandmother Lois and your mother Eunice and now, I am sure, lives in you* (1:5).

Paul also encouraged Timothy to stir up the flames of his faith and his spiritual gifts. Paul knew those gifts and had prayed that they be used to further Christ's ministry in His church when he had ordained Timothy. *For this reason I remind you to rekindle the gift of God that is within you through the laying on of my hands* (1:6). These gifts were not to be used timidly but with confidence, power, and discipline. *For God did not give us a spirit of cowardice, but rather a spirit of power and of love and of self-discipline* (1:7).

## SUGGESTIONS TO TEACHERS

A wise Christian counselor reminds us, "God does not call us to be successful; He calls us to be faithful." In a culture that glorifies the glitzy and glamorous, many of us may feel inferior and insignificant. After all, few of us will make *Who's Who* or be interviewed on a network TV talk show.

But in the Lord's scheme of things, what counts is being a faithful worker. This is the thrust of today's lesson. Timothy, Paul's companion in missionary work, may be studied as a shining example of such faithfulness.

1. PAUL'S COMPANION IN SERVICE. Begin by looking at Timothy's background. Mention the influence of Timothy's mother and grandmother. Family members exert a powerful influence in a youngster's spiritual development. Ask for sharing about how your students' parents may have been instrumental in their faith journey. Remind your class members that their heritage of Christian faith must be passed on to others in their families.

Point out also how young Timothy willingly left the security of home and accompanied Paul on the risky work of planting the faith in hostile towns.

2. PAUL'S "CHILD IN THE LORD." Timothy became a kind of adopted son to Paul. Sometimes the bonds between friends can be deeper than those between kinfolk. With Jesus Christ, we often find ourselves brought into a closeness in which we regard certain others as "family." A Christian congregation, in fact, is intended by God to be an extended family in which each cares for the others.

3. PAUL'S EMISSARY TO CORINTH. Timothy's time in Corinth was not always enjoyable. Paul mentioned Timothy's youthful anxieties and shortcomings as an evangelist in his Corinthian correspondence. But Timothy matured. Point out that God takes our weaknesses and failings and helps us to develop into stronger, more stalwart workers.

4. PAUL'S COLLEAGUE IN ADVERSITY. Jump ahead to the close of Paul's life when the old apostle was in prison and feeling deserted. Timothy was one of the few who was not busy looking "after their own interests" (Phil.2:21). Timothy stood by his mentor and friend. Over the years, the young protégé had grown from being Paul's "child" to his "brother," a trusted colleague in faithful service. If there is time, ask your students to tell about ways they believe they have grown in faith over the years.

## TOPIC FOR ADULTS
### BE A FAITHFUL WORKER

*Fan or Customer?* The slippery little word "faith" is often misunderstood. We often consider it to be something you feel or something you have—an abstract word like "honor" or "love." Not in the Bible, however. When the Scripture uses "faith," it refers to active commitment.

Frank Cashen is the executive vice president and general manager of the New York Mets. He is one of the best executives in baseball, having built the Mets into one of the sport's best teams. Cashen is a hard-nosed businessman who wants to fill the stands to pay the bills. Says Cashen, "I make a distinction between my fans and my customers. People come up to me all the time and say, 'I love the Mets . . .' Then I ask, 'When was the last time you came out to the ball park?' And they say, 'Oh, well, I've been meaning to.' Those people are my fans, but not my customers."

The difference between fans and customers is the distinction between "having some faith" and being faithful.

*Keeping the Faith—and Doing It!* It's like the elderly woman with bad eyesight and a limp who never missed attending her little church on Sundays in Illinois. One raw, blustery Sunday, her daughter and family tried to persuade her to stay at home. After all, the weather was bad, her sight was poor, the church was a long walk, her arthritis was acting up, and . . . besides, all that mattered was that she had some faith. Adjusting her hat and poking her umbrella out the door, the woman replied, "Faith, humph! What the Lord cares about and what I'd better show the neighbors is some faithfulness!"

Being faithful is doing the faith—keeping the faith and doing it, in spite of the odds and in spite of how we feel.

*Pegged.* Off the west coast of Scotland on the windswept isle of Raasay, several families live on the southeast end of the island. It is a dangerous place to raise children. The ground falls away abruptly to the sea in front of the houses, while at the back a steep slope rises. The hardworking parents worried about their little ones playing outside and finally devised a way to keep small children from tumbling over the cliff into the raging surf below.

On the small, level play area in front of the houses, the tiny kids were kept in safety. How? No, not fences. But pegs driven securely into the ground and a stout length of rope attached to the pegs. The other end of the rope would be tied firmly to the leg of the child. The little one could not stray too close to the brink of the cliff because of the rope and peg. Consequently, these youngsters of Raasay picked up the name "the peg children." In spite of the small degree of discomfort, the children were safe.

One "peg child" years later recounted how the experience reminded him that he was firmly tied to the family and his parent's love. This "peg child" went on to mention how he also felt firmly tied to the Lord in the sense of being God's "peg child." Reflecting on the bond he had with Christ, this Raasay man stated that he knew he had to be faithful to the Lord because he was pegged and tied in faith to God's faithfulness.

Timothy would have understood this description. We are also meant to know that we are pegged to Christ and must be faithful in all circumstances.

*Questions for Students on the Next Lesson.* 1. Why did Paul write to the Christians in Thessalonica? 2. What were some of the problems these early believers faced? 3. What was Paul referring to when he reminded the Thessalonians that he had earned his own way? 4. Why had Paul been forced to leave Thessalonica? 5. When have you faced opposition because of your faith or moral standards?

### TOPIC FOR YOUTH
### *PUT OTHERS FIRST!*

*Went Public.* As a boy, Dan Ginsburg loved baseball. He traveled by bus for hours to watch ball games. He studied baseball more than his course work at high school. As a teenager, he went to work for the Baseball Hall of Fame, making telephone calls and doing research.

When Dan was eight, he began collecting autographs of baseball players. Sometimes it meant standing at the field railing to get a scorecard signed. At other times it was going to a shopping center to obtain another signature. Soon, after young Dan took the nonpaying job at the Hall of Fame, his quest for autographs began in earnest. Over the years he collected all 219 baseball Hall of Famers' autographs, including a 1937 check Babe Ruth wrote and an annotated diary of Ty Cobb's.

Realizing he could not properly display his collection (it had to be kept in a lock-box at a bank, given its $500,000 appraised value), Dan donated the collection to the Elliott Museum in Stuart, Florida. Dan wanted to share his collection with as many as possible, so he chose this Americana museum. Dan put others first.

Paul urged Timothy to put others first. With us, others' concerns must be foremost, even over our own. This is the way of Christ.

*Needs Met.* On Friday, October 14, 1994, a fire destroyed the College Garden Apartment Complex near Slippery Rock University in Erie, Pennsylvania. The building was totally destroyed and seventy students were left homeless. They needed clothing, meals, money, books, and places to stay. The college community rallied. Dinner invitations poured in from the small town community, and $600 was raised from donations at the football game the next day. The student body donated jeans, sweatshirts, toiletries, and books. Others welcomed students into their rooms. The college food service fed the students at no cost.

Here is an outstanding example of a small community putting the needs of others first and expressing their concern. Hopefully, your church community does the same through its efforts to help the needy.

*Put Others First.* It was 7 a.m. and Rollin "Sissy" Ibrahim noticed flames shooting out of a window of an apartment building on Monday, October 24, 1994. She used a phone to summon help to the apartment in Shadyside, Pennsylvania, then ran to the building herself. The building's front door was cracked from the heat, and smoke was pouring out. So Sissy ran around the residence yelling at the top of her voice to wake those inside so they could get out of the burning building. Six people escaped because of her efforts.

Sissy placed the interests of others above herself. She saw their lives as important. This was the kind of concern that Paul spoke of to Timothy.

*Questions for Students on the Next Lesson.* 1. How did Paul communicate with his churches when he could not visit? 2. How are people "approved" to preach for God? 3. What image does Paul utilize to demonstrate the nurture of a Christian? 4. How did Paul handle the opposition that his preaching aroused? 5. How do you handle the opposition that witnessing arouses?

# MARCH, APRIL, MAY 1997

## HOPE FOR THE FUTURE

### LESSON 1—MARCH 2

#### PROCLAIM THE GOSPEL

*Background Scripture:* I Thessalonians 2:1-13
*Devotional Reading:* I Thessalonians 1:1-10

| KING JAMES VERSION | NEW REVISED STANDARD VERSION |
|---|---|

KING JAMES VERSION

I THESSALONIANS 2:1 For yourselves, brethren, know our entrance in unto you, that it was not in vain:

2 But even after that we had suffered before, and were shamefully entreated, as ye know, at Philippi, we were bold in our God to speak unto you the gospel of God with much contention.

3 For our exhortation was not of deceit, nor of uncleanness, nor in guile:

4 But as we were allowed of God to be put in trust with the gospel, even so we speak; not as pleasing men, but God, which trieth our hearts.

5 For neither at any time used we flattering words, as ye know, nor a cloke of covetousness; God is witness:

6 Nor of men sought we glory, neither of you, nor yet of others, when we might have been burdensome, as the apostles of Christ.

7 But we were gentle among you, even as a nurse cherisheth her children:

8 So being affectionately desirous of you, we were willing to have imparted unto you, not the gospel of God only, but also our own souls, because ye were dear unto us.

9 For ye remember, brethren, our labour and travail: for labouring night and day, because we would not be chargeable unto any of you, we preached unto you the gospel of God.

10 Ye are witnesses, and God also, how holily and justly and unblameably we behaved ourselves among you that believe:

11 As ye know how we exhorted and comforted and charged every one of you, as a father doth his children,

12 That ye would walk worthy of God, who hath called you unto his kingdom and glory.

13 For this cause also thank we God without ceasing, because, when ye received the

NEW REVISED STANDARD VERSION

I Thessalonians 2:1 You yourselves know, brothers and sisters, that our coming to you was not in vain, 2 but though we had already suffered and been shamefully mistreated at Philippi, as you know, we had courage in our God to declare to you the gospel of God in spite of great opposition. 3 For our appeal does not spring from deceit or impure motives or trickery, 4 but just as we have been approved by God to be entrusted with the message of the gospel, even so we speak, not to please mortals, but to please God who tests our hearts. 5 As you know and as God is our witness, we never came with words of flattery or with a pretext for greed; 6 nor did we seek praise from mortals, whether from you or from others, 7 though we might have made demands as apostles of Christ. But we were gentle among you, like a nurse tenderly caring for her own children. 8 So deeply do we care for you that we are determined to share with you not only the gospel of God but also our own selves, because you have become very dear to us.

9 You remember our labor and toil, brothers and sisters; we worked night and day, so that we might not burden any of you while we proclaimed to you the gospel of God. 10 You are witnesses, and God also, how pure, upright, and blameless our conduct was toward you believers. 11 As you know, we dealt with each one of you like a father with his children, 12 urging and encouraging you and pleading that you lead a life worthy of God, who calls you into his own kingdom and glory.

13 We also constantly give thanks to God for this, that when you received the word of God that you heard from us, you accepted it not as a human word but as what it really

word of God which ye heard of us, ye received it not as the word of men, but as it is in truth, the word of God, which effectually worketh also in you that believe. is, God's word, which is also at work in you believers.

*KEY VERSE: We had courage in our God to declare to you the gospel of God in spite of great opposition.* I Thessalonians 2:2b.

## HOME BIBLE READINGS

| | | | | |
|---|---|---|---|---|
| Feb. | 24 | M. | I Thessalonians 1:10 | *Serve the True God* |
| Feb. | 25 | T. | I Peter 1:1-10 | *Witness of the Prophets* |
| Feb. | 26 | W. | Romans 10:1-13 | *Confess Jesus Christ* |
| Feb. | 27 | T. | Acts 20:26-38 | *Be Guardians of God's Word* |
| Feb. | 28 | F. | II Corinthians 4:1-6 | *Keep Your Ministry Honest* |
| Mar. | 1 | S. | I Corinthians 14:20-25 | *Make Your Message Clear* |
| Mar. | 2 | S. | Psalm 67:1-7 | *All People Should Praise God* |

## BACKGROUND

We start this quarter of lessons by studying the letters Paul wrote to the congregation in Thessalonica. Written around A.D. 50, these epistles are the earliest complete parts of the New Testament we have, closer to the time of Christ than any other Bible book. The Thessalonian letters give us a superb look at the conditions existing among the earliest Christian converts.

Paul and his companions Silas and Timothy came to Thessalonica on an evangelistic trip that took them from Asia Minor to Greece. Thessalonica was a big, bustling city, the political and commercial center of northern Greece. Paul realized that by planting churches in important hubs like Thessalonica, the Gospel would also reach outlying communities.

Paul immediately targeted the large local synagogue as the place to start his preaching. He preached intently for three weeks about Jesus the Messiah and won a loyal group of converts. He also stirred up fierce opposition among fanatic opponents. Paul's stay in Thessalonica was cut short when his enemies stirred up a mob scene (see Acts 17:1-9).

Arriving eventually in Corinth, many miles to the south, Paul worried about his fledgling congregation in Thessalonica. He knew this group of working-class converts had received little grounding in the faith; they lacked stability. But he loved these people. From Corinth, he sent Timothy to revisit the little congregation to find out how they were doing.

Timothy returned to Corinth and reported on the conditions at Thessalonica. In some ways, the news was good. The Christians were valiantly trying to remain faithful to Christ. But there were problems, too. Some of the new believers had taken Paul's words about Christ's return to mean that the Second Coming was to be expected momentarily. That had caused some to stop working, to wait around for the Lord's appearing. Others, fresh from paganism, were still involved in sexual promiscuity. Perhaps most hurtful to Paul, some Thessalonians were complaining that Paul and his companions took advantage of the congregation's hospitality.

## NOTES ON THE PRINTED TEXT

The Thessalonians found fault with Paul's ministry, questioning his motives. Paul responded with a defense of his conduct. He reminded the Thessalonians of the ministry team's successes. These events attested to God's power and involvement. *You yourselves know, brothers and sisters, that our coming to you was not in vain* (2:1). Paul reviewed their coming to Thessalonica from Philippi. There, both he and Silas had been beaten with rods and thrown in jail. In spite of local opposition the three had boldly preached the Gospel to the Thessalonians. Paul's Greek word for opposition referred to a life-or-death struggle with determined opponents. *But though we had already suffered and been shamefully mistreated at Philippi, as you know, we had courage in our God to declare to you the gospel of God in spite of great opposition* (2:2).

Paul emphasized that his preaching of the Gospel was not based on deceit or trickery, but that he preached in order to please God. Responding to critics who charged him with self-seeking motives, he argued that the content of his preaching was God's entrusted message. *For our appeal does not spring from deceit or impure motives or trickery* (2:3). Thus, he spoke with God's approval, for God had examined and tested his motives. *But just as we have been approved by God to be entrusted with the message of the gospel, even so we speak, not to please mortals, but to please God who tests our hearts* (2:4).

Paul reminded his readers that he never tried to flatter them into accepting his message. Nor had he preached for money. Both the Thessalonians and God were witnesses to all of this. *As you know and as God is our witness, we never came with words of flattery or with a pretext for greed* (2:5).

The three ministers weren't seeking big reputations. It was enough to be the messengers of Christ and to enjoy God's approval. Paul also reminded the Thessalonians that he had refused to exercise his apostolic right to hospitality. He could have demanded food and lodging. *Nor did we seek praise from mortals, whether from you or from others, though we might have made demands as apostles of Christ* (2:6, 7).

In spite of their authority, Paul and his two companions were not harsh or overbearing. Instead, they were kind, like a nurse with her children. *But we were gentle among you, like a nurse tenderly caring for her own children* (2:7). Out of their deep affection they longed to share the Gospel and themselves with the church. This was a self-sacrificing love; nothing was being withheld. *So deeply do we care for you that we are determined to share with you not only the gospel of God but also our own selves, because you have become very dear to us* (2:8).

Paul pointed out that the three had worked and earned their own support as they preached the Gospel. They were never a financial burden to anyone. *You remember our labor and toil, brothers and sisters; we worked night and day, so that we might not burden any of you while we proclaimed to you the gospel of God* (2:9). All in all, the ministers had led exemplary lives among them. *You are witnesses, and God also, how pure, upright, and blameless our conduct was toward you believers* (2:10).

Paul appealed to the Thessalonians to recall the close and tender relationship they had with himself, Silas, and Timothy. It was a warm, father-like relationship with each member. The three encouraged each of the

Thessalonians to live a Christlike life-style and to conduct themselves as Jesus would. *As you know, we dealt with each one of you like a father with his children, urging and encouraging you and pleading that you lead a life worthy of God, who calls you into his own kingdom and glory* (2:11, 12).

The Thessalonians recognized that the apostles' message was the true Word of God. They accepted God's Word, believed it, and practiced it. Paul thanked God for their faith. *We also constantly give thanks to God for this, that when you received the word of God that you heard from us, you accepted it not as a human word but as what it really is, God's word, which is also at work in you believers* (2:13).

## SUGGESTIONS TO TEACHERS

A group of American ministers visited Mother Teresa in Calcutta. After seeing the desperate plight of the sick, and observing the heroic care given by Mother Teresa's wards, one visitor commented on how hard it must be to be a Christian in such a setting. "Oh no!" the famous nun replied. "Here," she stated, "the people want to know the love of Christ. In your country it is much harder. There, where you live, not many really want to hear about Jesus. It's much harder for you."

Do your students agree with Mother Teresa's assessment? What has been the reaction when you have spoken about Christ to your neighbors? Undoubtedly, some criticism or even hostility has resulted. Though Christians have not been thrown out of town like Paul, proclaiming the Good News in America does not always meet with warm acceptance.

1. COURAGEOUS WITNESSING. Paul's ancient letter to Thessalonica helps us see what the Lord expects of us today. Point out some of the hardships Paul and his colleagues faced in their efforts to share the message of Christ. How much easier it would have been to stay home, to hope that someone else would tell the people in Thessalonica about Jesus.

2. CONSCIENTIOUS WORKERS. Apparently some in Thessalonica had falsely accused Paul and his associates of preaching for personal gain. Paul refuted these slanderous charges by reminding his readers that he had never taken advantage of them in any way. Sometimes hurtful lies and mean-spirited gossip will be circulated in order to discredit sincere Christians. Evil-minded people will stoop to dirty tricks. Paul's answer was simply to keep on proclaiming the Gospel. His life so consistently reflected Christ's example that eventually his critics were silenced. Ask your students how they typically respond to criticism.

3. CARING WISDOM. Paul pointed out to his readers that he had been gentle among them and had treated them "like a nurse caring for her children" (2:7). In our era of "in-your-face" confrontational tactics, what a different approach Christians are called to have! Discuss the contrast between our society's aggressiveness and Paul's approach.

4. COMPELLING WORD. What, exactly, is the Gospel message? How should that message affect the way we treat each other? Many have written about the decline of civility in the last couple of decades. How can Christians encourage sensitivity and caring in a selfish, violent age?

TOPIC FOR ADULTS
*TELL THE GOOD NEWS!*

*How Qualified?* Suppose the apostle Paul was being evaluated by religious groups today. Perhaps they might write the following to him:

Dear Mr. Saul:

In reviewing your personality profile and performance records, our personnel committee has found several matters that have raised serious questions in our minds about your suitability to serve on the mission field. We note that you persist in reporting that you were converted in a dramatic way on your way to Damascus several years ago—by allegedly being confronted by Jesus Christ. Our psychological testing service states that such an experience signifies an unstable personality. We also understand that you are now using a different name, Paul, instead of your given name Saul. We question the wisdom of such a change and feel that this underscores your tendency to be somewhat unsteady.

Your physical problems cause us deep concern and indicate to us that you ought to seek a less taxing type of job. These ailments are now too numerous to permit us to recommend you for any form of active service. Your serious eye problems, your recurring bout with what you refer to as your "thorn," and your apparent inability to sleep soundly indicate that, frankly, you are unsuitable as a missionary.

Your police record is most unsettling to our committee. You have served time in prisons at Caesarea and Rome and have been arrested numerous times in Asia Minor and Greece. Apparently your methods and personality have upset many civic leaders in various cities. We have received numerous negative reports about your work from businessmen in Ephesus and government officials in Philippi, Thessalonica, Berea, and Lystra. Our committee prefers that our board representatives act diplomatically and respect local customs and opinions.

Your work record reflects a restlessness and inability to stay in one place for any length of time. We have examined your itineraries and find that you have wandered throughout Asia Minor and Greece without settling in one church. "Wanting to take the Gospel everywhere," you undertake too much.

In your correspondence to certain churches, you make some disturbing claims. For instance, in writing to the congregation in Corinth, you "decided to know nothing among them except Jesus Christ, and Him crucified." You apparently did not mention our denominational creeds. You obviously did nothing to promote our denominational programs. You said nothing about supporting our denomination's budget. This has been the case in all your letters. We prefer missionaries who recognize their loyalties.

In summary, it is my duty to inform you that our committee will not recommend you as a missionary. We urge you to return to Tarsus and settle down to your occupation of tent making. You obviously lack the qualifications needed for mission work with our board.

Sincerely,
Dr. I. M. Snootie
Chairman, Personnel Committee
Board of Foreign Missions

*Proclaimed by the Pilgrims.* The Mayflower pilgrims suffered terribly on their voyage to the New World. Half of the ship's crew, three of the mates, the master gunner, the cook, and the bosun all died. Most of these crew members had treated the pious men and women in the Pilgrim band with contempt, sometimes even with cruelty.

The worst of the crewmen was the bosun, a "proud young man," who used to "curse and scoff at the passengers." When one passenger was ill and pleaded for something to drink, the bosun and others mocked him and swore at him. In the end, though, the Pilgrims softened even the hard heart of the bosun, caring for him in his illness after he had been deserted by his "boone companions in drinking and jollity." The villain repented and publicly acknowledged his sins, but too late.

"O!" he confessed on his deathbed, "You, I now see, show your love like Christians indeed one to another. But we let one another lie and die like dogs."

*Orthodoxy Instead of Evangelism.* In the early 1930s, Erlangen University's theological faculty was renowned not only in Germany but throughout the western world for its orthodoxy. The proud professors of Erlangen were respected defenders of correct doctrine. Clergy and scholars alike in Germany acknowledged that Erlangen's theologians led all others in scholarship, wisdom, and knowledge.

Yet in 1934, these orthodox faculty members signed a statement supporting the right of Adolf Hitler to "purify" everything in Germany, which meant excluding Jews from political office. The faculty even agreed that sons and grandsons of Jews could be prevented from holding offices in the church. Throughout this shameful period in German history, Erlangen continued to pride itself on being a citadel of learning and correct doctrine.

The Lord wants us to tell the Good News in our words—but also in our deeds.

*Questions for Students on the Next Lesson.* 1. What is meant by living in "holiness"? 2. In what ways were the Thessalonians failing to show love? 3. Why is moral purity a key part of holy living? 4. How can your congregation help its youth avoid immorality? 5. When do you find it hardest to receive love? To give love?

### TOPIC FOR YOUTH
#### WALK THE TALK!

*The Motivator.* The Pennsylvania Association of Student Councils held its 58th Annual Conference in 1994. Over one thousand students attended leadership training seminars, skill-building groups, and student-led workshops. And they listened to motivational speakers as they wrestled with the theme, "Journey through the Mind of a Leader."

One speaker who impressed the young people was television newswoman Patrice King-Brown. She told the group that the desire to practice values such as honesty and compassion for others had to come, not from teachers, but from within themselves and from God.

Years earlier, Paul encouraged his readers to live lives worthy of God. Their motivation must also come from God. Their values must be displayed in their daily words and actions. That would please God and demonstrate their commitment to Him.

*Spoke Up.* In November, 1994, the Carnegie-Mellon University administration decided to ban obscene sex from its campus computer network. The university maintained that sexually explicit material, all found on the Internet, was illegal and that it should not be made available to students. The academic council agreed to shut down the areas of the computer system that carried the sexual material.

Some student groups immediately protested, arguing that the ban violated free speech. They organized the "Protest for Freedom in Cyberspace" that drew 350 students and faculty members. The group managed to garner plenty of news coverage, even from *Time* magazine.

Less noticed was a group that agreed with the ban. These were faculty members and young men and women who stood for moral purity. They pointed out that the material was not in keeping with the teachings of any religion. They spoke up and stood up for what they believed. They were roundly booed and mocked for their efforts.

Paul understood that proclaiming the Gospel and taking a stand would bring opposition. However, he knew that he had to please God. He urged the Thessalonians to do the same by living exemplary lives as Jesus taught.

*The Pressure of Peers.* The latest statistics from the Center for Disease Control in Atlanta are grim. Forty percent of all ninth graders have had sexual intercourse. In tenth grade the number increases to fifty percent. Sixty percent of all eleventh graders have experienced sexual intercourse, while seventy percent have engaged in sex by their senior year. The biggest reason for this activity is peer pressure. Young people are motivated to please their peers.

Paul reminds us that we must please God. One way is to realize that there are limits on our behavior. A Christian must live an exemplary life, after the example of Christ. We must show our faith in our actions as well as our words.

*Questions for Students on the Next Lesson.* 1. Where is Thessalonica? How and when did Paul first arrive there? 2. What instructions did Paul give to the Thessalonians? 3. What is the meaning of sanctification? 4. How is God an avenger? 5. What responsibilities do you have to live in holiness and love? What does that mean to you, in practical terms?

# LESSON 2—MARCH 9

## LIVE IN LOVE AND HOLINESS!

*Background Scripture:* I Thessalonians 3:6—4:12
*Devotional Reading:* I Peter 1:13-22

### KING JAMES VERSION

I THESSALONIANS 3:12 And the Lord make you to increase and abound in love one toward another, and toward all men, even as we do toward you:

13 To the end he may stablish your hearts unblameable in holiness before God, even our Father, at the coming of our Lord Jesus Christ with all his saints.

4:1 Furthermore then we beseech you, brethren, and exhort you by the Lord Jesus, that as ye have received of us how ye ought to walk and to please God, so ye would abound more and more.

2 For ye know what commandments we gave you by the Lord Jesus.

3 For this is the will of God, even your sanctification, that ye should abstain from fornication:

4 That every one of you should know how to possess his vessel in sanctification and honour;

5 Not in the lust of concupiscence, even as the Gentiles which know not God:

6 That no man go beyond and defraud his brother in any matter: because that the Lord is the avenger of all such, as we also have forewarned you and testified.

7 For God hath not called us unto uncleanness, but unto holiness.

8 He therefore that despiseth, despiseth not man, but God, who hath also given unto us his holy Spirit.

9 But as touching brotherly love ye need not that I write unto you: for ye yourselves are taught of God to love one another.

10 And indeed ye do it toward all the brethren which are in all Macedonia: but we beseech you, brethren, that ye increase more and more;

11 And that ye study to be quiet, and to do your own business, and to work with your own hands, as we commanded you;

12 That ye may walk honestly toward them that are without, and that ye may have lack of nothing.

### REVISED STANDARD VERSION

I THESSALONIANS 3:12 And may the Lord make you increase and abound in love for one another and for all, just as we abound in love for you. 13 And may he so strengthen your hearts in holiness that you may be blameless before our God and Father at the coming of our Lord Jesus with all his saints.

4:1 Finally, brothers and sisters, we ask and urge you in the Lord Jesus that, as you learned from us how you ought to live and to please God (as, in fact, you are doing), you should do so more and more. 2 For you know what instructions we gave you through the Lord Jesus. 3 For this is the will of God, your sanctification: that you abstain from fornication; 4 that each one of you know how to control your own body in holiness and honor, 5 not with lustful passion, like the Gentiles who do not know God; 6 that no one wrong or exploit a brother or sister in this matter, because the Lord is an avenger in all these things, just as we have already told you beforehand and solemnly warned you. 7 For God did not call us to impurity but in holiness. 8 Therefore whoever rejects this rejects not human authority but God, who also gives his Holy Spirit to you.

9 Now concerning love of the brothers and sisters, you do not need to have anyone write to you, for you yourselves have been taught by God to love one another; 10 and indeed you do love all the brothers and sisters throughout Macedonia. But we urge you, beloved, to do so more and more, 11 to aspire to live quietly, to mind your own affairs, and to work with your hands, as we directed you, 12 so that you may behave properly toward outsiders and be dependent on no one.

*KEY VERSES: May the Lord make you increase and abound in love for one another and for all. . . . And may he so strengthen your hearts in holiness that you may be blameless before our God and Father at the coming of our Lord Jesus with all his saints.* I Thessalonians 3:12a, 13.

## HOME BIBLE READINGS

| | | | | |
|---|---|---|---|---|
| Mar. | 3 | M. | I Corinthians 13:12 | *Love As God Loves* |
| Mar. | 4 | T. | Philippians 1:21-30 | *Live to Please God* |
| Mar. | 5 | W. | Philippians 2:1-8 | *Seek the Mind of Christ* |
| Mar. | 6 | T. | Philippians 2:12-18 | *Be Glad for Christian Obligations* |
| Mar. | 7 | F. | Ephesians 5:1-11 | *Promote Christian Conversations* |
| Mar. | 8 | S. | I Peter 4:1-11 | *Serve Others as if Serving God* |
| Mar. | 9 | S. | I Peter 1:13-22 | *Love One Another Sincerely* |

## BACKGROUND

Sometimes we view the early believers as though they were all ideal Christians. When we read Paul's letters, however, we quickly learn that these first-century church members had their flaws, just like us. The Thessalonian church was certainly not an ideal church.

Timothy's visit (after he had been forced to leave the city with his fellow preachers) uncovered some problems. One of the most disturbing was sexual immorality. Like many of the new converts in the Mediterranean world, a large segment of this congregation had once practiced other religions. Those who had been Jews, of course, had been raised according to the biblical teachings of sexual purity and continued to uphold high standards of faithfulness in marriage. But the former practitioners of various folk religions had been used to the easy-going ways of the Greek and Roman societies. Many found it hard to leave their promiscuity. The "everyone's-doing-it" culture flourished. As a result, Paul reminded the Thessalonians that they were called to be God's holy people. Paul insisted that Christians were intended to serve as a moral example to the rest of the community.

Another vexing matter, according to Timothy's report to Paul, was the slanderous attacks on Paul's personal integrity. Some in Thessalonica were criticizing him for being a parasite when he was in their midst. They denied Paul's down-to-earth honesty, obviously forgetting that he had insisted on earning his living during his time among them. Paul had to remind them that he was not like the traveling holy men, fake prophets, and quack healers who preyed on the gullible. He had refused to be a burden to anyone.

Throughout this letter, Paul emphasized that Christians must remember their call to live in exemplary ways. They must uphold the purity of family life and earn the respect of their neighbors. They must mind their own business and earn their livelihoods while reaching out with kind words and good deeds.

## NOTES ON THE PRINTED TEXT

*And may the Lord make you increase and abound in love for one another and for all, just as we abound in love for you* (3:12). Paul concluded his defense with a prayer for the Thessalonians. He prayed that their love might grow and overflow. This love was to be directed first to fellow believers and then to all people. Thus the believers would be blameless (having no defect) and have no fear at God's final judgment. *And may he so strengthen your hearts in holiness that you may be blameless before our God and Father at the coming of our Lord Jesus with all his saints* (3:13).

Paul reminded the Thessalonians of the practical instructions in Christian purity and love that they had received during his visit. He encouraged them to continue living lives pleasing to God. *Finally, brothers and sisters, we ask and urge you in the Lord Jesus that, as you learned from us how you ought to live and to please God (as, in fact, you are doing), you should do so more and more* (4:1). The instructions should present no difficulty; these were simply Christ's commands. *For you know what instructions we gave you through the Lord Jesus* (4:2).

The instructions applied particularly to sexual morality. *For this is the will of God, your sanctification: that you abstain from fornication* (4:3). Though promiscuity was prevalent, Paul reminded the believers that they were to be consecrated to God. Any sexual relations outside of marriage were forbidden. Paul wrote that Christians must *know how to control your own body in holiness and honor, not with lustful passion, like the Gentiles who do not know God, that no one wrong or exploit a brother or sister in this matter* (4:4-6). The Thessalonians were to remember that their bodies belonged to God. Because of this, they must exercise sexual self-control.

Disobedience would bring divine judgment. Paul reminded his readers that this should not be a surprise, because they had been previously warned. *Because the Lord is an avenger in all these things, just as we have already told you beforehand and solemnly warned you* (4:6).

Paul emphasized that God had called believers to holy living. This was God's demand, not Paul's. Holiness would be demonstrated in sexual morality. *For God did not call us to impurity but in holiness* (4:7). Those who disregarded this call to morality actually disregarded and rejected God! Disobedience also demonstrated that believers were ignoring the work of the Holy Spirit. *Therefore whoever rejects this rejects not human authority but God, who also gives his Holy Spirit to you* (4:8).

Paul commended the Thessalonians' love and encouraged them to love more and more. They had shown hospitality and offered gifts to believers in need. *Now concerning love of the brothers and sisters, you do not need to have anyone write to you, for you yourselves have been taught by God to love one another; and indeed you do love all the brothers and sisters throughout Macedonia. But we urge you, beloved, to do so more and more* (4:9, 10).

Finally, Paul urged his readers to live quietly, to mind their own business, and to earn their livelihood. Believers were not to be meddlesome and were to care for their own financial needs. In this manner Christians would gain the respect of their neighbors. *Aspire to live quietly, to mind your own affairs, and to work with your hands, as we directed you, so that you may behave properly toward outsiders and be dependent on no one* (4:11, 12).

## SUGGESTIONS TO TEACHERS

Everyone in your class recognizes the state of sexual morality in our society today. Statistics remind us of the alarming rise in teenage pregnancies and the frequency of sexual activity among junior and senior high schoolers. No one uses the term *illegitimate births* anymore to describe babies born to unwed mothers. The "sex sell" helps market almost every product. Pornography is a billion-dollar business. Big names in sports and entertainment have their dalliances reported in the regular press.

A quick survey of your class would probably reveal that every member knows at least one situation in which an unmarried couple are living together, or where a divorce is in progress. The phrase *holy matrimony* seems quaint to many, and matrimony itself seems questionable to so many others. This lesson on living in love and holiness could not be more timely.

1. REPORT BY TIMOTHY. Briefly review the background of the scriptural material in today's lesson. Describe the concerns Timothy shared with Paul regarding the Thessalonian believers. You may wish to comment on the similar situations believers face today. We, like the Thessalonians, live in a permissive culture that seems to encourage immoral living.

2. RESPONSE OF THANKSGIVING. Paul praised God for the valiant way some Christians had withstood the popular approach to morality. He gave thanks for their love and obedience. The example of the Thessalonian believers who had stood up strongly for the faith had encouraged others.

Point out the power of a good example. In the face of immoral living, Christ's people are called to demonstrate lives of caring and holiness.

3. REMEMBRANCE OF TEACHINGS. The term *holiness* probably needs explaining. To some, it smacks of a smug piety. No one likes a "holy Joe." But you can redeem the word. Basically, *holy* means "dedicated to God's special purposes." Just as the implements in the ancient temple were considered "holy" because they were dedicated for sacred use, so everyone who belongs to Christ is holy.

4. RESPECT FROM TOWNSPEOPLE. Paul implores the Thessalonian Christians to live lives of sexual purity as a way of illustrating to the public that they belong to Christ. The old axiom that "actions speak louder than words" applies particularly in the matter of sexual morality. Tell the class that the cynical and sinful world is watching our behavior closely. Our life-styles display the depth of our loyalties more than we realize.

## TOPIC FOR ADULTS
### LIVE IN LOVE AND HOLINESS!

*No Word on Love.* The word *atom* was defined in four lines in an encyclopedia dated 1768, while the article on love was five pages long. The new edition of the same encyclopedia has five pages on the subject of the atom but not a single word about love. This is the heart of our problems in the world today.

*Salty Counsel.* Salt is often mentioned in Russian circles. Salt figures in Russian Orthodox church ceremonies. Offering salt and bread is the traditional way of greeting guests at the door. Salt and bread are regarded as the basic elements of life—and the Russian soul—and therefore are symbols of welcome. A Russian proverb states that to know a person, you must eat a pood of salt together. A pood comes to about thirty-six pounds. This means that you must work at the relationship over a long period of time. First impressions are not enough. Second-hand information will not suffice.

To live in love and holiness with one another means working at it in the same way the old Russian proverb implies. It takes time; it demands persistence.

*Conceited Sailor.* A rich landlubber bought a condo in Florida. On his first vacation, he purchased a yacht and fancied himself a sailor. Ignoring all advice about taking a course on safety and navigation, he confidently set out on the ocean for his first cruise. Several miles from land, he became engulfed in dense fog. Then his engine quit. Finding himself drifting helplessly, the man got on his radio. "Help! I'm in trouble. My engine won't start and I'm fogbound. Send help immediately!"

A quick reply came from the Coast Guard. "We're coming out. What's your position? Tell us your position."

The would-be sailor called, "Hurry up. The waves are getting higher."

Patiently, the voice from the Coast Guard asked again, "What is your position?"

Annoyed, the man answered, "I am the First Vice President of the leading bank in _____. Now please come and help me."

Our conceited ways often keep us from receiving help. But part of learning to live in love and holiness—reaching out to others in need—is to first recognize our own need.

*Questions for Students on the Next Lesson.* 1. What did Paul tell the Thessalonian Christians who were suffering for their faith? 2. What forms of opposition do Christians encounter in our society? 3. How are you persecuted because of your faith? 4. Do you regularly pray for others, or only when the mood strikes? 5. How do those in your congregation support one another when troubles come?

## TOPIC FOR YOUTH
### LIVE TO PLEASE GOD

*Speaks Out.* One Sunday the youth group at St. John's Baptist Church in Unity, Pennsylvania, devoted their meeting time to studying hate groups such as the KKK. Their speaker was a fourteen-year-old ninth grader from Taylor-Allderdice High School in Pittsburgh. Matt Ittigson spoke about racism and his efforts to protest its spread. The teen spoke of the marches he had participated in and the times he and other teens had painted over KKK graffiti.

Matt's concern grew out of his own experience. He realized that he was both prejudiced as well as a victim of racism. He then did a major project at his school devoted to combating hate groups. Now this young man accepts every opportunity to speak out against hatred and call for a style of living that pleases God.

*Work Not Done.* Paul Krouse, publisher of *Who's Who Among High School Students,* maintains that a parent's work is far from done even when the teen's report card is excellent. He cites the 25th annual survey done by Who's Who.

One quarter of those surveyed had engaged in sexual intercourse. Nineteen percent of students admitted to drinking at least once a month. Two percent regularly use marijuana. One percent regularly use cocaine, crack, amphetamines, or other drugs. Seventeen percent admit to stealing, while a whopping seventy-eight percent admit to cheating.

Krouse said that the quality of life at home is a major influence on a student's behavior. Perhaps parents and youth alike need to hear and heed Paul's biblical plea. We must renew our commitment to love and holiness.

*Lot of Baloney.* Two North Braddock, Pennsylvania, girls, aged ten and twelve, came up with a pretty good scam to make some money. They went into the neighboring boroughs and took hoagie orders, claiming they were selling them for their church group or school band. Most of the time they collected between seven and ten dollars apiece, at each home, for the nonexistent sandwiches.

Sometimes they tried to get into people's homes, asking for a drink of water or to use the bathroom. While one kept the homeowner busy, the other would steal cash. For two months the girls continued to use the scam, unaware people were complaining to police about hoagies they bought, paid for, and never received. The two honest-looking girls were arrested and charged with theft, receiving stolen property, and theft by deception. What they thought was an innocent way to make easy money proved to be quite costly for them.

Like these two girls, we are all tempted to do wrong. Paul wrote that Christians must live in love and holiness. Moral purity was the call. He urged that Christians please God, exploit no one, and love everyone.

*Questions for Students on the Next Lesson.* 1. Have you ever been persecuted for your beliefs? If so, when? 2. How does God repay the persecutors? 3. What is the punishment for those who persecute God's people? 4. What support does Paul offer those who are persecuted? 5. How is Jesus' name glorified during persecution?

# LESSON 3—MARCH 16

## PRAY FOR OTHERS

*Background Scripture:* II Thessalonians 1
*Devotional Reading:* I Timothy 1:1-8

KING JAMES VERSION

II THESSALONIANS 1:1 Paul, and Silvanus, and Timotheus, unto the church of the Thessalonians in God our Father and the Lord Jesus Christ:

2 Grace unto you, and peace, from God our Father and the Lord Jesus Christ.

3 We are bound to thank God always for you, brethren, as it is meet, because that your faith groweth exceedingly, and the charity of every one of you all toward each other aboundeth;

4 So that we ourselves glory in you in the churches of God for your patience and faith in all your persecutions and tribulations that ye endure:

5 Which is a manifest token of the righteous judgment of God, that ye may be counted worthy of the kingdom of God, for which ye also suffer:

6 Seeing it is a righteous thing with God to recompense tribulation to them that trouble you;

7 And to you who are troubled rest with us, when the Lord Jesus shall be revealed from heaven with his mighty angels,

8 In flaming fire taking vengeance on them that know not God, and that obey not the gospel of our Lord Jesus Christ:

9 Who shall be punished with everlasting destruction from the presence of the Lord, and from the glory of his power;

10 When he shall come to be glorified in his saints, and to be admired in all them that believe (because our testimony among you was believed) in that day.

11 Wherefore also we pray always for you, that our God would count you worthy of this calling, and fulfil all the good pleasure of his goodness, and the work of faith with power:

12 That the name of our Lord Jesus Christ may be glorified in you, and ye in him, according to the grace of our God and the Lord Jesus Christ.

NEW REVISED STANDARD VERSION

II THESSALONIANS 1:1 Paul, Silvanus, and Timothy, To the church of the Thessalonians in God our Father and the Lord Jesus Christ:

2 Grace to you and peace from God our Father and the Lord Jesus Christ.

3 We must always give thanks to God for you, brothers and sisters, as is right, because your faith is growing abundantly, and the love of everyone of you for one another is increasing. 4 Therefore we ourselves boast of you among the churches of God for your steadfastness and faith during all your persecutions and the afflictions that you are enduring.

5 This is evidence of the righteous judgment of God, and is intended to make you worthy of the kingdom of God, for which you are also suffering. 6 For it is indeed just of God to repay with affliction those who afflict you, 7 and to give relief to the afflicted as well as to us, when the Lord Jesus is revealed from heaven with his mighty angels 8 in flaming fire, inflicting vengeance on those who do not know God and on those who do not obey the gospel of our Lord Jesus. 9 These will suffer the punishment of eternal destruction, separated from the presence of the Lord and from the glory of his might, 10 when he comes to be glorified by his saints and to be marveled at on that day among all who have believed, because our testimony to you was believed. 11 To this end we always pray for you, asking that our God will make you worthy of his call and will fulfill by his power every good resolve and work of faith, 12 so that the name of our Lord Jesus may be glorified in you, and you in him, according to the grace of our God and the Lord Jesus Christ.

KEY VERSE: *We always pray for you, asking that our God will make you worthy of his call and will fulfill by his power every good resolve and work of faith.* II Thessalonians 1:11.

## HOME BIBLE READINGS

| | | | | |
|---|---|---|---|---|
| *Mar.* | *10* | *M.* | II Chronicles 7:12-18 | *Pray in Humility* |
| *Mar.* | *11* | *T.* | John 17:6-12 | *Pray As Jesus Prayed* |
| *Mar.* | *12* | *W.* | Matthew 6:5-15 | *Pray in Private* |
| *Mar.* | *13* | *T.* | Jude 1:17-23 | *Pray in the Holy Spirit* |
| *Mar.* | *14* | *F.* | James 5:13-16 | *Pray for the Sick* |
| *Mar.* | *15* | *S.* | Acts 8:14-24 | *Pray for Friends* |
| *Mar.* | *16* | *S.* | I Samuel 12:19-25 | *Pray for the Penitent* |

## BACKGROUND

Paul, Silas, and Timothy faced some of their fiercest opposition in the city of Thessalonica. The account in Acts 17 describes an uproar that induced Paul to leave the city. Although no further riots against Christians occurred, the intimidation had not ended. Fanatic opponents from the synagogue continued to stir up trouble for believers.

Some of the new believers found the persecution almost too much to endure. These fainthearted converts needed some special words of encouragement. Although Paul had written an earlier letter (the one we know as I Thessalonians), some in the congregation failed to take his words seriously. They had not understood their call to share in Christ's sufferings.

Taking a positive approach, Paul affirmed them for continuing to stand bravely in a hostile environment. He commended the shaky Thessalonians for not faltering when encountering hatred and hardship. But he encouraged the wavering to maintain their trust in God. Enduring suffering would make them worthy of the kingdom of God.

Paul stated that throughout their times of hardship, the Thessalonian believers should remain confident that God does not permit persecutors to go unpunished. God relieves His people and takes vengeance on those refusing to obey the Gospel. At Christ's return, people would be judged appropriately. Meanwhile, Paul and Silas and Timothy would continue to pray for the Thessalonian congregation—that they would prove worthy of their calling.

## NOTES ON THE PRINTED TEXT

A few months after Paul, Silvanus, and Timothy (1:1) wrote the first letter to the church of the Thessalonians (1:1), Paul wrote a second letter to clear up a misunderstanding about Christ's second coming. In most of his epistles, after his introduction and greeting, Paul typically offered a note of thanksgiving. He followed the same practice in this letter. *We must always give thanks to God for you, brothers and sisters, as is right, because your faith is growing abundantly, and the love of everyone of you for one another is increasing* (2:3).

Thanksgiving was offered for two reasons. First, the Thessalonians had grown in their faith. Second, their love for one another had increased. Therefore the three missionaries offered thanksgiving to God, especially since all of this growth had been persistently accomplished in the midst of persecution. As a result, Paul, Silas, and Timothy encouraged other churches with the example of the Thessalonian church. *Therefore we ourselves boast of you among the churches of God for your steadfastness and faith during all your persecutions and the afflictions that you are enduring* (1:4).

Paul reminded the Thessalonians that their suffering was connected with the kingdom. *This is evidence of the righteous judgment of God, and is intended to make you worthy of the kingdom of God, for which you are also suffering* (1:5). Paul wrote that God would repay the persecutors, that they would be judged harshly. *For it is indeed just of God to repay with affliction those who afflict you* (1:6).

Those who were persecuted would be granted rest from their sufferings when Jesus came again. Paul wrote that God would give relief to the afflicted as well as to us, when the Lord Jesus is revealed from heaven (1:7). Paul used several phrases to describe Christ's authoritative coming. First, He would be revealed from heaven with his mighty angels (1:7). Only God dwelt in heaven. Only God had angels. These powerful agents would accompany Christ to execute His judgment, coming in flaming fire (1:8).

The judgment would be executed not only on the persecutors, but also on those who refused to obey the gospel of Christ. Paul wrote that God would inflict vengeance on those who do not know God and on those who do not obey the gospel of our Lord Jesus (1:8). Paul described this judgment for the Thessalonians. It was never-ending destruction and complete exclusion from God's presence and glory. *These will suffer the punishment of eternal destruction, separated from the presence of the Lord and from the glory of his might* (1:9).

Paul declared that while all people would be judged at Christ's return, His coming would elicit worship and astonishment from all believers. Paul reassured the readers about Christ's coming. *When he comes to be glorified by his saints and to be marveled at on that day among all who have believed, because our testimony to you was believed* (1:10).

As all believers waited for the Lord's coming, Paul would continue to pray for the Thessalonians. He prayed that they would show themselves worthy of God's kingdom through their continuing effort to live a Christian life-style. In that way, the believers gave glory to God and their Lord Jesus Christ. *To this end we always pray for you, asking that our God will make you worthy of his call and will fulfill by his power every good resolve and work of faith, so that the name of our Lord Jesus may be glorified in you, and you in him, according to the grace of our God and the Lord Jesus Christ* (1:11, 12).

## SUGGESTIONS TO TEACHERS

"If they arrested you for being a Christian, would they have enough evidence to convict you?" You could well start your lesson by asking this question of your class. Try following up with some related questions, such as, "Would anyone recognize you as a Christian to begin with?" or "Has your faith ever gotten you into any problems?" or "When was the last time you were criticized for standing up for your faith in Christ?"

The Thessalonian Christians faced hostility and harassment because of their identification with Christ. Believers today may not be fined by the authorities or fired from jobs in our country (although they frequently are in other places). But they certainly encounter opposition. How can Christians keep on being faithful in the face of persecution of any kind?

This is the key question in today's lesson.

1. GRACE IN THE FATHER'S TENDERNESS. Paul reminded his readers that they were constantly embraced by the undeserved mercy and caring presence of God. In spite of harsh conditions, Christ's people may be confident that they are accepted and protected by the loving Lord. This fundamental fact of human existence must undergird our thinking always.

2. GRATITUDE FOR FAITHFUL TESTIMONY. Paul also gave thanks to God for the way many Christians in Thessalonica had kept the faith through times of persecution. He, Silas, and Timothy and other believers were serving as a "support system" for the beleaguered Thessalonian believers.

All Christians need a support system. Talk with your students about ways church members can support each other in tough times. Paul stated that he was praying for the Thessalonians. How can those in your church grow in their prayer lives and be more supportive of one another through prayer?

3. GLORY IN THE FINAL TIME. Paul assured his audience in Thessalonica that Christ would indeed return and reward the faithful. Harsh times would not continue forever. God promises His blessing in a special way to those who endure persecution in any form without wavering.

4. GAINS FROM FERVENT TRUST. Perhaps Paul was recalling Jesus' words in the following beatitude: "Blessed are those who are persecuted for righteousness' sake, for theirs is the kingdom of heaven. Blessed are you when people revile you and persecute you and utter all kinds of evil against you falsely on my account. Rejoice and be glad, for your reward is great in heaven, for in the same way they persecuted the prophets who were before you" (Matt. 5:10-12). Focus on these words with your class. Be sure to direct everyone's attention to the example of Jesus Himself, who was arrested and executed unjustly because of His commitment to the Father and to us.

### TOPIC FOR ADULTS
#### PRAY FOR ONE ANOTHER!

*Prayer-filled Living.* Bible scholar Matthew Henry prayed consistently for others. His praying permeated all of his life. On one occasion, he was attacked by thieves and robbed of his wallet—not a pleasant experience, to be sure. But this is what Matthew Henry wrote in his diary the day he was mugged: "Let me be thankful. First, I was never robbed before. Second, although they took my purse, they did not take my life. Third, although they took my all, it was not very much. Fourth, let me be thankful because it was I who was robbed and not I who did the robbing."

Try this algebra problem to understand an important point: 270 over 38 equals X over 100. If you work out the equation, the answer is 711. Now let's contemplate the meaning behind the numbers.

The population of the United States stands at 270 million. We 270 million persons consume thirty-eight percent of the world's resources. If the rest of the people alive in the world today (5 billion persons) absorbed the world's resources in the same way we Americans do, only 711 million out of the 5 billion could be so privileged. The other 4-billion-plus people would be—and are—deprived.

Effective praying requires an active concern for others. That concern must be shown in specific ways. One way our prayers for others can have more meaning would be for us to live simpler life-styles. Let us pray to live more simply—that others may simply live.

*Prayer Positions.* Three ministers were talking about prayer and the appropriate and effective positions for prayer. As they were talking, a telephone repairman was working on the phone system in the background. One minister shared that he felt the key was in the hands. He always held his hands together and pointed them upward as a form of symbolic worship. The second suggested that real prayer was conducted on one's knees. The third responded that they both had it wrong—the way to pray was stretched out flat on one's face.

By this time the phone man couldn't stay out of the conversation any longer. He interjected: "I found that the most powerful prayer I ever made was while I was dangling upside down by my heels from a power pole, suspended forty feet above the ground."—James Hewett, *Illustrations Unlimited* (Wheaton, Ill.: Tyndale, 1988)

*Questions for Students on the Next Lesson.* 1. How did Paul meet his living expenses in Thessalonica? 2. Why were some church members in Thessalonica refusing to work? 3. What was Paul's advice to those not working? 4. How does your faith motivate you to keep serving the Lord? 5. How would you respond to someone who suggests a date that Christ will come again?

## TOPIC FOR YOUTH
### PRAYER HELPS

*Source of Support.* Andita Parker-Lloyd, a student at Wilkes University in Wilkes-Barre, Pennsylvania, returned to her home in Philadelphia in October, 1993. Her mother had died and she was home for the funeral. When she arrived, she found a social worker removing her younger brothers, eight-year-old Quentin and thirteen-year-old Kevin. They were to be placed in foster homes because their mother had been a single parent.

Andita never questioned what she must do. She went to court and was named the boys' legal guardian. She moved the boys to a public housing project in Wilkes-Barre so they could have a yard. After spending all day at classes and working at her part-time job, she goes home to take care of the boys. She still manages to edit the student newspaper, maintain a 3.1 grade point average, and see that her two brothers do their chores and homework.

How does Andita cope with the financial, physical, and emotional stress of being a full-time student and single supporter of her two brothers? She says, "I get by with a lot of prayer." That is the only thing that sees her through.

No doubt Paul would understand. He urged the Thessalonians to pray in all circumstances, as he himself had prayed.

*The Truth of Prayer.* When Dr. Bishop Knox, principal of a high school in Jackson, Mississippi, allowed a prayer to be read on the school's intercom, an idea was born. Students asked to be allowed to form a Bible club. The result was Aletheia Bible Clubs. (*Aletheia* is a New Testament word for "truth.")

Students at Aurora High School in Aurora, Missouri, and Cayuga High School in Montalba, Texas, organized the first clubs. Another in Jasper, Missouri, quickly followed. Junior Brian Gamel was the organizer in Aurora. He envisioned a club that simply put God back in his high school. Initially, nineteen other students shared his vision. In several weeks, the group grew to over forty members.

Through Bible study and prayer, the young people apply biblical truth in areas of faith, family, and freedom. Melissa Wright, a sophomore at the high school in Jasper, believes that acting and praying like a Christian at school might help turn things around in her school.

These students have accepted Paul's teaching about regular prayer.

*The Temptation of Revenge.* Among southern Slavs, mothers routinely lay their infant sons in cradles upon blood-stained shirts of their murdered fathers. These children are raised to avenge their fathers' deaths.

Perhaps you also, like other youth, have struggled with the desire for revenge. Certainly some young members of the Thessalonian church shared that struggle. Yet Paul wrote that God would repay the persecutors. He, and only He, would take vengeance on those who refused to obey the Gospel. Believers were to resist the temptation to carry out their own forms of vengeance.

*Questions for Students on the Next Lesson.* 1. How were believers to treat those who did not work? 2. Should the church exercise discipline on believers? 3. Do you think Paul was too harsh? 4. Is ignoring or shunning a believer an effective punishment? 5. Why were some Christians choosing not to work?

# LESSON 4—MARCH 23

## DO WHAT IS RIGHT

*Background Scripture:* II Thessalonians 3:1-18
*Devotional Reading:* Ephesians 4:25-32

### KING JAMES VERSION

II THESSALONIANS 3:1 Finally, brethren, pray for us, that the word of the Lord may have free course, and be glorified, even as it is with you:

2 And that we may be delivered from unreasonable and wicked men: for all men have not faith.

3 But the Lord is faithful, who shall stablish you, and keep you from evil.

4 And we have confidence in the Lord touching you, that ye both do and will do the things which we command you.

5 And the Lord direct your hearts into the love of God, and into the patient waiting for Christ.

6 Now we command you, brethren, in the name of our Lord Jesus Christ, that ye withdraw yourselves from every brother that walketh disorderly, and not after the tradition which he received from us.

7 For yourselves know how ye ought to follow us: for we behaved not ourselves disorderly among you;

8 Neither did we eat any man's bread for nought; but wrought with labour and travail night and day, that we might not be chargeable to any of you:

9 Not because we have not power, but to make ourselves an ensample unto you to follow us.

10 For even when we were with you, this we commanded you, that if any would not work, neither should he eat.

11 For we hear that there are some which walk among you disorderly, working not at all, but are busybodies.

12 Now them that are such we command and exhort by our Lord Jesus Christ, that with quietness they work, and eat their own bread.

13 But ye, brethren, be not weary in well doing.

14 And if any man obey not our word by this epistle, note that man, and have no company with him, that he may be ashamed.

15 Yet count him not as an enemy, but admonish him as a brother.

16 Now the Lord of peace himself give you peace always by all means. The Lord be with you all.

### NEW REVISED STANDARD VERSION

II THESSALONIANS 3:1 Finally, brothers and sisters, pray for us, so that the word of the Lord may spread rapidly and be glorified everywhere, just as it is among you,

2 and that we may be rescued from wicked and evil people; for not all have faith. 3 But the Lord is faithful; he will strengthen you and guard you from the evil one. 4 And we have confidence in the Lord concerning you, that you are doing and will go on doing the things we command. 5 May the Lord direct your hearts to the love of God and to the steadfastness of Christ.

6 Now we command you, beloved, in the name of our Lord Jesus Christ, to keep away from believers who are living in idleness and not according to the tradition that they received from us. 7 For you yourselves know how you ought to imitate us; we were not idle when we were with you, 8 and we did not eat anyone's bread without paying for it; but with toil and labor we worked night and day, so that we might not burden any of you. 9 This was not because we do not have that right, but in order to give you an example to imitate. 10 For even when we were with you, we gave you this command: Anyone unwilling to work should not eat. 11 For we hear that some of you are living in idleness, mere busybodies, not doing any work. 12 Now such persons we command and exhort in the Lord Jesus Christ to do their work quietly and to earn their own living. 13 Brothers and sisters, do not be weary in doing what is right.

14 Take note of those who do not obey what we say in this letter; have nothing to do with them, so that they may be ashamed. 15 Do not regard them as enemies, but warn them as believers.

16 Now may the Lord of peace himself give you peace at all times in all ways. The Lord be with all of you.

*KEY VERSE: Brothers and sisters, do not be weary in doing what is right.*
II Thessalonians 3:13.

## HOME BIBLE READINGS

| | | | | |
|---|---|---|---|---|
| Mar. | 17 | M. | Colossians 3:1-10 | *Turn Away from Evil* |
| Mar. | 18 | T. | Colossians 3:12-17 | *Do Everything in Jesus' Name* |
| Mar. | 19 | W. | Colossians 4:1-5 | *Be Gracious to Others* |
| Mar. | 20 | T. | Romans 15:1-6 | *Live in Harmony with Others* |
| Mar. | 21 | F. | Ephesians 4:1-8 | *Live Peacefully within the Church* |
| Mar. | 22 | S. | Ephesians 4:25-32 | *Live Peacefully within the Family* |
| Mar. | 23 | S. | I Peter 3:8-12 | *Rules for Christian Living* |

## BACKGROUND

Although Paul had written a letter to the Thessalonian church about the problems Timothy had reported, apparently some in that congregation were misinterpreting his words. Word came back to Paul that his counsel was being taken the wrong way in some cases—and ignored altogether in other cases. Paul sent a follow-up letter, II Thessalonians. Although it covers most of the same topics raised in the earlier letter, the tone is firmer and more formal.

The big problem requiring the second letter had to do with Paul's teachings about the return of Christ. When Paul preached in Thessalonica, his message implied (to some readers, at least) that Jesus would come apart from any preceding items. As a result, those expecting the Lord's momentary return became disillusioned. They became weary and burdened over the apparent delay in Jesus' return.

Coupled with this sense of disappointment was a feeling of despair among certain believers because their loved ones had died before the Second Coming. They feared that Christians who died before Christ returned were somehow left out.

Perhaps the most pressing difficulty concerned those who had simply quit their jobs in order to wait idly for Christ's return. These people soon had to turn to others for handouts, and developed a reputation for laziness. Although they whimpered that they were faithfully anticipating Jesus coming again, their fellow church members complained that they were merely sponging food.

Paul's second letter dealt firmly with the pastoral problems connected to belief in the return of Christ. The wise old apostle said bluntly that those who refused to work should not eat either. Real faithfulness did not give birth to indolence and idleness. Rather, faithfulness meant responsibility.

## NOTES ON THE PRINTED TEXT

*Finally, brothers and sisters, pray for us, so that the word of the Lord may spread rapidly and be glorified everywhere, just as it is among you* (3:1). Paul asked the Thessalonian church to continue to pray for Silas, Timothy, and himself that they might continue to preach the Gospel effectively. He also coveted their prayers for deliverance from the opposition of evil, unbelieving people. *And that we may be rescued from wicked and evil people; for not all have faith* (3:2).

While Paul asked for prayer for himself, he also remembered his readers. He reassured them. Confidently he reminded the church that God was dependable and would guard His people. *But the Lord is faithful; he will strengthen you and guard you from the evil one* (3:3). The three missionaries were certain that their readers would obediently carry out the instructions contained in the letter. *And we have confidence in the Lord concerning you, that you are doing and will go on doing the things that we command* (3:4). Paul encouraged his readers to remember the love God had shown for them in Christ. The same kind of steadfast endurance that they saw in Christ was what they as believers were to exhibit. *May the Lord direct your hearts to the love of God and to the steadfastness of Christ* (3:5).

Having asked for their prayers for himself, Paul then wrote regarding the second reason for his letter. He had received reports that people had stopped working, apparently drawing wrong conclusions about Christ's return. Paul responded with specific instructions. *Now we command you, beloved, in the name of our Lord Jesus Christ, to keep away from believers who are living in idleness and not according to the tradition that they received from us* (3:6). Paul condemned those who refused to work, instructing the Thessalonians to keep away from these people. He had never advocated such a life-style.

The three missionaries had provided an example for them to follow. The Thessalonians knew that Paul and his associates had not been lazy. *For you yourselves know how you ought to imitate us; we were not idle when we were with you* (3:7). Paul reminded the readers of the apostles' stay with Jason at Thessalonica. The three worked and paid for their room and board—and received nothing for their preaching. *We did not eat anyone's bread without paying for it; but with toil and labor we worked night and day, so that we might not burden any of you* (3:8). By avoiding any hardship for the church, Paul and his companions provided a good example. Paul reminded the Thessalonians that he could have insisted on their financial support, but did not. *This was not because we do not have that right, but in order to give you an example to imitate* (3:9).

The church was to adopt tough sanctions, if necessary. If those who were lazy did not work, they were to be given no food. *For even when we were with you, we gave you this command: Anyone unwilling to work should not eat* (3:10).

Paul specifically addressed the lazy church members who were becoming gossiping nuisances. *For we hear that some of you are living in idleness, mere busybodies, not doing any work* (3:11). Paul exhorted the idle loafers to work and earn a living. His authority to make such a command came from Jesus. *Now such persons we command and exhort in the Lord Jesus Christ to do their work quietly and to earn their own living* (3:12).

He also urged the readers not to grow tired of doing what was right. Some within the church might have been tempted to give up on charitable giving. Paul encouraged them to keep helping the needy. *Brothers and sisters, do not be weary in doing what is right* (3:13).

Believers were not to give encouragement to indolent fellow church members. The lazy individuals were acting in an unworthy manner. *Take* note of those who do not obey what we say in this letter: have nothing to do with them, so that they may be ashamed (3:14). Any discipline, though, must be administered in love. Those who disobeyed must not be treated as enemies. Do not regard them as enemies, but warn them as believers (3:15).

Paul closed with a benediction, praying that God bring about peace in the church. Now may the Lord of peace himself give you peace at all times in all ways. The Lord be with all of you (3:16).

## SUGGESTIONS TO TEACHERS

Like the church at Thessalonica, your congregation has people who sometimes cause problems. Perhaps these "problem people" haven't caused serious disunity, but every church experiences some mild conflict at times. Whenever two humans try to get together, even if they call themselves Christians, some disagreement takes place. The need, of course, is to keep the disagreement from escalating into discord, the discord into disputes, the disputes into divisiveness.

Paul's counsel to his beloved friends at Thessalonica offers helpful insights on the matter of preserving unity. On this Palm Sunday, when the attention focuses on Christ's triumphal entry, you and your class members can bring honor to the King of kings by learning together about trust and forgiveness.

1. PRAYERS FOR ENCOURAGEMENT. Paul and his colleagues sought unity among the believers in Thessalonica. In spite of problems from within the congregation and opposition from without, Christ's people must pray sincerely for others. Likewise, in congregations today, praying for others—even so-called troublemakers—is essential.

2. POWER OF THE LORD. Knowing the power of the Lord, and realizing his own need, Paul fervently sought the prayers of his friends in Thessalonica. Discuss how we can more effectively hold up each other in prayer today. For example, does each person in your class have a "prayer partner" who is consciously and regularly interceding for him or her?

3. PERILS OF IDLENESS. Some in the Thessalonian church had stopped working and were idly waiting for the Lord's return. This caused resentment among those providing handouts to the hungry. Some of these idlers were posing as super-Christians but in actuality were mere nuisances. Idle speculation about the date of Christ's return is not only unproductive, but unnecessary. God has His own timetable. Meanwhile, He calls each of us to active service while time is left.

4. PREMISE OF UNITY. Paul's letter instructs the church leaders to go to the idler, to "warn him as a brother." "Brother" suggests family. It implies a close relationship. In spite of conflict within a congregation, each member is bound to the other in a unity of love and responsibility that runs deeper than personality. It is a unity flowing from Christ's indwelling, mutually shared Spirit.

## TOPIC FOR ADULTS
### ACTIVE RIGHTEOUSNESS

Remembering the Earthly Life. A few years ago, the Rev. Edward Walker took a group of prospective pastoral candidates to a special convocation at a seminary. The gathering of young persons considering seminary study was opened with a prayer by a young man who was a first-year student. The words of his prayer, although uttered with good intentions, proved to be slightly startling to those present. The prayer began, "O Lord, we ask thy blessing upon those who are leaving this earthly life and entering the ministry. . . ."

Sometimes Christians mistakenly imagine that commitment to Christ means forgetting about "this earthly life" and being translated to another existence. Some Thessalonian believers apparently held such notions. Some of these super-spiritual souls even took to sitting around idly, waiting for the coming of Christ so they could leave this earthly life for good. Paul's advice continues to be sound. While we may have to wait for Christ's coming, we are expected to live active, productive lives.

*Ordering the Groceries.* In *Footnotes and Headliners*, artist and dedicated religious worker Corita Kent talks about celebrations. This marvelously creative person says that for any celebration, "someone has to order the groceries."

Some in Thessalonica forgot that "someone has to order the groceries," that is, work so that food can be bought, rent can be paid, bills can be met. Celebrating, even in the church, is fine. And fun. But if it means expecting life to be a continuous party without a willingness to earn one's livelihood, it's not a celebration. It's laziness!

Someone has to order the groceries; everyone must do his or her share in meeting the everyday needs of the group, whether a family, a church, or a community. Christ's people must never be accused of being drones.

*Bow Low.* In the city of Bethlehem, visitors throng to the historic Church of the Manger, the site where Mary supposedly gave birth to the baby Jesus. The venerable building can be entered only by stooping. Tourists sometimes complain at having to bend over to go through the low passageway, yet the designers of the entrance meant it to be that way. As pilgrims are forced to bow, they are reminded that they must bow humbly before Christ in their hearts. Conceited strutting is not compatible with a sincere approach to the Savior! Only those who bow can enter His presence and live active, righteous lives to His glory.

*Questions for Students on the Next Lesson.* 1. Were the women going to the tomb expecting the Resurrection? What was their mood? 2. What was the announcement by the angelic messenger? 3. How does the meaning of the Resurrection affect your attitude in facing your eventual death? 4. What are some practical ways a Christian can bring hope and comfort to a grieving friend?

TOPIC FOR YOUTH
*DO WHAT IS RIGHT!*

*How to Get Ahead.* A survey of financial attitudes in the United States, conducted by *Money* magazine, revealed that people still believe hard work is the primary way to get ahead. However, "inheriting money" and "winning a lottery" were the second- and third-place responses.

Obviously, humans still believe it's possible to get something for nothing. People, young and old, still do not fully understand the relationship between work and reward. Paul urged his church to work for a living. At the same time, he called them to accept God's gracious provision for their salvation.

*Called to Quality.* In 1994, a well-known, ready-to-wear clothing chain found that it had to return sixteen thousand garments to its supplier during a three-month period because of faulty workmanship. This was only one instance of such recalls.

Christians are called to quality workmanship. Their efforts must be of the highest standard. All believers should be able to say that their work is good because their work ethic reflects their commitment to Jesus Christ.

*Betting Bug.* Ten years ago, teenage gambling was unheard of. Today, seven percent of gambling counselors' case loads involve teenagers. A survey of 2,700 high school students concluded that youth are twice as likely as adults to become problem gamblers. Ninety-six percent of the nation's compulsive gamblers started gambling before the age of fourteen.

Despite such statistics, the public largely approves of gambling. According to a survey conducted for Harrah's and quoted in the *Christian Science Monitor,* fifty-five percent of American adults approve of gambling for anyone at any age, minors included.

Sadly, youth are influenced by society to try to get something for nothing. The betting bug is only one method of trying to acquire something without working for it. Paul told lazy believers they were to work for a living and avoid an idle life. In addition, they were not to grow weary in doing what was right.

*Questions for Students on the Next Lesson.* 1. What message was Mary to deliver to the disciples? 2. What confusion about the Resurrection existed at Thessalonica? 3. How did Paul describe the resurrection of the dead? What images did he utilize? 4. Do you find hope and encouragement in the Resurrection? 5. Why do Christians encourage one another with this hope?

# LESSON 5—MARCH 30

## THE RESURRECTION HOPE (EASTER)

*Background Scripture:* Matthew 28:1-10; I Thessalonians 4:13-18
*Devotional Reading:* Romans 5:1-11

### KING JAMES VERSION

MATTHEW 28:1 In the end of the sabbath, as it began to dawn toward the first day of the week, came Mary Magdalene and the other Mary to see the sepulchre.

2 And, behold, there was a great earthquake: for the angel of the Lord descended from heaven, and came and rolled back the stone from the door and sat upon it.

3 His countenance was like lightning, and his raiment white as snow:

4 And for fear of him the keepers did shake, and became as dead men.

5 And the angel answered and said unto the women, Fear not ye: for I know that ye seek Jesus, which was crucified.

6 He is not here: for he is risen, as he said. Come, see the place where the Lord lay.

7 And go quickly, and tell his disciples that he is risen from the dead; and, behold, he goeth before you into Galilee; there shall ye see him: lo, I have told you.

8 And they departed quickly from the sepulchre with fear and great joy; and did run to bring his disciples word.

9 And as they went to tell his disciples, behold, Jesus met them, saying, All hail. And they came and held him by the feet, and worshipped him.

10 Then said Jesus unto them, Be not afraid: go tell my brethren that they go into Galilee, and there shall they see me.

I THESSALONIANS 4:13 But I would not have you to be ignorant, brethren, concerning them which are asleep, that ye sorrow not, even as others which have no hope.

14 For if we believe that Jesus died and rose again, even so them also which sleep in Jesus will God bring with him.

15 For this we say unto you by the word of the Lord, that we which are alive and remain unto the coming of the Lord shall not prevent them which are asleep.

16 For the Lord himself shall descend from heaven with a shout, with the voice of the archangel, and with the trump of God: and the dead in Christ shall rise first:

17 Then we which are alive and remain shall be caught up together with them in the clouds, to meet the Lord in the air: and so shall we ever be with the Lord.

18 Wherefore comfort one another with

### NEW REVISED STANDARD VERSION

MATTHEW 28:1 After the sabbath, as the first day of the week was dawning, Mary Magdalene and the other Mary went to see the tomb. 2 And suddenly there was a great earthquake; for an angel of the Lord, descending from heaven, came and rolled back the stone and sat on it. 3 His appearance was like lightning, and his clothing white as snow. 4 For fear of him the guards shook and became like dead men. 5 But the angel said to the women, 'Do not be afraid; I know that you are looking for Jesus who was crucified. 6 He is not here; for he has been raised, as he said. Come, see the place where he lay. 7 Then go quickly and tell his disciples, 'He has been raised from the dead, and indeed he is going ahead of you to Galilee; there you will see him.' This is my message for you." 8 So they left the tomb quickly with fear and great joy, and ran to tell his disciples. 9 Suddenly Jesus met them and said, "Greetings!" And they came to him, took hold of his feet, and worshiped him. 10 Then Jesus said to them, "Do not be afraid; go and tell my brothers to go to Galilee; there they will see me."

I THESSALONIANS 4:13 But we do not want you to be uninformed, brothers and sisters, about those who have died, so that you may not grieve as others do who have no hope. 14 For since we believe that Jesus died and rose again, even so, through Jesus, God will bring with him those who have died. 15 For this we declare to you by the word of the Lord, that we who are alive, who are left until the coming of the Lord, will by no means precede those who have died. 16 For the Lord himself with a cry of command, with the archangel's call and with the sound of God's trumpet, will descend from heaven, and the dead in Christ will rise first. 17 Then we who are alive, who are left, will be caught up in the clouds together with them to meet the Lord in the air; and so we will be with the Lord forever. 18 Therefore encourage one another with these words.

these words.

KEY VERSE: *Since we believe that Jesus died and rose again, even so, through Jesus, God will bring with him those who have died.*
I Thessalonians 4:14.

## HOME BIBLE READINGS

| | | | | |
|---|---|---|---|---|
| Mar. | 24 | M. | Romans 5:1-11 | *Jesus Christ Died for Sinners* |
| Mar. | 25 | T. | Romans 5:12-19 | *God's Gift of Grace for All* |
| Mar. | 26 | W. | I Corinthians 15:1-11 | *The Fact of the Resurrection* |
| Mar. | 27 | T. | I Corinthians 15:12-19 | *The Need for the Resurrection* |
| Mar. | 28 | F. | I Corinthians 15:20-28 | *The Assurance of the Resurrection* |
| Mar. | 29 | S. | I Corinthians 15:35-44 | *The Nature of the Resurrection* |
| Mar. | 30 | S. | I Corinthians 15:51-58 | *The Victory of the Resurrection* |

## BACKGROUND

Easter has been the biggest celebration in the Christian community from the earliest days. In fact, the traditional celebration of Christmas came much later. Not until late in the fourth century did the church begin the formal observance of the birth of Christ. But the resurrection of Jesus Christ was commemorated as early as the first gatherings of Christians. This is thoroughly understandable, for had there been no resurrection, there would be no church. And no good news of God's victory over death would mean no hope. But the fact that Christ rose from the dead establishes hope in spite of the grave.

The news of the Resurrection was the keynote of the apostle Paul's preaching and, indeed, the preaching of all early evangelists. The hearers received this news gladly. In an age when life was short for most people, death's terrible finality seemed the greatest reality. Thus the Easter message, promising a relationship with God that could not be broken—even by death—stirred ordinary men and women to lives of heroism and hope.

Matthew and the other three Gospel writers emphasized the fact that Jesus had truly been dead, laid in a tomb as a cold corpse. These four writers stressed that no follower expected the Resurrection, in spite of Jesus' assurances that He would rejoin them. The account of the mourning women approaching the burial place underscores the drama of God's victory. Jesus lives! God raised Him from death! This news resonates in all the messages of the first Christian preachers.

## NOTES ON THE PRINTED TEXT

After the Sabbath, as the first day of the week was dawning, Mary Magdalene and the other Mary went to see the tomb (Matt. 28:1), which was cut into a limestone hillside. The outermost opening had been sealed with what may have been a heavy, three-foot rolling stone to keep wild animals from entering. The women came with myrrh, spices, and other scents.

And suddenly there was a great earthquake; for an angel of the Lord, descending from heaven, came and rolled back the stone and sat on it (28:2). While the area has a lot of seismic activity, the earthquake and the angel were obvious signs of God's activity. The guards were paralyzed into inactivity by their fright.

The angel had a message for the two women. *Do not be afraid; I know that you are looking for Jesus who was crucified. He is not here; for he has been raised, as he said. Come see the place where he lay* (28:5, 6). The women were not to be frightened. The tomb was empty! They could see for themselves that His body was gone. The angel also gave the women an assignment. They were to share the Resurrection hope with the male disciples, who were in hiding.

Believing the angelic messenger who said that Jesus had been raised, the two women ran to tell the disciples. Their emotions swung between fear and joy. Yet more startling discoveries awaited them that morning. Suddenly the risen Lord met them and said, "Greetings! (28:9). Recognizing Him, they worshiped Him. *And they came to him, took hold of his feet, and worshiped him* (28:9).

Jesus instructed them to deliver a message to His disciples. They were to meet Him in Galilee. *Then Jesus said to them, "Do not be afraid; go and tell my brothers to go to Galilee; there they will see me"* (28:10).

The resurrection hope was not initially understood by everyone in the Christian community. Within the Thessalonian church, for example, the death of certain members had created concern for their eternal welfare. People lamented and sorrowed, believing that these members had somehow missed the future blessing of Christ. Paul wrote to provide suitable comfort for such situations. *But we do not want you to be uninformed, brothers and sisters, about those who have died, so that you may not grieve as others do who have no hope* (I Thess. 4:13). Non-Christians grieved because they had no hope of life after death, but the Christian dead were with Christ. This continued life with Christ was the Christian's hope. Those who believed in the resurrection of Jesus need not grieve without hope, for they, too, would be brought by God to and with Jesus. *For since we believe that Jesus died and rose again, even so, through Jesus, God will bring with him those who have died* (4:14).

Paul stated that those who remained alive had no chronological advantage over those who had died. *For this we declare to you by the word of the Lord, that we who are alive, who are left until the coming of the Lord, will by no means precede those who have died* (4:15). Paul offered a picture of Christ's coming based on types of imagery that were popular in that day. God's command would initiate the resurrection of the dead, as a trumpet summoned those who had died. The dead would be raised to be united together with the living members of the church. *For the Lord himself, with a cry of command, with the archangel's call and with the sound of God's trumpet, will descend from heaven, and the dead in Christ will rise first* (4:16).

After the dead were raised, all believers would be gathered together. Literally, all those alive would be seized, or snatched, and brought before the Lord to meet Him. Therefore, the Christian's future, whether dead or alive, was a meeting with the Lord. *Then we who are alive, who are left, will be caught up in the clouds together with them to meet the Lord in the air; and so we will be with the Lord forever* (4:17).

Consequently, Christians were urged by Paul to encourage one another with the resurrection hope, passing along the comfort it would bring. *Therefore encourage one another with these words* (4:18).

## SUGGESTIONS TO TEACHERS

A man traveled to Graceland, Elvis Presley's residence, to join a large group commemorating what would have been the performer's sixtieth birthday in January, 1995. The man, twenty-seven years old, was a church member but apparently became depressed over Elvis's death.

Perhaps thinking of his own mortality, and pondering the hopelessness of Elvis Presley's dependence on drugs, this young man returned to his Memphis hotel room and faxed a long farewell note to his family. The note voiced his feelings of despair and gave detailed instructions about his funeral, cremation, and disposal of ashes. Then he killed himself. In spite of his love for Elvis's music, this young man could find no basis for hope.

The Easter news of Jesus raised alive is the only certain basis for hope. Today's lesson conveys life-or-death truths.

1. CONTRADICTION OF THE GRAVE. The resurrection of Jesus Christ is God's mighty assurance that He is supreme even over death. The demise of a human does not mean that God is helpless in the face of mortality. By raising up Jesus, God contradicts all human ideas about death as the final event in a person's existence. God has the last word, and that word signals hope.

2. CONTROL BY GOD. Celebrating Easter involves more than just recognizing the beauties of spring, with trees blossoming and bulbs flowering. Nor is Easter concerned with speculating about the immortality of the soul, with readings from Plato and the romantic poets. Neither of these approaches to the "holiday" brings the hope of new life through Christ. Our hope rests not on nature, nor on philosophies. Rather, our hope rests on God, the capable and compassionate One who bestowed new life on Jesus after His death. The Resurrection tells us that God remains in control.

3. CONFIDENCE IN THE LORD'S GOODNESS. Our Scripture passages in both Matthew and I Thessalonians describe the comfort the risen Lord brings to the grieving. The Resurrection assures us that God may be trusted, even in the face of our deepest grief. The tears and the loneliness, the questions and the loss are real, and should not be dismissed as wrong or unimportant. But what some writers call "clean grief" means clinging to the promise of God's goodness in spite of the hurt of losing a loved one.

4. COMFORT FOR THE GRIEVING. Grief is universal. Every tribe and community must cope with the devastating sense of loss caused by death. Thus a wide array of teachings and rituals have evolved in religions down through the centuries. But the resurrection hope is a divine revelation of truth about the matter—in a miraculous event of history. It conveys the promise of God that can bring comfort greater than any other word.

Some people in your class may want to share their experiences of grief. Allow for that in appropriate ways. But keep your lesson focused on the good news of the resurrected Christ. Only in the risen, living Lord do we realize genuine comfort.

## TOPIC FOR ADULTS
### THE RESURRECTION HOPE

*Miraculous Hours.* At the conclusion of Martin Scorsese's highly controversial film *The Last Temptation of Christ,* Jesus returns from an out-of-body "temptation sequence" to His final, agonizing moments of death. Suddenly, white flashes of light streak the screen and the image is lost. It appears as if someone opened the camera and exposed the film. Such an ending was apparently meant to suggest that neither Scorsese, the film maker, nor Nikos Kazantzakis, the novelist, had a desire to speculate on what actually happened between Jesus' death on the cross and Easter morning.

Nor did Matthew speculate about those hours. After Jesus' burial, he moves his readers directly to Easter morning, with its great flash of the appearance of the risen One.

Christ lives! His resurrection means light in our dark world, whether we can explain it adequately or not.

*Central Celebration.* The Resurrection is the central celebration in the church, though some Christians mistakenly think that it's Christmas. Actually, Christmas—the festival commemorating Christ's birth—did not come into practice until late in the fourth century. And then it was introduced to adapt and supplant Roman festivals in December. Some believers forget that had it not been for the Resurrection, there would be no interest in celebrating Christ's birth. The Resurrection created the community that eventually began honoring Christ's birth.

*Resurrected Body.* In the days when any country boy could stand in front of a blacksmith's shop and watch with fascinated eyes what happened there, something analogous to the resurrection of the body occurred. The smith would put a rusty, cold, dull piece of iron into the fire, and later take that identical piece of iron, now bright and glowing, out of the fire. Thus it will be with our bodies: they are laid in the grave, dead, heavy, earthly. But at the general resurrection this dead, heavy, earthly body shall arise living and glorious.—Spiros Zodhiates, *Illustrations of Bible Truths*

*Questions for Students on the Next Lesson.* 1. Why was John writing from Patmos? 2. Why did he write to the seven congregations? 3. What visions inspired John to write? 4. What are your feelings when you ponder the end of history? 5. What Christian symbols have deep meaning to you?

## TOPIC FOR YOUTH
### HAVE HOPE!

*Easter Gift.* St. James Presbyterian Church in Tarzana, California, was one of the structures damaged by the earthquake in January, 1994. It was so badly damaged that it was unsafe and unusable. The congregation of two hundred squeezed into a tiny fellowship hall for services, but pastors Ken Baker and Carl Horton knew that with the hot summer approaching, things would be difficult. The two checked into tent rentals, but that was too expensive (at $1,700 per week). They asked the congregation to pray and, throughout January and February, continued to believe that God would respond.

Christians on the other side of the country heard of the congregation's need. First Allegheny Presbyterian Church had burned to the ground in 1989. The church had bought a green and white circus tent and worshiped under it until their new church building was completed in 1990. The church then gave the tent to the presbytery, which used it as a rain shelter for children at the church camp.

Bart Williams, a member of Bakerstown Presbyterian Church and president of Parks Moving and Storage, arranged for a driver and the free transport of the tent to California. At 12:30 P.M., on Saturday, April 2, 1994 (the day before Easter), Steve Woods pulled up to the damaged church in his United Van Lines truck. Word spread throughout the area. For two hours Steve and volunteers labored to put up the tent, plant flowers, decorate the courtyard and lawn, and set up folding chairs. The next morning, Easter Sunday, the church worshiped and celebrated the joy of Easter.

*Die-hard Fans Remember.* In 1985, Saul Finkelstein, a baseball diehard, sat at the 457-foot mark of the outfield wall (the only piece of the wall that still remains) at old Forbes Field in Pittsburgh. He played a tape of the original broadcast of the seventh game of the 1960 World Series, the game in which Bill Mazeroski hit a game-winning homer. Ten years later, dozens of people again gathered with Finkelstein, reminiscing about that event that had been so special to them.

Nearly two thousand years ago, other "die-hard fans" went to a place that had special meaning for them to remember a man who had special meaning for them and an event that had shaped their lives. However, they discovered the event was not relegated just to the past. Jesus was alive, now and forever. He was present with them, giving them life, purpose, and hope. No longer would they sit at a tomb, just to remember for a while before going back to "real life." Now He was with them; He was their life.

*More than Science Fiction.* In November 1993 "The Death of Superman" became the best-selling comic book of all time. Over three million copies were sold. That issue described the demise of Superman, after an epic struggle, at the hands of an intergalactic bad guy named Doomsday. Superman's death, however, saved the city of Metropolis from destruction.

The publishers realized they could exceed the profits from this edition if they could produce a sequel in which Superman came back to life. They commissioned a "resurrection edition" to sell for $3.50. In this fictitious account of a resurrection, Superman is revived by what are called "healing baths" of the matrix chamber. He then returns and saves the earth from an evil cyborg. Interesting, perhaps, but it is all fiction, with make-believe "scientific" details.

The Easter story is different. Jesus is raised not by human design but by the Almighty. And He brings new birth to all who accept His living presence into their lives.

*Questions for Students on the Next Lesson.* 1. What does the word *revelation* mean, and what does this Bible book reveal? 2. Who wrote the Book of Revelation? 3. Where was it written? 4. What titles are applied to Jesus? 5. How is God described in Revelation?

# LESSON 6—APRIL 6

## COMMANDED TO WRITE

*Background Scripture:* Revelation 1:1-20
*Devotional Reading:* Revelation 21:1-3

### KING JAMES VERSION

REVELATION 1:4 John to the seven churches which are in Asia: Grace be unto you, and peace, from him which is, and which was, and which is to come; and from the seven Spirits which are before his throne;

5 And from Jesus Christ, who is the faithful witness, and the first begotten of the dead, and the prince of the kings of the earth. Unto him that loved us, and washed us from our sins in his own blood,

6 And hath made us kings and priests unto God and his Father; to him be glory and dominion for ever and ever. Amen.

7 Behold, he cometh with clouds; and every eye shall see him, and they also which pierced him: and all kindreds of the earth shall wail because of him. Even so, Amen.

8 I am Alpha and Omega, the beginning and the ending, saith the Lord, which is, and which was, and which is to come, the Almighty.

9 I John, who also am your brother, and companion in tribulation, and in the kingdom and patience of Jesus Christ, was in the isle that is called Patmos, for the word of God, and for the testimony of Jesus Christ.

10 I was in the Spirit on the Lord's day, and heard behind me a great voice, as of a trumpet,

11 Saying, I am Alpha and Omega, the first and the last: and, What thou seest, write in a book, and send it unto the seven churches which are in Asia; unto Ephesus, and unto Smyrna, and unto Pergamos, and unto Thyatira, and unto Sardis, and unto Philadelphia, and unto Laodicea.

12 And I turned to see the voice that spake with me. And being turned, I saw seven golden candlesticks;

13 And in the midst of the seven candlesticks one like unto the Son of man, clothed with a garment down to the foot, and girt about the paps with a golden girdle.

14 His head and his hairs were white like wool, as white as snow; and his eyes were as a flame of fire;

15 And his feet like unto fine brass, as if they burned in a furnace; and his voice as the sound of many waters.

### NEW REVISED STANDARD VERSION

REVELATION 1:4 John to the seven churches that are in Asia:

Grace to you and peace from him who is and who was and who is to come, and from the seven spirits who are before his throne, 5 And from Jesus Christ, the faithful witness, the firstborn of the dead, and the ruler of the kings of the earth.

To him who loves us and freed us from our sins by his blood, 6 and made us to be a kingdom, priests serving his God and Father, to him be glory and dominion forever and ever. Amen.

7 Look! He is coming with the clouds; every eye will see him, even those who pierced him; and on his account all the tribes of the earth will wail. So it is to be. Amen.

8 "I am the Alpha and the Omega," says the Lord God, who is and who was and who is to come, the Almighty.

9 I, John, your brother who share with you in Jesus the persecution and the kingdom and the patient endurance, was on the island called Patmos because of the word of God and the testimony of Jesus. 10 I was in the spirit on the Lord's day, and I heard behind me a loud voice like a trumpet 11 saying, "Write in a book what you see and send it to the seven churches, to Ephesus, to Smyrna, to Pergamum, to Thyatira, to Sardis, to Philadelphia, and to Laodicea."

12 Then I turned to see whose voice it was that spoke to me, and on turning I saw seven golden lampstands, 13 and in the midst of the lampstands I saw one like the Son of Man, clothed with a long robe and with a golden sash across his chest. 14 His head and his hair were white as white wool, white as snow; his eyes were like a flame of fire, 15 his feet were like burnished bronze, refined as in a furnace, and his voice was like the sound of many waters.

*KEY VERSE: Write in a book what you see and send it to the seven churches.* Revelation 1:11.

## HOME BIBLE READINGS

| Mar. | 31 | M. | John 1:1-8 | *Jesus, God's Eternal Word* |
|------|----|----|-----------|------------------------------|
| Apr. | 1 | T. | John 1:9-18 | *Jesus, the Light of the World* |
| Apr. | 2 | W. | Romans 6:1-11 | *We Live through Jesus Christ* |
| Apr. | 3 | T. | Colossians 1:15-23 | *Christ, the Head of All Things* |
| Apr. | 4 | F. | Psalm 100 | *Give Thanks to the Lord* |
| Apr. | 5 | S. | John 12:20-26 | *God Honors Those Who Serve Him* |
| Apr. | 6 | S. | Luke 2:25-33 | *A Savior for all People* |

## BACKGROUND

By the time the early church began, the Roman Empire sprawled across a good portion of the western world. The emperor could claim allegiances from Britain, Europe, North Africa, Asia Minor, and the Middle East. But claiming allegiance and holding it were not the same. Such a diverse collection of peoples, with such a variety of languages and customs, spread over such an enormous area, caused enormous governing problems.

Restless, conquered tribes in the outlying parts of the empire felt little loyalty to the despots in distant Rome. Therefore, rulers in the first century A.D. devised a scheme to try to knit together the empire, which was showing signs of coming apart. The scheme involved advancing a "civil religion" designed to assimilate everyone as part of the huge state. This cult demanded that the Roman emperor be worshiped by all citizens and subjects. Not to participate in the state shrine rituals was to be a traitor. Severe penalties were laid on anyone who refused to give the loyalty oath.

Naturally, Christians found themselves in a terrible bind. Most wanted to be law-abiding, but to declare that Caesar was lord meant pushing aside Jesus as the only Lord. So Christians who took their faith seriously suffered every time one of the emperors cracked down on dissidents. Harsh reprisals broke out under Emperor Domitian (A.D. 81—96), and hundreds of believers were rounded up and sent to concentration camps. Some were executed; others were fined. All lived under threats of arrest, loss of property, torture, imprisonment for life in the mines, and even death.

A man named John was banished to a desolate, rocky island called Patmos. John knew that fellow Christians on the mainland of Asia Minor were undergoing severe testing in seven urban centers. Undoubtedly John also realized that his own situation was perilous. Although many people had gone along with the emperor's edict requiring an annual visit to the imperial shrine, John knew that he had been called by the Lord to hold fast to his commitment to Christ as Lord. This great Christian also felt called to write to the seven congregations. He wanted to strengthen their resolve to endure in spite of severe persecution. John's letter is called Revelation.

## NOTES ON THE PRINTED TEXT

*John to the seven churches that are in Asia* (1:4). The letter properly began with a traditional opening formula, followed by a greeting and a blessing. The doxology was directed to God, who brought the great gifts of grace and peace to believers. He was described as timeless, using an adaptation of the name He made known to Moses: *who is and who was and who is to come* (1:4). According to one view, it was also seven angelic beings, who stood before God and were under His authority. Another view holds that the Holy Spirit is here represented under the picture of a sevenfold (or perfect) fullness.

Finally, the letter came from Christ, referred to through several unique titles that had great meaning for the persecuted believers. He was *the faithful witness* (1:5). The Greek word used here is *martus,* from which we get our English word *martyr.* Jesus faithfully testified about God at the cost of His own life. For those who witnessed before the Roman authorities at the cost of their lives, the resurrected Christ was described as the first born of the dead (1:5). As their sovereign Lord, Jesus was declared to be *the ruler of the kings of the earth* (1:5), even over the Roman emperors. Jewish writers often offered a doxology after mentioning God's name. John concluded with one praising Christ's redeeming death and resurrection. *Praise was given to him who loves us and freed us from our sins by his blood* (1:5).

When God finished leading Israel to Sinai, where the nation received the covenant, it became *a kingdom, priests, serving his God and Father* (1:6). In praise of Christ, John broke into a doxology. *To him be glory and dominion forever and ever. Amen* (1:6).

John called attention to the return of Christ by fusing together ideas from Daniel and Zechariah in his prophecy. Christ's coming would be visible to everyone. Even His enemies, those that pierced Him, would recognize Him and repent. *Look! He is coming with the clouds; every eye will see him, even those who pierced him; and on his account all the tribes of the earth will wail. So it is to be. Amen* (1:7).

God Himself assured His sovereignty and place in the world. God is the beginning and the end of all history. *"I am the Alpha and the Omega,"* says *the Lord God, who is and who was and who is to come, the Almighty* (1:8). The first and last letters in the Greek alphabet are alpha and omega. The Lord God Almighty will always be the beginning and the end of everything.

John explained to his readers what prompted him to write. He was also sharing in the persecution that his readers experienced. He had been banished from Ephesus to Patmos for his preaching. (A penal colony, Patmos was a small, volcanic island lying fifty miles off the Turkish coast.) *I, John, your brother who share with you in Jesus the persecution and the kingdom and the patient endurance, was on the island called Patmos because of the word of God and the testimony of Jesus* (1:9).

While at worship one Sunday, John heard *a loud voice like a trumpet* (1:10). The words were a command to write to seven churches in the Roman province of Asia Minor. Upon turning to see whose voice had commanded him to write, John saw the glorified Christ in the midst of seven golden lamp stands. The long robe denoted a man of rank, perhaps a priest. The golden sash differentiated Him from a working man. His eyes and His two-edged sword portrayed Jesus as the judge of all people.

## SUGGESTIONS TO TEACHERS

Starting this week, you will be teaching eight lessons based on Revelation. (Please note that the name is Revelation, not "the book of Revelations" as it is often referred to in the press.) Probably no part of the New Testament is more widely misunderstood, misinterpreted, and misused than this letter. Self-anointed prophets such as Luc Jouret, the Belgian physician who founded the Order of the Solar Temple, and David Koresh, the American who holed up in Waco, Texas, claimed that their study of Revelation led them to establish doomsday cults. Jouret and forty-eight followers died in fires in two Swiss villages, and another five perished in Quebec on the same day in 1994. Koresh and fanatic disciples were found dead after a shootout and fire in Waco in 1993. Others use Revelation to present bizarre teachings on radio and television.

Not surprisingly, many Christians shy away from Revelation because it is not always easy to understand. Much of its language is strange to our ears. A lot of the imagery is foreign to us. Yanked out of context, parts of Revelation may be unsettling when used to describe current events. But in spite of its difficulties, this book is indispensable. Appropriately, this great piece of Christian literature is truly God's final word in the collection of writings we call Holy Scripture. Let's get our bearings in this lesson.

1. SPECIAL CONCERN FOR THE SEVEN CHURCHES. John was writing to a group of congregations in what is now western Turkey. He knew that the members of these churches were under tremendous pressure to forsake the faith. The persecution was harsh and insidious.

Revelation was apparently a sort of "round-robin" letter, intended to be circulated among that cluster of churches. Throughout this missive, John lovingly pleaded with his readers to remain loyal to Christ as Lord.

2. SPIRIT'S COMMAND TO THE SEER OF PATMOS. Jesus, the living Lord, ordered John to write. It was not his idea to sit down and attempt to pen great literature. Rather, visions came to him from the Lord.

As the teacher, you may find it helpful to remind your students that Scripture is unlike all other writings. The Bible is God's revealed Word, not merely another piece of human opinion.

## TOPIC FOR ADULTS
### AVAILABLE FOR SERVICE

*Delivering the News.* During World War II, the French philosopher Gabriel Marcel worked for the Red Cross delivering telegrams. He didn't mind handing messages of good news to the recipients of telegrams. But he could not stand having to deliver reports of death, and he asked to hand out only hopeful words. When his superior told him that such a request was impossible, Marcel quit.

John, the Seer of Patmos, was ordered by Christ to bring messages to the churches that were not always pleasant and hopeful. In spite of his reluctance to bring such news, John did not flinch or quit. Christ's orders to us are not always easy to obey. Nevertheless, He provides the means and the strength, if we will only proceed by faith.

*From the King's Palace.* Samuel Rutherford, a saintly Scottish Christian, was thrown into prison for his faith. Enduring the freezing cold of his

Aberdeen jail cell, suffering hunger and illness, and cut off from his parishioners and friends, Rutherford continued to make himself available for
Christ's service in every way possible. He wrote many letters to the members of his congregation to encourage them to hold to their faith.

Interestingly, he never gave his address as the prison in Aberdeen, but
always labeled his letters "From my King's palace, Aberdeen." Rutherford
knew his king was Jesus, confident that Jesus Christ ruled all earthly
authorities. Certain that he was constantly in the presence and keeping of
Jesus, Rutherford could claim that even the damp, stone walls of Aberdeen
prison constituted the palace of King Jesus.

*Apt Reply.* Pastors calling on their parishioners sometimes receive
unusual answers to their questions. Alexander Whyte, minister of St.
George's Church, Edinburgh, once came to the bedside of a devout old
Christian elder. Whyte inquired, "How are you keeping, Donald?"

The old gentleman calmly replied, "Aye, Doctor, I am not keeping. I am
kept."

John of Patmos could testify the same. Being with Christ means we are
"kept."

*Questions for Students on the Next Lesson.* 1. What was happening to the
Christians in Smyrna that prompted John of Patmos to write to them?
2. How would you describe the situation in the church at Pergamum? 3.
What was John's advice to the congregation at Pergamum? 4. What did
John have to say to the believers at Smyrna? 5. What do you think your
church has in common with these two churches?

## TOPIC FOR YOUTH
### FOLLOWING INSTRUCTIONS

*Commanded to Write.* During the height of the Persian Gulf War in 1990,
Karen Fionella was assigned by her teacher to write a letter addressed to
"Any Soldier or Sailor." The eleven-year-old at Reservoir Middle School in
Newport News, Virginia, wrote her letter and turned it in to her teacher,
expecting it to go to a stranger. She simply introduced herself and offered
to write back if the soldier or sailor was interested.

One month later, Karen's letter was given to the chief executive officer of
the 10th Transportation Battalion, Major Charles Fionella, Karen's father.
The chance that he would be given the letter was 1 in 250,000. The major
was happily surprised . . . and mystified.

John was also commanded to write a letter. However, there was no mystery whatsoever as to the intent, the destination, and the purpose of his
message. John followed instructions from the risen Lord Himself.

*Symbol of Authority.* When a new pope is elected, one of the first acts of
the dean of the college of cardinals is to smash, with a chisel and a hammer, the fisherman's ring worn by the previous pope. The carved gold ring
that depicts Peter in a fishing boat is the symbol of papal authority, and its
destruction signifies the end of a papal reign. A new ring will be given to
the new pope.

No sign of authority was required when John saw the glorified Christ.
John immediately knew that Jesus had the necessary authority to issue the
command to write to the churches. You, too, must understand that the risen

and glorified Christ has the same authority and power over you. Like John, you must follow His commands.

*Carries the Authority.* The referee in a soccer game carries absolute authority over the game, an authority that begins the moment he or she enters the field of play. The referee has power over the game when the ball is out of play or when play has been suspended. The individual in black keeps the time, and can suspend or terminate the game. Furthermore, the referee can penalize a player for misconduct.

As responsible and authoritative as the referee of a soccer match is, John recognized a far greater authority. There is an authority with the power to judge all peoples and even terminate world history. When ordered to write, John complied and followed the instructions of this authority without question. We also need to recognize the authority that the glorified Christ commands. Like John, we must follow the Almighty's instructions.

*Questions for Students on the Next Lesson.* 1. Where were Smyrna and Pergamum? 2. What did John mean by writing "the angel of the church at Smyrna"? 3. What were "the synagogue of Satan" and "Satan's throne"? 4. Are the descendants of the Nicolaitans alive today? 5. Why are the letters to the seven churches important today?

# LESSON 7—APRIL 13

## TO SMYRNA AND PERGAMUM

*Background Scripture:* Revelation 2:8-17
*Devotional Reading:* I Corinthians 8:1-13

### KING JAMES VERSION

REVELATION 2:8 And unto the angel of the church in Smyrna write; These things saith the first and the last, which was dead, and is alive;

9 I know thy works and tribulation, and poverty, (but thou art rich) and I know the blasphemy of them which say they are Jews, and are not, but are the synagogue of Satan.

10 Fear none of those things which thou shalt suffer: behold, the devil shall cast some of you into prison, that ye may be tried; and ye shall have tribulation ten days: be thou faithful unto death, and I will give thee a crown of life.

11 He that hath an ear, let him hear what the Spirit saith unto the churches; He that overcometh shall not be hurt of the second death.

12 And to the angel of the church in Pergamos write; These things saith he which hath the sharp sword with two edges;

13 I know thy works, and where thou dwellest, even where Satan's seat is: and thou holdest fast my name, and hast not denied my faith, even in those days wherein Antipas was my faithful martyr, who was slain among you, where Satan dwelleth.

14 But I have a few things against thee, because thou hast there them that hold the doctrine of Balaam, who taught Balac to cast a stumblingblock before the children of Israel, to eat things sacrificed unto idols, and to commit fornication.

15 So hast thou also them that hold the doctrine of the Nicolaitanes, which thing I hate.

16 Repent; or else I will come unto thee quickly, and will fight against them with the sword of my mouth.

17 He that hath an ear, let him hear what the Spirit saith unto the churches; To him that overcometh will I give to eat of the hidden manna, and will give him a white stone, and in the stone a new name written, which no man knoweth saving he that receiveth it.

### NEW REVISED STANDARD VERSION

REVELATION 2:8 "And to the angel of the church in Smyrna write: These are the words of the first and the last, who was dead and came to life:

9 "I know your affliction and your poverty, even though you are rich. I know the slander on the part of those who say that they are Jews and are not, but are a synagogue of Satan. 10 Do not fear what you are about to suffer. Beware, the devil is about to throw some of you into prison so that you may be tested, and for ten days you will have affliction. Be faithful until death, and I will give you the crown of life. 11 Let anyone who has an ear listen to what the Spirit is saying to the churches. Whoever conquers will not be harmed by the second death.

12 "And to the angel of the church in Pergamum write: These are the words of him who has the sharp two-edged sword:

13 "I know where you are living, where Satan's throne is. Yet you are holding fast to my name, and you did not deny your faith in me even in the days of Antipas my witness, my faithful one, who was killed among you, where Satan lives. 14 But I have a few things against you: you have some there who hold to the teaching of Balaam, who taught Balak to put a stumbling block before the people of Israel, so that they would eat food sacrificed to idols and practice fornication. 15 So you also have some who hold to the teaching of the Nicolaitans. 16 Repent then. If not, I will come to you soon and make war against them with the sword of my mouth. 17 Let anyone who has an ear listen to what the Spirit is saying to the churches. To everyone who conquers I will give some of the hidden manna, and I will give a white stone, and on the white stone is written a new name that no one knows except the one who receives it.

*KEY VERSE: Be faithful until death, and I will give you the crown of life.* Revelation 2:10b.

## HOME BIBLE READINGS

| | | | | |
|---|---|---|---|---|
| Apr. | 7 | M. | Acts 3:17-26 | Repent and Return to God |
| Apr. | 8 | T. | Colossians 1:9-14 | Pray for Spiritual Wisdom |
| Apr. | 9 | W. | I John 5:1-5 | Overcome by Faith |
| Apr. | 10 | T. | I John 5:6-12 | Have Faith in Jesus Christ |
| Apr. | 11 | F. | Hebrews 3:1-6 | Hold Firm Your Hope |
| Apr. | 12 | S. | Proverbs 4:1-9 | Be Wise in the Lord |
| Apr. | 13 | S. | Proverbs 28:20-28 | Be Faithful and Righteous |

## BACKGROUND

Two of the seven congregations addressed in Revelation were in the cities of Smyrna and Pergamum. John was perhaps thinking of how a traveler would make a circuit to visit the seven churches. He might possibly start in the great seaport of Ephesus, then move up the coast to Smyrna and go next to Pergamum. Maybe John himself had made the trip to each of the seven churches in this way.

Smyrna was located thirty-five miles north of Ephesus. Known for its splendid paved streets, and nicknamed "the ornament of Asia," it was situated at the end of a major trade route through the Hermus Valley past Sardis. It was also a prosperous seaport. An old ally of Rome, boasting a temple to Tiberias, Livia, and the Senate, it was the first city in Asia to erect a temple for imperial worship. Possibly Paul established a church there on one of his missionary journeys through western Asia Minor.

Pergamum was the capital of the Roman province of Asia and the center for Rome's imperial cult. It lay fifteen miles inland and two miles north of the Caicus River. On its acropolis, an eight hundred foot hill, were many temples dedicated to various deities. Also on the hill were a library, palace, arsenal, theater, and three gymnasiums.

John's letter to the Christians in Smyrna was filled with praise and sympathy. He commended them for maintaining a vital congregation in the face of hardship and persecution. The story of the Smyrna church was a heroic tale of standing firm in the faith in spite of experiencing more suffering than any of the other seven churches. These believers had been subjected to constant persecution. They had little in the way of money or possessions and probably came from the lower class. John reminded them that in their material poverty, they would receive lavish spiritual riches because of their faith.

Remembering that Pergamum was the proud, royal, Roman capital of the province, John used a symbol of authority that had great meaning to its citizens: a sword (the two-edged Roman army sword, not the Oriental scimitar or the Greek cutting sword). Such a weapon stood for the official authority of Rome, which was vested in the Roman proconsul. He wielded the power of life and death over those in the city.

John assured his readers that Jesus Christ held even greater authority. The emperor and his minions in Pergamum were far inferior to the victorious Christ.

## NOTES ON THE PRINTED TEXT

*And to the angel of the church in Smyrna write: These are the words of the first and the last, who was dead and came to life* (2:8). The message to the angel of the church in Smyrna was from the glorified Christ, who died and came to life again.

Christians were facing persecution, imprisonment, and death. *I know your affliction and your poverty, even though you are rich. I know the slander on the part of those who say that they are Jews and are not, but are a synagogue of Satan* (2:9). The persecution was hostile. Fanatics from a synagogue were making slanderous accusations and attacking Christians. As a result, they proved to be more interested in the evil one than in the Messiah.

John encouraged the believers not to fear persecution but to endure it. *Do not fear what you are about to suffer* (2:10). He also warned that the campaign against them would intensify. The difficulties would span a short amount of time—only ten days (perhaps numerically symbolizing a brief period—but they would be intense. *Do not fear what you are about to suffer. Beware, the devil is about to throw some of you into prison so that you may be tested, and for ten days you will have affliction* (2:10). The prison was simply a place of detention where the Christian would await trial. Here, the believer was called to be faithful. The trial was a test involving a life-or-death decision. The faithful believer must be prepared to die for the faith. John reassured them that their loyalty would be rewarded. Just as the victor received a laurel wreath at the games, the faithful believer would receive glory. *Be faithful unto death, and I will give you the crown of life* (2:10).

John exhorted the believers to hear the message of the Spirit: they would not be hurt by the second death. While the believer might be martyred, he or she was not doomed to suffer the eternal judgment of God. The faithful would experience resurrection to life. *Let anyone who has an ear listen to what the Spirit is saying to the churches. Whoever conquers will not be harmed by the second death* (2:11).

*And to the angel of the church in Pergamum write: These are the words of him who has the sharp two-edged sword* (2:12). The one who carried the two-edged sword, the glorified Christ, proclaimed specific words of judgment. Knowing the city, John was perhaps referring to the acropolis with its enormous altar to Zeus and its temple to Asclepios, whose emblem was the serpent. Perhaps the entire hill with its temples suggested a mountain of gods that might be called a throne. Whatever the case, John was convinced it was a center of evil that threatened absolute allegiance to God.

While commended for its faithfulness, the church was called to repent, since division had been created by false teachings. *Some of you hold to the teaching of Balaam, who taught Balak to put a stumbling block before the people of Israel, so that they would eat food sacrificed to idols and practice fornication. So you also have some who hold to the teaching of the Nicolaitans* (2:14, 15). The controversy apparently centered around two things: food sacrificed to idols, and immoral sexual relations. The members were condemned for their lapses and were called to repent or suffer the consequences of God's judgment. The rest of the congregation was urged not to tolerate these beliefs and practices. *Repent then. If not, I will come to you soon and make war against them with the sword of my mouth* (2:16).

Christ promised blessings and a renewed character for those who responded to the Spirit. *To everyone who conquers I will give some of the hidden manna, and I will give a white stone, and on the white stone is written a new name that no one knows except the one who receives it* (2:17). Christians who kept the faith would eat the bread of heaven and be sustained by the Lord. Perhaps the white stone referred to acquittal before God. In the courts of those days, jurors displayed a white stone to indicate innocence or a black stone to indicate guilt. It also might refer to admission to the Lord's presence (a small stone was an admission ticket). The stone with a name upon it (either the believer's or, more likely, Christ's) signified the follower's new relationship with the Lord.

## SUGGESTIONS TO TEACHERS

Suppose John of Patmos were to write a letter to your church. What would he say? Would he commend your congregation for its faithfulness to the Gospel? Or would he write some reproving words about your wavering commitment?

Focus attention on the first two churches in this series, Smyrna and Pergamum. Perhaps like the Christian group at Smyrna, your church is strapped for funds. Your congregation also may be fighting an uphill battle to maintain enough members in the midst of a changing community and a secular culture.

Perhaps you can identify with Pergamum, as well. Your church may have a notable past and rich traditions in your community. Perhaps your members also feel the pressure to conform to the culture at large. To make this class session more pertinent, do a case study of these two churches described in the second chapter of Revelation.

1. THE SUFFERING CHURCH. This title would describe the church in Smyrna. Delve into the difficulties hinted at in Revelation. The Christians in that church suffered slander, for instance. What forms of slander do you or your students ever receive for your faith? If we never suffer opposition or persecution, are we truly reflecting the life of Jesus Christ in the world?

Christians in Smyrna did not have an easy time financially. They lacked money, but they didn't use their poverty as an excuse. Nor did they feel that becoming well-off was the main goal in life. How does your class feel about the ways money is used in your church and community?

Christians in Smyrna knew they were being tested, constantly tempted to compromise their faith. Persecution threatened, but the believers clung to Christ's promises and stood firm. Do we do the same?

2. THE STRAYING CHURCH. The church at Pergamum was slipping away from the faith. It had been sliding back into old religious rituals, listening to false teachers. Remind your students that conversion isn't just a once-and-done-with matter. Unless we are continually renewed by the Spirit and maintain a vigilant attention to serving Christ, we, like the Pergamum church people, easily drift away from the Lord.

Be sure to lift up the magnificent promise in Revelation 2:17. Christians are nourished by "hidden manna" and those who remain steadfast in their faith are assured joy and victory.

## TOPIC FOR ADULTS
### CALLED TO BE FAITHFUL

*The Tribe of Jesus.* David Dobler, moderator of the 1993 Presbyterian General Assembly, arrived at a Sudanese village that had been burned three times in five years because of war. Seeing that some of the simple thatched huts had a cross at the top, he asked, "What does that mean?" His African companion responded: "The people who live there belong to the tribe of Jesus; they will share whatever they have." He was told that from 100 to 200 war refugees cross the river weekly from Ethiopia, weary and hungry, looking for "the sign of the tribe of Jesus," meaning food and shelter.—Rev. Doyle Snyder.

*Dying for Life.* The late Alan Paton was a long-time foe of apartheid in South Africa. The famous author of novels set in his troubled home country, Paton was a committed Christian. Years before the winds of change came to South Africa, ending the terrible segregation laws and repressive police practices, Paton was faithful to the biblical dream of a new order in society.

Paton did not live to see the end of apartheid, but he remained faithful to the hope fostered by Christ. Paton acknowledged that Christians in South Africa would have to endure hatred and opposition while trying to bring about a new order of society. "While we are building it, we are going to be hated, cursed, stoned, shot at, perhaps even killed, by some of the very people for whom we are building it." But Paton reiterated that he was called to be faithful to Christ and summoned others to remember the call.

*Called in Calcutta.* A few years ago, I was invited to Calcutta to meet Mother Teresa. I had heard of this dedicated nun's service in the slums of one of India's dirtiest and most crowded cities. I was also aware of the work of her Missionary Order of the Sisters of Charity in sixty-seven countries. However, seeing her and her sisters ministering to the sick and dying was an unforgettable experience.

In centuries to come few will remember the Saddam Husseins and others trying to be Number One in our day. But countless people around the world will remember this tiny, stooped servant of Christ. On the wall of the stairway leading to the sisters' chapel is a hand-lettered sign reading, "Let each sister see Jesus Christ in the person of the poor; the more repugnant the work or the person, the greater also must be her faith, love, and cheerful devotion in ministering to the Lord in this distressing disguise."

*Questions for Students on the Next Lesson.* 1. What was taking place in the lives of Christians in Thyatira? 2. What did John say to this congregation? 3. Who was Jezebel in the Old Testament, and why was she mentioned in the message to Thyatira? 4. In what situations do you find it most difficult to avoid compromising your values in the name of tolerance? 5. How has your faith helped you hold fast to doctrinal and moral integrity?

## TOPIC FOR YOUTH
### GOOD, BUT ROOM TO GROW

*One Final Chance.* One fourteen-year-old boy has his entire town (West Yorkshire, England) against him. For six years this young man has been stealing. Beginning at age eight, he has been arrested eighty-eight times and convicted of 130 crimes, all committed within two miles of his home. Merchants have had to buy steel shutters and install costly surveillance equipment, mirrors, and alarm systems in order to maintain their insurance. After each arrest, the young man has promised to reform. However, becoming bored and having little money, he has repeatedly returned to crime.

Recently, he was given one final chance to change and start over. The judge has reminded the boy that while children younger than fifteen cannot be locked up in jail, he is now nearly fifteen. In addition, a law passed in January 1995 will make it possible to imprison offenders at age twelve. The judge warned him to behave, or else. The boy promised to go straight.

The risen Christ has called His followers to hold fast to His name. Their commitment must be sure, not like this boy's tentative attempts at reform.

*Deceived.* Kathy Andrade, a spirited young woman, was brought up in a religious family. At a certain age, however, she began to investigate her religious options. This included speaking with a rabbi and attending Bible study classes. The Martinez, California, girl was invited by Paul Fatta to come to Waco, Texas, and learn about the seven seals from David Koresh and his Branch Davidians. She decided to attend meetings there for five weeks. She never returned.

For two years Kathy listened to Koresh's talks. She persuaded her sister Jennifer to join her. Her mother, Isabel, journeyed several times to Waco in an attempt to bring Kathy and her sister home. While the women were thin, they did not appear to be brainwashed. She continued calling every week, urging them to forsake Koresh's grip of false teaching. Her efforts failed. The girls died in the fiery siege in May 1993.

John urged his readers to be on guard against false gods and false teaching. Heed his warning and hold fast to Jesus' name.

*New Beginning.* Leo Durocher, manager of the old New York Giants, gave a weeping rookie named Willie Mays some support after Mays had gotten on base only one time out of sixteen chances in his major-league debut. He told Mays, "Tomorrow's another day, kid. And you're going to be playing center field tomorrow." Mays got a new start, and he went on to become one of baseball's greats, a Hall of Famer.

John reminded his readers that the Lord offers His people a new beginning, too. The Lord has the same kind of trust in us that Durocher had in Mays. Don't waste your opportunities.

*Questions for Students on the Next Lesson.* 1. Where was Thyatira? 2. What charge was leveled against the congregation? 3. Would John's criticism of Thyatira be valid if applied to young people today? Why, or why not? 4. What was "the morning star"? 5. What would "He who is the first and the last" say today to the churches in North America?

# LESSON 8—APRIL 20

## *TO THYATIRA*

*Background Scripture:* Revelation 2:18-29
*Devotional Reading:* Romans 2:1-11

KING JAMES VERSION

REVELATION 2:18 And unto the angel of the church in Thyatira write; These things saith the Son of God, who hath his eyes like unto a flame of fire, and his feet are like fine brass;

19 I know thy works, and charity, and service, and faith, and thy patience, and thy works; and the last to be more than the first.

20 Notwithstanding I have a few things against thee, because thou sufferest that woman Jezebel, which calleth herself a prophetess, to teach and to seduce my servants to commit fornication, and to eat things sacrificed unto idols.

21 And I gave her space to repent of her fornication; and she repented not.

22 Behold, I will cast her into a bed, and them that commit adultery with her into great tribulation, except they repent of their deeds.

23 And I will kill her children with death; and all the churches shall know that I am he which searcheth the reins and hearts: and I will give unto every one of you according to your works.

24 But unto you I say, and unto the rest in Thyatira, as many as have not this doctrine, and which have not known the depths of Satan, as they speak; I will put upon you none other burden.

25 But that which ye have already hold fast till I come.

26 And he that overcometh, and keepeth my works unto the end, to him will I give power over the nations:

27 And he shall rule them with a rod of iron; as the vessels of a potter shall they be broken to shivers: even as I received of my Father.

28 And I will give him the morning star.

29 He that hath an ear, let him hear what the Spirit saith unto the churches.

NEW REVISED STANDARD VERSION

REVELATION 2:18 "And to the angel of the church in Thyatira write: These are the words of the Son of God, who has eyes like a flame of fire, and whose feet are like burnished bronze:

19 "I know your works—your love, faith, service, and patient endurance. I know that your last works are greater than the first. 20 But I have this against you: you tolerate that woman Jezebel, who calls herself a prophet and is teaching and beguiling my servants to practice fornication and to eat food sacrificed to idols. 21 I gave her time to repent, but she refuses to repent of her fornication. 22 Beware, I am throwing her on a bed, and those who commit adultery with her I am throwing into great distress, unless they repent of her doings; 23 and I will strike her children dead. And all the churches will know that I am the one who searches minds and hearts, and I will give to each of you as your works deserve. 24 But to the rest of you in Thyatira, who do not hold this teaching, who have not learned what some call 'the deep things of Satan,' to you I say, I do not lay on you any other burden; 25 only hold fast to what you have until I come. 26 To everyone who conquers and continues to do my works to the end, I will give authority over the nations; 27 to rule them with an iron rod, as when clay pots are shattered—28 even as I also received authority from my Father. To the one who conquers I will also give the morning star. 29 Let anyone who has an ear to listen to what the Spirit is saying to the churches.

KEY VERSE: *All the churches will know that I am the one who searches minds and hearts, and I will give to each of you as your works deserve.* Revelation 2:23b.

## HOME BIBLE READINGS

| | | | | |
|---|---|---|---|---|
| Apr. | 14 | M. | Romans 8:26-30 | *God Searches Our Hearts* |
| Apr. | 15 | T. | Romans 2:1-11 | *God Shows No Partiality* |
| Apr. | 16 | W. | Psalm 62:8-12 | *God Rewards According to Works* |
| Apr. | 17 | T. | II Peter 2:4-10 | *God Rescues the Godly from Trial* |
| Apr. | 18 | F. | Galatians 5:1-14 | *Hold Fast to Freedom in Christ* |
| Apr. | 19 | S. | Philippians 4:1-9 | *Rejoice in the Lord* |
| Apr. | 20 | S. | II Corinthians 13:5-10 | *Test Your Faith* |

## BACKGROUND

If you were traveling on a circuit among leading cities in western Asia Minor in the first century A.D., after leaving Smyrna and Pergamum you would have proceeded about thirty-five miles to the next principle center of population, the city of Thyatira. Although not as important as some of the other cities, Thyatira was renowned for its guilds of fine craftsmen. Textiles and metal work, in particular, gave the place a good reputation and brought it great wealth. Thyatira's polished brass, burnished bronze, and colorful dyed cloth were highly prized.

The city apparently housed a large Jewish community. Like many Gentiles, Lydia, who is mentioned in Acts 16:14, was attracted to the high morals of Judaism and was drawn to Jewish worship. Later, when this godly woman was in Philippi, she and a group of other women became the nucleus of the Christian church in Philippi. Her occupation, "a dealer in purple cloth," also reflected one of the main industries of Thyatira.

The city of Thyatira might not have been as important as some of the other major metropolitan centers in Asia Minor, but its church was a vital Christian community. Although we don't know who first established the believers there, some think that one or several of Paul's colleagues—or even the great missionary apostle himself—may have been instrumental in founding the congregation.

## NOTES ON THE PRINTED TEXT

*I know your works—your love, faith, service, and patient endurance. I know that your last works are greater than the first* (2:19). The church was generously praised for its works. The people there had been loving and filled with works of service.

However, the church did have one fault. *But I have this against you: you tolerate that woman Jezebel, who calls herself a prophet and is teaching and beguiling my servants to practice fornication and to eat food sacrificed to idols* (2:20). While the whole church did not accept Jezebel and her small group's sexual immorality and sacrificial meals, they did tolerate her. They let this female leader and her followers remain in the fellowship, even though she had been previously warned by John to repent. *I gave her time to repent, but she refuses to repent of her fornication* (2:21). She rejected John's call and continued to persuade the church to practice idolatry.

*Beware, I am throwing her on a bed, and those who commit adultery with her I am throwing into great distress, unless they repent of her doings; and I will strike her children dead* (2:22, 23). John promised that judgment would come. Christ would deal harshly with the offender and her immoral followers, most likely by an inflicted illness. (To "throw on a bed" was an expression for becoming ill.)

God's purpose in disciplining the church was to teach it and restore it. All the believers needed to remember His power. *And all the churches will know that I am the one who searches minds and hearts, and I will give to each of you as your works deserve* (2:23).

John cautioned the faithful within the church to hold fast to their doctrinal and moral integrity until Christ's return. He called them to ignore the false teaching of the prophetess. *But to the rest of you in Thyatira, who do not hold this teaching, who have not learned what some call 'the deep things of Satan,' to you I say, I do not lay on you any other burden; only hold fast to what you have until I come* (2:24, 25).

Christ promised that on the basis of His authority the faithful believers who listened to the Spirit would receive authority over the nations. Those who faithfully adhered to His works and words (they were referred to as conquerors) would exercise authority such as Christ received from God. *To everyone who conquers and continues to do my works to the end, I will give authority over the nations; to rule them with an iron rod, as when clay pots are shattered—even as I also received authority from my Father* (2:26-28).

In addition, Christ assured the believers of full participation in His kingdom. He offered His presence as a sign of His sovereignty and rule. The morning star was a symbol of victory and sovereignty, and it likely refers to Christ. Yet it also stands as a reassurance for believers of their glory in His kingdom. *To the one who conquers I will also give the morning star* (2:28).

## SUGGESTIONS TO TEACHERS

Although about ninety percent of Americans and Canadians profess faith in God, and the overwhelming number of these claim to be Christians, certain not-so-orthodox beliefs are also affirmed. For example, according to a recent Gallup poll, twenty-seven percent of respondents said that they believe in reincarnation and twenty-eight percent say it is possible to have contact with the dead. Strange teachings permeate the North American religious scene, along with the true biblical faith. Your lesson today, based on John's letter to the church at Thyatira, has up-to-the-minute relevance.

1. PATIENT IN SERVING. The congregation in Thyatira had its good points. For instance, it had a reputation for "love, faith, service, and patient endurance" (Rev. 2:19). What is your church chiefly noted for in your community? Have you ever surveyed non-church members in the vicinity of your church to learn their impressions?

2. PERMISSIVE TOWARD SIN AND IMMORALITY. "Oh no, our church never talks about sin," a deacon cheerfully assured a potential church member. The deacon added, "I guess we feel that's kind of puritanical and old-fashioned."

How do your students react to this deacon's claims? The lines between right and wrong have become so blurred in our generation that we may rarely think in terms of "sin" anymore. Anything we want to do is okay—as long as we feel all right about it. Feelings have become the judge, not the Lord. Especially in the matter of sexual behavior, society assures us that sensual pleasure is the main aim in life. How shall we respond, we who serve the righteous Lord?

3. PRINCIPLED IN SOUNDNESS. The Thyatira church was called to repudiate a teacher (called "Jezebel" by John of Patmos) who advocated immoral practices. What false teachings and immoral practices threaten to mislead believers today?

4. PROTECTED BY THE SAVIOR. We need not rely on our own willpower or human wisdom to stand up to the powerful temptations besetting us. We have Christ with us to stabilize and strengthen us. He is our authority, and He authorizes us to confront the Jezebels in our midst. With Christ, we will conquer.

## TOPIC FOR ADULTS
### HOLD TO SOUND TEACHING!

*Feeding the Cuckoo.* The cuckoo is a rather common bird in England. I am told that it never builds a nest of its own. When it's ready to lay an egg, the cuckoo finds an unattended nest with eggs in it. Then the cuckoo flies into the nest, hurriedly lays its egg among the other bird's eggs and flies off. That's all the parenting a cuckoo does!

It might be a thrush nest. The mother thrush returns and doesn't notice that there's an additional egg in her nest, even though the cuckoo's egg is much bigger than her own eggs. She sits on all the eggs until they hatch. The baby cuckoo will be three or four times the size of the baby thrushes. But it doesn't matter. If it's in the thrush's nest, she considers it hers. Being a good mother, she brings worms back to the nest. Four tiny thrush mouths open up and peep—and one giant cuckoo mouth. Guess who gets the worms. The cuckoo gets bigger and bigger and the baby thrushes get smaller and smaller.

I'm told that it's fairly easy to find a baby cuckoo in a nest. Simply walk along and look for dead baby thrushes on the ground. The cuckoo, as it grows bigger, throws them out, one by one. Mother thrush ends up feeding a cuckoo that's three times as big as herself.

Sin, once it gets into our lives, has a way of taking over, growing larger and larger and sometimes consuming us. That which we feed will grow.— Alex Gondola

*Holding to Sound Teaching.* Not only is prayer useful in fighting off demons, but also in sidestepping the dinosaurs that wish to drag us down into the tar pits of irrelevance. Under the guidance of the Holy Spirit we need inspired and visionary prayers to lead us. Too many of our prayers seem to restrict us to the status quo, missing our need to minister to an increasingly hostile and hurting world undergoing rapid change.

As William Easum has recently written in his provocative book *Dancing with Dinosaurs,* "We can't afford to be insensitive to the accelerated pace of change around us; otherwise we are drawn dangerously close to 'dancing with dinosaurs' before tar pits of doom. Churches and theological institutions with a slow pace of change are no longer adequate in a fast-changing world. Structures designed to coordinate ministry are unable to cause innovation. Ministries that worked in the industrial society no longer meet the spiritual needs of people in an informational society. In an age of computers, we cannot express truth in the language of a chariot age. The time has come for new wineskins."

Some of the assumptions that we need to make as Christians in order to succeed, according to Easum, are as follows:

1. North America is the new mission field.

2. Society will become increasingly hostile toward Christianity in the twenty-first century.

3. The distinction between clergy and laity will disappear in the twenty-first century.

4. If churches only improve what they have been doing, they will die.

5. The best way to fail today is to improve yesterday's successes.

6. Bureaucracies and traditional practices are the major cause of the decline of most denominations in North America.

7. Traditional churches that thrive in the twenty-first century will initiate radical changes before the year 2001.

Easum exhorts us to distinguish between essential beliefs that need to be maintained and non-essential practices that we should shed. Haven't we already witnessed church buildings turned into furniture stores, restaurants, antique shops, and townhouses? Do we need further evidence to sound the alarm? Dinosaurland may already be upon us as we cling to "security," seeking institutional guarantees that can't be made. We fail to remember that God's grace is our only guarantee in life.—Carnegie Samuel Calian, *Panorama,* Pittsburgh Theological Seminary, December, 1994.

*Neglecting Sound Teaching.* One of the effects of modern liberal Protestantism has been gradually to turn religion into poetry and therapy, to make truth vaguer and vaguer and more and more relative, to banish intellectual distinctions, to depend on feeling instead of thought, and to come to believe that God has no real power, that he cannot communicate with us, cannot reveal himself to us, indeed has not done so and that religion is our own sweet invention.—Flannery O'Connor, *The Habits of Being.*

*Questions for Students on the Next Lesson.* 1. What did John of Patmos have to say to the church in Philadelphia? 2. What were John's memorable terms about the Laodicean congregation? 3. In what ways is your congregation similar to these two churches? 4. What do you find to be the greatest difficulties facing the church in North America in our time? 5. What are the main strengths and weaknesses of your congregation?

TOPIC FOR YOUTH
*HOLD ON!*

*Fatal Mistake.* Fourteen-year-old Matilda Crabtree and her friend jumped out of a closet and shouted "Boo!" at about 1:00 a.m. on a Sunday morning in 1994. Matilda was shot and killed by her own startled father.

Matilda and her friend were supposed to spend the night at the friend's home. However, they decided to return to the Crabtree home because Matilda's parents were away. Her parents, though, returned early, and the girls decided to play a joke.

Robert Crabtree walked into the house, heard the girls making noises, and assumed that someone had broken into his home—just as the girls had hoped he would. The father got his .357 pistol, loaded it with hollow-point bullets, and investigated. When the girls jumped at him, he fired. He shot Matilda in the neck. She died saying, "I love you, Daddy."

Dire consequences can follow silly actions. In Revelation, John foresaw the terrible repercussions of tolerating an evil group within the fellowship. The "innocent fun" in Thyatira would have disastrous results.

*Serve Others.* The youth group at Mendon Presbyterian Church of Mendon, New York, has developed a series of projects to help the homeless in the Rochester area. Along with collecting canned goods, the youth prepare and serve meals. They pick apples and make applesauce. They also bake cookies. The group raises money to provide gifts of toiletries and personal items for the homeless.

In addition to their ministry to the homeless, the young people raise money for Camp Good Days and Special Times, a local camp for children who have cancer. They make special gifts for nursing homes and volunteer their services to the church.

Here is a group of young people that resembles the church of Thyatira. They make their church known by their service, faith, and love. What is your church doing for needy people in your area?

*Enough Is Enough.* Before his death, actor Bing Crosby questioned movie and television producers on what seemed to be so much immorality in the media. He asked them what they thought they were doing to the nation's youth by depicting so much immoral behavior. They responded that they were simply showing life as it was. He replied that they were incorrect. They were showing life as it would be. Ultimately, the children would suffer.

Crosby called the media to task. He urged them not to ignore traditional morality in the quest for profit. John, like Crosby, knew that certain people do not want to give up their immorality; it would cost them too dearly. Yet John called his church not to be cowardly, but to say enough is enough. Act to oppose immorality.

*Questions for Students on the Next Lesson.* 1. Where were Philadelphia and Laodicea? 2. What was "the key of David"? 3. What rewards did John hold before the church of Philadelphia? Were those rewards worth pursuing? 4. Why were lukewarm believers so harshly criticized? 5. Is a little faith better than none at all?

# LESSON 9—APRIL 27

## TO PHILADELPHIA AND LAODICEA

*Background Scripture:* Revelation 3:7-22
*Devotional Reading:* II Peter 2:4-10

### KING JAMES VERSION

REVELATION 3:7 And to the angel of the church in Philadelphia write; These things saith he that is holy, he that is true, he that hath the key of David, he that openeth, and no man shutteth; and shutteth, and no man openeth;

8 I know thy works: behold, I have set before thee an open door, and no man can shut it; for thou hast a little strength, and hast kept my word, and hast not denied my name.

9 Behold, I will make them of the synagogue of Satan, which say they are Jews, and are not, but do lie; behold, I will make them to come and worship before thy feet, and to know that I have loved thee.

10 Because thou hast kept the word of my patience, I also will keep thee from the hour of temptation, which shall come upon all the world, to try them that dwell upon the earth.

15 I know thy works, that thou art neither cold nor hot: I would thou wert cold or hot.

16 So then because thou art lukewarm, and neither cold nor hot, I will spue thee out of my mouth.

17 Because thou sayest, I am rich, and increased with goods, and have need of nothing; and knowest not that thou art wretched, and miserable, and poor, and blind, and naked:

18 I counsel thee to buy of me gold tried in the fire, that thou mayest be rich; and white raiment, that thou mayest be clothed, and that the shame of thy nakedness do not appear; and anoint thine eyes with eye-salve, that thou mayest see.

19 As many as I love, I rebuke and chasten: be zealous therefore, and repent.

20 Behold, I stand at the door, and knock: if any man hear my voice, and open the door, I will come in to him, and will sup with him, and he with me.

21 To him that overcometh will I grant to sit with me in my throne, even as I also overcame, and am set down with my Father in his throne.

### NEW REVISED STANDARD VERSION

REVELATION 3:7 "And to the angel of the church in Philadelphia write: These are the words of the holy one, the true one, who has the key of David, who opens and no one will shut, who shuts and no one opens:

8 "I know your works. Look, I have set before you an open door, which no one is able to shut. I know that you have but little power, and yet you have kept my word and have not denied my name. 9 I will make those of the synagogue of Satan who say that they are Jews and are not, but are lying—I will make them come and bow down before your feet, and they will learn that I have loved you. 10 Because you have kept my word of patient endurance, I will keep you from the hour of trial that is coming on the whole world to test the inhabitants of the earth.

15 "I know your works; you are neither cold nor hot. I wish that you were either cold or hot. 16 So, because you are lukewarm, and neither cold nor hot, I am about to spit you out of my mouth. 17 For you say, 'I am rich, I have prospered, and I need nothing.' You do not realize that you are wretched, pitiable, poor, blind, and naked. 18 Therefore I counsel you to buy from me gold refined by fire so that you may be rich; and white robes to clothe you and to keep the shame of your nakedness from being seen; and salve to anoint your eyes so that you may see. 19 I reprove and discipline those whom I love. Be earnest, therefore, and repent. 20 Listen! I am standing at the door, knocking; if you hear my voice and open the door, I will come in to you and eat with you, and you with me. 21 To the one who conquers I will give a place with me on my throne, just as I myself conquered and sat down with my Father on his throne.

*KEY VERSES: I know your works.* Revelation 3:8a, 15a.

## HOME BIBLE READINGS

| | | | | |
|---|---|---|---|---|
| Apr. | 21 | M. | I John 3:11-24 | *Love One Another* |
| Apr. | 22 | T. | Isaiah 55:1-9 | *Listen to God's Call* |
| Apr. | 23 | W. | II Thessalonians 1:5-10 | *Expect Christ's Coming* |
| Apr. | 24 | T. | Matthew 24:4-14 | *Endure Trials to the End* |
| Apr. | 25 | F. | Proverbs 10:11-24 | *Trust God, Not Wealth* |
| Apr. | 26 | S. | Deuteronomy 8:1-10 | *Bless the Lord for His Care* |
| Apr. | 27 | S. | I Corinthians 10:23-33 | *Do All for God's Glory* |

## BACKGROUND

If John had been making a tour of the seven churches, he would finally have visited Philadelphia and Laodicea after making a grand circle from Ephesus. The last two congregations on his list had much in common. Both were strategically located on important trade routes leading to the interior. Philadelphia and Laodicea each stood in a long river valley through which travelers from distant inland areas would travel. For this reason, both churches had great opportunities to evangelize. Both Philadelphia and Laodicea had strong churches, and both communities of Christians were poised to spread the faith up those long valleys into distant towns in central Asia. Yet only Philadelphia responded. Laodicea failed miserably to be a missionary church.

Of the two churches, surprisingly, Philadelphia was the poorer. The city had suffered a devastating earthquake in A.D. 17 and had not completely recovered. Church members had few resources; they struggled to subsist. Emperor Tiberius had sent some aid, and the city, in gratitude, had taken a new name, "Neocaesarea" (meaning "young caesar") in his honor. Workmen built an elaborate shrine dedicated to the young caesar, but aftershocks rattled the area almost continuously. After a while, the shrine fell into disuse and the name of the city reverted to Philadelphia. Many of the inhabitants moved out of town for safety reasons, preferring to live in adjacent fields.

Philadelphian believers not only suffered financial hardships but also religious persecution. The opposition and harassment came primarily from those calling themselves Jews. Yet, in spite of the difficulties they faced, the valiant Christians in Philadelphia took advantage of opportunities to witness for the Lord. John, therefore, commended the church for its outreach to the people up the valley in distant areas.

Laodicea was different. Although an affluent congregation in a wealthy city, this church apparently adapted itself to the culture at large. Smug Laodicea had recovered from a bad earthquake in A.D. 60 without outside help. With its big banks and rich tradesmen, this city felt content and self-sufficient. Laodicea's manufacturers turned out bales of soft woolen cloth and garments from this cloth. Its great medical center, with renowned physicians and pharmacists, attracted patients from throughout the Mediterranean world. Its eye clinic in particular, with its salves and ointments, brought Laodicea additional fame and respect. John made references to both the garment industry and eye treatments in his letter.

Laodicean Christians reflected the outlook of the great city, living self-satisfied lives. Successful in business, yes, but failures in service. Wealthy in worldly goods, yes, but poor in spiritual resources. No wonder John called this church "lukewarm."

## NOTES ON THE PRINTED TEXT

The message came from Christ, whose authority was clearly defined. *These are the words of the holy one, the true one, who has the key of David, who opens and no one will shut, who shuts and no one opens* (3:7). The risen Lord announced that He before the name of God—the "Holy One." He was the true Messiah who had divine authority. Holding the key to the kingdom, He had the right to refuse or to admit anyone.

*I know your works, I have set before you an open door, which no one is able to shut. I know that you have but little power, and yet you have kept my word and have not denied my name* (3:8). Christ set before the church at Philadelphia an open door, giving believers the opportunity to convert others. The church, small and seemingly powerless, had proven strong and loyal. It was commended for faithfully keeping the Word of God and not denying the name of Jesus.

The church was opposed by certain wicked synagogue leaders, who violently rejected Jesus as the Messiah. John said they had demonstrated relationship to the Evil One. For their rejection and lies, these narrow-minded fanatics would see Isaiah's prophecy reversed. Gentiles would be welcomed into the kingdom for their acknowledgment of Christ. Eventually those clinging to a twisted form of Judaism must acknowledge their mistake and join the Gentiles in proclaiming Christ as the Messiah. *I will make those of the synagogue of Satan who say that they are Jews and are not, but are lying—I will make them bow down before your feet, and they will learn that I have loved you* (3:9).

Because the Philadelphia church had kept God's Word and patiently endured persecution, they would be kept during the additional persecution and coming judgment. *Because you have kept my word of patient endurance, I will keep you from the hour of trial that is coming on the whole world to test the inhabitants of the earth* (3:10).

While John commended the church at Philadelphia, he severely condemned the church at Laodicea. He found no conviction or enthusiasm there. The church was lukewarm, indifferent about its faith. *I know your works; you are neither cold nor hot. I wish that you were either cold or hot* (3:15).

Because the church at Laodicea was lukewarm, Christ was about to reject it. John used a shocking but familiar illustration. Six miles away, in Hierapolis, were well-known hot springs. As the water flowed to Laodicea, it lost some of its heat. The water carried a lot of lime, which whitened the shores of the stream and made anyone sick who drank the water. *So because you are lukewarm, and neither cold nor hot, I am about to spit you out of my mouth* (3:16).

Christ admonished the Laodicean Christians to repent. Despite their banks, physicians, medicines, and their industries, they were spiritually poor. *For you say, "I am rich, I have prospered, and I need nothing." You do not realize that you are wretched, pitiable, poor, blind, and naked* (3:17). The Lord urged the believers to "buy" genuine wealth from Him. His words were filled with images—items to buy—things the Laodicean Christians would understand, for which the area was famed. *Therefore I counsel you to buy from me gold refined by fire so that you may be rich; and white robes to clothe you and to keep the shame of your nakedness from being seen; and salve to anoint your eyes so that you may see* (3:18).

The Lord's discipline proved His love for the believers. It was designed to produce repentance, which was their only hope. *I reprove and discipline those whom I love. Be earnest, therefore, and repent* (3:19). The Lord's invitation was a door opening to new life. *Listen! I am standing at the door, knocking; if you hear my voice and open the door, I will come in to you and eat with you and you with me* (3:20).

The mention of eating was an invitation to fellowship. Christ invited the Laodicean church to share the joys of fellowship with Him. As the victorious conqueror, He offered a place on the throne of the kingdom. *To the one who conquers I will give a place with me on my throne, just as I myself conquered and sat down with my Father on his throne* (3:21).

## SUGGESTIONS TO TEACHERS

You won't need any gimmicks or teasers to get this lesson started. The story of the two churches in today's Scripture automatically ignites discussion. Remember, though, that you are not standing back and pointing at these congregations as if they are specimens to be examined under a microscope. Rather, try to view them as mirrors held up to your own church. Which of the biblical churches do you see reflected?

1. PHILADELPHIA, THE MISSION CHURCH. This congregation seemed to have little going for it but managed to do an astonishing job of reaching out in Christ's name. Here was a mission-minded church! In spite of having little money and undergoing severe pressures from hostile townsfolk, the Philadelphian Christians showed true discipleship. John's message to this church in Revelation 2 may be summed up in the following words.

*Conscientious.* This group of believers "kept my word of patient endurance" (2:10). The Greek words here show that the Philadelphian church people doggedly held on to their beliefs.

*Commendation.* The Lord remembered the sacrifice and perseverance of this congregation, and praised them. Although they might have thought that Jesus had forgotten them at times, they heard His words of commendation.

*Coming.* The Lord may have tarried, but His coming is assured, John told this congregation.

*Crown.* Jesus Christ is conqueror. To those who hang on, regardless of the problems and persecution, will go the victory.

2. LAODICEA, THE COMFORTABLE CONGREGATION. The Lord dismissed this church as a lukewarm group. It was so smug in its affluence that it felt it needed nothing, not even Jesus Christ. And it squandered its opportunities to reach out in mission.

*Comfortable.* What similarities are there between the Laodicean church and many contemporary North American churches? How does the rest of the Christian family in today's world regard the church in our country?

*Call for Repentance.* In what ways does the Lord call our congregations to repent? How has the church in the western world failed to respond?

*Claim.* Christ continues to knock at the door of the Laodicean church to gain admittance and make His claims. He wants to be the strength of our churches, but He must be invited to use His power among us.

*Conqueror.* Jesus was a powerless failure by all our human standards. He was arrested, convicted, and executed. He left no fortune or organization, no army or government. Yet God has vindicated Him by raising Him as the conqueror of the cosmos.

## TOPIC FOR ADULTS
### GOOD NEWS, BAD NEWS

*Church of the Eight Families.* In Bali, not far from the main town of Denpasar, is a village called Katung. It is a Hindu village of some two hundred families who worship their gods in the traditional way. They take part in the many ceremonies, and make their daily offerings to appease the gods and maintain the harmonious balance between good and evil. They believe that the gods absorb the essence from these offerings and thus look with favor on the supplicants.

Like many others, a young woman from one of these families left the village to find work in Denpasar. While there, she became involved with some Christian families, and was so impressed by the quality of their faith that she, too, became a Christian. Eventually she returned to her village—one Christian among two hundred Hindu families, all of whom were angry with her for bringing a foreign deity into their midst.

She set up a small shop in the village and stocked it with produce. It was a complete failure. The Headman and the local priest were irate and instructed the villagers to have nothing to do with the girl, as their Hindu gods would be affronted by her presence.

The young woman must have had great strength of character because she refused to leave the village in spite of the ostracism. Instead, her new Christian faith was so evident in the way she lived that her family decided to stand with her and embrace her faith. The Headman and the village priest were beside themselves with anger and hatred. In fact, they were livid.

A remarkable thing happened. Three other families, closely connected, also became Christians, making four in all. Soon after, there was a Hindu ceremony in the village, led by the Balinese priest. As he was performing the rites, a strong wind arose and a large branch of a banyan tree crashed down on the gathering, killing the priest and three other Hindus.

The people began to mutter. Was this some kind of sign? What did it mean?

The Headman decided that the tragedy was caused by the intrusion of the Christians. He vented his fury by inciting the villagers to burn down the houses of the four Christian families. As the flames took hold, all the Christians—except the young woman—fled to Kintam-ani where other Christian families took them in and cared for them. The woman took refuge under a bed and escaped when the arsonists left.

The Headman now felt that he had exorcised the alien spirits. But his satisfaction was short-lived. He became seriously ill with a mysterious complaint that was never diagnosed. He died without knowing the cause.

This sequence of events really impressed the villagers—so much so that they accepted the Christians back into the village. Before long there were eight families embracing the faith.

Meanwhile, Christian families in Denpasar and elsewhere helped the four burnt-out families to rebuild their homes. In one instance, they were given laying chickens whose eggs were then collected and sold for the building fund. Eventually all four houses were restored and, as a thanksgiving sign, a cross was erected at the entrance to each home. These crosses are in full public view to all the tourists traveling to the popular destination of the volcano at Kintam-ani, but few people would realize their significance.

You might think that this persecution of Christians happened many years ago. Not so. Those four houses were destroyed in 1983.

And now? There is a small, beautiful Christian church in that village of Katung, with twelve strong Christian families worshiping there and every prospect of future growth.

Many people say, "But what can I do? I am only one." This young, courageous Christian girl showed what the power of one can achieve when working in partnership with God.—Maisie McKenzie

*Never Fanatics!* A minister visiting Mexico was watching young people coming to the village church on a Sunday morning for services. He noticed that every man approaching the entrance of the church with his senorita waved the young lady through the door, then stood outside on the steps smoking a cigar. Once in a while, the minister observed one of the young men peering inside the door to see how the service was progressing. A large group of young men had congregated outside on the steps leading to the town plaza. Finally the minister could not contain his curiosity. Walking up to the gathering of men, he said: "I notice that you escort the young women to the service and then wait out here."

"Yes," they answered. "That's right."

"You do not go in to worship yourselves?"

"Oh, no. Not usually."

"I don't understand. Are you not Christians?"

The young men looked at him in surprise. "Of course we're Christians," they answered. "But we are not fanatics!"

This attitude no doubt characterized the Laodicean church members. And it is found in many North American churches today.

*Questions for Students on the Next Lesson.* 1. What is meant by the reference to the scroll in Revelation 4 and 5? 2. Why is Jesus Christ referred to as the Lamb? 3. In your opinion, what is the primary purpose of worship? 4. What did John the Seer mean when he wrote that Christ "ransomed" us? 5. How is your congregation attempting to relate to Christians in other lands and cultures?

## TOPIC FOR YOUTH
### BE OPEN TO GROWTH

*American Dream.* The American dream is simple: make lots of money. People think more about money than any other topic, according to a survey done by *Money Magazine.* One interesting finding was that young people, while they make less money than adults, enjoy spending it more.

John responded to the obsession with wealth, arguing that anyone who makes money the goal of his life is actually spiritually poor. Genuine wealth comes from God. Listen to His teaching and grow in your understanding as a follower of Christ.

*Loyal to His Belief.* Leonard Winograd was the navigator on a B-24 Liberator bomber near the conclusion of World War II. On his forty-third mission, on January 31, 1945, his plane was forced to land in what is now Bosnia, then part of Yugoslavia. For three days he avoided capture.

When finally taken, he was sent to Moosberg Camp in southern Germany. Upon his arrival, his German interrogators asked him his religion. He had lived in fear of that question, knowing what the Nazis were doing to Jews. Yet, without hesitation, the young man replied, "Jewish."

The Germans replied that they could do anything they wanted with Winograd—torture him or have him killed. However, nothing happened to him, and his faith and trust in God deepened during his internment. Following the war, Leonard Winograd became a rabbi. No half-hearted loyalty or commitment for him. He stuck to his beliefs.

John commended his readers for their loyalty to God and their persevering faith. He applauded the fact that they did not deny their Savior. And we, too, must be loyal to Him, the one who has all authority in our lives.

*Open to Growth.* Listen to some of the troubles this man had in his life. At age seven, his family was forced out of its home, and he had to go to work. When he was nine, his mother died. He lost his job as a store clerk when he was twenty. He wanted to go to law school but he lacked the education to get in.

At age twenty-three he went into debt with a partner to buy a small store. Three years later the partner died, leaving him to pay off the entire debt. When he was twenty-eight, after courting a girl for four years, he asked her to marry him. She turned him down. He ran for Congress and lost two times before he finally won. He served one two-year term in the House of Representatives, then lost his bid for re-election. Soon after, his beloved son died, at age four. In fact, three of his four children died before they became adults. He ran for the Senate and lost. He ran for the vice-presidency and lost.

Quite a string of losses, failures, and disappointments, isn't it? But this man, Abraham Lincoln, was open to the Lord's strength and guidance. He grew in faith and persevered in politics. Eventually he led a nation.

*Questions for Students on the Next Lesson.* 1. Who was "the Lion of Judah"? 2. Why did the lamb have seven horns and seven eyes? 3. Why is the slaughter of the lamb so significant? 4. What does the word *ransom* mean to you, personally?

# LESSON 10—MAY 4

## THE REDEEMING LAMB

*Background Scripture:* Revelation 4:1—5:14
*Devotional Reading:* Revelation 4:1-11

KING JAMES VERSION

REVELATION 5:1 And I saw in the right hand of him that sat on the throne a book written within and on the backside, sealed with seven seals.

2 And I saw a strong angel proclaiming with a loud voice, Who is worthy to open the book and to loose the seals thereof?

3 And no man in heaven, nor in earth, neither under the earth, was able to open the book, neither to look thereon.

4 And I wept much, because no man was found worthy to open and to read the book, neither to look thereon.

5 And one of the elders saith unto me, Weep not: behold, the Lion of the tribe of Juda, the Root of David, hath prevailed to open the book, and to loose the seven seals thereof.

6 And I beheld, and, lo, in the midst of the throne and of the four beasts, and in the midst of the elders, stood a Lamb as it had been slain, having seven horns and seven eyes, which are the seven Spirits of God sent forth into all the earth.

7 And he came and took the book out of the right hand of him that sat upon the throne.

8 And when he had taken the book, the four beasts and four and twenty elders fell down before the Lamb, having every one of them harps, and golden vials full of odours, which are the prayers of saints.

9 And they sung a new song, saying, Thou art worthy to take the book, and to open the seals thereof: for thou wast slain, and hast redeemed us to God by thy blood out of every kindred, and tongue, and people, and nation;

10 And hast made us unto our God kings and priests: and we shall reign on the earth.

NEW REVISED STANDARD VERSION

REVELATION 5:1 Then I saw in the right hand of the one seated on the throne a scroll written on the inside and on the back, sealed with seven seals; 2 and I saw a mighty angel proclaiming with a loud voice, "Who is worthy to open the scroll and break its seals?" 3 And no one in heaven or on earth or under the earth was able to open the scroll or to look into it. 4 And I began to weep bitterly because no one was found worthy to open the scroll or to look into it. 5 Then one of the elders said to me, "Do not weep. See, the Lion of the tribe of Judah, the Root of David, has conquered, so that he can open the scroll and its seven seals."

6 Then I saw between the throne and the four living creatures and among the elders a Lamb standing as if it had been slaughtered, having seven horns and seven eyes, which are the seven spirits of God sent out into all the earth. 7 He went and took the scroll from the right hand of the one who was seated on the throne. 8 When he had taken the scroll, the four living creatures and the twenty-four elders fell before the Lamb, each holding a harp and golden bowls full of incense, which are the prayers of the saints. 9 They sing a new song: "You are worthy to take the scroll and to open its seals, for you were slaughtered and by your blood you ransomed for God saints from every tribe and language and people and nation; 10 you have made them to be a kingdom and priests serving our God, and they will reign on earth."

KEY VERSE: *By your blood you ransomed for God saints from every tribe and language and people and nation.* Revelation 5:9b.

## HOME BIBLE READINGS

| | | | |
|---|---|---|---|
| Apr. | 28 | M. | Isaiah 53:4-9 | *The Lamb Sacrificed* |
| Apr. | 29 | T. | Daniel 7:9-14 | *The Lamb Receives a Kingdom* |
| Apr. | 30 | W. | I Peter 1:18-25 | *Sinners Ransomed by Blood of Christ* |

## BACKGROUND

A tourist on the Isle of Patmos today can visit the place where tradition claims Revelation was written. High on the rocky little island is a small cave. This was John's cell, we're told. Here, far from the beleaguered Christians he knew and loved, he prayed. And here the risen Christ's presence became so real to John in a series of visions. From this cramped, isolated cleft in the rocks of a remote speck in the Aegean Sea some of the most sublime words from the Lord were revealed. Countless believers through the centuries have found hope and inspiration in John's recorded visions.

To many modern readers, however, some of these visions seem quite strange. We tend to see everything in a literal, or scientific, way. When we read John's visions in Revelation, we must keep in mind that he was writing in a different genre than we are used to reading. This type of literature is called apocalyptic, and it always employs visions and symbols to convey its message. Many parts of the Hebrew Scriptures are apocalyptic, such as the Book of Daniel, and parts of Amos and Joel. Such Scriptures disclose God's word of judgment and hope in images that are always awesome and sometimes frightening.

John's Revelation contains many such symbols. Although some of these are obscure, most will appear to have significance with some research. In Revelation 4 and 5, the subject matter for this lesson, the symbols' meanings, such as the Lamb, the scroll, the throne, and the numbers twenty-four and seven can be understood fairly readily with the aid of a good commentary and reference to the "Notes on the Printed Text." Keep in mind that John's audience would have immediately identified the symbolic value of these terms, just as someone today would know what we are talking about if we refer to America as "Uncle Sam."

## NOTES ON THE PRINTED TEXT

John had a vision of the Lord seated on His throne in glory. He sat amidst great celebration and praise. *Then I saw in the right hand of the one seated on the throne a scroll written on the inside and on the back, sealed with seven seals* (5:1). In God's hands was an unusual scroll. Normally, writing was done only on one side of such scrolls. This particular scroll had information recorded on both sides and was sealed with seven seals. Seals were marks of authenticity or authority. A scroll was sealed by tying a piece of cord around it, to which was attached a lump of clay. The seal bearing the mark of the owner was then pressed into the clay. The document could be read only by breaking the seal. The document held by God contained His future plan of redemption for the kingdom. Since no one knew its contents, all those who were present were curious.

One problem existed. No human was worthy to open the scroll. No human had earned the right to look at the contents of the scroll or to carry out its plans. *And I saw a mighty angel proclaiming with a loud voice, "Who is worthy to open the scroll and break its seals?" And no one in heaven or on earth or under the earth was able to open the scroll or to look into it* (5:2, 3).

John wept because no one was worthy to open the scroll. Did he cry because of frustrated curiosity, or was it because of the realization that God's plan for redemption not only remained unknown but unaccomplished? In any case, John could not hide his disappointment. *And I began to weep bitterly because no one was found worthy to open the scroll or to look into it* (5:4).

An elder consoled John and told him there was one who had proven his worth. The victorious Christ, with His messianic titles, could open the scroll. *Then one of the elders said to me, "Do not weep. See, the lion of the tribe of Judah, the Root of David, has conquered, so that he can open the scroll and its seven seals"* (5:5).

Encouraged, John looked for a mighty, conquering lion. However, to his surprise he saw that the one worthy to open the scroll was a lamb, standing as if it had been recently slaughtered. *Then I saw between the throne and the four living creatures and among the elders a lamb standing as if it had been slaughtered, having seven horns and seven eyes, which are the seven spirits of God sent out into all the earth* (5:6). The horn was a symbol of strength. The lamb possessed immense power. The seven eyes denoted the fullness of knowledge, which saw and understood everything. The lamb possessed all the energy of God released in Creation.

The lamb advanced from the throng of worshipers and took the scroll. *He went and took the scroll from the right hand of the one who was seated on the throne* (5:7). As the lamb received the scroll, then presumably took His place upon the throne, the four angels and twenty-four elders offered their worship, praise, and prayers. *When he had taken the scroll, the four living creatures and the twenty-four elders fell before the lamb, each holding a harp and golden bowls of incense, which are the prayers of the saints* (5:8).

As the lamb received the scroll, all present celebrated by singing a new song accompanied by harps. The song celebrated the salvation offered to all people through the sacrifice of the lamb. *You are worthy to take the scroll and to open its seals, for you were slaughtered and by your blood you ransomed for God saints from every tribe and language and people and nation* (5:9). The song began in an identical manner to the one offered earlier in praise to God. The lamb was divine. Through the lamb's death, all people were freed, liberated from sin. (A "ransom" was a release price, paid to deliver an individual or people. The death of Jesus was the ransom for humankind from the power of death and sin.)

Finally, the throng proclaimed that the ransomed were to be a kingdom and priests serving God. *You have made them to be a kingdom and priests serving our God, and they will reign on earth* (5:10).

## SUGGESTIONS TO TEACHERS

A man I know insists upon referring to God as "my old Buddy upstairs." This sense of familiarity with the Almighty seems widespread. Some religious figures defend the practice, stating that the folksy, friendly-fellow terminology for the Divine is an appropriate reaction against the fear-based faith of our ancestors.

But does the Bible advocate this "my-old-Buddy" talk? Without diminishing the awareness of God's loving acceptance, Scripture insists that Almighty God, the Eternal One, Creator and Sustainer of this universe, is not to be approached flippantly or casually. A sense of respect must be preserved. God is God; we are mere humans. The gulf is great, and only Christ can bridge that gap.

Your lesson this morning is meant to put in perspective who God is, who we are, and who Christ is.

1. AWE. Start by pointing out how John honored the Lord in a worshipful way. Here was no deity scaled down to human dimensions. Throughout Revelation, John showed a profound sense of awe and wonder. Confronted by the Almighty, John became deeply aware of how unworthy he was to be allowed such visions. He knew he had not earned or deserved this glimpse of the Almighty's plans.

2. ACKNOWLEDGMENT. John's vision convinced him that only Jesus Christ is the worthy personality of history. Only Jesus is victorious. All others fade and fail. As the one who alone is worthy to open the scroll in John's vision, only Jesus can disclose God's purposes for the future. John's vision, in other words, means that Jesus is unique. Jesus makes claims no other can make. Be sure the students recognize these exclusive qualities related to Christ and His role in their salvation.

3. APPOINTMENT. Have group members look carefully at the words of the hymn in Revelation 5:9, 10. Lift up the words about how Christ has "ransomed" us for God, saving us with His life from the clutches of destructive powers infesting the universe.

In addition, Christ has made us "a kingdom of priests serving our God" (5:10). As a kingdom of priests, we are intercessors for others with the Lord. As the church, do we realize our awesome task?

4. ACCLAIM. Move on to the portions of a doxology in verses 12 and 13. These words cry out to be sung, not merely read aloud. The vision here is that everyone forevermore will accord the Almighty the honor and obedience that is His due. Meanwhile, our task as faithful Christians is to do everything we can to bring Him that honor and obedience in our day. It starts with us.

## TOPIC FOR ADULTS
### WHO IS WORTHY?

*Worthy One.* Do you know what the letters IHS mean? They are sometimes inscribed in a church's altar tables or crosses. These Greek letters, iota, eta, and sigma, are the first three letters in the name *Jesus* in the Greek New Testament. Not realizing that IHS is actually a sort of abbreviation for Jesus' name, some have mistakenly said that the letters stand for "in his service." One woman probably did not understand the Greek letters but certainly grasped the significance of what Jesus went through on the Cross when she interpreted IHS as "I Have Suffered!"

Jesus is truly the "Worthy Lamb," the only one whose sufferings could make eternal atonement for eternal salvation.

*God's Plus Sign.* In California, a teenage mother who had not had any teaching in the Christian faith used a church day-care center for her child. One day she asked the woman in charge, "Why is it that churches all seem to have that plus sign on their steeples?"

The day-care supervisor smiled and immediately answered, "That's the Cross. Jesus died on a cross because of His love for all of us. It's wonderful that you think of His cross as a plus sign, for that's what it is. It's the means of adding people to God's family."

*Full Disclosure.* On November 26, 1943, a German air-to-surface guided missile sank the British troopship HMT Rohna in the Mediterranean Sea. More than one thousand American soldiers died. For security reasons, news of this disaster was suppressed by the military authorities during the war. Finally, after fifty years, U.S. and British military documents regarding the ship's sinking were declassified. A disclosure of the disaster was finally made to the survivors and the families of those who died.

John initially lamented that a sealed document existed—a "classified" document, in effect. No one had the authority to open it. Full disclosure was impossible until the coming of the lamb.

*Questions for Students on the Next Lesson.* 1. How does belonging to Christ establish our kinship with people of all races and cultures? 2. In what ways has your faith helped you in times of suffering? 3. When have you sensed the greatest comfort from Christ? 4. When have you had to pay a price for your Christian convictions? 5. When was the last time you expressed appreciation to someone who helped you in a time of difficulty?

## TOPIC FOR YOUTH
### WHO IS WORTHY?

*What Kind of Worship?* Judge Thomas P. Quirk, of the Lake Charles City Court of New Orleans, has sentenced over three hundred young and old individuals to attend church. He initiated this program for no-contest pleas in 1992. His alternative program makes it possible for individuals who cannot afford fines to plead guilty to minor offenses such as drunk driving. They are then sentenced to attend church once a week for a period of one year. The American Civil Liberties Union has challenged the sentencing program, claiming the punishment is a violation of the separation of church and state.

The sentencing program also raises the question: What kind of worship are these people attending? The congregation that joined in the worship of the Lamb truly wanted to offer glory and honor to God. They realized the ransom the Lamb had been made for them. In response, they sang songs of blessing and glory in sincere worship.

John saw this heavenly worship participation as a privilege, not a sentence. How do you view worship?

*Risked Life.* Jason Bratkovich, 18, watched the oncoming car hit a ditch and begin to come into his lane. Initially he thought the car was drifting slowly, without anyone in it. Then he realized the car contained two individuals. The driver, Diane K. Nicholas, had suffered a seizure. She was screaming for help as the vehicle rolled lazily onto the two-lane road near Harrison City, Pennsylvania. A terrified child was also strapped into the front seat.

The teenager stopped his pick-up truck, ran alongside the car, pulled open the door, hit the brake pedal, and shifted the car's transmission into park. Jason's effort saved Diane's and her child's lives.

Perhaps you are influenced by stories of heroes who risk their lives for others. Remember the story of Him who gave His life as a ransom for all people.

*Questions for Students on the Next Lesson.* 1. What is the seal on the servants' foreheads? 2. What great ordeal have these people come through? 3. Do people still face persecution today for their faith? 4. How were the robes of these people made white? 5. Of whom are the creatures and the people singing?

## PROVISION FOR THE REDEEMED

### Background Scripture: Revelation 7:1-17
### Devotional Reading: Hebrews 9:7-14

KING JAMES VERSION

REVELATION 7:1 And after these things I saw four angels standing on the four corners of the earth, holding the four winds of the earth, that the wind should not blow on the earth, nor on the sea, nor on any tree.

2 And I saw another angel ascending from the east, having the seal of the living God: and he cried with a loud voice to the four angels, to whom it was given to hurt the earth and the sea,

3 Saying, Hurt not the earth, neither the sea, nor the trees, till we have sealed the servants of our God in their foreheads.

9 After this I beheld, and, lo, a great multitude, which no man could number, of all nations, and kindreds, and people, and tongues, stood before the throne, and before the Lamb, clothed with white robes, and palms in their hands;

10 And cried with a loud voice, saying, Salvation to our God which sitteth upon the throne, and unto the Lamb. . . .

13 And one of the elders answered, saying unto me, What are these which are arrayed in white robes? and whence came they?

14 And I said unto him, Sir, thou knowest. And he said to me, These are they which came out of great tribulation, and have washed their robes, and made them white in the blood of the Lamb.

15 Therefore are they before the throne of God, and serve him day and night in his temple: and he that sitteth on the throne shall dwell among them.

16 They shall hunger no more, neither thirst any more; neither shall the sun light on them, nor any heat.

17 For the Lamb which is in the midst of the throne shall feed them, and shall lead them unto living fountains of waters: and God shall wipe away all tears from their eyes.

NEW REVISED STANDARD VERSION

REVELATION 7:1 After this I saw four angels standing at the four corners of the earth, holding back the four winds of the earth so that no wind could blow on earth or sea or against any tree. 2 I saw another angel ascending from the rising of the sun, having the seal of the living God, and he called with a loud voice to the four angels who had been given power to damage earth and sea, 3 saying, "Do not damage the earth or the sea or the trees, until we have marked the servants of our God with a seal on their foreheads." . . .

9 After this I looked, and there was a great multitude that no one could count, from every nation, from all tribes and peoples and languages, standing before the throne and before the Lamb, robed in white, with palm branches in their hands. 10 They cried out in a loud voice, saying, "Salvation belongs to our God who is seated on the throne, and to the Lamb!" . . .

13 Then one of the elders addressed me, saying, "Who are these, robed in white, and where have they come from?" 14 I said to him, "Sir, you are the one that knows." Then he said to me, "These are they who have come out of the great ordeal; they have washed their robes and made them white in the blood of the Lamb. 15 For this reason they are before the throne of God, and worship him day and night within his temple, and the one who is seated on the throne will shelter them. 16 They will hunger no more, and thirst no more; the sun will not strike them, nor any scorching heat; 17 for the Lamb at the center of the throne will be their shepherd, and he will guide them to springs of the water of life, and God will wipe away every tear from their eyes."

KEY VERSE: *The Lamb at the center of the throne will be their shepherd, and he will guide them to springs of the water of life, and God will wipe away every tear from their eyes.* Revelation 7:17.

## HOME BIBLE READINGS

| May | 5 | M. | John 4:19-26 | *Worship in Spirit and in Truth* |
|-----|---|----|--------------|----------------------------------|
| May | 6 | T. | Psalm 121:1-8 | *The Lord, Your Keeper* |
| May | 7 | W. | Psalm 23:1-6 | *The Lord, Your Shepherd* |
| May | 8 | T. | Isaiah 25:6-9 | *The Lord, Our Comforter* |
| May | 9 | F. | John 10:7-18 | *Jesus, the Good Shepherd* |
| May | 10 | S. | I Chronicles 16:28-36 | *The Lord, Worthy of Worship* |
| May | 11 | S. | John 14:15-24 | *Jesus Rewards Faithfulness* |

## BACKGROUND

John's message to the seven churches was meant to encourage Christians to remain faithful to Christ in spite of persecution. John assured the believers that history was still in God's hand and that Jesus Christ, not a human emperor, was due all loyalty. Only Christ reigned supreme.

To express these views, John used vivid imagery from the Hebrew Scriptures that his readers would readily understand. In Revelation 6, John wrote about the scroll of destiny—a way of discerning God's purposes in history. John commented on the seven seals on the scroll. The number seven, we remember, conveyed the idea of completeness to the ancients.

The first four seals concerned affairs on earth. Evil powers would seem to triumph for a time as aggressors, war, famine and death—the four horsemen—would execute judgment and bring suffering. The last three seals dealt with the spiritual realm. To John's readers, familiar with such references in Zephaniah and other Old Testament writings, the seals meant a time of universal terror. Throughout the lurid descriptions of world devastation, John intended his readers to realize that the Lord would ultimately prevail over the forces of evil.

Revelation 7, the focus of this lesson, described an interlude before the opening of the seventh seal of the scroll. This section in John's message brought hope and comfort to suffering readers trying to keep their faith. John assured them that they were "sealed" as God's own, that they belonged to Him as His possession. Those who were sealed included persons from among the Hebrews and the Gentiles. This great assembly constituted 144,000—the number of the twelve tribes times twelve, signifying a perfect square and symbolizing completeness. The number was then multiplied by 1,000 to show how great the number of the saved will be.

The lovely poetry of this chapter conveys God's promise that He would shelter His people, and they would receive the joy and comfort of being in God's presence continually.

John referred to Jesus Christ as "the Lamb," alluding to the slaughter of the lambs at Passover time and at the time of the crucifixion. John wanted everyone to recall that Jesus had gone through all the sufferings that any of His followers might experience. Switching metaphors, John promised that the Lamb would also be the Shepherd of His people.

## NOTES ON THE PRINTED TEXT

The lamb slowly broke the seals on the scroll, revealing coming judgment. However, between opening the sixth and seventh seals, just when the reader expected the worst, there was an interlude. John reminded his fellow believers that they need not be afraid.

*After this I saw four angels standing at the four corners of the earth, holding back the four winds of the earth so that no wind could blow on the earth or sea or against any tree* (7:1). In his vision, John saw four living creatures restraining the wind so that there would be no destruction or wind damage anywhere on the earth until God ordered the winds released. Another angel arrived from the east with a symbol of God's authority, perhaps a signet ring. He had an order for the four angels holding the winds.

God's faithful servants first had to be marked before the winds were released. The four were to further restrain the winds. *I saw another angel ascending from the rising sun, having the seal of the living God, and he called with a loud voice to the four angels who had been given power to damage earth and sea, saying, "Do not damage the earth or the sea or the trees until we have marked the servants of our God with a seal on their foreheads"* (7:2, 3).

John saw a multitude of the redeemed from all races and cultures worshiping God. They were wearing white as a sign of victory, holiness, and purity. They carried palm branches in their hands, also a sign of victory. *After this I looked, and there was a great multitude that no one could count, from every nation, from all tribes and peoples and languages, standing before the throne and before the lamb, robed in white, with palm branches in their hands* (7:9).

The redeemed people shouted, praising God for the victory of Christ and also for their deliverance from sin and death. *Salvation belongs to our God who is seated on the throne, and to the lamb!* (7:10). In the midst of the worship, John and one of the twenty-four elders spoke. The elder-musician probed John's understanding of the scene. *Then one of the elders addressed me, saying, "Who are these, robed in white, and where have they come from?"* (7:13). John admitted his ignorance. *I said to him, "Sir, you are the one that knows"* (7:14a)

The elder then explained that the multitude consisted of the redeemed who had been faithful to God through great suffering. They were ordinary believers who had kept their faith and loyalty to God despite the terrible trials, persecutions, and even death that they faced. *Then he said to me, "These are they who have come out of the great ordeal; they have washed their robes and made them white in the blood of the lamb"* (7:14b) The worshipers' clean, white robes symbolized their purity and their victory through Christ's crucifixion and resurrection.

Because of their triumphal victory, they stood in God's presence, and He provided for their shelter and protection. They continued to worship Him. *For this reason they are before the throne of God, and worship him day and night within his temple, and the one who is seated on the throne will shelter them* (7:15).

Because of their victory, the redeemed of God would no longer suffer hunger, thirst, and discomfort from heat. These sufferings came to an end for God's faithful. *They will hunger no more, and thirst no more; the sun will not strike them, nor any scorching heat* (7:16).

The victorious would no longer be leaderless. The lamb would be their shepherd, guiding and comforting them. John pictured a typical

Palestinian scene where one sheep leads the rest of the flock to a feeding or resting spot. *For the lamb at the center of the throne will be their shepherd, and he will guide them to springs of the water of life, and God will wipe away every tear from their eyes* (7:17).

## SUGGESTIONS TO TEACHERS

How do you encourage a group of persecuted Christians to remain true to Christ? If you are writing, for example, to a community of German Lutherans, you might quote Martin Luther and recite the stirring verses of "A Mighty Fortress Is Our God." Someone from Asia or Africa who is not acquainted with the Lutheran traditions might find these references puzzling and relatively meaningless. The same may be true for us today when we try to understand Revelation as a form of Christian encouragement.

Part of our problem stems from the rich array of images in Revelation. We may take them in ways John did not intend. Don't spoil this beautiful and important book by trying to read cryptic messages into each metaphor or reference, as some interpreters try to do. For example, probably the number 144,000 simply signifies completeness and stands for the enormous group of the faithful. God has not put a limit on the number who can be saved.

Throughout this study, emphasize the reasons John wrote to the early believers. Then explore ways of applying these great words to our world today. We, too, often find it hard to remain loyal to Christ when the going gets tough. John's words can help us.

1. GUARDED FROM LASTING TRIBULATION. We sometimes wonder, "Is it worth it to go through all the trouble of being a Christian?" Yet God provides reassurance. Many of our tribulations are relatively light and insignificant; they soon pass. But other trials threaten to overwhelm us. What are the most challenging difficulties you face as a church? As individuals? What are the most powerful forms of evil attempting to defeat us in our communities?

2. GATHERED CLOSE TO THE LIVING LORD. The ones who have "come out of the great ordeal" (7:14) will be sheltered by the Almighty, John promised. Christians may face all trials, temptations, and terrors, confident that their faithfulness brings an ever-closer relationship to the Lord.

3. GUIDED TO THE LIVING WATER. Revelation 7 is God's announcement that suffering will come to an end for those who persevere in trust and obedience. The words about the "springs of the water of life" (7:17) should lead you to references in the Gospel of John (4:14; 6:35; 7:37) and elsewhere in the New Testament (such as Matthew 5:6). In these passages Jesus alluded to Himself as the answer to our deepest "thirsts" in this life.

4. GLADDENED IN LOSS AND LONELINESS. Is there any word of comfort when death and destruction seem to prevail? Revelation 7 is God's emphatic "Yes!" The Lord of all, who raised up Jesus Christ from the tomb, "will wipe away every tear from [our] eyes" (7:17).

## TOPIC FOR ADULTS
### PROVISION FOR THE REDEEMED

*Enough!* Missionary Gregory Fisher teaches at a Bible college in West Africa. He writes about an incident that took place in one of his classes when he was helping his African students understand the Second Coming of Christ.

Fisher and his students were discussing the fourth chapter of I Thessalonians, where Paul speaks of the return of Christ. Verses 16 and 17 read like this: "For the Lord himself, with a cry of command, with the archangel's call and with the sound of God's trumpet, will descend from heaven, and the dead in Christ will rise first. Then we who are alive, who are left, will be caught up in the clouds together with them to meet the Lord in the air; and so we will be with the Lord forever." This is stirring, exciting imagery!

One of the students took the passage quite literally. Since it said Christ would return with a shout of command, the student asked, "Professor Fisher, please tell us—what will Jesus shout?"

Fisher had no answer, of course. But he thought about the question for a moment. He thought about all the pain and suffering he saw daily in Africa: the lack of adequate medical care, the starvation, the filth, the beggars, the orphans, the lepers, the violence, the tribal wars. And he thought about all the evil there is in the rest of the world: wars, genocide, economic exploitation, pollution of the environment. After a moment, Fisher responded, "When Jesus returns, perhaps He will shout 'Enough!'"

Seeing that his students were startled by his answer, the professor explained. "Enough! Enough suffering. Enough starvation. Enough terror. Enough death. Enough indignity. Enough lives trapped in hopelessness. Enough sickness and disease. Enough time. ENOUGH!"—Alex Gondola

*In His Hand.* The famous sculptor Rodin [row-DANH] created two small statues. One was called "The Hand of the Devil" and the other "The Hand of God." "Hand of the Devil" has smoothly polished marble portraying a cupped hand in which lies an inert human figure.

The other statue, "The Hand of God," is made of rough quarry stone that has not been polished smooth. In the center of this stone, a powerful hand thrusts upward. It appears to cleave the marble with its potent motion. This strong hand also holds a human figure, but here the hand grasps the human figure, symbolically bringing it from the nothingness of oblivion into life.

According to the writer of Revelation, believers may live in the knowledge that they are held in the hand of God. They are grasped by the love and power of the living Lord.

*Hold Tight!* A small boy was visiting a big city with his father. The little fellow had grasped the finger of his daddy to keep from being lost in the crowds. Eventually the boy grew tired, his pace slowed, and he struggled to keep his grip on his father's finger. Finally, he looked up and said, "Daddy, you'll have to take my hand now. I can't hold on much longer." The father smiled, picked the boy up, and put him on his shoulders.

When we cannot hang on any longer, the Lord stoops down and carries us. He is always with us, no matter what the trial.

*Questions for Students on the Next Lesson.* 1. What is the significance of the rider on the white horse? 2. What does the symbolism of the Great White Throne suggest to you? 3. Does God still judge people? If so, on what basis? 4. How would you describe your sense of personal accountability? 5. Why might some readers tend to ignore the imagery in Revelation?

## TOPIC FOR YOUTH
### DELIVERANCE ASSURED

*Drawn Together.* High school baseball player Tim McCarver was adored and boosted by the local sportswriters in Memphis, Tennessee. When he signed with the St. Louis Cardinals for a bonus of $75,000, he was a southern white boy who had never played or shared anything with blacks. Pitcher Bob Gibson, by contrast, never gained much journalistic or community attention as a high school or college athlete because he was black. He signed with the Cardinals for a $4,000 bonus. Yet, in an era of civil rights struggles, these two men were drawn together in deep friendship.

The friendship took time to develop, though. At spring training Gibson got on the bus and saw McCarver sipping an orange soda. When Gibson asked if he could have a swig, McCarver was caught off guard. White boys never played with blacks—let alone shared a drink with them! McCarver promised to save Gibson some.

Later in spring training, a young black boy slipped over the fence and stole some baseballs. McCarver yelled at the boy, calling him a cannibal. Gibson and teammate Curt Flood quietly looked over at McCarver. Embarrassed, McCarver apologized to the black men. Gibson responded that McCarver did not need to apologize to him; McCarver needed to figure out why he made such a remark in the first place.

The distance between the two closed. Another day Gibson and Flood acted out for McCarver how a black man and a white man shook hands. Gibson played the white man and, after shaking Flood's hand, looked at his own hand and then wiped it against his pants. He then looked at McCarver and teased him that he had done that before. The more Gibson kidded him, the deeper their friendship grew. By 1964, the two were firm friends and often went to dinner with their wives and other team members. While baseball initially drew them together, Gibson broke down the race barrier between them.

Like Gibson and McCarver, all youth need to accept people from other races and cultures. John promised that Christ's redeemed would come from all races and cultures and find their common ground, not merely in human friendship, but in the worship of Jesus Christ.

*Sought and Found Relief.* Medical doctors in Pittsburgh, Pennsylvania, are realizing the need to learn the Russian language. In October, 1994, eight-year-old Konstantin Kouzmine was transferred to Children's Hospital from St. Petersburg's Pediatrics Institute. "Kostya," as he was nicknamed, had been attacked on an elevator by a man with a hook. He had lost his small intestine and a part of his large intestine. Five hours of surgery at the institute failed to help him. More skilled care was required to save the boy, and a plea for help was issued. Children's Hospital, several corporations, and various individuals responded to bring the young Kostya relief. Following successful surgery, he was released on November 18.

On December 1, twelve-year-old Sveta Mishina of Moscow arrived at Allegheny General Hospital for pediatric neurosurgery to treat her spina bifida. Hundreds of such operations had been done at the Spina Bifida Center of the hospital, but the surgery was not available at Moscow's Children's Hospital.

Once again, appeals went out and diplomatic red tape was bypassed. Sveta was brought to America and the surgery performed. Less than twelve hours later, Sveta moved her legs.

What seems greater tp us than an end to our suffering? John promised that the redeemed would no longer suffer. God Himself would provide comfort, care, and shelter.

*Expressed His Gratitude.* On October 13, 1960, the Pittsburgh Pirates defeated the New York Yankees in the final game of the World Series. That evening, the Pirate team threw a large party. However, Roberto Clemente skipped the team party in order to walk the streets of Pittsburgh and thank the fans for their support and faith.

Clemente was an exceptional individual. While many seem unable to express appreciation, he had no difficulty offering thanks. Likewise, those gathered around the throne of God will have no difficulty expressing their gratitude to God for His eternal faithfulness.

*Questions for Students on the Next Lesson.* 1. How does John describe Christ's coming? 2. Why doesn't the army of heaven wear armor? 3. What is the book of life? 4. By what standards will people be judged in the last judgment? 5. What fate awaits those whose names are not in the book of life?

# LESSON 12—MAY 18

## THE VICTORIOUS CHRIST

*Background Scripture:* Revelation 19:1—20:15
*Devotional Reading:* Revelation 19:1-10

### KING JAMES VERSION

REVELATION 19:11 And I saw heaven opened, and behold a white horse; and he that sat upon him was called Faithful and True, and in righteousness he doth judge and make war.

12 His eyes were as a flame of fire, and on his head were many crowns; and he had a name written, that no man knew, but he himself.

13 And he was clothed with a vesture dipped in blood: and his name is called The Word of God.

14 And the armies which were in heaven followed him upon white horses, clothed in fine linen, white and clean.

15 And out of his mouth goeth a sharp sword, that with it he should smite the nations: and he shall rule them with a rod of iron: and he treadeth the winepress of the fierceness and wrath of Almighty God.

16 And he hath on his vesture and on his thigh a name written, KING OF KINGS, AND LORD OF LORDS.

20:11 And I saw a great white throne, and him that sat on it, from whose face the earth and the heaven fled away; and there was found no place for them.

12 And I saw the dead, small and great, stand before God; and the books were opened: and another book was opened, which is the book of life: and the dead were judged out of those things which were written in the books, according to their works.

13 And the sea gave up the dead which were in it; and death and hell delivered up the dead which were in them: and they were judged every man according to their works.

14 And death and hell were cast into the lake of fire. This is the second death.

15 And whosoever was not found written in the book of life was cast into the lake of fire.

### NEW REVISED STANDARD VERSION

REVELATION 19:11 Then I saw heaven opened, and there was a white horse! Its rider is called Faithful and True, and in righteousness he judges and makes war. 12 His eyes are like a flame of fire, and on his head are many diadems; and he has a name inscribed that no one knows but himself. 13 He is clothed in a robe dipped in blood, and his name is called The Word of God. 14 And the armies of heaven, wearing fine linen, white and pure, were following him on white horses. 15 From his mouth comes a sharp sword with which to strike down the nations, and he will rule them with a rod of iron; he will tread the wine press of the fury of the wrath of God the Almighty. 16 On his robe and on his thigh he has a name inscribed, "King of kings and Lord of lords."

20:11 Then I saw a great white throne and the one who sat on it; the earth and the heaven fled from his presence, and no place was found for them. 12 And I saw the dead, great and small, standing before the throne, and books were opened. Also another book was opened, the book of life. And the dead were judged according to their works, as recorded in the books. 13 And the sea gave up the dead that were in it, Death and Hades gave up the dead that were in them, and all were judged according to what they had done. 14 Then Death and Hades were thrown into the lake of fire. This is the second death, the lake of fire; 15 and anyone whose name was not found written in the book of life was thrown into the lake of fire.

KEY VERSE: *On [the rider's] robe and on his thigh he has a name inscribed, "King of kings and Lord of lords." Revelation 19:16.*

## HOME BIBLE READINGS

| | | | | |
|---|---|---|---|---|
| May | 12 | M. | Revelation 19:1-5 | *Praise God for His Judgments* |
| May | 13 | T. | Revelation 19:6-10 | *Power Belongs to God* |

| May | 14 | W. | Revelation 19:17-21 | *Punishment of False Prophets* |
| May | 15 | T. | Revelation 20:1-6 | *Christ Will Reign One Thousand Years* |
| May | 16 | F. | Hebrews 12:22-29 | *A Kingdom that Cannot Be Shaken* |
| May | 17 | S. | Philippians 3:15-21 | *Our Bodies Will Be Changed* |
| May | 18 | S. | II Timothy 1:8-14 | *Jesus Shall Abolish Death* |

## BACKGROUND

Christians were questioning whether evildoers would ever be put down. And John knew from firsthand experience that powerful people and forces opposed God. The emperor and the court in Rome thought that they could usurp the place of the Almighty. Cruel Roman rulers indulged in extravagant luxuries, squandering the resources of entire provinces for lavish banquets. Emperors practiced disgusting vices. Even Romans themselves were appalled at the antics of their leaders. John also knew the brutal reprisals leveled at those who refused to go along with the imperial edicts regarding emperor worship. He wrote to encourage Christians to hold on to the faith.

Believers from the lower class—which meant most believers—suffered from high prices, sudden shortages, and general financial uncertainty. Rich, unscrupulous merchants and shipping tycoons created monopolies. Market manipulators rigged prices, which allowed them to have an economic stranglehold on most cities. Meanwhile, these exploiters enjoyed extraordinary luxury. In their gluttony, they ignored the starving and made slaves of the poor. Scholars point out that the Roman economic system was based on slavery. Some estimate that as many as sixty million humans existed in such servitude.

John of Patmos was confident that God would not countenance these evil practices forever. With a vivid description of seven cycles of judgment, John assured his readers that history would culminate with God victorious and His faithful followers vindicated.

In today's lesson, based on Revelation 19 and 20, John stated that God will bring an end to the cruel and arrogant authorities who have challenged Him. The devil, the one behind all the evil forces loose in the world, will ultimately receive his appropriate destiny.

## NOTES ON THE PRINTED TEXT

*Then I saw heaven opened, and there was a white horse! Its rider is called Faithful and True, and in righteousness he judges and makes war* (19:11). Christ appeared as a military commander, riding on His white stallion, leading the army of heaven. His name indicated that He was no deceiver. He could be trusted as the authoritative witness to God. His word was His weapon, and with that He judged and did battle.

Christ was able to judge because of His ability to see into the human heart. Nothing escaped His eyes. His knowledge and understanding penetrated everything. Though a judge, He was also a king with many crowns.

Still, there was mystery. To the ancients, a name revealed one's true nature. John and his readers could never fully understand Christ and His nature. *His eyes are like a flame of fire, and on his head are many diadems;*

*and he has a name inscribed that no one knows but himself* (19:12).

John continued his description of the rider on the white horse. He wore a bloodstained robe, the gruesome stains being the result of divine judgment. *He is clothed in a robe dipped in blood, and his name is called The Word of God* (19:13). Having described the commander, John then pictured the heavenly army that followed. Instead of wearing battle armor, they were dressed for a joyous celebration. Their clothing, even their horses, symbolized victory. *And the armies of heaven wearing fine linen, white and pure, were following him on white horses* (19:14).

The soldiers were not fighters, but witnesses. They were to view Christ's authority and judgments. John depicted these by utilizing three Old Testament images. *From his mouth comes a sharp sword with which to strike down the nations, and he will rule them with a rod of iron; he will tread the wine press of the fury of the wrath of God the Almighty* (19:15).

Christ's authority and sovereignty over all the earth was proclaimed by the name embroidered on His robe and on His thigh. In that era statues of kings sometimes had their royal title and name inscribed on them. *On his robe and on his thigh he has a name inscribed, "King of kings and Lord of lords"* (19:16).

John finally described the last judgment for his readers. God was the judge, sitting on the white throne. *Then I saw a great white throne and the one who sat on it* (20:11). His glory, holiness, and authority were so evident that all creation had fled in an effort to escape His terrible judgment. *The earth and the heaven fled from his presence, and no place was found for them* (20:11).

None escaped death. All the dead were gathered before the great throne for judgment. The one sitting on the throne judged the dead according to their works, as recorded in the book of life. Everything an individual had done, whether good or bad, was recorded in these books. *And I saw the dead, great and small, standing before the throne, and books were opened. Also another book was opened, the book of life. And the dead were judged according to their works, as recorded in the books* (21:12). No one was exempt. Even those lost at sea were not overlooked. *And the sea gave up the dead that were in it, Death and Hades gave up the dead that were in them, and all were judged according to what they had done* (20:13).

God's judgment resulted in the final resolution of death, along with those whose names did not appear in the book of life. *Then Death and Hades were thrown into the lake of fire. This is the second death, the lake of fire* (20:14). *Anyone whose name was not found written in the book of life was thrown into the lake of fire* (20:15).

## SUGGESTIONS TO TEACHERS

"Why do evil people seem to get away with their wicked ways?" Christian believers asked the question centuries ago, and many suffering exploitation today are asking it, as well. So often God seems indifferent. Yet today's lesson affirms that God finally brings a successful conclusion to His plans for the world.

1. VISION OF FULFILLMENT. Start by calling attention to the great hallelujah chorus at the opening of chapter 19. In spite of his confinement

in a bleak detention camp on Patmos, John was able to celebrate God's goodness. "Hallelujah" was a way of life for him, and it is meant to be the life theme of all believers. Ask your students how well they are able to praise the Lord in all circumstances.

2. VINDICATION OF THE FAITHFUL. In Revelation 18, John promised his readers that those who remained faithful to Christ would enjoy eternal fellowship with the Lord. Even those who died would be gathered to the side of Christ. In chapter 19, John told how faithful believers would be invited to the "marriage supper of the Lamb," welcomed to a joyous celebration. Middle East weddings were the most festive of parties.

3. VICTORY OVER FUTILITY. "What's the use of being good or trying to help others?" Church members may sometimes wonder about this. John of Patmos reassured Christians that their lives of caring and serving are never in vain. God ultimately prevails and rewards His followers.

4. VANQUISHING OF THE FOOLISH. John offered a series of pictures of the eventual doom of those opposing the Lord. In chapter 20, he dealt with the time between when the wicked would be vanquished.

Warn your students about persons who use Revelation to set up a strict timetable for the future. John's writings must not be used to prepare a printout of the hour, day, and year of the end.

5. VALIDATION OF FAITH. The main thrust throughout this lesson is that Jesus Christ is victor. God wins.

Your lesson may close with reference to the conclusion of chapter 20. Here the Almighty on His throne holds all persons accountable, including dictators and tyrants of every stripe.

## TOPIC FOR ADULTS
### THE VICTORIOUS CHRIST

*Trivialization of Sin.* Society often makes sin into something trivial. We refer to rich desserts as "sinful" and divorces as "no-fault." Some worshipers complain if the church bulletin contains a printed confession of sin for the Sunday service.

Cornelius Plantinga, Jr.'s book *Not the Way It's Supposed to Be: A Breviary of Sin* reminds us that our culture rarely encourages any sense of self-reproach. Sermons with titles such as "Cancel that Guilt Trip" try to talk people out of a sense of sin. Therapeutic religion has trivialized accountability before God. Judgment is seldom mentioned. Plantinga maintains that the accusation "You have sinned," which once had the power to jolt people, is now often offered with a grin and a tone that signals ironic humor.

Plantinga, and a growing number of other scholars, are trying to recapture a biblically based concept of human failure and our need for repentance and grace. Even into the 1950s, a heritage of taking sin seriously was still evident in most Christian churches. While growing up among western Michigan Calvinists in the 1950s, Plantinga said he heard as many sermons about sin as he did about grace. "Don't go to church if you want to hear about sin," says the Rev. William Willimon, Duke University chaplain. "But go to a movie or pick up a book and you're more likely to hear about it."

While many churches today tell their flocks they are good people and mean well, Willimon said in an interview, authors such as Flannery O'Connor and Margaret Atwood will discuss the human capacity for evil.

Plantinga said in an interview that all kinds of churches share guilt over the trivialization of sin. In some churches, sin is generally spoken of only in corporate terms, and largely related to social issues. In other churches, which have numerical growth as their *only* goal, the uncomfortable topic of certain prevalent sins may never get mentioned.

Plantinga says confessing sin is not only religiously important, but psychologically important. "What happens otherwise is that we start to close wounds that we haven't really healed," he said. But theologians arguing for a return to a classical concept of sin realize they face long odds. Human beings have a capacity for self-deception that is fathomless, says Plantinga. Look no farther than the current state of affairs in churches, some say.

"We can deny our rebellion and our sin, but there are few facts more attested by American history than this: We are fallen," Willimon says. "It is odd, as we sit around here in one of the bloodiest centuries humanity has ever known, and we talk about what good people we are."

*The Real Victor.* A series of movies have appeared with the theme of judgment and the end of the human race In the films *The Terminator* and its sequel, *T2, Judgment Day,* Arnold Swarzenegger became an action star. Some have practically elevated Swarzenegger to the status of a deity because of his fictional exploits in these movies.

John of Patmos presented visions of the great judgment and the final days. But his script pointed not to a merely human hero, but to the victorious Christ. Only Jesus Christ is the King of kings and the Lord of lords.

*Questions for Students on the Next Lesson.* 1. What is the significance of the fact that no temple was found in John's vision of the new Jerusalem? 2. What did John mean in his reference to the gates never being shut? 3. How did this vision bring hope and consolation to John's readers? 4. What relevance does the Scripture in this lesson have for Christians today? 5. Do you think that all nations will someday live together peacefully?

## TOPIC FOR YOUTH
### VICTORY AT LAST!

*No Escape.* Just prior to his death in 1867, Richard Slyhoff made arrangements for his burial. Slyhoff, from Sigel, Pennsylvania, was concerned about judgment in the afterlife, admitting that he had been an ungodly man. He believed that a mighty earthquake would precede the resurrection of the dead, and he devised a plan to escape judgment. He had his grave dug under a huge leaning rock. When the earthquake occurred, the rock would presumably fall on his grave and shield him from judgment.

Unfortunately, over the years since Slyhoff's death, erosion and other forces of nature have foiled his plan. The rock has tilted in the wrong direction and has been moved nine feet by a tornado.

Slyhoff's plan to avoid judgment has failed. The current owner of the property summed up the situation by noting that the God who created the universe could certainly look underneath a rock.

How true! John knew that ultimately everyone would be judged for their deeds. There would be no escape for those not redeemed by the blood of the Lamb.

*Accountable.* Archaeologists have documented that John and other biblical authors borrowed literary symbols from earlier cultures. For example, an Egyptian papyrus from the eleventh century B.C. shows the weighing of the heart of the dead. The heart was believed to be the center of thought and action. Maat, the god of justice and order, is depicted as placing the individual's heart on a huge scale while the deceased stands holding his hands aloft, waving feathers (the sign of Maat), and holding a heart amulet in order to impart by magic the correct weight to his deceased heart.

Thoth, the divine scribe with the head of a bird, stands to the left of the scale. He is ready to report the result of the weighing to Osiris, the judge of the dead and lord of eternity. A crocodile waits at the feet of Osiris to devour the dead ones that do not pass Maat's test. Being eaten by the crocodile was the second death for those who did not measure up to Maat's test.

All cultures demonstrate a desire to test accountability. God has built into us an "ought" that we recognize within. It calls us to standards, and we realize we fail. Revelation shows us the only way of escape: bow before the Lamb.

*The List.* Steven Spielberg made a remarkable film, *Schindler's List,* about Oscar Schindler, a businessman who rescued over a thousand Jews from certain death during World War II. Consider Oscar Schindler. He knew his people by name. He paid a price to buy them from death. His list was a list of life. His people were chosen. They did not earn the right to be on the list.

John reminded his readers about Jesus Christ. He knew His people by name. He paid the price to buy them from death. His list was a list of life. His people were chosen. They did not earn the right to be on the list.

While Oscar was a savior from physical harms, John presented his readers with the Savior, the one who triumphed over all evil. Christ could be trusted. And those who trust Him are afforded a spot on *The List,* His book of life.

*Questions for Students on the Next Lesson.* 1. How would you describe the new earth? 2. Who will be admitted into the new earth and the new Jerusalem? 3. Why was there no temple in the new Jerusalem? 4. How does God make all things new? 5. Is the hope of salvation an expectancy for you? Why?

# LESSON 13—MAY 25

## A NEW HEAVEN AND EARTH

*Background Scripture:* Revelation 21:1—22:5
*Devotional Reading:* Revelation 22:1-9

### KING JAMES VERSION

REVELATION 21:1 And I saw a new heaven and a new earth: for the first heaven and the first earth were passed away; and there was no more sea.

2 And I John saw the holy city, new Jerusalem, coming down from God out of heaven, prepared as a bride adorned for her husband.

3 And I heard a great voice out of heaven saying, Behold, the tabernacle of God is with men, and he will dwell with them, and they shall be his people, and God himself shall be with them, and be their God.

4 And God shall wipe away all tears from their eyes; and there shall be no more death, neither sorrow, nor crying, neither shall there be any more pain: for the former things are passed away.

5 And he that sat upon the throne said, Behold, I make all things new. And he said unto me, Write: for these words are true and faithful.

6 And he said unto me, It is done. I am Alpha and Omega, the beginning and the end. I will give unto him that is athirst of the fountain of the water of life freely.

7 He that overcometh shall inherit all things; and I will be his God, and he shall be my son. . . .

22 And I saw no temple therein: for the Lord God Almighty and the Lamb are the temple of it.

23 And the city had no need of the sun, neither of the moon, to shine in it: for the glory of God did lighten it, and the Lamb is the light thereof.

24 And the nations of them which are saved shall walk in the light of it: and the kings of the earth do bring their glory and honour into it.

25 And the gates of it shall not be shut at all by day: for there shall be no night there.

26 And they shall bring the glory and honour of the nations into it.

27 And there shall in no wise enter into it any thing that defileth, neither whatsoever worketh abomination, or maketh a lie: but they which are written in the Lamb's book of life.

### NEW REVISED STANDARD VERSION

REVELATION 21:1 Then I saw a new heaven and a new earth; for the first heaven and the first earth had passed away, and the sea was no more. 2 And I saw the holy city, the new Jerusalem, coming down out of heaven from God, prepared as a bride adorned for her husband. 3 And I heard a loud voice from the throne saying, "See, the home of God is among mortals. He will dwell with them as their God; they will be his peoples, and God himself will be with them; 4 he will wipe every tear from their eyes. Death will be no more; mourning and crying and pain will be no more, for the first things have passed away."

5 And the one who was seated on the throne said, "See, I am making all things new." Also he said, "Write this, for these words are trustworthy and true." 6 Then he said to me, "It is done! I am the Alpha and the Omega, the beginning and the end. To the thirsty I will give water as a gift from the spring of the water of life. 7 Those who conquer will inherit these things, and I will be their God and they will be my children.

. . .

22 I saw no temple in the city, for its temple is the Lord God the Almighty and the Lamb. 23 And the city has no need of sun or moon to shine on it, for the glory of God is its light, and its lamp is the Lamb. 24 The nations will walk by its light, and the kings of the earth will bring their glory into it. 25 Its gates will never be shut by day—and there will be no night there. 26 People will bring into it the glory and the honor of the nations. 27 But nothing unclean will enter it, nor anyone who practices abomination or falsehood, but only those who are written in the Lamb's book of life.

*KEY VERSE: I saw a new heaven and a new earth; for the first heaven and the first earth had passed away, and the sea was no more. Revelation 21:1.*

## HOME BIBLE READINGS

| | | | | |
|---|---|---|---|---|
| May | 19 | M. | Revelation 21:9-14 | *The New Jerusalem* |
| May | 20 | T. | Revelation 21:15-21 | *The City's Measurements* |
| May | 21 | W. | Revelation 22:1-5 | *The City's Blessings* |
| May | 22 | T. | Revelation 22:6-14 | *A Trustworthy Book* |
| May | 23 | F. | Revelation 22:16-20 | *A Certain Return* |
| May | 24 | S. | Isaiah 60:1-5 | *Zion's Future Glory* |
| May | 25 | S. | II Peter 3:8-18 | *Grow in Knowledge as You Wait* |

## BACKGROUND

Without hope, a person soon loses the will to survive. Ask any former hostage or POW. Or, for that matter, speak with any member of the medical community who has tended the ill and injured. Hope must be present for survival.

John of Patmos, writing to seven congregations, sensed the need for hope among the beleaguered believers in those churches. He knew that some had already paid the price of their faith with their lives. Others, he had heard, were undergoing intense persecution. He concluded his magnificent series of visions with a memorable promise of hope. This hope was expressed in symbolic language conveying a picture of a new creation.

The portion of Revelation considered in our lesson opens with an announcement of what seems to be a re-creation of the Garden of Eden—God's promise of the new heaven and earth. The idea of newness pervades this entire section of Revelation. With references to Jerusalem, which his readers would have readily appreciated, John claimed that God would bring about a new holy city, unlike any existing before. The vastness of the city, with each side stretching the equivalent of 1,400 miles, meant there was a place for every faithful follower of Christ. The cube shape signified perfection.

The absence of a temple proclaimed that the presence of the Lord was everywhere, not localized in one space marked "Holy." Worship would be continuous, because God would be with His own in a new and wondrous way through Christ.

Our passage today concludes with a startlingly new thought, especially for people coming from a Jewish background. The faithful would be able to look on God's face! In the Hebrew tradition, no one was ever permitted to see the Lord directly. Neither Moses, nor Isaiah, nor anyone else was privileged to have this form of encounter. But in this final chapter of Revelation (see 22:4) the Lord assures His faithful followers of a face-to-face encounter with Him.

## NOTES ON THE PRINTED TEXT

John wrote to reveal God's purpose in history. His writing has depicted God's judgments, the collapse of the evil powers, the last judgment of humankind, and the future plans of God. In today's lesson, John reached the climax of his writings. *Then I saw a new heaven and a new earth; for the first heaven and the first earth had passed away, and the sea was no more* (21:1). John saw a vision of a newly created heaven and a newly created earth that had no oceans.

The new earth required a new metropolitan center for God's redeemed people. God created a glorious and beautiful city. *And I saw the holy city, the new Jerusalem, coming down out of heaven from God, prepared as a bride adorned for her husband* (21:2).

One of heaven's residents announced wonderful news. The city would be God's dwelling place. Now all redeemed humankind would enjoy unhindered fellowship with its Lord. *See, the home of God is among mortals. He will dwell with them as their God; they will be his peoples, and God himself will be with them* (21:3).

Because God was with His people, all unhappiness would end. All that was evil or that brought sorrow would pass away. The life giver and Comforter would always be present with them. *He will wipe every tear from their eyes. Death will be no more; mourning and crying and pain will be no more, for the first things have passed away* (21:4).

God addressed John directly, reaffirming His intent to make a new creation. He also guaranteed the truth of John's vision and testimony. *And the one who was seated on the throne said, "See, I am making all things new." Also he said, "Write this, for these words are trustworthy and true"* (21:5).

God also announced the completion of His creative work. He was the starter and finisher of all creation. *Then he said to me, "It is done! I am the Alpha and the Omega, the beginning and the end"* (21:6a). God also affirmed His constant care for those sharing His fellowship. *To the thirsty I will give water as a gift from the spring of the water of life* (21:6b). He also promised that the faithful believers would be His heirs. Through Christ, they were children of God. *Those who conquer will inherit these things, and I will be their God and they will be my children* (21:7).

John described the city, its wall, and the building materials. One thing, though, initially seemed strange to John. The temple, the symbol of God's presence, was absent. Now God Himself was present, united with Christ. Their presence surrounded everyone. *I saw no temple in the city, for its temple is the Lord God the Almighty and the Lamb* (21:22).

God's presence also gave light to all. God's glory made the normal sources of light, the sun and the moon, unnecessary. *And the city has no need of sun or moon to shine on it, for the glory of God is its light, and its lamp is the Lamb* (21:23). With the defeat of the antichrist, all nations and peoples would come and offer their praise and tribute. *The nations will walk by its light, and the kings of the earth will bring their glory into it* (21:24).

With God present, no further protection was needed. The enemy was defeated. The gates would remain open permanently. *Its gates will never be shut by day—and there will be no night there* (21:25). All treasures would be brought as an offering to God. However, only the redeemed, those who conformed to God's will, would be admitted. *People will bring into it the glory and the honor of the nations. But nothing unclean will enter it, nor anyone who practices abomination or falsehood, but only those who are written in the Lamb's book of life* (21:26, 27).

## SUGGESTIONS TO TEACHERS

The words of Dr. Martin Luther King, Jr., gave hope to disheartened African-Americans at a crucial time in this nation's history. On August 26, 1963, Dr. King stood on the steps of the Lincoln Memorial in Washington, D.C., and addressed the nation with his "I Have a Dream" speech. His words seemed to spark a turning point in the struggle for civil rights. King offered a vision of a new America and stirred hopes for a new society.

John's final section of Revelation offered a vision of a new order and inspired hope among the oppressed in the seven churches. The new heaven and new earth promised in this great book continue to instill hope. This is the central idea to keep in mind in your lesson today.

1. DIVINE DWELLING PLACE. Focus on this great promise: "The home of God is among mortals. He will dwell with them as their God. . ." (Rev. 21:3). Remind your students that the Almighty involves Himself lovingly in human concerns. Although the "God-Is-Dead" talk has gone the way of all theological fads, many people live as though the Lord is absent from the world. John's word from God assured his fellow believers that they could rely on the Lord's companionship. And so may we.

2. DEATH'S DEMISE. Through Christ, we may be confident of the death of death. Christ's resurrection and victory mean that death no longer has the last word. This portion of Revelation could open a discussion about how Christians should view death. Make sure your students understand how Christ's work on the cross has conquered the final enemy.

3. DISCIPLES' DELIGHT. John's words about the new Jerusalem (21:9-27) describe a community of perfection and beauty. Note that there is no temple; God's presence is everywhere. Nor is there even sun or moon, because the city is illumined by that presence.

Like Dr. King's "I Have A Dream" speech, John's vision gave hope. Emphasize that neither King nor John were mumbling pie-in-the-sky platitudes. Revelation tells us that God will fulfill the vision of a new heaven and new earth with a community of light, joy, and harmony.

4. DARKNESS'S DOOM. The end of night and an era of perpetual light is promised. Think of the connotations of darkness: fear, gloom, cold, uncertainty, danger. Evil seems to lurk in the shadows. Threats of harm increase where there is no light. Who wants to walk alone on a dark, deserted street in any city?

The passage about light has a theme of safety and security because of the victorious Lord. Light fosters the flourishing of the "tree of life," bringing healing for all peoples. Have your students look at Revelation 21:22—22:5 and consider how the Lord brings "healing of the nations" (22:2). Move on to verse 4, and consider the significance of looking upon the face of God, the source of all light. Healing and a face-to-face encounter come to all who hold to their faith in the Lord.

## TOPIC FOR ADULTS
### A NEW HEAVEN AND EARTH

*Saw the Vision.* Almost fifty years ago, the area of what is now Malawi, in the heart of Africa, was torn by a bloody revolution. Missionaries who had faithfully ministered in hospitals and clinics there knew they were in danger. These valiant servants of Christ had been called to bring healing to people living with malaria and other tropical diseases. Authorities arranged to have an airplane fly over and drop a message asking if they wished to be rescued. The message instructed the missionaries to put a large white "X" on a mountain clearing if they wished to leave. If they wanted to remain, they were to lay out an "I." The missionaries speedily consulted with each other and their African colleagues, and then immediately used white rocks to form an enormous "I."

With the mark showing emphatically that they would not desert their calling, they added a message taken from Ephesians 2:14: "ALL ONE." The London Times carried a picture of the message, taken from the air. The rocks spelling out the decision of that band of Christ's servants may still be seen on that mountain near Livingstonia, Malawi.

These believers in Malawi knew that the future was in God's hands. The new heaven and the new earth meant that they could announce to the world that they were committed to being with their African brothers and sisters. In Christ, they were "all one." Until the Kingdom is fully manifested, the mission hospital in Livingstonia continues to be a demonstration of God's ways.

*Open the Door.* Undoubtedly you have seen a copy of the painting by Holman Hunt, "The Light of the World." This familiar piece of art depicts Jesus poised at the doorway of a building, with uplifted hand, as if knocking. The original resides in Keble College, Oxford, England.

The artist was inspired by Christ's words in Revelation. Hunt wanted to convey the glorious news that with Jesus Christ, a new life awaits. The painting has an unusual detail, however, which some overlook. Hunt deliberately did not paint a handle on the outside of that door. He stated that he wanted to indicate that Jesus will not coerce anyone to accept Him as Lord. He invites. But the person inside who refuses to open the door will not enter the new heaven and new earth.

*Appropriate Misquote.* A small girl in Sunday school had been taught a memory verse from the closing part of Matthew's Gospel. But when she got home and tried to recite it to her parents, the little scholar offered an inspiring misquote. She proudly stated, "Glow, I am with you always, to the close of the age!"

The new heaven and new earth envisioned by John will come through the power of the living Christ. That means we may glow with hope and joy.

*Questions for Students on the Next Lesson.* 1. What are the Pastoral Epistles? Why were they given that name? 2. Why did Paul write to Timothy? 3. What kinds of instructions did Paul give Timothy? 4. What do the words in I Timothy 4:6-16 call us to do? 5. Who looks to you to see an example of what it means to be a Christian?

## TOPIC FOR YOUTH
### A NEW PLACE

*A Golden Age.* The November 29, 1994, edition of the *Sun*, one of the supermarket tabloids, carried a front-page story announcing a great archaeological discovery. A "sermon of Jesus," in His own handwriting, had supposedly been excavated by a Dr. Bradford Nelson. In this sermon Jesus stated that He would return to initiate "a golden age" after peace comes to the Middle East.

While we may smile at weird claims such as this, the story does demonstrate a hope and longing for a better world. Although some have lost hope, many foster and nurture it in the most unusual ways.

John reminded his readers of Jesus' promise of a new beginning, complete with a new heaven and earth. His promise offered far more than just peace. It was the promise of His constant presence with us, for all eternity.

*The Better World.* What is the secret behind the popularity of Star Trek? What motivates the deep loyalty of Trekkers? With over twenty million fans and one billion dollars in revenues, the show makes an interesting topic.

Quite simply, the series runs on religious undercurrents, the strongest theme involving a world where harmony and humanism have triumphed. Everyone can live in peace and hope. One example would be the latest film, *Generations,* where a scientist drops a world into the Nexus, a time zone of pure joy and bliss.

Actress Whoopi Goldberg, who has a recurring role in the films, believes the success lies in the show's multicultural aspects. It portrays a universe where vastly different people get along together, making a world where problems are solved in genuine equality.

Instead of elevating humankind to a god-like status, John described a new and better world created by God. Humankind was the recipient, not the star actor.

*New Beginning.* Japanese veterans of World War II stood weeping tears of shame and sorrow, asking for forgiveness on November 29, 1994, at Kanchanaburi, Thailand. They were learning how they had been responsible for the deaths of 116,000 people while serving in the Imperial Army, forcing war prisoners to build the notorious "death railway." The several dozen men then walked across a bridge over the River Kwai. It was a small portion of railway track that these troops had forced allied POW's and Asian slave laborers to build through a thick, malaria-ridden jungle.

These Japanese soldiers accepted responsibility for their actions. They journeyed to Thailand to seek forgiveness, hoping to receive a new start in life as they crossed an old bridge. And we, when we come to Christ, cross a bridge to a new beginning, as well, for in Him, all things are made new.

*Questions for Students on the Next Lesson.* 1. What "instructions" was Timothy to bring to his church? 2. How does a believer "train" in godliness? 3. What is the Christian's hope? 4. How important is a believer's example? 5. Why is reading the Scripture so important for spiritual growth?

# JUNE, JULY, AUGUST 1997

## GUIDANCE FOR MINISTRY

## LESSON 1—JUNE 1

### CHRIST'S SERVANT SETS AN EXAMPLE

*Background Scripture:* I Timothy 4:6-16
*Devotional Reading:* Psalm 37:1-11

KING JAMES VERSION
I TIMOTHY 4:6 If thou put the brethren in remembrance of these things, thou shalt be a good minister of Jesus Christ, nourished up in the words of faith and of good doctrine, whereunto thou hast attained.

7 But refuse profane and old wives' fables, and exercise thyself rather unto godliness.

8 For bodily exercise profiteth little: but godliness is profitable unto all things, having promise of the life that now is, and of that which is to come.

9 This is a faithful saying and worthy of all acceptation.

10 For therefore we both labour and suffer reproach, because we trust in the living God, who is the Saviour of all men, specially of those that believe.

11 These things command and teach.

12 Let no man despise thy youth; but be thou an example of the believers, in word, in conversation, in charity, in spirit, in faith, in purity.

13 Till I come, give attendance to reading, to exhortation, to doctrine.

14 Neglect not the gift that is in thee, which was given thee by prophecy, with the laying on of the hands of the presbytery.

15 Meditate upon these things; give thyself wholly to them; that thy profiting may appear to all.

16 Take heed unto thyself, and unto the doctrine; continue in them: for in doing this thou shalt both save thyself, and them that hear thee.

NEW REVISED STANDARD VERSION
I TIMOTHY 4:6 If you put these instructions before the brothers and sisters, you will be a good servant of Christ Jesus, nourished on the words of the faith and of the sound teaching that you have followed.
7 Have nothing to do with profane myths and old wives' tales. Train yourself in godliness, 8 for, while physical training is of some value, godliness is valuable in every way, holding promise for both the present life and the life to come. 9 The saying is sure and worthy of full acceptance. 10 For to this end we toil and struggle, because we have our hope set on the living God, who is the Savior of all people, especially of those who believe.

11 These are the things you must insist on and teach. 12 Let no one despise your youth, but set the believers an example in speech and conduct, in love, in faith, in purity. 13 Until I arrive, give attention to the public reading of scripture, to exhorting, to teaching. 14 Do not neglect the gift that is in you, which was given to you through prophecy with the laying on of hands by the council of elders. 15 Put these things into practice, devote yourself to them, so that all may see your progress. 16 Pay close attention to yourself and to your teaching; continue in these things, for in doing this you will save both yourself and your hearers.

*KEY VERSES: Train yourself in godliness, for, while physical training is of some value, godliness is valuable in every way, holding promise for both the present life and the life to come. I Timothy 4:7b, 8.*

## HOME BIBLE READINGS

| | | | | |
|---|---|---|---|---|
| May | 26 | M. | Psalm 37:1-11 | *Set a Good Example* |
| May | 27 | T. | Proverbs 23:15-25 | *Be Wise* |
| May | 28 | W. | I Corinthians 4:1-5 | *Be Trustworthy* |
| May | 29 | T. | I Corinthians 4:6-13 | *Be Humble* |
| May | 30 | F. | I Thessalonians 5:23-28 | *Be Faithful as God Is Faithful* |
| May | 31 | S. | I Timothy 4:1-5 | *Beware of False Doctrines* |
| June | 1 | S. | I Corinthians 1:10-25 | *Preach Christ Crucified* |

## BACKGROUND

The letters to Timothy and Titus, which we will be studying during the coming weeks, are quite different from other writings in the New Testament. For one thing, they were addressed to individuals. Except for the brief epistle to Philemon, all other New Testament books were written to churches. Furthermore, the letters to Timothy and Titus were sent to individuals who had pastoral oversight over congregations. More than other portions of the New Testament, these letters are filled with practical advice to pastors. The books of Timothy and Titus have therefore been labeled "the Pastoral Epistles" for centuries, beginning with Thomas Aquinas (of the thirteenth century), who spoke of I Timothy as a "pastoral textbook."

These three letters discuss matters that pastoral leaders must handle in their congregations. Although all three letters touch on doctrinal themes, their main focus is on practical problems affecting a church, such as what kind of officers to choose and how to tell false teachings from true.

The apostle Paul wrote these pastoral letters in the latter part of his career. When he wrote the first letter to Timothy, he was still free. The second letter, however, discloses that he had been arrested and was in prison in Rome. Some scholars think Paul suffered two imprisonments in Rome, and that he sent his letter to Titus between these two. Everybody agrees that Paul was finally executed in Rome. Since all of these letters were written during the times immediately before and during Paul's stay in a Roman prison, we can date them in the mid-60s A.D.

When we read the Pastoral Epistles, we might feel that Paul was skipping from one subject to another—sometimes quoting a verse from a hymn, returning several times to warnings about false teachings, and interspersing personal remarks about such mundane matters as Timothy's stomach problems. Throughout, however, Paul was pleading with his associates to stand firm as pastoral leaders. He wanted them to teach their congregations to maintain high standards of morality and service. We can learn much from studying these manuals for godliness in the church.

## NOTES ON THE PRINTED TEXT

"The best way to teach is by example," an old camp director used to tell his staff. His words echoed another man's teachings centuries earlier. Paul advised Timothy to be a good example, to model the faith in all he did.

*If you put these instructions before the brothers and sisters, you will be a good servant of Christ Jesus, nourished on the words of the faith and of the sound teaching that you have followed* (4:6). Paul advised Timothy to place before his church members the words of faith and sound teaching that he himself had followed. One way to share this sound doctrine was by modeling it in daily life. Throughout their years together, Timothy had heard, seen, and studied these ideas with Paul. The best way to refute any false teaching was a positive presentation of the Christian faith. Timothy's words and works must show that he was a faithful minister of Christ.

*Have nothing to do with profane myths and old wives' tales* (4:7b). Paul urged Timothy to ignore the superstitions of the heretics. Instead of interacting with such false teachings, Timothy was directed to train himself in godliness, just as an athlete trained for a sports contest. *Train yourself in godliness, for, while physical training is of some value, godliness is valuable in every way, holding promise for both the present life and the life to come* (4:7b, 8). While physical exercise was beneficial in the present life, spiritual exercise was of far greater value. It prepared the individual for the life to come. Since the false teachers advocated various self disciplines and abstinences, Paul taught that self-control, devotion to the gospel tradition, and acceptance of suffering was better.

Paul returned to his original thought, using a traditional formula. *The saying is sure and worthy of full acceptance* (4:9). Paul taught that believers labor and strive because their hope is set on the living God. Eternal life was the goal and hope of all believers. *For to this end we toil and struggle, because we have our hope set on the living God, who is the Savior of all people, especially of those who believe* (4:10).

Paul returned to personal instructions for Timothy. He commanded Timothy to speak authoritatively. *These are the things you must insist on and teach* (4:11). Paul encouraged Timothy to resist those who questioned his abilities and authority due to his age. *Let no one despise your youth, but set the believers an example in speech and conduct, in love, in faith, in purity* (4:12). To counter his age handicap, Timothy was to be an example to the believers in at least five areas.

In addition, Paul exhorted Timothy to diligently attend to his pastoral duties. He was to read the Scripture publicly and apply its lessons to the believers through his preaching. Until Paul arrived, he was also to instruct his congregation in Christian doctrine. *Until I arrive, give attention to the public reading of scripture, to exhorting, to teaching* (4:13).

If Timothy doubted that he could lead by example, Paul reminded him that he possessed the grace and power of the Holy Spirit. A special ability from the Spirit had been given to him at his ordination. *Do not neglect the gift that is in you, which was given to you through prophecy with the laying on of hands by the council of elders* (4:14).

Equipped with the Spirit, Timothy was expected to lead the church energetically. Timothy was to put all of Paul's instructions into practice in order to benefit himself as well as his hearers. *Put these things into practice, devote yourself to them, so that all may see your progress* (4:15). When the congregation noticed that Timothy was fulfilling his calling as a leader, they would no longer think of him as young and inexperienced, but recognize his authority and follow his example.

Timothy must live what he preached. His exemplary lifestyle would be the lesson and the preaching. *Pay close attention to yourself and to your teaching; continue in these things, for in doing this you will save both yourself and your hearers* (4:16).

## SUGGESTIONS TO TEACHERS

A young pastor in New England was discovered spending an unusual amount of time with an attractive young woman in the congregation. Both were married. Because the pastor's car was parked in the driveway of the woman's house almost every afternoon, several of the deacons called on him. When questioned about the matter, the pastor became defensive. He dismissed the deacons' concerns as none of their business. "What I do in my spare time is my own business," he insisted.

Unfortunately, this man's example undermined his ministry. Eventually, when he was discovered to be having an affair with the woman in question, he excused his conduct on the grounds that "it happens all the time these days, so why the big fuss?" The example of his infidelity continues to hamper the growth of that congregation. If only this young pastor would have taken to heart the words in I Timothy!

1. FED. Timothy was urged to be "nourished on the words of the faith" (4:6). We, like Timothy, must be nourished spiritually. Ask your students what kind of spiritual nourishment feeds them. The junk food of popular movies and television programs? A diet of sugary devotionals? When was the last time you or your students read a good book on Christian doctrine? How often does each group member take time for serious Bible study?

2. FIT. Paul used terminology from the gymnasium and athletic field to remind Timothy of the importance of staying spiritually fit. Sports training illustrates the way Christians must work to keep from becoming flabby spiritually, for believers face powerful opponents. What forms of "workout" should followers of Christ practice each day to remain strong in godliness?

3. FOCUSED. Paul insisted that Timothy "give attention to the public reading of scripture" (4:13) by continuously doing everything possible to preach and teach the Word of God. The pastor or congregation that neglects the Bible soon loses its focus on the Lord. Discuss with your students what it means to be a Scripture-based church.

4. FERVENT. Young Timothy apparently lacked confidence because of his youth and inexperience. Paul advised him, however, to set "an example in speech and conduct, in love and purity" (4:12). Emphasize that every servant of Christ is to live an exemplary life. The world will see Christ's significance through those who dare call themselves Christians.

## TOPIC FOR ADULTS
### *PRACTICE WHAT YOU PREACH*

*Truth or Fiction?* A Bishop in London once had a conversation with a famous actor. "Why is it," asked the Bishop, "that we preachers make so little impression with the great and true subjects that we proclaim, while you actors move people so deeply with the fictitious matters you portray?"

The actor answered, "Perhaps it is simply because we actors speak of fictitious things as if they were true; you clergy speak about true things as if they were fictitious."

*Conciliator's Credo.* Since leaving office, former President Jimmy Carter has distinguished himself by practicing Christian convictions in specific ways. As president, Carter was often ridiculed for his convictions and traditional beliefs. But he did not retire to play golf and write memoirs to answer his critics. Carter quietly joined work crews rehabilitating inner-city buildings for Habitat for Humanity. He was observed tidying up the churchyard in Plains, taking his monthly turn tending the grounds. And he has also risked his life by repeatedly consenting to try to broker a cease fire or bring together warring factions in violence-torn countries. Why does he take the risks and criticisms that come with being a conciliator?

"I have one life and one chance to make it count for something," he explains. "I'm free to choose what that something is, and the something I've chosen is my faith. Now, my faith goes beyond theology and religion and requires considerable work and effort. My faith demands—this is not optional—my faith demands that I do whatever I can, wherever I can, whenever I can, for as long as I can, with whatever I have, to try to make a difference."

*Authentic Answers.* A farmer was asked if he was a Christian. He answered, "Let me give you two lists. First, let me give you ten names of people who like me. Then let me give you a list of ten who hate me. Why not ask them?"

What better way of replying to the question! How would you answer?

*Questions for Students on the Next Lesson.* 1. What precisely do the words *righteousness* and *godliness* mean to you? 2. What are some unsound teachings that threaten to undermine the faith of some church people in our time? 3. Why does the Bible warn about wanting to get wealth? 4. Does I Timothy 6 state that money in itself is evil? 5. What are the keys to contentment in living?

### TOPIC FOR YOUTH
#### KEEP ON SERVING

*No Profane Myths?* Paul urged Timothy to have nothing to do with profane myths and false tales. Instead, he was to train himself in godliness. Perhaps you feel that you have followed these instructions, but you may need to think again. Children spend an average of one-and-a-half hours per day staring at computer games. In fact, a ten-year-old would apparently rather play a video game than eat, sleep, or go to school.

The forty-million-dollar-per-year industry allows a child to move into a different world. One of the best-selling video games is Mortal Kombat, a brutal punch-and-kick game in which Johnny Cage kills by decapitating his victims. Another character, Rayden, favors electrocution. Kano punches his opponent's chest open to tear out his heart, while Sonya Blade utilizes a burning kiss of death.

The result is that children who play these games become far more aggressive and prone to solving their problems with violence, according to Parker V. Page, head of Children's Television Resources and Education. So when you think that you have nothing to do with profane myths . . . think again.

*Trained in Wrong Priority.* For as long as Eric could remember, he had been involved in church activities and youth groups. As he grew, Eric also became interested in swimming. He participated in the local swim club and did very well. In high school Eric devoted more and more time to his competitive swimming. His parents began skipping Sunday morning worship to drive Eric to the local university where he received private coaching. The extra work paid off. Eric did quite well in the swimming meets, qualifying for the state tournament. He also received a college scholarship.

But Eric and his family had become inactive at church. Eric had given priority to developing his athletic ability while neglecting his spiritual development. While he was physically fit in this life, he was unprepared for the life to come. How fit are you—physically and spiritually?

*Deepen Your Knowledge.* A Gallup Poll noted some ominous trends in our culture, while lamenting the shocking lack of biblical knowledge. Some specific findings of the survey: six out of ten teenagers were unable to name any New Testament Gospels; four in ten teens who attend church cannot name them; three in ten teens do not know what event is celebrated at Easter. One-third of teens do not know the number of disciples Jesus had, while one in five regular churchgoers cannot answer the same question.

Paul urged Timothy not to neglect the reading of Scripture and not to neglect the study of Christian doctrine. Listen to his advice. Deepen your knowledge of the faith so that you, too, may serve and be an example to those still seeking the Lord.

*Questions for Students on the Next Lesson.* 1. What happens to a church when something other than the gospel is preached? 2. What was the basis of Paul's "contentment"? 3. How did Paul feel about money? 4. What danger does wealth bring? 5. What suggestions did Paul make to those who were rich?

# LESSON 2—JUNE 8

## CHRIST'S SERVANT TEACHES GODLINESS

*Background Scripture:* I Timothy 6:2b-21
*Devotional Reading:* I Timothy 6:14-20

KING JAMES VERSION

KING JAMES VERSION

I TIMOTHY 6:2b . . . teach and exhort.

3 If any man teach otherwise, and consent not to wholesome words, even the words of our Lord Jesus Christ, and to the doctrine which is according to godliness;

4 He is proud, knowing nothing, but doting about questions and strifes of words, whereof cometh envy, strife, railings, evil surmisings,

5 Perverse disputings of men of corrupt minds, and destitute of the truth, supposing that gain is godliness: from such withdraw thyself.

6 But godliness with contentment is great gain.

7 For we brought nothing into this world, and it is certain we can carry nothing out.

8 And having food and raiment let us be therewith content.

9 But they that will be rich fall into temptation and a snare, and into many foolish and hurtful lusts, which drown men in destruction and perdition.

10 For the love of money is the root of all evil: which while some coveted after, they have erred from the faith and pierced themselves through with many sorrows.

11 But thou, O man of God, flee these things; and follow after righteousness, godliness, faith, love, patience, meekness.

12 Fight the good fight of faith, lay hold on eternal life, whereunto thou art also called, and hast professed a good profession before many witnesses.

13 I give thee charge in the sight of God, who quickeneth all things, and before Christ Jesus, who before Pontius Pilate witnessed a good confession;

14 That thou keep this commandment without spot, unrebukeable, until the appearing of our Lord Jesus Christ:

15 Which in his times he shall shew, who is the blessed and only Potentate, the King of kings, and Lord of lords;

16 Who only hath immortality, dwelling in the light which no man can approach unto; whom no man hath seen, nor can see: to whom be honour and power everlasting. Amen.

17 Charge them that are rich in this world, that they be not highminded, nor

NEW REVISED STANDARD VERSION

I TIMOTHY 6:2b Teach and urge these duties.

3 Whoever teaches otherwise and does not agree with the sound words of our Lord Jesus Christ and the teaching that is in accordance with godliness, 4 is conceited, understanding nothing, and has a morbid craving for controversy and for disputes about words. From these come envy, dissension, slander, base suspicions, 5 and wrangling among those who are depraved in mind and bereft of the truth, imagining that godliness is a means of gain. 6 Of course, there is great gain in godliness combined with contentment; 7 for we brought nothing into the world, so that we can take nothing out of it; 8 but if we have food and clothing, we will be content with these. 9 But those who want to be rich fall into temptation and are trapped by many senseless and harmful desires that plunge people into ruin and destruction. 10 For the love of money is a root of all kinds of evil, and in their eagerness to be rich some have wandered away from the faith and pierced themselves with many pains.

11 But as for you, man of God, shun all this; pursue righteousness, godliness, faith, love, endurance, gentleness. 12 Fight the good fight of the faith; take hold of the eternal life, to which you were called and for which you made the good confession in the presence of many witnesses. 13 In the presence of God, who gives life to all things, and of Christ Jesus, who in his testimony before Pontius Pilate made the good confession, I charge you 14 to keep the commandment without spot or blame until the manifestation of our Lord Jesus Christ, 15 which he will bring about at the right time—he who is the blessed and only Sovereign, the King of kings and Lord of lords. 16 It is he alone who has immortality and dwells in unapproachable light, whom no one has ever seen or can see; to him be honor and eternal dominion. Amen.

17 As for those who in the present age are rich, command them not to be haughty, or to set their hopes on the uncertainty of riches, but rather on God who richly provides us with everything for our enjoyment. 18 They

trust in uncertain riches, but in the living God, who giveth us richly all things to enjoy;

18 That they do good, that they be rich in good works, ready to distribute, willing to communicate;

19 Laying up in store for themselves a good foundation against the time to come, that they may lay hold on eternal life.

20 O Timothy, keep that which is committed to thy trust, avoiding profane and vain babblings, and oppositions of science falsely so called:

21 Which some professing have erred concerning the faith. Grace be with thee. Amen.

are to do good, to be rich in good works, generous, and ready to share, 19 thus storing up for themselves the treasure of a good foundation for the future, so that they may take hold of the life that really is life.

20 Timothy, guard what has been entrusted to you. Avoid the profane chatter and contradictions of what is falsely called knowledge; 21 by professing it some have missed the mark as regards the faith.

Grace be with you.

*KEY VERSES: Pursue righteousness, godliness, faith, love, endurance, gentleness. Fight the good fight of the faith. I Timothy 6:11b, 12b.*

## HOME BIBLE READINGS

| June | 2 | M. | I Timothy 6:13-21 | *Keep above Reproach* |
|---|---|---|---|---|
| June | 3 | T. | I Timothy 5:17-24 | *Keep Yourself Pure* |
| June | 4 | W. | Philippians 1:3-11 | *Approve the Good* |
| June | 5 | T. | I John 2:12-17 | *Do Not Love the World* |
| June | 6 | F. | Ephesians 3:14-21 | *Accept the Love of Christ* |
| June | 7 | S. | Luke 12:13-21 | *Follow Christ's Example* |
| June | 8 | S. | II Peter 1:3-11 | *God's Divine Power Grants Godliness* |

## BACKGROUND

Timothy, Paul's colleague, was a native of Lystra, a city in what is now central Turkey. His father was not a believer, but his mother and grandmother, Eunice and Lois, were devout Christians. Timothy was drawn to Jesus Christ through Paul's preaching in Lystra and became a loyal friend and associate. To silence the shrill criticism of traditionalists within the Christian fellowship—as well as Jewish opponents—Timothy accepted Paul's request to be circumcised.

The trio of Paul, Silas, and Timothy continued on their momentous missionary journey across to Greece. In spite of his youth, Timothy became a trusted emissary of Paul. He returned to Thessalonica as Paul's representative and served in the same capacity in Corinth, Ephesus, Macedonia, and other Gentile congregations. Reading the New Testament, however, we get the impression that Timothy sometimes felt intimidated by his critics. Paul felt the need to bolster his younger associate's faith and self-confidence on several occasions. Nevertheless, the two had a special relationship in which Timothy was referred to as a son on four occasions in the letters we call I and II Timothy.

Paul dictated his first letter to Timothy shortly after visiting churches in Macedonia. He had asked Timothy to stay in Ephesus to supervise the fledgling church there. Paul expected to rejoin Timothy in Ephesus as early as possible. Meanwhile, he dispatched a letter crammed with practical counsel to the timid, inexperienced, and sometimes frail young preacher.

## NOTES ON THE PRINTED TEXT

*Teach and urge these duties* (6:2b). Paul concluded his letter with another reminder about the danger of false teachings. He contrasted Timothy's preaching with that of the false teachers. Timothy taught the sayings of Christ.

Apparently a large oral tradition existed, perhaps already by this time some written tradition, of Christ's words. Those who taught other than Christ's words were guilty of misunderstanding, blind ambition, or rhetorical theorizing. *Whoever teaches otherwise and does not agree with the sound words of our Lord Jesus Christ and the teaching that is in accordance with godliness, is conceited, understanding nothing, and has a morbid craving for controversy and for disputes about words* (6:3, 4a).

Paul detailed the results of unsound teaching, which would ultimately destroy the church. The believers' mental and moral attitudes would be changed and they would lose their hold on the truth. Other opportunists would use the faith for profit. *From these come envy, dissension, slander, base suspicions, and wrangling among those who are depraved in mind and benefit of the truth, imagining that godliness is a means of gain* (6:4b, 5).

Using irony, Paul echoed his opponents' claim that the true faith could be a means of profit. However, he reinterpreted the claim to prove that the benefits would not consist of material gifts but the promise of true life. This understanding led to true contentment and satisfaction. *Of course, there is great gain in godliness combined with contentment* (6:6). Godliness should produce spiritual contentment, not necessarily material gain.

Paul taught that godliness was not a means of gain. Nothing that a believer desired or coveted had any permanency. *For we brought nothing into the world so that we can take nothing out of it* (6:7). In fact, believers should be satisfied with the basic necessities. *But if we have food and clothing, we will be content with these* (6:8). Godliness with contentment was the great gain.

Paul warned that those who want to be rich become trapped in harmful desires that can ruin their lives. These people are like animals lured into a trap or are—literally—drowning in a sea. *But those who want to be rich fall into temptation and are trapped by many senseless and harmful desires that plunge people into ruin and destruction* (6:9). Paul recited a proverb to prove the problem of riches. The love of money led to all kinds of evil. He then added another thought that described riches as being like thorns that painfully puncture and scratch us. The love of money leads believers away from the heart of faith in Christ. *For the love of money is a root of all kinds of evil, and in their eagerness to be rich some have wandered away from the faith and pierced themselves with many pains* (6:10).

Paul addressed Timothy personally, appealing to him to keep clear of such greedy behavior. Instead, he was to pursue certain positive qualities. *But as for you, man of God, shun all this; pursue righteousness, godliness, faith, love, endurance, gentleness* (6:11). His character and conduct were to be like God's. Paul saw life as being like a long, continual athletic contest. He challenged Timothy to struggle for the prize connected with eternal life, a goal he had accepted at his baptism (or his ordination). *Fight the good fight of the faith; take hold of the eternal life, to which you were called and for which you made the good confession in the presence of many witnesses* (6:12).

Timothy was charged to be as unflinchingly loyal to his calling as Jesus was before Pontius Pilate. He was also reminded to serve Christ with the same enthusiasm that he had pledged at either his baptism or ordination. He must keep himself free from heresy and contamination until Christ's coming. *In the presence of God, who gives life to all things, and of Christ Jesus, who in his testimony before Pontius Pilate made the good confession, I charge you to keep the commandment without spot or blame until the manifestation of our Lord Jesus Christ, which he will bring about at the right time* (6:13-15a).

The mention of Christ's coming caused Paul to offer a doxology praising God's sovereignty. *He who is the blessed and only Sovereign, the King of kings and Lord of lords. It is he alone who has immortality and dwells in unapproachable light, whom no one has ever seen or can see; to him be honor and eternal dominion. Amen* (6:15b, 16).

Paul returned to his thoughts on wealth. He reminded Timothy to counsel the wealthy Ephesians about the temptations riches presented. The wealthy should put their trust and reliance in God, not riches. *As for those who in the present age are rich, command them not to be haughty, or to set their hopes on the uncertainty of riches, but rather on God who richly provides us with everything for our enjoyment* (6:17).

The wealthy should help the poor if they truly wanted to please God. *They are to do good, to be rich in good works, generous, and ready to share, thus storing up for themselves the treasure of a good foundation for the future, so that they may take hold of the life that really is life* (6:18, 19).

Paul closed by urging Timothy to keep the Gospel safe and pure. "Guard" denotes the placing of a trust in another's keeping. *Timothy, guard what has been entrusted to you. Avoid the profane chatter and contradictions of what is falsely called knowledge; by professing it some have missed the mark as regards the faith* (6:20, 21). Paul ended the letter with a benediction of grace.

## SUGGESTIONS TO TEACHERS

A young Marine sat down before the chaplain and confessed, "I need some kind of guideline, Chaplain. I want to be a Christian, but I'm confused. One guy tells me it merely means you don't cuss or sleep with someone who's not your wife. Another guy tells me anything's okay as long as you say your prayers. And others think you're going soft if you show any signs of being a Christian at all. What am I to do, Chaplain?"

The Marine's problem was similar to the one faced by Timothy's people in Ephesus—or the people in your class. What does it mean to be a Christian? How shall we live a godly life as servants of Christ?

The Gospel (and thus the material in this lesson) does not offer a system of rules for earning God's favor. Christ has delivered us from legalism and offered His work on the cross as our means of salvation. Nor does the New Testament allow Christ's people to wander into moralistic ways, in which they may imagine they can save themselves by being "good." However, our lesson from I Timothy does give helpful teaching about living out our salvation in godliness.

1. CARING vs. CONTENTIOUS. Discuss I Timothy 6:2b-5, noting that persons truly trying to be servants of the Servant Lord will strive always to show love. A spirit of conceit and a "craving for controversy and for disputes" is the quickest way to short-circuit the Holy Spirit's power. How easy it is to think that "my position" is to be defended at all costs! How tempting it is to want to coerce others through religious debate. Yet so often the debater wins the argument but loses a brother. Many a church has been crippled by unnecessary squabbles.

2. CONTENT vs. CRAVING. Take a good look at Paul's admonitions regarding money. Make students realize that it is the *love* of money, not money itself, that is "the root of all kinds of evil" (6:10). Here is a great opportunity to talk about Christian stewardship. Poverty is not glorified here; neither is wealth. Each status in life has its problems, its dangers to spiritual growth. The key is to learn contentment in fellowship with God. In these "neurotic nineties," Christians may discover a sense of serenity in the midst of a consumer-oriented culture.

3. CONFESSING vs. COMPROMISING. The pressures to "give in and go along" are sometimes irresistible. Think together and talk about the practical meaning of pursuing "righteousness, godliness, faith, love, endurance, gentleness" (6:11). Go on to the following verse, which reminds believers of their original, public confessions of faith. This "public pledge of allegiance to Christ" is a lifetime promise. How shall we carry it out in daily life?

4. CONSIDERATE vs. CALCULATING. Throughout this lesson, we have suggested bold contrasts as a way of clarifying the nature of godliness. Here is another contrast that comes through: we can show consideration toward others rather than calculating how to put them down. In this regard, Paul held up the example of Christ himself.

### TOPIC FOR ADULTS
### *PURSUE GODLINESS*

*What Shapes You? Time* magazine's December 5, 1994, issue featured the subject of leadership. The magazine editors screened hundreds of candidates, then selected fifty men and women, age forty and under, who are expected to be the outstanding leaders in the coming years. The story gave profiles of the fifty leaders.

The list included promising leaders in politics, government, education, and business. The cutoff age of forty was an attempt to balance accomplishment with future promise. One of those selected was a young African American law professor at Yale, Stephen Carter. Carter's writings include *The Culture of Disbelief,* in which he criticized the courts and academia for "treating God as a hobby." At the time Carter was selected as one of the fifty most promising leaders, he was working on a new book, "about a life in which one works hard to do what most of us don't do often enough—distinguish right from wrong."

Stephen Carter is an active church member. He states, "Each of us is a complex of our ideas and experiences. I am shaped by being an African-American. But I am also shaped by being a Christian."

What—and who—shapes your life?

*Righteous as a Coffee Mug.* When we hear the word *righteous* today, it is quite likely that we associate it with vague notions of unworldly piety. Thus someone described as righteous is pictured as highly religious, law-abiding, and scrupulous in the extreme. We may in our own minds even add "self" before "righteous."

Yet in Old English, one meaning of "righteous" was much more ordinary and earthy. Someone or something that acted according to their true nature could have been described as righteous. Thus a coffee mug that held the coffee well, and was good to use, might be called "righteous." So, too, might a mayor, a wife, a sheep dog, a hammer, or a law.

The Bible's picture of righteousness is closer to this than it is to head-in-the-clouds piety. For us today, being righteous means being what God created us to be . . . children who reflect the Father's likeness. For God is a righteous God, and His righteousness is not abstract. He acts to maintain and restore righteousness in all things.

The idea that we can live righteously by disengaging from the struggle of everyday life is totally foreign to the biblical way of thinking. It would be akin to putting a mug on a mantel, keeping it dusted, but never actually using it. It may get some compliments or even be described as a thing of beauty. But by definition it is not a "righteous" coffee mug until it is taken down and used as it is meant to be used.

*Greedy Grumblers.* Few of us live in true contentment. We love money; we want more. Most of us are grumblers—if not public grumblers, we are closet complainers. We're all a bit like the man in the joke who was sitting at his desk looking dejected. An acquaintance walked by and asked, "Hey, Sam! Why the long face?"

"Why the long face?" Sam replied. "Well, do you remember that two months ago my grandfather died and left me $25,000?"

"Yeah, I remember. But why so downcast and depressed?"

Last month my Uncle Bert passed away, and he left me $15,000."

The friend nodded, "That's right, I remember! But why are you down in the dumps now? What's so bad about all that?"

"What's so bad about it? This month, not a dime!"

*Questions for Students on the Next Lesson.* 1. What military example did Paul use in writing to Timothy? 2. What sports reference did he use? 3. What was taking place in Paul's life when he wrote this letter? 4. To what extent does your Christian commitment make demands on you? What is the most difficult aspect of being a Christian? 5. How would you counsel someone who is suffering because of his or her faith in Christ?

## TOPIC FOR YOUTH
### STRIVE FOR GODLINESS

*What's Important?* Eric, 18, summed up his philosophy of life when he told his girlfriend, "If you don't have money, you're nobody. It's the world we live in."

Some youth are trapped by the desire for money. They love money so much that they neglect their spiritual, moral, and social development. Paul warned about the trap of wealth and money. The desire for money can be the ruin of our lives.

*Blinders, Please.* Plog Research conducted a survey of United States travelers. The question to be answered was actually a sentence to complete: "The trip is ruined if . . ." While the majority (77 percent) indicated their vacation would be spoiled by a dirty hotel, almost half (43 percent) felt their trip would be ruined if they had to look at poverty. Almost half of the public felt it was important to see no evidence of the world's poor when they—the relaxing tourists—were trying to enjoy themselves.

Wealth can lead people away from the practice of compassion. Sadly, a nation that calls itself Christian and possesses most of the world's wealth does not want to look upon the world's poor. What does this say about the true state of our commitment to Christ and His values?

*Poverty of Compassion.* Over thirty years ago, President Lyndon B. Johnson declared a War on Poverty, promising to eliminate poverty from the land. Between 1965 and 1992, the gross national product grew by 53.2 percent. However, thirty-eight million Americans (including 14.6 million children, or one in every five) still live in poverty. Under some current welfare reform plans, it is projected that five million children, half of those supported by the Aid to Families with Dependent Children program, will be denied assistance.

Paul warned that those who want to become rich often become trapped in harmful desires that ruin their lives. Paul reminded Timothy and his church to love. Love means caring for all in compassion and generosity, especially the children.

*Questions for Students on the Next Lesson.* 1. What examples of faithfulness did Paul offer to Timothy in his second letter? 2. How is Jesus "a descendant of David"? 3. Why was Paul suffering? 4. Have you had to suffer for your faith? When? 5. Why is the "Word of God . . . not chained"?

# LESSON 3—JUNE 15

## CHRIST'S SERVANT ENDURES SUFFERING

**Background Scripture:** II Timothy 2:1-13
**Devotional Reading:** II Timothy 2:14-26

### KING JAMES VERSION

II TIMOTHY 2:1 Thou therefore, my son, be strong in the grace that is in Christ Jesus.

2 And the things that thou hast heard of me among many witnesses, the same commit thou to faithful men, who shall be able to teach others also.

3 Thou therefore endure hardness, as a good soldier of Jesus Christ.

4 No man that warreth entangleth himself with the affairs of this life; that he may please him who hath chosen him to be a soldier.

5 And if a man also strive for masteries, yet is he not crowned, except he strive lawfully.

6 The husbandman that laboureth must be first partaker of the fruits.

7 Consider what I say; and the Lord give thee understanding in all things.

8 Remember that Jesus Christ of the seed of David was raised from the dead according to my gospel:

9 Wherein I suffer trouble, as an evil doer, even unto bonds; but the word of God is not bound.

10 Therefore I endure all things for the elect's sakes, that they may also obtain the salvation which is in Christ Jesus with eternal glory.

11 It is a faithful saying: For if we be dead with him, we shall also live with him:

12 If we suffer, we shall also reign with him: if we deny him, he also will deny us:

13 If we believe not, yet abideth faithful: he cannot deny himself.

### NEW REVISED STANDARD VERSION

II TIMOTHY 2:1 You then, my child, be strong in the grace that is in Christ Jesus; 2 and what you have heard from me through many witnesses entrust to faithful people who will be able to teach others as well. 3 Share in suffering like a good soldier of Christ Jesus. 4 No one serving in the army gets entangled in everyday affairs; the soldier's aim is to please the enlisting officer. 5 And in the case of an athlete, no one is crowned without competing according to the rules. 6 It is the farmer who does the work who ought to have the first share of the crops. 7 Think over what I say, for the Lord will give you understanding in all things.

8 Remember Jesus Christ, raised from the dead, a descendant of David—that is my gospel, 9 for which I suffer hardship, even to the point of being chained like a criminal. But the word of God is not chained. 10 Therefore I endure everything for the sake of the elect, so that they may also obtain the salvation that is in Christ Jesus, with eternal glory. 11 The saying is sure: If we have died with him, we will also live with him; 12 if we endure, we will also reign with him; if we deny him, he will also deny us; 13 if we are faithless, he remains faithful—for he cannot deny himself.

*KEY VERSE: Share in suffering like a good soldier of Christ Jesus.*
II Timothy 2:3.

## HOME BIBLE READINGS

## BACKGROUND

Paul's Second Letter to Timothy is probably the most deeply personal of all of the great apostle's writings. Here he lays bare his heart and comes through as truly human. In the earlier letter to Timothy, Paul was still a free man. But by the time he wrote II Timothy, he had been arrested and condemned, and he faced the end of his life. A sense of time running out was made harsher by the desolation he was experiencing. Friends had all left, except for Luke. For different reasons, faithful associates could no longer be with him. The loneliness was no doubt hard to bear.

Paul was being tried for his membership in what was thought to be a subversive cult. And he was resigned to the fact that there was no way for him to escape the death sentence. He also knew that Christians throughout the empire could expect similar forms of persecution. No longer would the emperor and other authorities tolerate those worshiping Jesus Christ.

Paul had leaned on Timothy, who was a faithful emissary to various churches. The childless, elderly missionary had felt such a close bond with Timothy that he referred to him as his son. As his father in the faith, old Paul wanted to give Timothy some final words of comfort and counsel. Second Timothy throbs with Paul's love for his spiritual son and heir.

Timothy was not always robust—physically, emotionally, or spiritually. Paul was concerned that Timothy might not have the stamina to persevere in the days of testing ahead. In some ways, the Second Letter to Timothy became a manual for effective church leadership in tough times. The advice continues to be as pertinent today as it was in A.D. 67.

## NOTES ON THE PRINTED TEXT

Paul exhorted Timothy to display courage and steadfastness, to keep sharing the Gospel reliably with others. Timothy had learned this from his grandmother, mother, Barnabas, Paul, and other faithful witnesses. After all, he had been ordained for this very thing: to preach and teach. *You then, my child, be strong in the grace that is in Christ Jesus, and what you have heard from me through many witnesses entrust to faithful people who will be able to teach others as well* (2:1, 2).

Knowing that the life of an evangelist and a preacher was full of hardship, Paul urged Timothy to accept his share of suffering. Paul used a series of illustrations. *Share in suffering like a good soldier of Christ Jesus* (2:3). A soldier is fully committed to his commanding officer. He has been called and dispatched to active duty. He serves bravely, even in tough circumstances. He seeks only to carry out his commander's orders. Timothy was charged to do the same. *No one serving in the army gets entangled in everyday affairs; the soldier's aim is to please the enlisting officer* (2:4).

Next Paul referred to the professional athlete, who practiced strict training and who was rewarded only when he competed within the rules. Ancient rules dictated that an athlete swear that he had consistently trained for ten months, followed a strict diet, and completed pre-game physical training. The Christian leader must exhibit the dedication of an athlete. *And in the case of an athlete, no one is crowned without competing according to the rules* (2:5).

Paul developed his final metaphor from the life of the farmer. Anyone who plants and envisions a good harvest must be willing to work hard. *It is the farmer who does the work who ought to have the first share of the crops* (2:6). Paul urged Timothy to ponder and discover for himself the implications of his three illustrations. *Think over what I say, for the Lord will give you understanding in all things* (2:7).

If Timothy needed an example of suffering, he had only to think of Christ Himself, who suffered and died before His exaltation. Paul used a short creedal formula, which was also the heart of his preaching. *Remember Jesus Christ, raised from the dead, a descendant of David—that is my gospel* (2:8). Paul also held himself up to Timothy as an example. *I suffer hardship, even to the point of being chained like a criminal* (2:9a). While stymied by his unjust confinement, he knew that the Gospel was not stopped simply because he had been imprisoned. *But the word of God is not chained* (2:9b).

Paul's sufferings, though, were not tragic. He reminded Timothy that he suffered hardship and prison so that it was easier for people to receive salvation in Christ. *Therefore I endure everything for the sake of the elect, so that they may also obtain the salvation that is in Christ Jesus, with eternal glory* (2:10).

Paul emphasized his point by quoting a hymn that would have been familiar to Timothy. Perhaps the hymn was associated with the experience of baptism. The first two of four "if" clauses were positive statements that emphasized a believer's participation in Christ's death and resurrection. *If we have died with him, we will also live with him; if we endure, we will also reign with him* (2:11b, 12).

## SUGGESTIONS TO TEACHERS

Over the past few decades news reports have presented numerous accounts of Christian martyrdom at the hands of fanatic Muslim extremists in Algeria, the Sudan, Iraq, Iran, and Pakistan—and by right-wing death squads in several Latin American countries. Reports from China indicate that some Christians are still in prison because of their evangelistic activities.

Persecution of Christians happens in the twentieth century, just as it did in the first century. Probably in this country no "hit man" will gun us down because of our commitment to Christ. And most likely, no jail term or torture cell awaits us. But persecution may take more subtle forms. If we are not experiencing some personal discomfort or social pressure because of our faith, perhaps we need to ask why. Timothy had no such need to ask.

1. STRENGTHENED IN GRACE. Timothy learned to be "strong in the grace that is in Jesus Christ" (2:1). God's grace is His goodness poured out on the undeserving through Jesus Christ. "Amazing Grace" has been trivialized as part of the sentimental repertoire of pop singers. But the existence of unconditional acceptance—God's grace—is a radical message that stiffens our resolve to remain strong in the faith.

2. STEADFAST IN COMMITMENT. Living as a Christian means being constantly on active duty (see II Tim. 2:3-7). Point out that a believer will not become entangled in "civilian" pursuits that might keep him or her from carrying out the orders of the commander. Likewise, a successful ath-

lete wins only by competing according to the rules. Half-hearted commitment in sports, as well as in the military, means disaster. The same is true in the life of a Christian.

3. SYMPATHETIC TO CHRIST. Paul offered Timothy a tip on how to endure suffering: "Remember Jesus Christ!" (2:8). Jesus had died and been subjected to cruelty, disgrace, and a horrible death. Suffering hardship and being "chained like a criminal" (2:9) would not break the person who remembered Christ's sufferings.

4. SECURE IN THE GOSPEL. Second Timothy 2:11-13 may contain the lines of a lovely ancient hymn, or words of an early creed; they should be repeated in your class. Examine each of these phrases, savoring the marvelous promises of God to those who endure.

## TOPIC FOR ADULTS
### THE COST OF COMMITMENT

*High Price of Faith.* With our comfortable pews and feel-good religion, we in this country might not realize what fellow Christians are experiencing in other places. In Iran, in January 1994, the body of Bishop Haik Hovsepian-Mehr was found after he had spoken out in criticism of the government's persecution of Christians. Hovsepian-Mehr, superintendent of the Assemblies of God congregations in Iran, and head of an umbrella organization for all Protestant churches in that country, was murdered at the hands of Iranian security forces. His death was the result of his efforts to secure release for Mehdi Dibaj, another Assemblies of God minister, who had been sentenced to death for converting from Islam.

In Pakistan, in March 1995, a fourteen-year-old Christian boy, Salamat Masih, and his uncle, a forty-year-old Christian named Rehmet Masih, were finally released after being sentenced to death for allegedly defaming the prophet Mohammed. The appeals court judge threw the case out when the prosecution could not produce any evidence of the charges, but militant Muslim extremists vowed to kill Masih, the defense attorney, and the judges. Earlier, on April 5, 1994, while the blasphemy trial was in progress, three gunmen on motorbikes opened fire on the Masih family as they were being escorted into the Lahore High Court building, killing Manzoor Masih, son of Rehmet Masih. Although the gunmen were arrested a few days later, they were quickly released on bail. The charges against the two Masihs were eventually disclosed to be fabricated by fanatics. Their only crime, in effect, was that of being practicing Christians.

In 1995, the Chinese government was reportedly again harassing Christians. It was seeking to remove Yang Yudong, senior pastor of Gangwashi Church, one of the most popular congregations in Beijing. In a dispatch from Beijing, the Associated Press said it had been given a written appeal signed by six Christians. It called "brothers and sisters in Christ to pray for us, members of the body who have suffered abuse, and to be concerned about how the situation develops."

Yang has long irritated the Chinese government with his pro-democracy views and his efforts to distance the Gangwashi congregation from the officially recognized church in China. The appeal said that Chinese police have followed and harassed church members and that in at least two instances, members had been beaten by plainclothes policemen.

After officials in Xunhang County in the province of Shaanxi got word that five young preachers from neighboring Ankang would be attending a service at a local house church, eight or nine policemen paid it a visit. They beat some people with clubs and handcuffed the three male and two female Ankang preachers. The three men were stripped from the waist down and beaten. The twenty-six other Christians present were then forced to beat the three men a hundred times each with a bamboo rod—or be beaten themselves. After this, the three were strung up with rope and beaten unconscious by the cursing police officers. The two women were also harshly beaten, and the officers tore open their clothes and abused them. The beatings continued until dawn, at which time they were all locked in one bare detention room for eight days. One of the men, twenty-two-year-old Lai Manping, later died.

Every year, thousands of less severe incidents occur, ranging from the fining of Christians who "unlawfully" attend unregistered religious meetings, to the arrest and imprisonment of itinerant evangelists. Most of these cases involve house churches, which are illegal because they are not registered with the government.

Even so, Christianity is the fastest growing religion in China today, especially among young people. Its dynamism owes much to the passionate commitment and spiritual hunger of Chinese Christians themselves. Their vibrant faith is captured in the words of one young female house church leader. When asked if she was afraid of persecution, she smiled and replied, "That would be my time of glory."

How much is your commitment costing you?

*Questions for Students on the Next Lesson.* 1. Why was Paul writing the words in II Timothy 4 to his young associate? 2. What did Paul think would be the outcome of his imprisonment? 3. What are some of the current false teachings that threaten to undercut true faith in Christ? 4. When do you find it unpopular to speak up as a Christian? 5. Aware of your mortality, how would you write to a trusted friend about facing your imminent death?

## TOPIC FOR YOUTH
### SUBMIT TO DISCIPLINE

*Many Menorahs.* On December 2, 1993, five-year-old Isaac Schnitzer and his two-year-old sister, Rachel, were getting ready for bed. The two had placed a yellow plastic menorah in the bedroom window of their Billings, Montana, home. Suddenly the window was shattered by a cinder block. The two terrified children hid under Isaac's bed. A Neo-Nazi hate group had been active in the area for over a year, intimidating black worshipers, spray-painting swastikas on Native Americans' homes, and overturning headstones in the Jewish cemetery.

Sarah Anthony Roberts, of the Billings Coalition for Human Rights, went to work. She organized a vigil outside the synagogue. Margie MacDonald and her pastor, Rev. Keith Torney of the First Congregational United Church of Christ, made pictures of menorahs and asked the congregation to put the pictures in their windows as a show of solidarity. The idea caught on. The eighth graders at St. Francis Upper School, with their teacher, Martha Zauher (who had just read *The Diary of Anne Frank* to her class), organized a menorah project. Menorahs began to appear in factories, stores, gas stations, cars, on billboards and rooftops, and in thousands of Christian homes. The Catholic High School placed a banner over its new windows that read, "Happy Chanukah to our Jewish Friends." The Billings Gazette published a full-page color menorah, urging its 56,000 readers to display it as a symbol of their determination to live together in harmony.

On the eighth and final day of Chanukah, menorahs were everywhere. Blacks, whites, Native Americans, Mexican Americans, Catholics, and Protestants all displayed their menorahs to show their determination to live and suffer together. The young people learned that loving commitment to others may require personal suffering. The apostle Paul had reiterated this point by reminding Timothy of his own and Christ's suffering.

*Concentration.* Jason Garfield is one of the best jugglers in the United States. The fifteen-year-old sophomore from Roosevelt High School in Seattle, Washington, can juggle nine rings at once. Fewer than a dozen jugglers in the country can do that. Jason has won the International Jugglers Association junior competition for seventeen-year-olds and younger.

Jason practices four hours every day, except on Sunday. The routines demand intense concentration and eye-hand coordination. His goal is to win the national championship and become a full-time professional juggler.

Paul wrote of the discipline involved in being a Christian. It takes the same kind of dedication, intense concentration, and focus to be Christ's servant as it does to perfect any skill. The difference is that the work is motivated and produced by God's Spirit. And it reaps eternal reward.

*Woke Up in Time.* In his late teens and early twenties, Benjamin Franklin and a school friend were learning to speak and translate Italian. They also began playing chess. Soon, they were only playing chess. Franklin woke up to the situation and realized that their study habits would have harmful consequences. He therefore refused to play any longer—unless it was agreed that the loser would translate fifty pages of Dante before the next game! The strategy paid off. Since they were evenly matched, both learned Italian.

Living the Christian life, like academic studying, requires discipline. We must work at both with determination and perseverance.

*Questions for Students on the Next Lesson.* 1. What particular message was Timothy to proclaim? What else was Timothy to do? 2. What did Paul mean by "itching ears"? 3. What unsound doctrines or myths are being put forth today? 4. Do Christians always endure suffering when they preach? 5. Is living the Christian life always a struggle for you?

# LESSON 4—JUNE 22

## CHRIST'S SERVANT TEACHES FAITHFULNESS

*Background Scripture:* II Timothy 4:1-18
*Devotional Reading:* Philippians 4:8-20

### KING JAMES VERSION

II TIMOTHY 4:1 I charge thee therefore before God, and the Lord Jesus Christ, who shall judge the quick and the dead at his appearing and his kingdom;

2 Preach the word; be instant in season, out of season; reprove, rebuke, exhort with all longsuffering and doctrine.

3 For the time will come when they will not endure sound doctrine; but after their own lusts shall they heap to themselves teachers, having itching ears;

4 And they shall turn away their ears from the truth, and shall be turned unto fables.

5 But watch thou in all things, endure afflictions, do the work of an evangelist, make full proof of thy ministry.

6 For I am now ready to be offered and the time of my departure is at hand.

7 I have fought a good fight, I have finished my course, I have kept the faith:

8 Henceforth there is laid up for me a crown of righteousness, which the Lord, the righteous judge, shall give me at that day: and not to me only, but unto all them also that love his appearing.

### NEW REVISED STANDARD VERSION

II TIMOTHY 4:1 In the presence of God and of Christ Jesus, who is to judge the living and the dead, and in view of his appearing and his kingdom, I solemnly urge you:

2 proclaim the message; be persistent whether the time is favorable or unfavorable; convince, rebuke, and encourage, with the utmost patience in teaching. 3 For the time is coming when people will not put up with sound doctrine, but having itching ears, they will accumulate for themselves teachers to suit their own desires, 4 and will turn away from listening to the truth and wander away to myths. 5 As for you, always be sober, endure suffering, do the work of an evangelist, carry out your ministry fully.

6 As for me, I am already being poured out as a libation, and the time of my departure has come. 7 I have fought the good fight, I have finished the race, I have kept the faith. 8 From now on there is reserved for me the crown of righteousness, which the Lord, the righteous judge, will give me on that day, and not only to me but also to all who have longed for his appearing.

KEY VERSES: *I solemnly urge you: proclaim the message; be persistent whether the time is favorable or unfavorable.* II Timothy 4:1b, 2a.

## HOME BIBLE READINGS

| | | | |
|---|---|---|---|
| June | 16 | M. | Psalm 119:89-96 | *The Lord's Laws Are Forever* |
| June | 17 | T. | Psalm 32:19-24 | *Praise the Lord for His Faithfulness* |
| June | 18 | W. | II Timothy 4:9-18 | *Faithful in Spite of Trials* |
| June | 19 | T. | Romans 8:12-17 | *Be as Faithful as God's Child* |
| June | 20 | F. | Luke 16:10-17 | *Be Faithful over Small Things* |
| June | 21 | S. | Deuteronomy 10:12-20 | *The Lord Requires Faithfulness* |
| June | 22 | S. | I Peter 5:1-11 | *Faithfulness Will Be Rewarded* |

## BACKGROUND

Words written by death-row inmates are often drenched in pathos and self-pity. Not so with Paul! Second Timothy's final chapter reveals no "poor-me" message. The weary old warrior for the Lord knew his days were limited. Nero's axe man would bring a grisly conclusion to Paul's plans. In spite of the grim future, Paul calmly dictated a farewell message to his beloved colleague Timothy. It was filled with words of encouragement and comfort. But a note of urgency does pervade the entire portion of the letter under discussion in this lesson.

Paul repeated his plea that Timothy teach sound doctrine. The prevalence of false teachers concerned Paul. He had traveled to the world's great cities. He had seen and heard the stunts and messages of a variety of quack healers, clever orators, and cunning heretics who tried to undermine the faith of Christians. The wise apostle knew human nature. He recognized that people are readily attracted to the novel and sensational. Worried that the peddlers of error were working their wiles on susceptible believers in Ephesus, Paul repeatedly urged Timothy to prepare his people to stay true to the Gospel. In the closing parts of this letter, Paul renewed his warnings and pleas.

Paul also knew Timothy's strengths and weaknesses. Timothy's nature was that of a somewhat shy, sensitive young man who found it hard to stand up to tough critics. Paul's closing remarks, therefore, also called on Timothy to preach the news of Jesus Christ whether he felt like it or not and whether his people wanted to hear it or not. Sometimes, Paul knew, church leaders tend to be accommodating. And sometimes they think they're doing their people a favor by shielding them from the hard demands of the Gospel. Paul encouraged his associate to call his congregation to faithfulness to Christ in the face of opposition and false teachings.

## NOTES ON THE PRINTED TEXT

As Paul's letter to Timothy came to a close, Paul reiterated his appeal to Timothy: faithfully preach to the Ephesian church. To show how serious he was, Paul placed his appeal in the context of the final judgment. This was to remind Timothy of his ultimate accountability. *In the presence of God and of Christ Jesus, who is to judge the living and the dead, and in view of his appearing and his kingdom, I solemnly urge you: Proclaim the message* (4:1, 2a). In every circumstance Timothy was to preach God's word of the Gospel. Whether the time was opportune or not, Timothy was to testify to Christ. *Be persistent whether the time is favorable or unfavorable* (4:2b).

Paul also had other commands for Timothy. *Convince* (4:2c). Literally, Timothy was to refute, argue against, and correct any false teaching. *Rebuke* (4:2c). Timothy was not to hesitate to reprove or censure those with perverse wills. *And encourage, with the utmost patience in teaching* (4:2c). He was also to exhort his church members to repent of any false teaching and follow the Gospel.

The old pastor also gave Timothy a warning. *For the time is coming when people will not put up with sound doctrine, but having itching ears, they will accumulate for themselves teachers to suit their own desires, and will turn away from listening to the truth and wander away to myths* (4:3, 4). Instead of listening to the Gospel, people would follow those who proclaim false doctrines. This false teaching would sound exciting or be based on fables. It would arouse curiosity and eventually gather a following. The people would almost be intoxicated by such teachings.

Timothy was to teach his congregation sound doctrine and keep his head.

*As for you, always be sober, endure suffering, do the work of an evangelist, carry out your ministry fully* (4:5). Evangelists were not pastors in permanent residence.Timothy was to faithfully and diligently preach and teach in Ephesus before moving on to another assignment.

The reason for the admonition was now revealed: Paul saw Timothy as his successor. Paul's ministry was nearly over. Imprisoned, he was certain to be executed soon. Using the powerful metaphor of the drink offering, he made his point: this was the final act of the sacrifice. *As for me, I am already being poured out as a libation, and the time of my departure has come* (4:6). He spoke of departing from this world, using words that denote a ship departing from the harbor or a traveler striking his tent.

Paul faced death with no fear or denial. Knowing that Timothy had seen prizes being awarded at the Isthmian games, Paul used athletic imagery to encourage him. He had completed the contest, he had finished the foot race, he had kept his pledge to compete honestly. Paul could look back over his life and confidently declare that he had not halfheartedly carried out his responsibilities. He had given his whole self to Christ. *I have fought the good fight, I have finished the race, I have kept the faith. From now on there is reserved for me the crown of righteousness, which the Lord, the righteous judge, will give me on that day, and not only to me but also to all who have longed for his appearing* (4:7, 8). The crown was the prize distributed on the last day of the Isthmian games. Paul contrasted his crown of righteousness with the athlete's wreath of withered celery leaves. His crown of salvation would be awarded to him by God Himself—and to all who anticipated Christ's coming again.

## SUGGESTIONS TO TEACHERS

Suppose that you have been arrested by secret police in a foreign country known for its hostility to Christians. You have been told that you will be detained indefinitely. But a friendly guard lets it be known that he will smuggle out a letter to your congregation back home.

What would you say to your pastor and fellow church members, whom you may not see for a long time, if ever? What would people in your class write back to you? Paul's final words to Timothy take on an immediacy and relevance when we put ourselves into the action!

1. PREACHER WITH URGENT MESSAGE. Work through II Timothy 4:1-18, verse by verse. No "business-as-usual" attitude here about Christ's work! As teachers and pupils, leaders and worshipers, don't we sometimes think, "Well, I just don't feel like _____ (attending church/praying /studying Scripture/teaching the class, etc.) today." How does this Scripture passage answer our feeble excuses?

2. LISTENERS WITH ITCHING EARS. Many church members today demand entertainment and shy away from worship. Instead of being centered on Christ, worship becomes centered on ourselves. Therapeutic interests ("Does it make me feel better?") or utilitarian concerns ("Does it help me?") displace serving Jesus Christ. Ulterior motives for worship push aside praise. The old Westminster Catechism becomes reversed: the chief end of God is to glorify us and to please us forever.

3. WRITER WITH GLORIOUS CROWN. Paul's autobiographical com-

ments (4:6-8) remind us that in spite of suffering, we can trust our Lord. Paul can teach us how to live, how to face trials, and even how to face death.

4. COMPANIONS WITH SPECIFIC ASSIGNMENTS. Paul made certain requests of Timothy and others, such as bringing a cloak or books. Christian fellowship calls for caring in concrete ways. We must always show our concern for one another in practical forms. The handwritten note, the personal visit, and the thoughtful act of service will always be important forms of ministry.

5. DESERTERS WITH PERSONAL AGENDAS. Lamentably, some of Paul's coworkers, such as Demas (4:10), apparently forgot their responsibilities. Personal agendas took over.

True believers continue in Christ's service, not just when they feel like it or when others seem eager to know about the Lord.

TOPIC FOR ADULTS
*KEEP THE FAITH*

*Midsummer Test.* Today, June 22, the citizens of Florence, Italy, will carefully examine a certain brass plate in the ancient cathedral. The inconspicuous piece of metal is embedded in the floor directly below the great dome. Each year, on June 22, the sun's position produces a shaft of sunlight that falls directly through a certain opening in the soaring roof and reflects brightly for a brief time on the brass plate.

The architect deliberately designed the soaring dome so that if the sunbeam did not shine down through the opening onto the plate on the floor below, the people of Florence would know that their great cathedral had shifted on its foundation. Each year, the Florentines anxiously await the report on June 22. When the severe floods swept through the valley and submerged the historic city in 1967, everyone stood by with trepidation as the annual midsummer test approached. When the brass plate gleamed on that June 22, as it had in previous years for over five centuries, the sense of relief was immense.

Christ's light tests our faithfulness each day. Through Jesus, God examines us, His church, to determine whether we are still resting securely in His grace. Faith in Christ is the sure foundation upon which we must stand. And through the illumination of His loving presence, God reveals how far we sometimes shift from relying on Him.

*Lethargic Believers.* In a certain town, a family stopped worshiping at the Lutheran church and began attending the Presbyterian church. The young daughter was asked why her family had switched. The youngster tried to explain that her father did not care for the liturgical forms the new Lutheran pastor had introduced.

But she could not pronounce "liturgy." Her explanation, therefore, came out as, "Daddy says he likes the Presbyterian lethargy better."

How easy it is to sink into a denominational lethargy! As Paul summoned Timothy to keep the faith, our Lord calls us to persevere in our heartfelt, enthusiastic commitment.

*Handling the Bones.* Pastor Phil Mitchell described an experience that illustrates how easy it is to get used to handling sacred matters with little sense of awe. In his student days, Phil promised to help a friend move back home at the end of a school term. The friend was studying at McGill University medical school in Montreal, and Phil got up early to drive the several hundred miles to meet his friend. When he arrived at his friend's dorm, Phil discovered that the man had not yet begun to pack up his belongings. Phil offered to help.

Pointing to some objects on the top of the dresser, his friend said, "Fine. You can pack Oscar."

To his horror, Phil found himself looking at a disassembled human skeleton.

"That's Oscar," called the friend. "Pack him in these boxes in tissue paper."

As Phil looked at the skeletal remains of what had been a person, he felt a sense of awe and recoiled from touching any of them. Finally, he took a piece of tissue paper and tried to wrap it around his thumb and index finger. Then, with the tissue paper shielding him from directly touching anything, he gingerly picked up one piece of the skeleton. Holding it at arm's length, he carried it to the box and dropped it into the crumpled tissue paper. For the next several minutes, he painstakingly repeated the procedure, carefully avoiding contact with any of the bones.

Gradually, however, Phil found himself regarding the human skeleton as any other object to be packed that day. Before long, he tossed aside his tissue paper "glove" and handled the bones with his bare hands. By the time he had finished packing the skeleton, he looked upon the bones the same way he might have regarded a bundle of kindling to be picked up. He reflected on his ability to become callous in touching those bones.

Phil commented later that he knows that the same kind of "getting-used-to" feeling can also arise in people handling sacred matters. As a fine pastor he humbly confesses that he must guard against spiritual matters with inappropriate familiarity. He warns Christians to be careful not to handle God's affairs in a perfunctory way, as merely another chore. "It's easy to lose the sense of reverence and responsibility we once had," Phil Mitchell warns.

*Questions for Students on the Next Lesson.* 1. Who was Titus? 2. Why was Paul writing to him? 3. What advice in this letter do you find helpful to you, personally? 4. Why can disunity in a congregation be so destructive to its witness? 5. What can the church do to encourage more courtesy and civility in our society?

## TOPIC FOR YOUTH
### REMAIN FAITHFUL

*More Than Feeling.* A "Peanuts" cartoon features Charlie Brown approaching a friend and asking her if she is concerned about world hunger. She shrugs her shoulders indifferently. Charlie Brown goes to a second and then a third friend, asking the same question. Each time he receives the same indifferent response. Finally, Charlie Brown shouts, "Well, at least I feel guilty about it!"

Although Charlie Brown felt something for the hungry, he had not served them. A Christian commitment would lead Charlie into practical acts of ministry. Some personal sacrifice would be necessary to achieve a better world for all peoples.

*Faithful Volunteers.* For all its charities, America does not have a volunteer shortage. When President Clinton proposed a national service program to promote projects for the good of communities, skeptics laughed. They felt the Corporation for National Service would fail. The program provides funds to volunteers so they can work on projects in public safety, environment, education, and health. However, Eli Segal, the head of the program, indicated there has been great interest by all age groups. The volunteer spirit is healthier than ever.

Youth can be a determined group when they feel a cause is just and true. Paul commanded Timothy to demonstrate the same determination for Christ. In spite of opposition, he was to convince all people of God's love through Jesus Christ.

*Costly Determination.* Jonathan Daniels was the son of a doctor in Keene, New Hampshire. Although he grew up as a rebellious, white, New England youth, he never lost his religious beliefs. He heard Dr. Martin Luther King, Jr., appeal for volunteers from the north to help out in Selma, Alabama, during the height of the civil rights movement. Daniels moved south, determined to aid the cause of civil rights.

He moved in with a black family. He brought black friends to St. Paul's Episcopal Church, an all-white congregation. At the post office he was called ugly names by a man ahead of him in line. When he was stopped at a traffic light in his car, a man got out of his own auto and came up to Daniels's window, berated him and called him "scum." Daniels continued to work for voter registration, even after he had been shot at and threatened by the Ku Klux Klan.

At 3:00 P.M. on August 20, 1965, Jonathan, Richard Morrisroe from Chicago, and two girls decided to walk across the street to a grocery store to get something to eat. They were halfway across the street when Thomas Coleman, a deputy sheriff, walked out of the grocery store swearing at them and telling them to get off the property or he would kill them. In his hand was a shotgun. With no further warning Coleman shot Jonathan, killing him instantly as he pushed one of the girls down. Morrisroe was also shot and gravely wounded. Both lay in the street for over an hour as traffic drove back and forth.

Coleman was arrested and tried on first-degree manslaughter. The all-white jury acquitted him and he was freed.

Jonathan Daniels's name was entered in the Chapel of Saints and Martyrs of Our Own Time in Canterbury Cathedral. He was listed as giving his life to save one of his companions determined to bring civil rights to all.

Like Paul, Jonathan Daniels understood that a commitment to Christ involves sacrifice. And, like Paul, he willingly accepted sacrifice in order to create a better world.

*Questions for Students on the Next Lesson.* 1. Should Christians always obey society's laws? Why, or why not? 2. How were we as believers once "foolish" and "disobedient"? 3. What does it mean to be saved? 4. To what kinds of good works should believers devote their lives? 5. How should believers respond to those who refuse to listen to the truth?

# LESSON 5—JUNE 29

## CHRIST'S SERVANT ENCOURAGES COMMUNITY

*Background Scripture:* Titus 3:1-11
*Devotional Reading:* Romans 13:1-10

### KING JAMES VERSION

TITUS 3:1 Put them in mind to be subject to principalities and powers, to obey magistrates, to be ready to every good work,

2 To speak evil of no man, to be no brawlers, but gentle, shewing all meekness unto all men.

3 For we ourselves also were sometimes foolish, disobedient, deceived, serving divers lusts and pleasures, living in malice and envy, hateful, and hating one another.

4 But after that the kindness and love of God our Saviour toward man appeared,

5 Not by works of righteousness which we have done, but according to his mercy he saved us, by the washing of regeneration, and renewing of the Holy Ghost;

6 Which he shed on us abundantly through Jesus Christ our Saviour;

7 That being justified by his grace, we should be made heirs according to the hope of eternal life.

8 This is a faithful saying, and these things I will that thou affirm constantly, that they which have believed in God might be careful to maintain good works. These things are good and profitable unto men.

9 But avoid foolish questions, and genealogies, and contentions, and strivings about the law; for they are unprofitable and vain.

10 A man that is an heretick after the first and second admonition reject;

11 Knowing that he that is such is subverted, and sinneth, being condemned of himself.

### NEW KING JAMES VERSION

TITUS 3:1 Remind them to be subject to rulers and authorities, to be obedient, to be ready for every good work, 2 to speak evil of no one, to avoid quarreling, to be gentle, and to show every courtesy to everyone. 3 For we ourselves were once foolish, disobedient, led astray, slaves to various passions and pleasures, passing our days in malice and envy, despicable, hating one another. 4 But when the goodness and loving kindness of God our Savior appeared, 5 he saved us, not because of any works of righteousness that we had done, but according to his mercy, through the water of rebirth and renewal by the Holy Spirit. 6 This Spirit he poured out on us richly through Jesus Christ our Savior, 7 so that, having been justified by his grace, we might become heirs according to the hope of eternal life. 8 The saying is sure.

I desire that you insist on these things, so that those who have come to believe in God may be careful to devote themselves to good works; these things are excellent and profitable to everyone. 9 But avoid stupid controversies, genealogies, dissensions, and quarrels about the law, for they are unprofitable and worthless. 10 After a first and second admonition, have nothing more to do with anyone who causes divisions, 11 since you know that such a person is perverted and sinful, being self-condemned.

*KEY VERSE: I desire that you insist on these things, so that those who have come to believe in God may be careful to devote themselves to good works; these things are excellent and profitable to everyone. Titus 3:8b.*

## HOME BIBLE READINGS

| | | | |
|---|---|---|---|
| June 23 | M. | II Timothy 2:14-19 | *Avoid Disputes* |
| June 24 | T. | Philippians 4:10-20 | *Support Faithful Workers* |
| June 25 | W. | Titus 2:1-8 | *Teach Sound Doctrines* |
| June 26 | T. | Titus 2:9-19 | *Teach with Authority* |
| June 27 | F. | II Corinthians 2:5-11 | *Forgive One Another* |
| June 28 | S. | Romans 3:9-20 | *All Are Guilty under the Law* |
| June 29 | S. | Romans 3:21-31 | *All Are Justified by God's Grace* |

# BACKGROUND

The third New Testament book in the pastoral Epistles was addressed to Titus, another trusted associate of Paul. In contrast to the timid and hesitant Timothy, Titus apparently was decisive and confident. A Gentile convert, Titus accompanied Paul and other believers to the great conference in Jerusalem that attempted to resolve doctrinal disagreements. Titus was a devout believer who had not undergone circumcision or subscribed to the requirements of the Old Testament Law. He belonged to the renowned, mission-minded congregation in Antioch.

Titus became a close associate of the apostle Paul and served as Paul's messenger-representative to the difficult church in Corinth. Later, Titus accompanied Paul on an evangelistic tour of Crete. Paul left Titus to continue the work in Crete and moved on to further missionary visiting.

The island of Crete had been the center of a remarkable ancient civilization. But in the time of the New Testament, its citizens had an unsavory reputation. Others in the Roman world looked upon Cretans as corrupt and unreliable. Just as the theaters of that day always portrayed a person from Corinth as an immoral drunk, they inevitably showed someone from Crete as an untrustworthy sneak. "To play the Cretan" was a popular saying, meaning to be a cheat and liar. Even Paul quoted a line from Epimenides, a poet from Crete, who spoke of his fellow citizens in unflattering terms: "Cretans are always liars, vicious brutes, lazy gluttons" (Titus 1:12). Crete would be a difficult place to establish a flourishing community of Christian converts.

Knowing that Titus had a challenging assignment in Crete, Paul wrote him a personal note. The letter to Titus contains words of encouragement, instruction, and challenge. Titus must persevere in evangelizing the Cretans. Paul's pastoral advice, while written to Titus, was also circulated by Christians as a message to the entire church, especially its leaders.

# NOTES ON THE PRINTED TEXT

*Remind them to be subject to rulers and authorities, to be obedient, to be ready for every good work, to speak evil of no one, to avoid quarreling, to be gentle, and to show every courtesy to everyone* (3:1, 2). Having addressed Titus and the Cretan believers about their church and duties to each other, Paul spoke of their relationship to the civil authorities and the law. Perhaps Paul recalled the Cretans' reputation for rebelliousness. Titus was to remind his people to be loyal and obedient subjects. The Christians were urged to be good citizens, always ready to help others.

If the Cretan believers needed a motive to be more caring toward those around them, Paul supplied one. He recalled their history prior to accepting the Gospel. *For we ourselves were once foolish, disobedient, led astray, slaves to various passions and pleasures, passing our days in malice and envy, despicable, hating one another* (3:3). The Cretans and Titus had originally been blind and contemptuous of God. Misguided by false beliefs, they were slaves to their lusts and desires. This produced anti-social behavior shown in envy and hatred. This sinful behavior was to remain in the past.

God's grace produced change. Generously, God introduced a Savior in Christ. *But when the goodness and loving kindness of God our Savior appeared, he saved us* (3:4, 5a). God's salvation was given lovingly and freely, not because of any good deeds or meritorious works done by the believers. Salvation was based on God's mercy, not on human righteousness. Baptism proclaimed God's saving work in a dramatic fashion. *He saved us, not because of any works of righteousness that we had done, but according to his mercy, through the water of rebirth and renewal by the Holy Spirit* (3:5).

The Holy Spirit brought about rebirth and renewal, which were richly and abundantly poured out on Christian readers. The purpose of His action was to make all believers His heirs. The faithful could anticipate the inheritance of eternal life. *This Spirit he poured out on us richly through Jesus Christ our Savior, so that, having been justified by his grace, we might become heirs according to the hope of eternal life* (3:6, 7). Paul ended his explanation with a formula statement. *The saying is sure* (3:8a). Perhaps he quoted or paraphrased a hymn or an early piece of baptismal liturgy familiar to Titus and the Cretan Christians.

Returning to his initial theme of social duty, Paul urged the faithful to devote their lives to good deeds. Believers were to energetically perform useful actions for others. *I desire that you insist on these things, so that those who have come to believe in God may be careful to devote themselves to good works; these things are excellent and profitable to everyone* (3:8b).

The old pastor also urged Titus to stay clear of needless controversy. Titus was not even to investigate silly heresies because that would be a waste of time. Apparently the heresies had some Jewish fables and laws as their foundation. *But avoid stupid controversies, genealogies, dissensions, and quarrels about the law, for they are unprofitable and worthless* (3:9).

Paul offered Titus a method of dealing with those who continued to delve into speculations and cause dissension. Two clear warnings should be given. If the second warning was ignored, the faithful were to have no dealings with the troublemakers. *After a first and second admonition, have nothing more to do with anyone who causes division, since you know that such a person is perverted and sinful, being self-condemned* (3:10, 11).

## SUGGESTIONS TO TEACHERS

An attorney, indicted for tax evasion, tried to line up witnesses to attest to his good character. Someone suggested a pastor or priest, but the accused said he wasn't part of any congregation. Yet he insisted, "I am a deeply Christian man. But my religion is a very personal matter, and I see no need for it to have anything to do with my professional life or with a church body."

Paul's words to Titus challenge this lawyer's outlook—and ours, when we try to split off our faith from our daily living.

1. PUBLIC RECTITUDE. Paul reminded believers that they are called to be public examples. The world is eyeing Christians for what they do—more than for what they say. Try making a list of nouns and adjectives that may seem quaint today but which describe God's intentions for our behavior. Try such words as *integrity, honorable, humility, just, responsible, trustworthy, courtesy, kind,* and *civil.*

2. PAST REMEMBRANCE. The Cretans were reminded that their pasts

were far from savory in the Lord's eyes. God's undeserved mercy saved them, not their own wisdom or goodness. Likewise, when we confront our past, we remember some sad things about ourselves. We realize we can never make any claims on God's goodness. Our acceptance by Him is based on sheer grace.

Without morbidly dwelling on the sins of yesterday, we may maintain an appropriate sense of humility by recalling our failings and shortcomings. And we make space in our lives for Jesus Christ's life-giving forgiveness.

3. PERPETUAL RENEWAL. We use the term burn-out frequently today. How often have you heard, "I'm burned out as a Sunday school teacher," or "I feel burned out by helping in the food pantry"? Some in your class undoubtedly have this sense of fatigue in serving.

Titus correctly reminds all Christians that the Holy Spirit renews them for ministry. In fact, without continuously calling on the Lord for the Spirit's renewing empowerment, believers quickly run out of energy and enthusiasm. Discuss the symptoms and treatment for spiritual burn-out with your students.

4. PERSONAL RELATIONSHIPS. Particularly emphasize the call to build community and to treat one another lovingly. The church—beginning with your class and your congregation—must be a working model of true community. Thus the world may catch a glimpse of God's intentions for all creation. Our world is ripped apart by ethnic cleansings, religious rivalries, and clan hatreds. At this writing, at least one hundred armed conflicts are taking place around the world. In our own country, a lack of civil discourse and a rise in hate groups point toward danger ahead. How shall we confront such problems through Christian ministry?

## TOPIC FOR ADULTS
### BE GOOD TO ONE ANOTHER

*Mutual Support.* Several boys were hiking on a trail that crossed an old, unused set of railroad tracks. Some boys tried walking on one of the rails without losing their balance. None of the youngsters was able to take more than a few steps before wobbling and falling off.

Two of the boys quietly watched the others try to walk the rail. Then they conferred and announced, "We bet we can walk from here up to that bend without falling off," pointing to the curve several hundred feet up the track.

"Betcha can't," replied the others, challenging the bold pair to prove they could stay on the rail.

Stepping onto the rail, standing next to each other, the two boys joined hands. Together, supporting and balancing each other, they easily walked down the track without falling off until they came to the curve

When we reach out and steady each other, we receive and give support as Christians. As Christ's community, we can walk without losing our balance. But we must extend ourselves for each other with open hands and hearts.

*Vanishing Reverence?* In 1995, Jason G. Brent wrote an article in the monthly newsletter of the Mensa Society's Los Angeles chapter. He stated, "Society must face the concept that we [should] kill off the old, weak, the stupid, and the inefficient." Brent and the others receiving the newsletter are members of an organization that admits people with high IQs.

In spite of their towering IQs, some of these supposedly superior intellects lack all sense of respect for others. Another Mensa contributor, Jon Evans, wrote that many homeless "should be humanely done away with, like abandoned kittens," and "a piece of meat in the shape of a man, but without a mind, is not a human being, whether the body be deathly ill, damaged by accident, mentally blank because of brain deficiency, or criminally insane."

The words of these so-called geniuses seem to echo a phrase used in Hitler's Third Reich: "useless eaters." Such views eventually led to the systematic extermination of the retarded, insane, and terminally ill in Germany.

Is reverence for life fading in our society? Scripture calls us to regard each fellow human as created in God's image and as one for whom Christ died.

*All in the Same Boat.* An ancient rabbinic story illustrates how we are all bound together and meant to look after each other's welfare. A man was in a boat with others, but he acted as if he were the only one on board. One night, he took out his knife and began to cut a hole beneath his seat. His neighbors shrieked, "Have you gone mad? Do you want to sink us all?"

"Why are you upset?" replied the man. "What I'm doing is none of your business. I paid my way. I am cutting only under my own seat."

The selfish man with the knife would not accept what you and I must never forget: We all are in the same boat. Let us care for one another, in Christ's name.

*Questions for Students on the Next Lesson.* 1. Who were the "Hebrews" for whom this letter was written? 2. What was the writer's purpose in sending this letter? 3. What is meant by the term *God's Son,* in referring to Jesus? 4. How did God speak in Old Testament times? 5. How has Jesus Christ brought a new understanding of God to humans?

## TOPIC FOR YOUTH
### BE GOOD TO ONE ANOTHER

*Discipline Advocated.* Many mothers believe that spanking is still a good way to discipline. Yet the U.S. Surgeon General, the American Academy of Pediatrics, and the National Association of Social Workers all oppose spanking as a form of child discipline.

Dr. Rebecca R.S. Socolar, a lead researcher and medical school professor, wrote in *Pediatrics* that 42 percent of the mothers surveyed had spanked their child in the last week. Mothers also overwhelmingly believed in spanking for dangerous misbehavior, such as getting too close to a hot iron. Overall, Socolar concluded that spanking was a more appropriate response to misbehavior than yelling or ridicule. Strong discipline must be employed to guide the growing child.

Centuries earlier, Paul had reached a similar conclusion. He urged Titus to resort to strong discipline if warnings failed. Believers were to have nothing to do with those who delved into worthless speculations.

*Never Got the Point.* A thirteen-year-old boy who attended Mount Pleasant Area Secondary School in Westmoreland County, Pennsylvania, was arrested and charged with aggravated assault, simple assault, reckless endangerment, and possession of a weapon on school property. He had jabbed twenty-eight students with a hypodermic syringe at school.

The boy had stolen the syringe from a doctor's office. It was new and unused so the threat of AIDS was very remote. Friends said the boy was not serious in his attacks, but was simply joking around by pricking the victims. He began at his bus stop and was arrested by 8:00 A.M. Those he jabbed responded in different ways. One girl was upset enough to punch the boy in the face, while others complained to the school principal. Apparently the boy chose to disregard the difference between respectful and offensive behavior.

Christian believers are to commit themselves to doing good to others. Courtesy and gentleness are to be exhibited. This was the point Paul urged upon Titus and his readers.

*New Contentment.* By his twenty-fifth birthday, Steve Jones was a professional golfer earning about two million dollars yearly. He played for one reason: to meet beautiful women. His whole goal in life was to play golf and be chased by women. He characterized his life as consisting mostly of excessive drinking, sexual immorality, and athletic pride.

Then he began to attend church. He listened to sermons for six months and then became a Christian. His life underwent a drastic change.

The new Steve Jones stopped drinking, swearing, and chasing women. He married and had a child. He lost twenty or more of his old friends who could not understand Steve's transformation.

The Spirit brought rebirth and renewal in Jones's life. As a result of his conversion, new behavior had to result. Now Steve leads fellowship meetings on tour. He plays in numerous charity tournaments and devotes significant time to his family and his church.

*Questions for Students on the Next Lesson.* 1. By whom, and for whom, was Hebrews written? 2. In what ways is Jesus the reflection of God's glory? 3. How is Jesus greater than the angels and Moses? 4. Why is Jesus "the high priest of our confession"? 5. Does God still speak today? How?

# LESSON 6—JULY 6

## JESUS IS GOD'S SON

*Background Scripture:* Hebrews 1:1-14; 3:1-6
*Devotional Reading:* Hebrews 1:6-14

### KING JAMES VERSION

HEBREWS 1:1 God, who at sundry times and in divers manners spake in time past unto the fathers by the prophets,

2 Hath in these last days spoken unto us by his Son, whom he hath appointed heir of all things, by whom also he made the worlds;

3 Who being the brightness of his glory, and the express image of his person, and upholding all things by the word of his power, when he had by himself purged our sins, sat down on the right hand of the Majesty on high;

4 Being made so much better than the angels, as he hath by inheritance obtained a more excellent name than they.

5 For unto which of the angels said he at any time, Thou art my Son, this day have I begotten thee? And again, I will be to him a Father, and he shall be to me a Son?

3:1 Wherefore, holy brethren, partakers of the heavenly calling, consider the Apostle and High Priest of our profession, Christ Jesus;

2 Who was faithful to him that appointed him, as also Moses was faithful in all his house.

3 For this man was counted worthy of more glory than Moses, inasmuch as he who hath builded the house hath more honour than the house.

4 For every house is builded by some man; but he that built all things is God.

5 And Moses verily was faithful in all his house, as a servant, for a testimony of those things which were to be spoken after;

6 But Christ as a son over his own house; whose house are we, if we hold fast the confidence and the rejoicing of the hope firm unto the end.

### NEW REVISED STANDARD VERSION

HEBREWS 1:1 Long ago God spoke to our ancestors in many and various ways by the prophets, 2 but in these last days he has spoken to us by a Son, whom he appointed heir of all things, through whom he also created the worlds. 3 He is the reflection of God's glory and the exact imprint of God's very being, and he sustains all things by his powerful word. When he had made purification for sins, he sat down at the right hand of the Majesty on high, 4 having become as much superior to angels as the name he has inherited is more excellent than theirs.

5 For to which of the angels did God ever say, "You are my Son; today I have begotten you"? Or again, "I will be his Father, and he will be my Son"?

3:1 Therefore, brothers and sisters, holy partners in a heavenly calling, consider that Jesus, the apostle and high priest of our confession, 2 was faithful to the one who appointed him, just as Moses also "was faithful in all God's house." 3 Yet Jesus is worthy of more glory than Moses, just as the builder of a house has more honor than the house itself. 4 (For every house is built by someone, but the builder of all things is God.) 5 Now Moses was faithful in all God's house as a servant, to testify to the things that would be spoken later. 6 Christ, however, was faithful over God's house as a son, and we are his house if we hold firm the confidence and the pride that belong to hope.

KEY VERSES: *Brothers and sisters, holy partners in a heavenly calling, consider that Jesus, the apostle and high priest of our confession, was faithful to the one who appointed him.* Hebrews 3:1, 2a.

## HOME BIBLE READINGS

| July | 3 | T. | Galatians 4:1-7 | *Christ, Son and Heir of God* |
| July | 4 | F. | John 14:1-7 | *To Know Christ Is to Know God* |
| July | 5 | S. | John 4:13-21 | *Confess Christ as Gods' Son* |
| July | 6 | S. | John 6:35-40 | *Christ Came to Do God's Will* |

## BACKGROUND

This week's material begins a nine-week series of lessons based on the Letter to the Hebrews. We do not know who wrote Hebrews, since no author is named in the letter itself. Some scholars think the apostle Paul was the writer. Others suggest Apollos. Still others surmise that perhaps Barnabas, or even Priscilla was the unnamed author. From the contents of this great piece of Christian literature, we may conclude that the writer came from a Jewish background.

Who were the original readers? Again, we do not know. Was it a congregation from one of the great cities like Rome or Ephesus, which had sizable Jewish populations? Or were the recipients members of the community of Jewish Christians in Jerusalem? Or could Hebrews have been sent to the Greek-speaking Jewish population in Alexandria?

We must remember that Judaism in the first century A.D. had diverse manifestations. There were a variety of sects within the Jewish community throughout the Roman world. The two main groups could be classified as Hebraic Jews and Hellenistic Jews. The Hebraic Jews strictly adhered to the law of Moses. Paul was originally from this group. The other group, the Hellenistic Jews, had adjusted to Greek culture. They lived outside of Jerusalem, often in distant Greek-speaking cities, spoke Greek as a first language, and had a different culture and outlook than the Hebraic Jews.

Stephen and the Seven described in Acts 7 were Hellenistic Jews. After Stephen's martyrdom and the persecution of believers in Jerusalem, Christians belonging to this faction were scattered throughout Judea and Samaria. They survived this terrible period of hardship, but faced additional persecution. Certain evidence points to this group as the audience for whom Hebrews was originally intended. But the great message of Hebrews applies to readers in 1997, as well.

## NOTES ON THE PRINTED TEXT

Hebrews proclaims the superiority of Jesus. It was written to Jewish Christians who had grown in their faith but were still drawn to the Jewish liturgy and its institutions. Some had become overly devoted to Judaism, while others were in danger of renouncing their Christian faith. The writer was concerned to remind his or her readers that Christ was greater than the prophets whose words, while important, were fragmentary and spasmodic. *Long ago God spoke to our ancestors in many and various ways by the prophets* (1:1). While God had spoken in the past through visions, dreams, angels, smoke, fire, and natural events, at different places and times, He had now spoken to His people through His Son. *But in these last days he has spoken to us by a Son, whom he appointed heir of all things, through whom he also created the worlds* (1:2).

A son was the heir, the one who would receive the father's property upon reaching adulthood. He oversaw all, even while the father was still living.

The writer of Hebrews affirmed Jesus the Son to be the Lord over all and the agent of Creation. As God's Son, He reflected God's glory. Literally, Christ was marked, engraved, or stamped with God's characteristics. *He is the reflection of God's glory and the exact imprint of God's very being* (1:3a). As Son, he also carried God's authority. *He sustains all things by his powerful word* (1:3a).

Jesus was greater than the prophets because He was the purifier of the people. Christ's crucifixion was the sin-offering that cleansed the community. As one who was sinless and undefiled, He could sit beside God the Father in the position of honor. *When he had made purification for sins, he sat down at the right hand of the majesty on high* (1:3c).

The writer affirmed that Jesus was superior to angels. Angels were called sons of God; however, no angel was ever called *the* Son. And no angel was ever worshiped. *Having become as much superior to angels as the name he has inherited is more excellent than theirs. For to which of the angels did God ever say, "You are my Son; today I have begotten you?" Or again, "I will be his Father, and he will be my Son?"* (1:4, 5).

Jesus was also greater than Moses. Moving from one argument to another, the writer affectionately called the believers to consider Jesus, God's apostle and high priest. As Moses was faithful and trustworthy in the Lord's house, so was Jesus. *Therefore brothers and sisters, holy partners in a heavenly calling, consider that Jesus, the apostle and high priest of our confession, was faithful to the one who appointed him, just as Moses also "was faithful in all God's house"* (3:1, 2).

However, Christ was greater in the same way the architect and builder of a house was greater than the house itself. *Yet Jesus is worthy of more glory than Moses, just as the builder of a house has more honor than the house itself. (For every house is built by someone, but the builder of all things is God)* (3:3, 4).

The unknown writer reminded the believers that the Son who was *over* God's house was superior to Moses, who was a faithful servant *in* God's house. *Now Moses was faithful in all God's house as a servant, to testify to the things that would be spoken later. Christ, however, was faithful over God's house as a son, and we are his house if we hold firm the confidence and the pride that belong to hope* (3:5, 6).

## SUGGESTIONS TO TEACHERS

A Korean family visited a church near their new residence in America. The Koreans, from a country where Christianity is spreading more rapidly than almost anywhere in the world, asked the greeters what their church stood for. "Oh," gushed the first greeter, "we're the friendly church. We have activities for everybody—a bowling league, a couple's club, a bell choir, a women's bazaar workshop, and lots of other fun organizations."

The father in the Korean family politely pursued his original question. "Yes, but what do you stand for?" The greeters blinked and stammered weakly that they guessed they stood for "trying to be friendly."

Later, the Koreans tried to explain that they wanted to learn if that congregation's members affirmed the greatness of Jesus Christ. How would your own church members have answered their question? The writer of

Hebrews stood for the supremacy of Jesus Christ over all things.

1. THE COMPLETE COMMUNICATION. Hebrews emphasizes the place of Christ in God's plan for Creation. In our busy lives, including our busy lives at church, we need constant reminding that the bowling league, couple's club, bell choir, and bazaar workshop are secondary. Jesus comes first. While we may appropriately communicate friendliness and foster friendships, Jesus Himself is the only complete communication of God's friendliness and friendship.

Take a long look at the opening words: "God has spoken to us by a Son" (1:1, 2). Remind your students that in Hebrew thinking, a son was assumed to have all the personality traits of the father. Jesus, in other words, revealed God's character as no other.

2. THE SOLE HEIR. Jesus' preeminence in the universe is stated in unmistakable terms. The fact that He is "appointed heir of all things" (1:2) places Jesus above every other teacher, saint, hero, prophet, or holy person. Plumb the meaning of those words to help your students grasp the uniqueness of Jesus.

3. THE SUPREME REVELATION. "He is the reflection of God's glory and the exact imprint of God's very being" (1:3) proclaimed the author of Hebrews. Here is the answer to New Age claims of "revelations" or to those looking for angels to bring private miracles or personal messages from heaven. Christians need no additional disclosures from heaven. Jesus is the supreme revealer of the Father. Nothing can improve on Him.

4. THE HEAD OF THE HOUSEHOLD. The writer of Hebrews referred to the church as God's household and to Jesus as the head of that "family." Is your congregation conscious of being such a community? Hebrews 3 speaks of Jesus' faithfulness to His calling as the one in charge of that household. But the author called his readers to remember their calling, too: to witness to the supremacy of Jesus Christ.

## TOPIC FOR ADULTS
### GOD DOES A NEW THING

*Into the Pit.* A Chinese pastor was asked to explain the differences among Buddhism, Confucianism, and Christianity. He said: "A man fell into a deep pit and called and called for help. Buddha came by and heard the call and looked with pity on the man. 'Do not struggle, friend,' he said. 'Tear out of your heart all desire to change your situation. For there is no pit and no self in the pit. Enter the great Void and be at peace.' And Buddha went serenely on his way.

"Then, in time, Confucius passed that way and heard cries from the pit. He came and frowned down upon the hapless fellow and said, 'Reason should tell you that you have come to this tragedy by your own doing. Had you walked wisely—not too far this way, not too far that way—you would not now find yourself in trouble. It would be folly to help you out of this pit only to see you fall into another. If you do get out, follow the middle way.'

"Then another came by and, hearing the weak and helpless cries, hurried to the edge of the pit. He did not stop to pity or to reason or to count the fearful cost. Love and compassion filled his heart. 'Courage, Brother,' he called, and though he knew full well the act would cost him his life, he flung off his outer garment and leapt into the pit. He lifted the man to his shoulder and said, 'Climb to safety, Brother. Take my cloak and find your way home.'"

*Christ the Mirror.* There is in Rome an elegant fresco by Guido, "The Aurora." It covers a high ceiling. Looking up at it from below, your neck grows stiff, your head dizzy, and the figures become indistinct. The owner has placed a large mirror near the floor. Visitors may sit at their leisure, look into the mirror, and without fatigue study the fresco above.

In Christ, as in a mirror, we may behold the glory, truth, and grace of God.

*Down to Our Level.* Visitors to Trafalgar Square in London gaze upward to the top of a tall pillar to look at the statue of Lord Horatio Nelson, hero of the decisive Battle of Trafalgar. Because the figure of the victorious admiral stands at the pinnacle of the colossal column, onlookers cannot make out the features of the great man. In his attempt to honor Nelson, the sculptor placed the statue much too high for the face to be discernible from the street below.

A few years ago, however, at an exhibition in London, an exact replica of the Nelson statue was placed at eye level where everyone could see it. For the first time, people got a close-up of the features that they could barely see before.

In the person of Jesus Christ, God brought Himself "down to eye level" so all could see the qualities of His nature. In Jesus, we meet God face to face.

*Questions for Students on the Next Lesson.* 1. Where do humans stand in relation to angels? 2. According to Hebrews 2, what part of Creation is subject to human control? What does this mean in regard to our use of earth's resources? 3. Was Jesus truly human like us, or only partly so? 4. How does Jesus Christ help us when we are tempted? 5. How does your faith in Christ affect your view of death?

## TOPIC FOR YOUTH
### JESUS, THE SON

*Greater than These.* Here's a story circulating in the eastern United States: Dr. S.W. Mitchell, a Philadelphia neurologist, had gone to bed. The day had been exhausting and he was tired. Outside, it was bitter cold and snowing, yet his sleep was interrupted by a continual knocking on his front door. He opened the door to find a little girl, poorly dressed, who asked him to come help her sick mother. Reluctantly the doctor agreed.

Mitchell found the mother desperately ill with pneumonia. He arranged for her care and then complimented the woman on the persistence and intelligence of her daughter. The woman looked at him strangely and told the doctor that her daughter had died one month ago. The child's clothing was still in the closet. Inside, the doctor found the coat he had seen the girl wearing. It was absolutely dry! The doctor concluded that an angel had brought him to the woman's side.

Stories like this are gripping some of our citizens, who are becoming fascinated with angels and the supernatural. Sadly, this interest is rarely tied to any semblance of biblical truth. As impressive as this strange story is,

Hebrews affirms Jesus' superiority to these beings. The Son is superior to all the angels, and His truth is so much greater than myths and rumors. Therefore, Christians should focus their attention on Jesus, avoiding the mythical and magical.

*Young Activist.* In February, 1994, a fight involving twenty-six students erupted during lunch period at Pittsburgh's Allderdice High School. It was triggered by graffiti that contained racial epithets and the letters KKK.

Kia Omotalade, a sophomore at the high school, wanted to do something positive to help calm racial tensions. She went to her principal, Judy Johnson, with an idea to begin the Allderdice African-American Action Society. The group was to focus on promoting appreciation for all cultures. The group attracted white, Asian, and Hispanic students. All the students joined together to challenge the student body to serve and help each other.

Their society grew. As they gathered data and analyzed problems, they developed a curriculum to foster tolerance and conflict resolution. They also held a public forum and a two-day workshop on race relations. For her efforts, Kia was awarded an outstanding citizen award by the city of Pittsburgh.

Active in a Baptist church and its youth group, Kia sees all people as brothers and sisters called by a common Savior to live and work together. Each individual is called by God to know Him and reflect His glory.

*Questions for Students on the Next Lesson.* 1. How was Jesus made lower than the angels? 2. In what way is Jesus the "pioneer of salvation"? 3. How and why did Jesus "taste death for everyone"? 4. Why did Jesus share our humanity? 5. What did Jesus accomplish through His death?

# LESSON 7—JULY 13

## JESUS, OUR SAVIOR

*Background Scripture:* Hebrews 2:1-18
*Devotional Reading:* Hebrews 10:1-10

### KING JAMES VERSION

HEBREWS 2:5 For unto the angels hath he not put in subjection the world to come, whereof we speak.

6 But one in a certain place testified, saying, What is man, that thou art mindful of him? or the son of man, that thou visitest him?

7 Thou madest him a little lower than the angels; thou crownedst him with glory and honour, and didst set him over the works of thy hands:

8 Thou hast put all things in subjection under his feet. For in that he put all in subjection under him, he left nothing that is not put under him. But now we see not yet all things put under him.

9 But we see Jesus, who was made a little lower than the angels for the suffering of death, crowned with glory and honour; that he by the grace of God should taste death for every man.

10 For it became him, for whom are all things, and by whom are all things, in bringing many sons unto glory, to make the captain of their salvation perfect through sufferings.

11 For both he that sanctifieth and they who are sanctified are all of one: for which cause he is not ashamed to call them brethren. . . .

14 Forasmuch then as the children are partakers of flesh and blood, he also himself likewise took part of the same; that through death he might destroy him that had the power of death, that is, the devil;

15 And deliver them who through fear of death were all their lifetime subject to bondage.

16 For verily he took not on him the nature of angels; but he took on him the seed of Abraham.

17 Wherefore in all things it behoved him to be made like unto his brethren, that he might be a merciful and faithful high priest in things pertaining to God, to make reconciliation for the sins of the people.

18 For in that he himself hath suffered being tempted, he is able to succour them that are tempted.

### NEW REVISED STANDARD VERSION

HEBREWS 2:5 Now God did not subject the coming world, about which we are speaking, to angels. 6 But someone has testified somewhere, "What are human beings that you are mindful of them, or mortals, that you care for them? 7 You have made them for a little while lower than the angels; you have crowned them with glory and honor, 8 subjecting all things under their feet." Now in subjecting all things to them, God left nothing outside their control. As it is, we do not yet see everything in subjection to them, 9 but we do see Jesus, who for a little while was made lower than the angels, now crowned with glory and honor because of the suffering of death, so that by the grace of God he might taste death for everyone.

10 It was fitting that God, for whom and through whom all things exist, in bringing many children to glory, should make the pioneer of their salvation perfect through sufferings. 11 For the one who sanctifies and those who are sanctified all have one Father. For this reason Jesus is not ashamed to call them brothers and sisters. .

. .

14 Since, therefore, the children share flesh and blood, he himself likewise shared the same things, so that through death he might destroy the one who has the power of death, that is, the devil, 15 and free those who all their lives were held in slavery by the fear of death. 16 For it is clear that he did not come to help angels, but the descendants of Abraham. 17 Therefore he had to become like his brothers and sisters in every respect, so that he might be a merciful and faithful high priest in the service of God, to make a sacrifice of atonement for the sins of the people. 18 Because he himself was tested by what he suffered, he is able to help those who are being tested.

LESSON FOR JULY 13

*KEY VERSE: We do see Jesus, who for a little while was made lower than the angels, now crowned with glory and honor because of the suffering of death, so that by the grace of God he might taste death for everyone.* Hebrews 2:9.

## HOME BIBLE READINGS

| | | | | |
|---|---|---|---|---|
| July | 7 | M. | John 10:22-30 | *Jesus Christ Gives Eternal Life* |
| July | 8 | T. | I John 4:1-6 | *Jesus Christ Is of God* |
| July | 9 | W. | I John 4:7-12 | *Jesus Christ Is Love* |
| July | 10 | T. | Matthew 4:1-11 | *Jesus Christ Resisted Temptations* |
| July | 11 | F. | John 3:16-21 | *Jesus Christ Was Sent by God* |
| July | 12 | S. | I John 2:1-6 | *Jesus Christ, Our Advocate* |
| July | 13 | S. | Hebrews 3:1-6 | *Jesus Christ Was Faithful* |

## BACKGROUND

The early Christians were viewed with suspicion by nearly everyone. They were suspected of treason by the Romans. At the same time, they were pressured by fanatic Jewish loyalists to give up their belief in Jesus as the Messiah. The hostility from both sides took many forms. Sometimes it came in the form of intimidation. Other times, it came as the loss of work, or social ostracism, or even criminal arrest on trumped-up charges. Beatings, imprisonments, and sometimes death—all were part of the cost of maintaining faith in Jesus.

In the earliest years of the church, many members came to Christ out of Judaism. Other converts had adhered to synagogue worship but were not necessarily Jews themselves. Such people had been attracted to Judaism's high moral standards and strict monotheism. Although these folks professed faith in Jesus as Lord, they remembered the old Jewish teachings and practices and held them in high regard.

The writer of the Epistle to the Hebrews was aware that persecutions and pressures were pushing many many who had confessed Christ to slip back into a religion of legalism and lifeless ceremony. He correctly saw that these professing believers were losing sight of Christ's significance. If they lost their grasp of Christ's death and resurrection, they would revert to being less than Christians.

Hebrews was intended to strengthen the understanding about Jesus Christ among shaky followers. Written in superb Greek, with ringing words of confidence, Hebrews affirms the complete sufficiency and supremacy of Jesus Christ as Lord. No other being can make the claims attributed to Him.

## NOTES ON THE PRINTED TEXT

*Now God did not subject the coming world, about which we are speaking, to angels* (2:5). The writer pointed to the coming world. This was the age to come, a time when the Messiah would rule in fullness of power. At that time, everyone would be subject to the Messiah, not to God's angels.

The writer supported his words with other Scriptures. He quoted a piece of the Psalms, introducing the lines with a formula. The believers were reminded that humans were a little lower than the angels and were given honor in the cosmos. All Creation was subject to human control. *But someone has testified somewhere, "What are human beings that you are mindful of them, or mortals, that you care for them? You have made them for a little while lower than the angels; you have crowned them with glory and honor, subjecting all things under their feet"* (2:6-8a).

For a short time, Jesus was also, in a sense, made lower than the angels. His reduction in status was only temporary, however. Ultimately He was honored and exalted beyond His suffering and death. His death benefited humankind because it canceled sin. *But we do see Jesus, who for a little while was made lower than the angels, now crowned with glory and honor because of the suffering of death, so that by the grace of God he might taste death for everyone* (2:9).

The author reaffirmed that God's purpose was to provide salvation for humankind. In order to accomplish this goal, people had to be cleansed of their sins. Through Jesus' suffering and death, all believers were welcomed into God's glory. *It was fitting that God for whom and through whom all things exist, in bringing many children to glory, should make the pioneer of their salvation perfect through sufferings* (2:10).

Christ was described as the "pioneer" of salvation—the founder, leader, or the one who went first. Sometimes this Greek word was used in a nautical context to describe one who, as the ship sank, took the rope, swam to shore through the rocks and surf, and fastened the line so that the others might follow him to safety. Jesus was the pioneer who blazed the trail into the presence of God. He showed humankind the way to peace and friendship with God.

The author wrote that Christ suffered in order to sanctify His brothers and sisters. "Sanctify" conveys the idea of holiness, of cleansing from sin and defilement. *For the one who sanctifies and those who are sanctified all have one Father. For this reason Jesus is not ashamed to call them brothers and sisters* (2:11).

Christ took on human nature and shared human experience so that He might die in order to destroy death and the devil. *Since, therefore, the children share flesh and blood, he himself likewise shared the same things, so that through death he might destroy the one who has the power of death, that is, the devil* (2:14). Christ acted to free humankind from the fear of death. His resurrection freed *those who all their lives were held in slavery by the fear of death* (2:15). Christ acted because of His love for and preference for Israel, the descendants of Abraham. *For it is clear that he did not come to help angels, but the descendants of Abraham* (2:16).

Jesus became like His brothers and sisters so that he could become their high priest. Of course, the high priest could not be a foreigner; he had to be of a pure Jewish heritage. His priestly work was to make atonement for the nation's sin. *Therefore he had to become like his brothers and sisters in every respect, so that he might be a merciful and faithful high priest in the service of God, to make a sacrifice of atonement for the sins of the people* (2:17).

The author asserted that because Jesus suffered and was tempted, He is able to help all of us who experience the same struggles. *He is able to help those who are being tested* (2:18a).

## SUGGESTIONS TO TEACHERS

Offering lip service to Jesus as "Savior" may sound pious and impressive when repeated in a creed at Sunday worship. But what, exactly, does it mean to speak of Jesus in this way?

When it comes to turning to someone or something for "rescue," Jesus often seems to be relegated to a minor role. Our culture preaches that power, money, success, good looks, the right attitude, and large doses of common sense are what save a person. But we also have to deal with the human tragedies that our dependency on false "saviors" has produced. Ask the drug-addicted teenager and the ulcer-ridden executive what they're relying on for salvation. Jesus offers a better way.

Your lesson today on Jesus as Savior may appear at first to be merely repeating another of those old churchy-sounding phrases. But the message of the old-but-ever-new claim of Jesus as the only Savior needs to be told again and again.

1. SENTENCED BY SINS. Admittedly, sin is not a popular topic in our day. We bob and weave to avoid even using the word. Hebrews reminds us that sin is an attitude of disobedience toward God. That disobedience takes countless forms, but its consequences are deadly. It ends in separation from the Lord.

But why do we take sin so lightly these days? Discuss with your students the question that psychiatrist Karl Menninger asked (as the title of one of his books): "Whatever happened to sin?"

2. SEALED AS SUPERIOR. The astounding message of the Gospel is that God is truly interested in our welfare, in spite of our willful disobedience. Out of concern for us, God has acted. He has come among us in human form. In Jesus we confront the supreme being who invaded the order of Creation.

Jesus must be recognized as more than another noteworthy teacher and leader, or even as the most outstanding personality of history. He is sealed as the superior One of all the universe, for all time.

3. SANCTIFIED AS SAVIOR. As the preeminent personality, Jesus must be recognized as embodying all of God's nature. All we need of God is present in Jesus. This lesson should expand your students' concept of Jesus. He alone is worthy of the praise implied in the word *Savior*.

4. SUBJECTED TO SUFFERING. Although fully God, Jesus was also fully human, subject to the common struggles, including facing death, that you and I experience. Jesus also suffered, knew defeat, experienced loneliness and betrayal. Jesus is the only one who completely identifies with our pain and problems. As the God-Man, Jesus may be relied upon to rescue us from any destructive force.

## TOPIC FOR ADULTS
### JESUS, PIONEER OF SALVATION

*Charter of Newness.* During the Lewis and Clark expedition up the Missouri Valley in the early part of the last century, a young lieutenant was assigned to explore the region of what is now southeastern Montana. The lieutenant studied the existing maps very carefully—and became concerned. The young officer reported to his captain in great distress.

"Sir, there is no map of the region beyond this river. What are we to do?" he inquired. The captain, realizing the risks of advancing into uncharted country, commanded him to proceed as ordered and chart the territory.

Jesus, pioneer of our salvation, opened the uncharted areas beyond death so that we may move through life with confidence. Because He has already gone into the far country beyond the grave, we may live and die with a sense of serenity.

*Forsook the Perks.* Today's celebrities demand many kinds of special treatment. David Letterman has an assistant whose duties include slicing portions of bite-size pieces of pineapple for his boss every day. Bill Cosby insists upon being driven in nothing but a Jaguar. Wesley Snipes will not travel unless he has at least six bodyguards. Eddie Murphy refuses to perform unless his dressing room has a supply of peach-scented potpourri. On a recent tour in Miami, Luther Vandross would not touch a doorknob until one of his staff had first wiped it for him.

Fancy restaurants and hotels are eager to cater to the stars and provide their unusual perks. By contrast, Jesus made no celebrity-type demands. He sought no perks, expected no deferential treatment. He took on our human nature, experiencing the hurts, temptations, and deprivations of ordinary folk in order to bring us God's presence. Forsaking all claims to star status, Jesus became like his brothers so he could be their high priest.

*Cadillac Heaven.* When Betty Young died in November 1994, she stipulated in her will that she was to be buried in her beloved 1989 Cadillac Coupe de Ville. At great expense and effort, workmen removed the seats from the Cadillac to accommodate a honey-colored casket containing Betty Young's body. Then a crew excavated an enormous grave in the cemetery of Foster, Long Island. A flatbed truck conveyed the Cadillac to the cemetery, where a crane hoisted the large automobile into a huge pit, Betty Young's final resting place.

"Cadillac heaven" is no substitute for Christ's promises! Because of our risen Lord, who has already experienced the terrors of death, we may trust in God for our eternal rest. Christ, the pioneer of our salvation, has opened the way beyond the grave.

*Questions for Students on the Next Lesson.* 1. What was the function of the high priest in the Jerusalem temple? 2. Why does the writer of Hebrews portray Jesus as the great High Priest? 3. How does prayer help a believer withstand temptations? 4. How has God dealt with our sins? 5. What does Hebrews suggest as the remedy for personal guilt?

## TOPIC FOR YOUTH
### JESUS, THE SAVIOR

*Meeting Needs through Us.* The *New York Times Magazine* detailed the lives of several children in Manila. Their father is in jail for murder, and they spend the days selling flowers in the "red-light district." Their mother buys the flowers and depends on the children to sell them at a higher price. The entire family lives in the jail cell, where the father spends the day gambling at cards or getting drunk. The social and judicial systems tolerate this situation, which causes immense suffering for the children.

Our Savior is not aloof from suffering, poverty, or injustice. He came and lived as one of us, experiencing all that we endure. Willingly He suffered injustice, pain, and even death to bring His children to the salvation of His Father. Yet, during the time He is away, before He comes back to earth again, He expects us to be His hands and feet in meeting human need. What steps can you take on His behalf today?

*Disciplined by Suffering.* Football players practice a drill called "three on one." A defensive lineman lines up against three blockers. These three are to use every ounce of energy to completely remove the defensive player from an area five feet wide, usually lined with cones, so that a runner can slip through. The defensive player must try to tackle the ball carrier.

The drill is vicious, but the purpose is to test and toughen the defensive player. The conditions of the drill are actually harder than what might occur in a game. If a player learns to perform in this drill, then he should be able to perform even better in a game, when more is at stake. Suffering in drills makes the player stronger, equipping him for the real thing.

We're often hit by hurtful circumstances through no fault of our own. We're ready to quit. But like the toughening exercises in sports, the discipline of life's trials builds strength and character. And we can remember that God is strengthening us for Christ's service.

*Knew Suffering.* John Sech had been a foreman at the Mesta Machine Company. A vibrant, energetic, and outgoing individual, he had worked hard for his supervisors. But in his fifties he suffered a series of strokes. Each successive mini-stroke left him in worse condition. Despite therapy, he lost his speech. Then he developed diabetes, which eventually required both legs to be amputated. Finally, he even lost an arm.

Throughout his ordeal, which lasted for years, John's son, Bill, stuck with him. Every day he stopped to see his father. When Bill's mother died, and his father was placed in a personal care home, Bill still found an hour each afternoon after work to spend with his dad.

Bill was asked by his friends how he was able to carry on. Did he ever become discouraged or lose hope? Bill responded, "Dad is not the only person suffering. I know everyone has sorrow and suffering, so they understand. You reach down and find something inside you that helps you go on."

The writer of Hebrews made similar statements, but he proclaimed more—that the "something inside of you" can be faith in the supreme Savior. This Savior came and destroyed death. Nothing can defeat His love for us, no matter what our suffering.

*Questions for Students on the Next Lesson.* 1. What was the function of the high priest? 2. Why was Jesus the "great high priest?" 3. Were priests subject to weaknesses? Was Jesus? Why, or why not? 4. Who was Melchizedek? Why was he mentioned? 5. How was Jesus "made perfect"?

# LESSON 8—JULY 20

## JESUS IS THE HIGH PRIEST

*Background Scripture:* Hebrews 4:14—5:10; 7:1-28
*Devotional Reading:* Hebrews 7:20-28

### KING JAMES VERSION

HEBREWS 4:14 Seeing then that we have a great high priest, that is passed into the heavens, Jesus the Son of God, let us hold fast our profession.

15 For we have not an high priest which cannot be touched with the feeling of our infirmities; but was in all points tempted like as we are, yet without sin.

16 Let us therefore come boldly unto the throne of grace, that we may obtain mercy, and find grace to help in time of need.

5:1 For every high priest taken from among men is ordained for men in things pertaining to God, that he may offer both gifts and sacrifices for sins:

2 Who can have compassion on the ignorant, and on them that are out of the way; for that he himself also is compassed with infirmity.

3 And by reason hereof he ought, as for the people, so also for himself, to offer for sins.

4 And no man taketh this honour unto himself, but he that is called of God, as was Aaron.

5 So also Christ glorified not himself to be made an high priest; but he that said unto him, Thou art my Son, to day have I begotten thee.

6 As he saith also in another place, Thou art a priest for ever after the order of Melchisedec.

7 Who in the days of his flesh, when he had offered up prayers and supplications with strong crying and tears unto him that was able to save him from death, and was heard in that he feared;

8 Though he were a Son, yet learned he obedience by the things which he suffered;

9 And being made perfect, he became the author of eternal salvation unto all them that obey him;

10 Called of God an high priest after the order of Melchisedec.

### NEW REVISED STANDARD VERSION

HEBREWS 4:14 Since, then, we have a great high priest who has passed through the heavens, Jesus, the Son of God, let us hold fast to our confession. 15 For we do not have a high priest who is unable to sympathize with our weaknesses, but we have one who in every respect has been tested as we are, yet without sin. 16 Let us therefore approach the throne of grace with boldness, so that we may receive mercy and find grace to help in time of need.

5:1 Every high priest chosen from among mortals is put in charge of things pertaining to God on their behalf, to offer gifts and sacrifices for sins. 2 He is able to deal gently with the ignorant and wayward, since he himself is subject to weakness; 3 and because of this he must offer sacrifice for his own sins as well as for those of the people. 4 And one does not presume to take this honor but takes it only when called by God, just as Aaron was.

5 So also Christ did not glorify himself in becoming a high priest, but was appointed by the one who said to him, "You are my Son, today I have begotten you"; 6 as he says also in another place, "You are a priest forever, according to the order of Melchizedek."

7 In the days of his flesh, Jesus offered up prayers and supplications, with loud cries and tears, to the one who was able to save him from death, and he was heard because of his reverent submission. 8 Although he was a Son, he learned obedience through what he suffered; 9 and having been made perfect, he became the source of eternal salvation for all who obey him, 10 having been designated by God a high priest according to the order of Melchizedek.

KEY VERSE: *Let us therefore approach the throne of grace with boldness, so that we may receive mercy and find grace to help in time of need.* Hebrews 4:16.

## HOME BIBLE READINGS

| July | 14 | M. | Hebrews 7:1-9 | Melchizedek Is King of Peace |
| July | 15 | T. | Hebrews 9:1-10 | High Priests Offer Blood Sacrifices |
| July | 16 | W. | John 17:1-5 | Christ's Prayer to Be Glorified |
| July | 17 | T. | Hebrews 7:10-19 | Christ Is High Priest Forever |
| July | 18 | F. | Hebrews 8:1-7 | Christ Sits at God's Right Hand |
| July | 19 | S. | Hebrews 7:20-28 | Christ Intercedes for Us |
| July | 20 | S. | Romans 8:31-39 | Nothing Can Separate Us from God |

## BACKGROUND

There were three levels in the temple hierarchy: high priest, priest, and Levite. At the top, the high priest was considered the embodiment of all that was sacred. This man wore a breastplate on which the names of the twelve tribes of Israel were inscribed. When he entered the sanctuary, his breastplate signified that he represented all of God's chosen people. The high priest was allowed to go behind the great curtain and enter the holy of holies, the innermost part of the temple, once a year on the Day of Atonement. There he would make atonement for the sins of the nation.

In the years after Israel was no longer an independent state, the high priest acquired much of the honor and respect that had been formerly given the king. By the time of Jesus, the high priest presided over an influential body of priests, scribes, and a powerful ruling body known as the Sanhedrin.

Only a descendant of Eleazar, the son of Aaron, could serve as a high priest. The office was held for life. An elaborate ceremony consecrated the man appointed high priest. As the spiritual head of Israel, the high priest was expected to maintain a degree of ceremonial purity unmatched by any other. For example, he could not defile himself even by touching the dead bodies of his own parents.

The writer to the Hebrews knew that his readers already understood the role and requirements of the high priest. Therefore, this author went into detail to show how Jesus was the great High Priest who provided atonement for all people. To those who claimed that Jesus had no high priestly credentials, the writer of Hebrews reached back into the Scriptures for an example of a non-hereditary priest who was honored as God's agent: Melchizedek.

Melchizedek ("king of righteousness" in Hebrew) prepared a special meal for Abram (the father of all Hebrew history), bestowed a blessing in the name of the Most High God, and accepted Abram's gift of a tithe (Gen. 14:18-20). One other reference to Melchizedek occurs in the Old Testament. Psalm 110:4 mentions that Melchizedek is the prototype of the ideal king, a David-like messiah-ruler endowed with priestly authority.

The readers of Hebrews quickly got the message that Jesus filled the requirements of the ideal priest-king in the way Melchizedek had done. Here was the scriptural proof offered to anyone who questioned Jesus' right to be called "High Priest." That proof came through in Genesis, where Abram himself looked to Melchizedek as one greater even than he. Jesus, the High Priest after the order of Melchizedek, would institute a reign of peace and righteousness forever—something no mere mortal could ever do.

## NOTES ON THE PRINTED TEXT

The high priest presided over sacrifices offered in the Jerusalem temple. The chief function of the priesthood was to maintain an open channel of communication with God. To this end, sacrifices had to be offered continually to ensure God's favor. Thus, the role of high priest was that of mediator between God and humankind. The author of Hebrews had already described Jesus as the high priest. Today you will consider the writer's argument on this subject designed to solidify the believers' faith. *Since, then, we have a great high priest who has passed through the heavens, Jesus, the Son of God, let us hold fast to our confession* (4:14).

Every effort was made to keep the high priest undefiled, particularly on the Day of Atonement. On that day, the high priest offered a bull as a sin offering for himself and his family. Thus he would be treated as free of sin and could minister on behalf of his people. The writer told his readers that though Jesus had experienced temptation, He had never sinned. *For we do not have a high priest who is unable to sympathize with our weaknesses, but we have one who in every respect has been tested as we are, yet without sin* (4:15).

The approach to God was strictly controlled. The various rings of the temple courts separated Jew from Gentile, male from female, and priest from God. Only on the Day of Atonement could the high priest enter the holy of holies and approach the altar, which might be thought of as the throne of grace. Through Jesus, approach to the throne of God was opened to all. Believers could approach God with confidence, knowing they would receive mercy and grace. *Let us therefore approach the throne of grace with boldness, so that we may receive mercy and find grace to help in time of need* (4:16).

High priests represented the people before God. They brought the offerings and sacrifices dedicated to God—most of which were guilt offerings. *Every high priest chosen from among mortals is put in charge of things pertaining to God on their behalf, to offer gifts and sacrifices for sins* (5:1).

The high priest could offer atonement and forgiveness of sins only if the sins were committed out of ignorance and not deliberately. He had to balance the law with love. *He is able to deal gently with the ignorant and wayward, since he himself is subject to weakness* (5:2). Because he, too, was weak and sinful, he also had to offer a sacrifice for his own misdeeds on the Day of Atonement. *And because of this he must offer sacrifice for his own sins as well as for those of the people* (5:3).

The high priest was chosen by God for his position. No one could choose the honor of being high priest. *And one does not presume to take this honor, but takes it only when called by God, just as Aaron was* (5:4). Christ did not glorify Himself but was appointed by God to the high priesthood. The writer quoted scripture (Ps. 2:7 and 110:4) as proof. These texts proved Jesus was both a king and part of the priesthood based on Melchizedek's order.

The author spoke of Jesus' passion, describing His agony. Christ prayed to be spared from death on the cross. *In the days of his flesh, Jesus offered up prayers and supplications, with loud cries and tears, to the one who was able to save him from death, and he was heard because of his reverent submission* (5:7). However, while praying to be spared, Jesus chose to obey. *Although he was a Son, he learned obedience through what he suffered* (5:8). The writer summarized the result of Jesus' passion: His obedience provided eternal salvation to all who obey Him. *And having been made perfect, he became the source of eternal salvation for all who obey him, having been designated by God a high priest according to the order of Melchizedek* (5:9, 10).

## SUGGESTIONS TO TEACHERS

Several years ago, a fictional story portrayed the suffering people of the world bringing criminal charges against God. The victims of cruel oppressors demanded that God be put on trial and sentenced. The sentence was this: that God live as a member of a despised minority, experience homelessness and rejection, be falsely arrested and tortured, then put to death by violent means. The climax of the drama comes when accusers suddenly realize that the Almighty has, indeed, already known all of these forms of suffering. In Jesus Christ, God has plumbed the depths of human pain.

In today's lesson, Jesus comes through as the great High Priest, the perfect intermediary between humans and God, because He has known our pain and heartache. The biblical language about the Jewish high priest illustrates exactly what this means. Don't feel you have to spend most of your lesson explaining all the symbolism of ancient temple worship. Keep your attention fixed on Jesus, the one who brings His followers to the throne of God.

1. HUMAN. Hebrews makes it clear that our High Priest understands us completely. He identifies with us in every way. As one who also faced temptation, He realizes our needs and weaknesses. Because Jesus is "one of us," as well as one with God, we can look to Him as our perfect intercessor.

2. HUMBLE. Our High Priest was not anointed by human authority. Nor was He self-anointed. Hebrews makes it clear that Jesus was called by God yet willingly accepted the indignity and suffering of the cross. This High Priest did not strut with self-importance, demanding honors and glory. Comment about the consistent humility Jesus demonstrated. Point out that a willingness to set aside personal glory is the hallmark of a Christian disciple.

3. HALLOWED. The author of Hebrews builds an impressive case for Jesus' preeminence as the great High Priest for Christians. He does this by showing that even in Jewish tradition, a priest-messiah-king did not have to fulfill all the traditional legal requirements; he could be a Melchizedek-type of priest. Just as Melchizedek deserved gifts from Abram, his illustrious ancestor, Jesus, is even more deserving. Jesus, more than any other personality in God's order, is worthy to be honored. He alone is hallowed as the perfect mediator between us and God.

4. HOLY. Human high priests in the Jewish tradition had to be replaced whenever they died. The author of Hebrews proclaimed that Jesus is the permanent High Priest. In addition, there is no longer any need for a high priest to offer up a daily sacrifice. Once and for all, Jesus has offered up

Himself. The complete and perfect sacrifice has been made.

Stress that no person needs to placate God. No matter how lavish or sacrificial the gift or deed, it could never suffice to make us right with our Creator. But the good news is that through Jesus' sacrifice, we are given a new relationship with the Lord by pure, unconditional grace. We are accepted because of Christ's work, not ours.

## TOPIC FOR ADULTS
### JESUS, THE GREAT HIGH PRIEST

*Shared Their Struggle.* Gallaudet University in Washington, D.C., has had a distinguished history of serving students with hearing disabilities. Over 21,000 deaf young men and women are enrolled.

In the late 1980s, the university was in turmoil because the president had no hearing problems. The student body grew increasingly unhappy with her lack of empathy and understanding, and the unrest threatened to bring campus programs to a standstill. Finally the trustees asked the president to resign.

Dr. I. K. Jordan was appointed to the presidency, and he immediately took steps to bring healing after the controversy over his predecessor's leadership. Jordan met with the president of the student body and the chairman of the university's board of trustees to discuss the future of Gallaudet. As they walked out of the meeting, the head of the student association turned to Dr. Jordan and with great emotion stated, "There was no interpreter."

The reason? Dr. Jordan is also deaf. The young president of the student body realized that their new leader was a person like themselves who had experienced all their struggles with hearing impairment.

In the person of Jesus Christ, we have a great High Priest who has shared the trials and tribulations of our humanity. Let us trust Him as the one to intercede for us

*You Would Kiss Me?* George M. Conn, Jr., tells about something that happened over thirty years ago when he was a newly commissioned Navy reserve chaplain. The local Navy recruiter had called to ask Conn to perform a wedding for a young seaman who had been absent without leave. He had left his his ship in order to look after his girl friend.

The young seaman was eighteen, and the girl was seventeen. The recruiter spilled out the other details. The girl was six months pregnant. The seaman had left his ship out of concern for the girl's welfare. The authorities had picked him up at her home and put him in jail. The recruiter said the boy was to be released from jail for an hour for the wedding, if Conn would be the officiating minister. The young man had asked for the wedding in order to have the Navy provide the girl with prenatal and obstetric care (and the baby with pediatric care). The recruiter pleaded with Conn to come down to his office and "do the wedding."

Conn struggled briefly with the principles he had learned in seminary. For example: not to officiate at weddings of convenience, especially for strangers—most especially with pregnant teenage kids he didn't know, who had no tie with his church. But Conn also realized that sometimes occasions arise in which caring for persons can take precedence over rules and doctrines. Was this such a case?

He hurried to the recruiter's office, met the couple, and proceeded with the wedding service. Vows were spoken, a ring given, a kiss exchanged. Then, after the benediction, Conn did what he always did at a wedding. He shook the groom's hand and leaned over to kiss the bride on the cheek.

The young bride jumped back as if she had been touched by a live wire. She did not step back, Conn reports; she jumped back. Tears flowed down her cheeks as she faced the minister. Then she gasped, "You would kiss me?"

Conn suddenly realized that he stood in front of her in his officer's uniform, with sleeves marked with the stripes of power, privilege, and authority. His chaplain's cross, he knew, communicated judgment to the frightened seventeen-year-old bride. But his willingness to bestow a kiss communicated a powerful message of grace.—Adapted from an article by George M. Conn, Jr., in *Presbyterian Outlook,* March 20, 1995.

In the person of Jesus, God brought His kiss of acceptance to all humans. The all-powerful, all-authoritative Ruler of the universe laid aside His privilege in the humanity of Jesus. He opened the way for us to know God's loving acceptance.

*Plain Package.* A South African miner found one of the world's largest diamonds, which was the size of a small lemon. He needed to get it to the company's office in London, so he put the diamond in a small steel box and hired four men to deliver it. Even when it was in the ship's safe, the diamond was guarded day and night by at least two armed men. But when the package arrived at the company's office in London, it was found to contain a lump of black coal. Three days later, the diamond arrived by ordinary parcel post in a plain package. The owner had assumed correctly that most people would pay no attention to an ordinary cardboard box.

That is the way God sent His Son into the world, and that is the way He took Him out of the world. Jesus came as an ordinary baby, born to unimportant people in an unimportant place. He died as a revolutionary between two thieves—not an uncommon event in the first century. Within that death, however, there was the precious glint of divine love and a guarantee of our victory over death. And those of us who dare to identify with this plain life and death find the treasure above all treasures. Sadly, many still pass by, unimpressed with the plain package of God's goodness.

*Questions for Students on the Next Lesson.* 1. What was the purpose of the system of sacrifices in the Jerusalem temple? 2. Did the sacrifices succeed in removing guilt permanently? 3. In what way did Christ's sacrifice do away with the ceremonies at the temple? 4. How has Christ's death opened the way to God? 5. What are some of the faulty ways we may try to deal with our guilt?

## TOPIC FOR YOUTH
### JESUS, THE LEADER

*A Sinner?* In a nationwide survey of adults eighteen years and older, the Barna Research Group of Glendale, California, discovered that while Americans believe in the existence of Jesus, a large percentage believe that Christ Himself was a sinner! Forty percent of all adults believe that Jesus made mistakes. Forty-two percent of the adults believe that Jesus committed sins during His life on earth.

This flies in the face of Scripture, particularly Hebrews, which claims that Jesus was tempted but without sin. Perfect and full atonement could be made only by one who was Himself perfect.

*Legislated Humility.* Unsportsmanlike conduct, including taunting an opponent, is prohibited in professional and college football. This includes all the little victory celebrations (the victory dances, high-5's, etc.) that so often occur in the end zone after one team scores a touchdown. The prohibition is designed to prevent ill will and to keep a player from focusing on himself. Violation of the rule brings a fifteen-yard penalty.

Since the referee must make the call based on his judgment, the rule is enforced differently at different times. Certain college football coaches, though, have been very concerned that this rule be strictly enforced.

Perhaps you have struggled with the call to be humble. Recall the example of Jesus. Hebrews reminds us that Christ did not glorify Himself—the one who had every right to do so. Rather, God bestowed glory on Him. But He did so only after the cross.

*Not Strong Enough.* Eric Green is one of the National Football League's largest tight ends. As he rumbles down the field he is a huge target for a pass from the Pittsburgh Steelers' quarterback, Neil O'Donnell. Green's quickness and sure hands have made him a significant offensive threat. A graduate of Liberty University, this Christian athlete is 6 feet 5 inches tall and weighs 274 pounds. Surely he would be strong enough to resist temptation!

Think again. His faith and enormous physical strength were not enough to keep him from substance abuse.

Often temptations come unexpectedly. Despite our best defenses and impressive strength, we collapse. Over-confidence, perhaps, is our worst mistake.

Being a Christian does not mean we will not be tempted. Jesus was tempted and struggled all His life. Yet sin never overcame Him. Never overestimate your strength. Temptation is stronger and more subtle than you may think.

*Questions for Students on the Next Lesson.* 1. What was the purpose of Israel's sacrifices? 2. What is sanctification? 3. Why was Jesus the perfect sacrifice? 4. What was the "footstool" upon which Jesus' feet rested? 5. In what ways do people today still make sacrifices, in hopes of pleasing God?

# LESSON 9—JULY 27

## JESUS IS THE SACRIFICE

*Background Scripture:* Hebrews 9:11—10:18
*Devotional Reading:* Hebrews 10:11-18

### KING JAMES VERSION

HEBREWS 10:1 For the law having a shadow of good things to come, and not the very image of the things, can never with those sacrifices which they offered year by year continually make the comers thereunto perfect.

2 For then would they not have ceased to be offered? because that the worshippers once purged should have had no more conscience of sins.

3 But in those sacrifices there is a remembrance again made of sins every year.

4 For it is not possible that the blood of bulls and of goats should take away sins.

5 Wherefore when he cometh into the world, he saith, Sacrifice and offering thou wouldest not, but a body hast thou prepared me:

6 In burnt offerings and sacrifices for sin thou hast had no pleasure.

7 Then said I, Lo, I come (in the volume of the book it is written of me,) to do thy will, O God.

8 Above when he said, Sacrifice and offering and burnt offerings and offering for sin thou wouldest not, neither hadst pleasure therein; which are offered by the law;

9 Then said he, Lo, I come to do thy will, O God. He taketh away the first, that he may establish the second.

10 By the which will we are sanctified through the offering of the body of Jesus Christ once for all.

11 And every priest standeth daily ministering and offering oftentimes the same sacrifices, which can never take away sins:

12 But this man, after he had offered one sacrifice for sins for ever, sat down on the right hand of God;

13 From henceforth expecting till his enemies be made his footstool.

14 For by one offering he hath perfected for ever them that are sanctified.

### NEW REVISED STANDARD VERSION

HEBREWS 10:1 Since the law has only a shadow of the good things to come and not the true form of these realities, it can never, by the same sacrifices that are continually offered year after year, make perfect those who approach. 2 Otherwise, would they not have ceased being offered, since the worshipers, cleansed once for all, would no longer have any consciousness of sin? 3 But in these sacrifices there is a reminder of sin year after year. 4 For it is impossible for the blood of bulls and goats to take away sins. 5 Consequently, when Christ came into the world, he said, "Sacrifices and offerings you have not desired, but a body you have prepared for me; 6 in burnt offerings and sin offerings you have taken no pleasure. 7 Then I said, 'See, God, I have come to do your will, O God' (in the scroll of the book it is written of me)." 8 When he said above, "You have neither desired nor taken pleasure in sacrifices and offerings and burnt offerings and sin offerings" (these are offered according to the law), 9 then he added, "See, I have come to do your will." He abolishes the first in order to establish the second. 10 And it is by God's will that we have been sanctified through the offering of the body of Jesus Christ once for all.

11 And every priest stands day after day at his service, offering again and again the same sacrifices that can never take away sins. 12 But when Christ had offered for all time a single sacrifice for sins, he sat down at the right hand of God, 13 and since then has been waiting until his enemies would be made a footstool for his feet." 14 For by a single offering he has perfected for all time those who are sanctified.

**KEY VERSE:** *By a single offering he has perfected for all time those who are sanctified.* Hebrews 10:14.

## HOME BIBLE READINGS

| | | | | |
|---|---|---|---|---|
| *July* | *21* | *M.* | Hebrews 9:23-28 | *Christ Sacrificed One Time Only* |
| *July* | *22* | *T.* | Hebrews 8:8-13 | *The New Covenant Superior to First* |
| *July* | *23* | *W.* | Hebrews 9:11-22 | *The New Covenant Verified* |
| *July* | *24* | *T.* | Psalm 40:4-10 | *God Does Not Want Sacrifices* |
| *July* | *25* | *F.* | I Samuel 15:17-23 | *To Obey Is Better than Sacrifice* |
| *July* | *26* | *S.* | Mark 12:28-34 | *To Love Is Better than Sacrifice* |
| *July* | *27* | *S.* | Micah 6:1-8 | *Walk Humbly with Your God* |

## BACKGROUND

Large segments of Exodus, Leviticus, and Deuteronomy describe the details involved in offering sacrifices to God. The animal to be sacrificed had to be without disease or injury. The animal's blood must be sprinkled or smeared on the altar, presenting the sacrificed life to the Lord. Only bullocks or cattle, sheep, goats, doves, and pigeons could be sacrificed. And only qualified priests could carry out the necessary rituals.

By the time of Jesus, the sacrificial system and its ceremonies had evolved into the most important aspect of Jewish worship. Each morning and each evening, an unblemished male lamb was slaughtered by the high priest, a portion of the blood poured on the altar, and a piece of the meat burned there. All these acts were accompanied by chants and responses by Levite choirs. At the beginning of each sabbath, and at the start of every new month, additional animals were sacrificed. Likewise, on all festivals in the Jewish year, more sacrifices were required.

The Day of Atonement was the most solemn and important occasion for sacrifice. Leviticus 16 describes the role of the high priest and the details of the sacrifices on this day. Two sin offerings were made, one for the high priest and the other for the people. Even the high priest was considered unworthy to approach God, requiring a sacrifice before he could go into the holy of holies. On that day, the blood of the sacrificial animal was taken into the holy of holies itself.

What was the meaning behind all these complex rules of temple worship? A cluster of symbolic associations were involved. One was the awareness of human unworthiness to approach the Lord. Offering a perfect animal was a way of expressing that the worshiper deserved to die; he was offering up his life to God through the slaughter of the animal.

There was also the idea of renewing the ancient covenant. Eating with the other party in a covenant was a central part of the ceremony sealing the relationship. The sacrifices stood for the reestablishment of relationship with God and His people. Putting a portion of the meat on the altar, and distributing another portion for the use of the priest, was an outward sign of the covenantal bond.

## NOTES ON THE PRINTED TEXT

The writer of Hebrews had previously depicted Christ as the ideal High Priest who offered the perfect sacrifice for sin. That argument culminated with proof not only of the futility of Jewish sacrifices, but of the finality of Christ's sacrifice. The high priestly sacrifice of Jesus superseded the old sacrificial system.

The author initially proposed that the old system had failed. The law with its sacrifices failed because it simply could not make people perfect. *Since the law has only a shadow of the good things to come and not the true form of these realities, it can never, by the same sacrifices that are continually offered year after year, make perfect those who approach* (10:1).

If the worshipers had been effectively cleansed from sin, they would no longer have been conscious of sin and would not have continued to offer sacrifices. If perfection had been achieved, the sacrifices would be unnecessary. *Otherwise, would they not have ceased being offered, since the worshipers, cleansed once for all, would no longer have any consciousness of sin?* (10:2).

The repetition of sacrifices demonstrated the non-permanence of their efficacy. They reminded sinners of their guilt but simply could not remove that guilt. *But in these sacrifices there is a reminder of sin year after year* (10:3). The author then reached a verdict: sin still exists. *For it is impossible for the blood of bulls and goats to take away sins* (10:4).

Since animal sacrifices, established in the first covenant, were unable to take away the sins of humankind, God abolished that first covenant and established a second one. The author quoted Psalm 40:6-8, attributing those words to Christ. The Lord was quoted as saying that the Old Testament law demanding sacrifices was finished. A perfect sacrificial body (the whole animal was offered and burned) had been furnished because God took no pleasure in those repeated animal sacrifices. *Consequently, when Christ came into the world, he said, "Sacrifices and offerings you have not desired, but a body you have prepared for me; in burnt offerings and sin offerings you have taken no pleasure"* (10:5, 6).

Still quoting the psalm, the writer emphasized that Jesus came to fulfill God's will. *Then I said, "See, God, I have come to do your will, O God (in the scroll of the book it is written of me.)"* (10:7).

God's will was a better, or perfect, sacrifice. Christ came to replace the sacrifices prescribed by the law and to establish a new order. *When he said above, "You have neither desired nor taken pleasure in sacrifices and offerings and burnt offerings and sin offerings" (these are offered according to the law,) then he added, "See, I have come to do your will." He abolishes the first in order to establish the second* (10:8, 9).

Jesus' sacrifice was decisive and final. He was the perfect sacrifice for sin. God's people were made pure by Christ's atoning death. *And it is by God's will that we have been sanctified through the offering of the body of Jesus Christ once for all* (10:10).

The writer reiterated his argument. Human priests daily performed religious rites that could never take away sin. *And every priest stands day after day at his service, offering again and again the same sacrifices that can never take away sins* (10:11). Instead of the repetitive, meaningless sacrifices, Jesus offered a single sacrifice that spiritually cleansed believers. Again finding support in the Psalms (110), the writer affirmed that Christ took His position of honor at God's right hand and triumphantly waited for the defeat of His enemies. *But when Christ had offered for all time a single sacrifice for sins, "he sat down at the right hand of God," and since then has been waiting "until his enemies would be made a footstool for his feet." For by a single offering he has perfected for all time those who are sanctified* (10:12-14).

## SUGGESTIONS TO TEACHERS

Today we don't feel a need to appease God by slaughtering a sheep, sprinkling its blood on the church communion table, and burning a chunk of the meat as a gift to the Lord. Yet a subtle desire to sacrifice remains. We do want to secure a sense of the Lord's acceptance. Some church people immerse themselves in "good works." Others attempt to live self-sacrificing lives (which are often only an effort to ease guilt). Many people devise their own systems of self-sacrifice in vain attempts to acquire a relationship with the Almighty.

The point of this lesson is that THE sacrifice has already been made. Through Jesus Christ's sacrificial death, as the writer to the Hebrews pointed out, a new relationship with God has been secured once and for all.

1. POSSESSOR OF PERFECTION. Jesus' death was all-sufficient. His sacrifice on the Cross was complete and everlasting in its effect. No other can approach this sacrifice, or need try. Although Christians should not put down people practicing other religions, we may confidently state that what was done by Jesus ended the need for any other sacrificial act to secure divine mercy. Christ, and only Christ, is the perfect sacrifice.

2. PROVIDER OF THE NEW COVENANT. The ancient sacrificial system of Israel renewed the old covenant between God and His people. But the perfect sacrifice on the cross instituted the new covenant. God has promised His complete acceptance when we turn and entrust our lives to Christ. Hebrews speaks of the "promised eternal inheritance" (9:15). Reflect on what this inheritance means. Discuss the term *mediator*.

3. PERMANENCE OF HIS SACRIFICE. Formerly, sacrificial offerings had to be repeated. Only partial and temporary acceptance by the Lord could be assured under the former practices. The effect of Christ's sacrifice, however, lasts forever. We may be certain we have access to God always. Through the Cross and Resurrection, He welcomes us eagerly.

4. PROVISION FOR OUR FORGIVENESS. Hebrews has some unusual ways of proclaiming that God has forgiven us through Christ. Take this opportunity to discuss what the forgiveness of God implies for us. Go beyond the superficial, and lift up the fact that forgiveness costs. It cost the life of the Son of God. To appropriate God's acceptance also means granting mercy, in turn, to others. And that costs, too.

## TOPIC FOR ADULTS
### JESUS THE PERFECT SACRIFICE

*A Sacrifice for Ed.* No one spent more time around the church than Ed. He was the congregation's Mr. Fix-it. He was also the best volunteer. Others would sign up for an evening, maybe two, to help paint Sunday school rooms. Ed would be there every evening.

Ed accepted the tedious job of keeping the financial records, tallying the Sunday offerings, recording pledges, sending out the statements, making monthly reports, arranging for the annual audit, and writing the checks. He volunteered at the local hospital on Saturdays. Most holidays, he delivered Meals on Wheels when others wanted time off.

The finance committee and a few others in the congregation knew that Ed tithed a hefty ten percent of his modest salary as an accountant. His boss and the company knew that he had twice turned down promotions in order to stay in his hometown and help in the church and community. Unfortunately, his hours away from his family had meant that his two children grew up feeling that Ed had put his volunteer work ahead of them. They had resented his evenings away, and they wanted no part of his church.

One January evening, Ed returned home complaining of chest pains. Tests revealed coronary problems, and doctors insisted on a heart by-pass operation. The pastor came to call.

"You look worried," the minister said.

"Yeah, I guess I am," said Ed.

"Well, of all people in the church, you've showed you're a man of faith," replied the minister.

After a long silence, Ed spoke. "Pastor, I really am not. In fact, I haven't ever been able to feel that the Lord wanted me because I'm not a good enough person. So, I've been trying to get right with Him. I've sacrificed so much, even my family. But I still don't feel as though I've done enough to be accepted by the Lord."

In the next half hour, the minister quietly explained to Ed that no human could hope to make an adequate sacrifice in order to be right with the Lord; the sacrifice had already been made at the Cross. No system of human sacrifices could accomplish what needed to be done.

Ed's face gradually brightened with hope, and the two prayed. Ed went into surgery the next morning a changed man.

*Costly Sacrifice.* A tragic accident took place in 1946 in Los Alamos, New Mexico. A group of scientists was preparing materials for an atomic bomb test. One of them, a young man named Louis Slotin, was bringing two hemispheres of uranium together to try to determine exactly how much U-235 was needed to make a chain reaction. He had done this particular procedure many times before, bringing the two bits of material dangerously close together, then pushing them apart with a screwdriver before a deadly chain reaction could start.

But on that particular day, the screwdriver slipped, and the bits of uranium came too close together. Instantly, the room was filled with a dazzling blue haze. The young scientist reacted quickly. Instead of ducking and possibly saving himself, he tore the uranium apart with his bare hands, thus stopping the reaction. He saved, with his own body, the lives of seven other scientists in the room. But he knew he had done it at the cost of his own life. As he waited for the ambulance, he said quietly to his companions, "You'll come through it all right. But I haven't the faintest chance myself." Nine days later, in excruciating agony, Louis Slotin died.—Adapted from "Planet in Rebellion" by George Vandeman.

Jesus Christ's costly sacrifice brought new life to millions. He could have saved Himself, but He willingly accepted the pain and disgrace of the Cross for the sake of others.

*A Thousand Points.* We humans persist in thinking we can save ourselves by "the point system" of accruing merit through our own good works. Somehow, we imagine that our goodness will impress the Lord enough to win His acceptance. The uselessness of such an attitude is summed up in a humorous story.

It seems that a man well-known for his piety died and went to heaven. As he approached the pearly gates, St. Peter came out and told him to halt. "Just a minute," said St. Peter. "You can't just walk into heaven. You have to have 1,000 points. We assign you points for what you've done in your life. What have you done to expand the kingdom of God?"

"Well," said the man, his mind racing, "I was baptized."

"Baptism is good," said St. Peter. "That gives you one point."

"I also attended worship regularly all my life, nearly ever Sunday."

"Church attendance is good," said St. Peter. "Now you have two points."

"And I was a Deacon, and I taught Sunday school for a couple of years. I was also faithful in keeping up my tithes and offerings."

"Church attendance, taking leadership positions, faithful giving," said St. Peter. "Let's see, that gives you three more points, for a total of five."

"For the love of God!" the man cried. "How can anyone get into heaven?"

"Did I hear you mention the love of God?" asked Peter. "That's worth the other 995 points!" And he opened the Pearly Gates.

This obviously nonbiblical story does at least make a point about works-righteousness. Though, of course, it doesn't go far enough. All of our so-called good deeds are worth nothing toward our salvation; they don't earn a single point. Jesus paid it all. For only He is qualified to do so.

*Questions for Students on the Next Lesson.* 1. Why did the writer of Hebrews have to remind his readers of the basic tenets of the faith? 2. Do you feel you are growing more mature in the faith? If so, what leads you to think so? If not, why not? 3. How do you respond to church members who may think they don't need to learn more about the faith? 4. Will we always be rewarded for being loyal to Christ? 5. What specific steps could you take to grow spiritually in the year ahead?

## TOPIC FOR YOUTH
### *JESUS, THE SACRIFICE*

*Ref's Unorthodox Rules.* The basketball game at Cerritos, California between Whitney High and Valley Torah High was delayed forty minutes in December 1994 by official Dale Earnshaw. He threatened to cancel the game if the Torah players did not remove their yarmulkes. Torah's team members are all Orthodox Jews who are required to wear the small, cloth skullcaps as a symbol of their constant recognition of being under God's will and care.

The Torah High School team and coaches pleaded for tolerance, reminding the referee that they did have official permission to observe the age-old religious practice. Because of religious law, they had to disregard the sport's rules. Earnshaw said he was not against the yarmulkes, but objected to the metal clips and pins used to hold them in place. He was afraid someone might get hurt, since basketball was a contact sport. He was reminded that basketball was not supposed to be a contact game, according to the rules. The game finally took place.

Some youth, like those of Torah High School, struggle with obeying every law. However, all the laws simply cannot be obeyed. The author of Hebrews pointed out that observing religious law could not bring about perfection. Rather, a new sacrifice had to be offered—a perfect, eternal one.

*Changed Because of Law.* When pop star Michael Jackson planned to perform in Tel Aviv, Israel, his corporate sponsor urged him to reschedule his concert. He was to perform on Saturday, September 18, 1993. However, Pepsi-Cola was already taking the heat from angered rabbis because the company had violated Jewish law by selling soft drinks to young people waiting for a Guns N' Roses concert before the sabbath ended. The law forbade all trading between sundown Friday and the appearance of at least three stars in the heavens on Saturday night. Jackson's performance was moved to Monday night, September 20. Religious law won out.

The writer of Hebrews stressed that the coming of Jesus freed people from these kinds of laws. Because of Jesus' sacrifice, the old law had been superseded. Now, a whole new way of life existed because of Christ.

*Sacrificed to Save the Other.* Michael Coleman and his cousin Dwayne Coleman discovered they could get into the Fairywood Pool after it was closed for the day. No attendants or lifeguards were on duty, so the boys decided they would sneak a swim. Besides, it was a hot evening in July 1990, and Michael assured Dwayne that he could swim. Dwayne had some misgivings, since he was a nonswimmer.

The two boys, both thirteen, jumped into the refreshing water. Unfortunately, Dwayne leaped into the deep end of the pool and panicked. He struggled frantically to grab Michael, who valiantly tried to keep his cousin from going under. As they screamed and thrashed in the pool, their cries were heard by a pair of older boys.

Robert Smith, twenty, was playing three-on-three basketball nearby when he heard the cries and shouts from the pool. He and Dennis Lamar ran, scaled the fence, dove in the pool, and pulled the two boys out. Both the boys had already gone under.

Young Michael drowned saving his cousin Dwayne's life. He sacrificed himself to keep Dwayne above the water.

The same idea of sacrifice is found in Hebrews. Christ made a single sacrifice for His people. He died to save each of us and give us eternal life.

*Questions for Students on the Next Lesson.* 1. How did the writer of Hebrews define perfection? 2. What were the basic elements of Christian teaching? 3. What is repentance? 4. What reward was promised to the faithful? 5. Have you imitated the unknown writer of Hebrews in any way?

# LESSON 10—AUGUST 3

## *GROW IN FAITHFULNESS*

*Background Scripture:* Hebrews 5:11—6:12
*Devotional Reading:* Hebrews 6:13-20

### KING JAMES VERSION

HEBREWS 5:11 Of whom we have many things to say, and hard to be uttered, seeing ye are dull of hearing.

12 For when for the time ye ought to be teachers, ye have need that one teach you again which be the first principles of the oracles of God; and are become such as have need of milk, and not of strong meat.

13 For every one that useth milk is unskilful in the word of righteousness: for he is a babe.

14 But strong meat belongeth to them that are of full age, even those who by reason of use have their senses exercised to discern both good and evil.

6:1 Therefore leaving the principles of the doctrine of Christ, let us go on unto perfection; not laying again the foundation of repentance from dead works, and of faith toward God.

2 Of the doctrine of baptisms, and of laying on of hands, and of resurrection of the dead, and of eternal judgment.

3 And this will we do, if God permit.

4 For it is impossible for those who were once enlightened, and have tasted of the heavenly gift, and were made partakers of the Holy Ghost,

5 And have tasted the good word of God, and the powers of the world to come,

6 If they shall fall away, to renew them again unto repentance; seeing they crucify to themselves the Son of God afresh, and put him to an open shame.

7 For the earth which drinketh in the rain that cometh oft upon it, and bringeth forth herbs meet for them by whom it is dressed, receiveth blessing from God:

8 But that which beareth thorns and briers is rejected, and is nigh unto cursing; whose end is to be burned.

9 But, beloved, we are persuaded better things of you, and things that accompany salvation, though we thus speak.

10 For God is not unrighteous to forget your work and labour of love, which ye have shewed toward his name, in that ye have ministered to the saints, and do minister.

### NEW REVISED STANDARD VERSION

HEBREWS 5:11 About this we have much to say that is hard to explain, since you have become dull in understanding. 12 For though by this time you ought to be teachers, you need someone to teach you again the basic elements of the oracles of God. You need milk, not solid food; 13 for everyone who lives on milk, being still an infant, is unskilled in the word of righteousness. 14 But solid food is for the mature, for those whose faculties have been trained by practice to distinguish good from evil.

6:1 Therefore let us go on toward perfection, leaving behind the basic teaching about Christ, and not laying again the foundation: repentance from dead works and faith toward God, 2 instruction about baptisms, laying on of hands, resurrection of the dead, and eternal judgment. 3 And we will do this, if God permits. 4 For it is impossible to restore again to repentance those who have once been enlightened, and have tasted the heavenly gift, and have shared in the Holy Spirit, 5 and have tasted the goodness of the word of God and the powers of the age to come, 6 and then have fallen away, since on their own they are crucifying again the Son of God and are holding him up to contempt. 7 Ground that drinks up the rain falling on it repeatedly, and that produces a crop useful to those for whom it is cultivated, receives a blessing from God.

8 But if it produces thorns and thistles, it is worthless and on the verge of being cursed; its end is to be burned over.

9 Even though we speak in this way, beloved, we are confident of better things in your case, things that belong to salvation. 10 For God is not unjust; he will not overlook your work and the love that you showed for his sake in serving the saints, as you still do.

KEY VERSE: *Let us go on toward perfection.* Hebrews 6:1a.

## HOME BIBLE READINGS

| July | 28 | M. | Hebrews 6:12-30 | *God's Covenant Promise Unchanged* |
|------|----|----|-----------------|-------------------------------------|
| July | 29 | T. | Matthew 10:34-42 | *Servants Rewarded for Good Work* |
| July | 30 | W. | Ephesians 2:1-8 | *By Grace We Are Saved* |
| July | 31 | T. | I Corinthians 10:1-13 | *Escape Temptations with God's Help* |
| Aug. | 1 | F. | Job 4:1-9 | *God Punishes the Wicked* |
| Aug. | 2 | S. | I Peter 2:1-10 | *Grow Up to Your Salvation* |
| Aug. | 3 | S. | II Peter 1:12-21 | *Prophecy Comes from the Holy Spirit* |

## BACKGROUND

The New Testament Greek word for apostasy literally means "standing away." In the early church it refers to standing away from Christ, or forsaking the true faith. Those guilty of apostasy once had professed their allegiance to Christ but had then relinquished it.

The persecutions in the first three centuries took a fearsome toll on the Christian community. Many glorious stories of heroism come from this period. Many other stories will never be known, stories of nameless men and women who stood firm in their faith and paid huge penalties as a result. Martyrdom was quite common. The fate of other believers involved deportations to the mines, maiming, branding, flogging, and imprisonment.

Though some stood strong for the faith, others were guilty of apostasy. After each wave of persecution subsided, the churches struggled over the matter of what to do about those who had deserted the faith under pressure. Some who were guilty came back and asked to be readmitted to the Christian fellowship. "Should we welcome them?" asked the faithful. And what about those who hadn't asked to rejoin? Should the church seek them out and re-evangelize them? Some said the apostasizers should be given a second chance, while others in the church wanted to treat them as infidels.

The writer of Hebrews recognized that there was another group, those who were simply allowing their original ardor for Christ to cool. The author of this letter wanted to stir up those who were becoming apathetic. At that time, as in our time, many Christians unintentionally allowed other interests to crowd out Christ. The writer reminded them that they should have matured so much that they would now be teachers. But instead of being graduates in the school of faith, they were still in kindergarten.

## NOTES ON THE PRINTED TEXT

Hebrews had described Jesus as the great High Priest. But now an interruption occurred in which the author exhorted the believers. Perhaps the letter was originally delivered orally; therefore, the sender stressed hearing as he or she warned against apostasy. *About this we have much to say that is hard to explain, since you have become dull in understanding* (5:11).

Hebrews was written during the lifetime of the second generation of Christians. A considerable interval of time had elapsed after their conversion, and the readers should have learned enough to teach others. Instead they needed to be reminded of the most basic elements of the faith. They were slow, indifferent learners who, in the author's opinion, had taken too much time to learn. *For though by this time you ought to be teachers, you need someone to teach you again the basic elements of the oracles of God. You need milk, not solid food; for everyone who lives on milk, being still an infant, is unskilled in the word of righteousness. But solid food is for the mature, for those whose faculties have been trained by practice to distinguish good from evil* (5:12-14).

*Therefore let us go on toward perfection, leaving behind the basic teaching about Christ* (6:1a). The writer encouraged the believers to move, as God leads, beyond the basic teachings of faith toward deeper maturity. The basic teachings about Christ may have included the Lord's words, which may have been passed down orally. Also included were specific, fundamental teachings of the faith such as *repentance from dead works and faith toward God, instruction about baptisms, laying on of hands, resurrection of the dead, and eternal judgment* (6:1b, 2). Repentance from dead works contrasted the life of Christians before and after baptism. Perhaps the laying on of hands referred to the entry of the Holy Spirit into the lives of new believers. They would be enabled to move to maturity according to God's leading. *And we will do this, if God permits* (6:3).

Christians hold differing views on this passage. Some think it refers to once-genuine believers. Others think it refers to mere professors. The seriousness of the situation is highlighted by indicating a danger of recrucifying Christ. *For it is impossible to restore again to repentance those who have once been enlightened, and have tasted the heavenly gift, and have shared in the Holy Spirit, and have tasted the goodness of the word of God and the powers of the age to come, and then have fallen away, since on their own they are crucifying again the Son of God and are holding him up to contempt* (6:4-6).

The writer illustrated with a word picture from the world of agriculture. Farm land that received abundant rain was expected to produce a good harvest. As a result, it received God's blessing. If the land produced weeds, thorns, and thistles, it was cursed. It would be burned to destroy the weeds. The believer was to remain faithful in order to receive his or her reward. *Ground that drinks up the rain falling on it repeatedly, and that produces a crop useful to those for whom it is cultivated, receives a blessing from God. But if it produces thorns and thistles, it is worthless and on the verge of being cursed; its end is to be burned over* (6:7, 8).

The writer now offered encouragement, affectionately addressing his audience as beloved, the only instance of this in the whole letter. Assurance lay in the hope of salvation. *Even though we speak in this way, beloved, we are confident of better things in your case, things that belong to salvation* (6:9). God would not overlook the believers' faith and works. *For God is not unjust; he will not overlook your work and the love that you showed for his sake in serving the saints, as you still do* (6:10).

The writer offered one final encouragement. Those who remained diligent in faithfulness would realize the full assurance of hope. *And we want each one of you to show the same diligence so as to realize the full assurance of hope to the very end* (6:11).

## SUGGESTIONS TO TEACHERS

When a human body stops growing, it begins dying. Growth and renewal in the cells must continue if a person is to remain healthy. That same law also applies to the spiritual life. Keep growing . . . or else.

Today's lesson addresses the "arrested growth" that can happen in a believer's spiritual life. Hebrews was written to Christians nearly nineteen centuries ago, but the urgent advice has relevance for all of us today.

ARRESTED DEVELOPMENT. What nourishes a Christian's spiritual growth? Hebrews states that those who had once made professions of faith seemed to stop growing up and maturing in their faith. The writer described the diet for spiritual babes, and insisted that his readers must keep growing and take solid food for good spiritual development. Ask for comments on what feeds the souls of your students. Do they read Scripture regularly as part of their "religious diet"?

2. ANIMATED DYNAMIC. In the plea to keep on growing, emphasis is laid on the enablement that comes from Christ. The Spirit acts as the dynamic presence of Jesus, who animates and activates our growth as believers. Discuss the role of the Holy Spirit in our maturing as Christians, especially the use of spiritual gifts for mutual edification.

3. ARROGANT DEMEANOR. Lamentably, some who make professions of faith eventually fall away. Some even turn against Christ and hold him in contempt. What could be more tragic!

The temptations that lead to apostasy are powerful even today. But the writer to the Hebrews reminded his hearers that there can be no turning back. Once Christ calls a person, he calls that man or woman for a lifetime of obedient service.

4. ARDENT DESIRE. The author of Hebrews held out hope that his readers would do better. God's aspirations for us, likewise, are that we will grow in likeness to Christ. As a parent longs to see his or her child grow into a stable, caring adult, the Lord wants us to develop into responsible disciples. He desires to see us move out of the kindergarten stage of Christianity and mature as "grown-ups" in the faith.

In your class, you might ask each person to share what they believe Christian maturity would look like in their life. Ask each student to jot private, "personal resolutions" about steps they could take to advance their spiritual growth.

## TOPIC FOR ADULTS
### GROW IN FAITHFULNESS

*Redemption Always Possible.* James Galipeau is a law officer in perhaps the worst area for gangs and street crime anywhere, the "backhood" of Los Angeles. The Rolling 60s Crips and the Bloods are known and feared for their violence in this concentration of rundown houses, poverty-stricken churches, and sleazy brothels. Officially, the area is known as South-Central, and Galipeau is the Metropolitan Specialized Gang Unit probation officer. To the people of the area, Galipeau's street name is Kojak, because of his clean-shaven head.

Galipeau is a thirty-year veteran gang probation officer. At 6 foot 1 inch and 230 pounds, wearing hoop earrings and a medallion dangling from a gold chain, he looks more like a gang member himself than a police officer. His reputation in Los Angeles, however, has made him the best known probation officer in the country. Nearly every night, Jim Galipeau practices the dying art of street probation, supervising and counseling some of the most violent of South-Central's Crips and Bloods. But unlike many law enforcement people, he does not think that hard-core gang members are beyond redemption. He admits a small percentage are sociopaths, but insists that most would opt for jobs and a normal life if they could find a face-saving way to go about it. Galipeau tries to give them that opportunity.

But he is no softie with his clients. He demands that each one call him on Mondays to set up a meeting each week. In this world of crack houses, absent fathers, drug-addicted mothers, and armed assaults, Galipeau's work with angry, street-smart hoodlums has saved scores of young men from destruction.

How did Galipeau become such a successful and respected rescuer? What motivates him to work tirelessly to try to save arrested gang members from further crime? Jim Galipeau states that his belief in redemption comes from his own background as a teenager in Long Beach, California. He says that he ran with a rough crowd. "I was a real delinquent when I was a kid," he recalled in a radio interview with Terry Gross on the talk show "Fresh Air." "I was into stealing cars, fighting, and breaking into liquor store warehouses."

His mother suffered from multiple sclerosis, so his father worked the swing shift so he could spend part of the day caring for her. But his father was often called away from work to go to the police station because of Jim's arrests. One of those nights became a turning point. "This time they were going to send me away. The cops and my probation officer were sick and tired of my act. And when my father arrived at two in the morning they told him they were going to send me away for good."

"Personally, I was ready to do time, but when my father heard them, he broke down and began sobbing. He was the strongest man I had ever known, but he began pleading with them not to take me away. He would work two jobs to earn money to send me to private school. . . . He would do something—anything—to get me to turn around. The probation officer looked at me with disgust, and it hit me like a ton of bricks. Dad was living his life for me and Mom, but I was out there executing him. It happened in a moment, and I was struck dumb by it. I looked at the probation officer and said, 'Give me a chance.' He gave me six months to clean up my act. The next day I quit the gang."

The power of the love of Jim Galipeau's father affected young Jim so profoundly that he has been growing in faithfulness to community service ever since. We see the suffering love in God our Father's eyes when Christ encounters us. We realize His seeking love, and His claim on us. Our response can only be to turn, and with His strengthening mercy, grow in faithfulness.

*Use It or Lose It.* Janice took piano lessons for twelve years and developed into a promising performer. She planned to teach music someday. Then she went to college. Instead of majoring in music education as she originally intended, she became interested in contemporary literature and chose an English major. Extra-curricular activities in the drama club and gymnastics took up her spare time. Occasionally she would sit down at the piano, but found her keyboard skills not as sharp as they once had been.

Upon graduation, she moved to Chicago and found a job. She told herself that she would return to her music as soon as possible, but meanwhile she needed to earn a living. She planned to save to buy herself a piano, but a new car and vacations always consumed what she meant to set aside for the piano. New hobbies, especially golf, attracted her. Soon, she devoted nearly all her weekends to sharpening her abilities as a golfer.

Then she met a man at a golfing party and married him. When the children came, she quit her job for several years, and then reentered the job market when the last child was in junior high. Meanwhile, she sometimes remarked that she would get back to playing the piano again, but it was always "someday."

On their twentieth wedding anniversary, her husband presented her with a lovely spinet piano. Delighted, Janice sat down to play. To her surprise, the years of no practice had ruined her fingering. Gripping a golf club had done something to one wrist. Her ability to sight-read the music seemed to have diminished. Her playing sounded like the clumsy efforts of a beginning piano student. Looking up at her husband, Janice smiled ruefully. "Well, the old saying is true, I guess. 'Use it, or lose it.'"

Use your faith and keep progressing in Christian growth. If not, like Janice's piano playing, you lose touch with what you once loved.

*Questions for Students on the Next Lesson.* 1. Why can we approach God with assurance? 2. How do we know that God is faithful? 3. How does staying in Christian fellowship help us to do good deeds? 4. Does your congregation support those who experience grief or hardships? 5. How has your church helped you to remain faithful during hard times?

## TOPIC FOR YOUTH
### *KEEP ON GROWING*

*Costly Commitment.* Val Gaddis liked and needed her job at Westmarc Cable in Winona, Minnesota. But she was unhappy when her employer decided to offer X-rated pay-per-view movies on the Spice Channel. She prayerfully wrestled with what to do. She decided her moral convictions were more important than her job, so she quit. She told her supervisor that her conscience would not allow her to be a part of that type of environment.

Val exhibited a mature faith that was not indifferent to evil. She would not sidestep the teachings of Jesus, but stood firm in her beliefs. She demonstrated the kind of diligence Hebrews speaks of. She trusted in God's approval, and this was a giant step of growth for her.

*Understood Consequences.* John Scott had a fight with his girlfriend. Angry and upset, the young man sought some consolation in alcohol. After a day-long drinking binge, he awoke with a wad of cash in his pocket that he could not explain. He slowly recalled robbing his neighborhood convenience store. He walked to the store and confessed to the clerk while returning the money. Finally, he calmly waited for the Pittsburgh Police to arrest him. When asked to explain why he returned, Scott said that he had a jolt of conscience. He realized that he had broken the law and must face the consequences.

Scott was able to distinguish between good and evil. He understood that he had done wrong. He found it impossible to compound his problems with an act that was morally and legally wrong. He therefore repented and awaited the consequences, in the assurance that he had finally done the right thing. This is what it means to grow.

*A Cause Worth Winning.* Former Pennsylvania Governor Robert P. Casey spoke to the Fifth Anniversary convention of the Christian Coalition. Casey has long been a leader in the pro-life movement. He closed his address with a letter from a little girl in Hollsopple, Pennsylvania, a small town in Somerset County. She told the governor that she was ten years old and had been adopted at birth. Had it not been for his efforts, she might not have been alive. She thanked him and told him that while he was fighting a hard battle for the cause, she would do the same thing. That message strengthens Casey and enables him to see that the pro-life movement is a worthy cause.

Both Casey and the ten-year-old understood what it meant to make a commitment to an important cause. The writer of Hebrews stressed the same commitment to his readers. Their faith must be developed every day of their lives.

*Questions for Students on the Next Lesson.* 1. What is meant by "entering the sanctuary through the curtain"? 2. How important is purity to a Christian? Why? 3. How important is attendance at church to a believer? 4. Have you suffered for your faith? When? 5. What is the basis of a Christian's confidence?

# LESSON 11—AUGUST 10

## *REMAIN NEAR TO GOD*

*Background Scripture:* Hebrews 10:19-39
*Devotional Reading:* I Corinthians 1:1-10

### KING JAMES VERSION

HEBREWS 10:19 Having therefore, brethren, boldness to enter into the holiest by the blood of Jesus,

20 By a new and living way, which he hath consecrated for us, through the veil, that is to say, his flesh;

21 And having an high priest over the house of God;

22 Let us draw near with a true heart in full assurance of faith, having our hearts sprinkled from an evil conscience, and our bodies washed with pure water.

23 Let us hold fast the profession of our faith without wavering; (for he is faithful that promised;)

24 And let us consider one another to provoke unto love and to good works:

25 Not forsaking the assembling of ourselves together, as the manner of some is; but exhorting one another: and so much the more, as ye see the day approaching. . . .

32 But call to remembrance the former days, in which, after ye were illuminated, ye endured a great fight of afflictions;

33 Partly, whilst ye were made a gazingstock both by reproaches and afflictions; and partly whilst ye became companions of them that were so used.

34 For ye had compassion of me in my bonds, and took joyfully the spoiling of your goods, knowing in yourselves that ye have in heaven a better and an enduring substance.

35 Cast not away therefore your confidence, which hath great recompence of reward.

36 For ye have need of patience, that, after ye have done the will of God, ye might receive the promise.

37 For yet a little while, and he that shall come will come, and will not tarry.

38 Now the just shall live by faith: but if any man draw back, my soul shall have no pleasure in him.

39 But we are not of them who draw back unto perdition; but of them that believe to the saving of the soul.

### NEW REVISED STANDARD VRSION

HEBREWS 10:19 Therefore, my friends, since we have confidence to enter the sanctuary by the blood of Jesus, 20 by the new and living way that he opened for us through the curtain (that is, through his flesh), 21 and since we have a great priest over the house of God, 22 let us approach with a true heart in full assurance of faith, with our hearts sprinkled clean from an evil conscience and our bodies washed with pure water. 23 Let us hold fast to the confession of our hope without wavering for he who has promised is faithful. 24 And let us consider how to provoke one another to love and good deeds, 25 not neglecting to meet together, as is the habit of some, but encouraging one another, and all the more as you see the Day approaching. . . .

32 But recall those earlier days when, after you had been enlightened, you endured a hard struggle with sufferings, 33 sometimes being publicly exposed to abuse and persecution, and sometimes being partners with those so treated. 34 For you had compassion for those who were in prison, and you cheerfully accepted the plundering of your possessions, knowing that you yourselves possessed something better and more lasting. 35 Do not, therefore, abandon that confidence of yours; it brings a great reward. 36 For you need endurance, so that when you have done the will of God, you may receive what was promised. 37 For yet "in a very little while, the one who is coming will come and will not delay; 38 but my righteous one will live by faith. My soul takes no pleasure in anyone who shrinks back." 39 But we are not among those who shrink back and so are lost, but among those who have faith and so are saved.

*KEY VERSE: Let us hold fast to the confession of our hope, without waver-*
*ing, for he who has promised is faithful.*  Hebrews 10:23.

## HOME BIBLE READINGS

| Aug. | 4 | M. | II Corinthians 4:7-12 | *Power Belongs to God* |
|---|---|---|---|---|
| Aug. | 5 | T. | John 3:1-15 | *Be Born of the Holy Spirit* |
| Aug. | 6 | W. | II Corinthians 4:13-18 | *Things of the Spirit Are Unseen* |
| Aug. | 7 | T. | John 17:20-26 | *Jesus' Prayer for the Church* |
| Aug. | 8 | F. | Psalm 19:7-14 | *God Speaks through His Word* |
| Aug. | 9 | S. | I Peter 1:3-9 | *A Genuine Faith Is Important* |
| Aug. | 10 | S. | I Corinthians 1:1-10 | *God Is Faithful* |

## BACKGROUND

The Day of Atonement was the greatest and holiest worship experience for Jews in the first century (as well as in the twentieth). Our Jewish neighbors call it Yom Kippur. In Hebrew, it means both "day of atonement" and "day of propitiation." The instructions in Leviticus and Numbers show that this great annual holy day was observed with a complex series of ceremonies, all of which had deep symbolic meaning to worshipers. Yom Kippur was (and still is) the one day in which worshipers must fast. But the key participant when the great temple still stood in Jerusalem was the high priest.

The high priest went through seven days of arduous preparation. These days were marked by personal purification. When the Day of Atonement itself began, the high priest first made a personal sacrifice of an unblemished bull and appeared in the clothing of a penitent. Next, he made a sacrifice for the priests. This entailed the ritual slaughter of a second bull. The high priest confessed his sins and the sins of the Aaronic priesthood, then entered the holy of holies.

The holy of holies, the innermost shrine of the temple, was so sacred a place that only the high priest was allowed to go behind the entrance curtain—and then only on the Day of Atonement. The presence of the Lord was to be found within the secret confines of the holy of holies. On this occasion, the first of four times when the high priest entered the holy of holies, he carried coals from the altar and incense. The second time, he took blood of the bull which had been sacrificed for the sins of the priests.

The next portion of the day's ceremonies entailed ritual sacrifice for the sins of the people. Two male goats were presented. By lot, one was chosen to be slaughtered and the other to be the scapegoat to be driven into the wilderness, bearing away the sins of Israel's faithful. With the blood of the slain goat, the high priest went behind the great curtain into the holy of holies the third time and interceded for the people. The other goat was later led out of the temple and driven to the wild area to the east, where it was finally pushed over a high cliff to its death. The high priest then made his fourth and final visit into the sacred inner shrine to retrieve the censer in which incense had been smoking. Only after sundown was anyone permitted to eat or drink after the twenty-four-hour fast.

Those to whom Hebrews was addressed would have been familiar with all the ceremonial practices connected to this feast. They knew this as the highlight of the year, the day of divine forgiveness.

The writer of Hebrews made the point that through Jesus Christ, the great High Priest, a permanent Yom Kippur has been instituted so that every day is one in which God's mercy is given. Furthermore, because of the incarnation, the Cross, and the Resurrection, every believer is welcomed into the very presence of the living Lord. The holy of holies has been opened for all the faithful, forever.

## NOTES ON THE PRINTED TEXT

The holy of holies was the innermost room of the temple, God's dwelling place. Only on the day of atonement could one person, the high priest, enter this room. Even then, the priest hurried. So strict were the Jews that the rooms surrounding this room were monitored to assure purity. No one could enter without clean hands and a pure heart.

Because Christ is our priest and also the sacrifice, believers are able to approach God without fear. With His sacrifice, He inaugurated a new age. *Therefore, my friends, since we have confidence to enter the sanctuary by the blood of Jesus, by the new and living way that he opened for us through the curtain (that is, through his flesh), and since we have a great high priest over the house of God, let us approach with a true heart in full assurance of faith, with our hearts sprinkled clean from an evil conscience and our bodies washed with pure water* (10:19-22). The writer urged believers to approach with clean hands and an honest and pure heart. Through Christ's purifying death, we can experience the washing away of sin.

Faith was all important if the believers were to approach God. Because of God's faithfulness, believers were to hold fast to their faith, described as a confession of hope. *Let us hold fast to the confession of our hope without wavering, for he who has promised is faithful* (10:23).

In another exhortation, the faithful were reminded to love one another. Their love for one another must be demonstrated in acts of kindness toward others. In addition, the listeners were urged to gather together for fellowship, study, and worship. Apparently some of the believers, discouraged perhaps by Christ's delayed return, had stopped attending worship. They had given up hope. *And let us consider how to provoke one another to love and good deeds, not neglecting to meet together, as is the habit of some, but encouraging one another, and all the more as you see the Day approaching* (10:24, 25).

After warning his readers about the punishment for not holding fast to their faith, the writer reminded his listeners to recall the past. When they had committed themselves to Christ, their faith had been strong. They happily endured suffering, even the plundering and theft of their possessions, knowing that they had a promised heavenly treasure waiting for them. *But recall those earlier days when, after you had been enlightened, you endured a hard struggle with sufferings, sometimes being publicly exposed to abuse and persecution, and sometimes being partners with those so treated. For you had compassion for those who were in prison, and you cheerfully accept- ed the plundering of your possessions, knowing that you yourselves pos- sessed something better and more lasting* (10:32-34).

The believers must be confident and endure the hardships of persecution in order to receive what God had promised. They had been outspoken about their faith in the past; they were to continue to be equally bold in sharing their faith now. *Do not, therefore, abandon that confidence of yours; it brings a great reward. For you need endurance, so that when you have done the will of God, you may receive what was promised* (10:35, 36).

The author wove in scriptural support from Isaiah (26:20) and Habakkuk (2:3, 4), which called for faithfulness. The prophets said the Lord would come and fulfill His promise, but the righteous must endure a time of persecution. During this time they would be tempted to give up their faith; nevertheless, they must remain faithful. *For yet "in a very little while, the one who is coming will come and will not delay; but my righteous one will live by faith. My soul takes no pleasure in anyone who shrinks back"* (10:37, 38).

Believers were not to abandon their faith. They were to endure and enjoy the Lord's pleasure. *But we are not among those who shrink back and so are lost, but among those who have faith and so are saved* (10:39).

## SUGGESTIONS TO TEACHERS

Have you ever encountered someone who confesses to have trusted in Christ in the past, but after suffering or disappointment, admits to little faith? All believers experience times when their faith is tested. Undoubtedly, some in your class are now facing such a situation, a period of time when God seems distant and their faith needs strengthening. Perhaps this lesson will help.

1. CONFIDENCE IN CHRIST. Jesus Christ is the bedrock of our faith. Hebrews says this over and over again in imagery that comes from Jewish tradition. The main point is that we may come into the presence of the Almighty with confidence because of Jesus our High Priest. We may approach God as the welcoming Lord.

2. CONSIDERATION OF OUR CONFESSION. Hebrews was directed to people who had once made a commitment to Jesus as Lord, but who were inclined to stray from their loyalty to Him. The writer reminded them of their original vows. In this lesson, go back to the promises made by mem- bers of your class. What was asked when they completed a membership class and joined the church? Ask your people to recall those commitments. Can they state fairly exactly what they agreed to? You may wish to bring in a copy of the questions and ceremony used in your congregation to receive someone or to baptize some as a Christian.

3. CONCERN FOR COMPANIONS. This section of Hebrews emphasizes the corporate aspect of the Christian life. No merely private religion is ever sanctioned in Christ's community. A Christian is always part of a fellow- ship, never a lone wolf or solitary practitioner. At this point in the lesson, you must stress the important role of the body of Christ, local and univer- sal. Our culture so glorifies individualism that even our religion becomes tainted with "me-ism"—to the exclusion of the rest of Christ's family.

4. CONSISTENCY OF COMMITMENT. Hebrews warns against back-

sliding. No off-again, on-again or "when-it's-convenient" religion with Jesus! The writer calls all readers to live consistently close to Christ. Discuss what this consistency implies for a Christian today. Personal devotional practices? Regular worship? On-going involvement in programs to help the hungry and homeless? What else can your students suggest?

## TOPIC FOR ADULTS
### *ENDURING HARD TIMES*

*Enduring, as in the Early Church.* The Marxist government in Ethiopia forced out all missionaries in 1979, allowing only twenty-four hours notice to leave. During the following ten years, Ethiopian Christians went through a period that they simply call "The Persecution." Ethiopian pastors and elders were murdered, imprisoned, or exiled. The pressure was so severe that a few renounced their faith. Most churches were forced to close. Trying to survive in extreme poverty under a hostile regime, and challenged even by forces of nature, most Ethiopian believers clung to their faith in Christ.

In 1995, a small group of American Christians was able to visit Ethiopia. They found people often living in abject poverty, some communities dwelling like living fossils in the stone age, all subject to the ravages of curable diseases like tetanus and pneumonia. The visitors also found these Christians struggling against tribal religions, powerful witch doctors, and a popular belief in demonic possession.

Despite all the handicaps, and regardless of the acute shortage of leaders (in one district, there are only ten pastors to serve seventy congregations of twenty thousand Christians), the churches are filled. Children, young people, parents, and elderly members—all have been changed by the power of Jesus Christ and the presence of a loving church family. They witness to their faith in Jesus Christ as they tell their stories and sing their hymns of praise, accompanied by homemade flutes, drums, string instruments, and gourds filled with dried beans.

In them we see clearly what the first-century church must have been like.

*Waffling Church Leader.* Admittedly the 1500s were difficult years for the church in England. Reform and counter-reform, conflicting religious policies, and a series of forced changes under four Tudor monarchs made life difficult for parish clergy. Some spun like weathervanes, easily accommodating their practices to whatever the current ruler decreed. Others tried to hold fast to Christ.

One waffling cleric, who held on to his post for fifty years, was Christopher Trychay. The Rev. Trychay came to the parish of Morebath, England, in the early 1500s. At that time, he adhered to all the practices of the Roman church. He seemed particularly interested in promoting the cult of St. Sidwell, and personally presented a gilt statue in her honor—even placing it on the Jesus altar. By the mid-1530s, the Jesus altar had become St. Sidwell's altar, and parishioners began to name their children after that saint. Trychay urged the members of the Morebath parish to adorn her image with silver shoes!

When King Henry VIII broke with Rome and placed himself at the head of the new Church of England, Trychay seemed to have no problems in breaking with Rome also and adopting the changes called for by the king. He apparently presented himself as a faithful Anglican, while others adhering to the older ways had to leave their parishes.

When Mary Tudor came to the throne in 1553, the pendulum suddenly swung violently back to Rome. Protestants suffered martyrdom, but the Rev. Christopher Trychay had no problems. He simply led the Morebath parish back into former ways. The old vestments, the icons, and the adoration of St. Sidwell immediately returned.

Queen Elizabeth succeeded Mary Tudor, and Protestantism again became the religion of the realm. Once again, Trychay and the Morebath parish flip-flopped. The parish purchased new prayer books, hymnals, and Bibles in 1560. In 1562, the rood screen separating the worshipers from the altar area was removed. And in 1573, Trychay sounded like a lifelong reformer as he recorded the gift of a new prayer book and psalter with the entry, "Deo Gracias" ("Thanks be to God")—obviously the pious sentiment of a proper Protestant clergyman during Elizabeth's reign!

Christopher Trychay's religious gyrations allowed him to hold on to his plush assignment. Perhaps by the 1570s, he was sincerely convinced of Protestant truths, but during the previous half century of his ministry, he had displayed a dazzling ability to waffle to fit the times. The writer of Hebrews would have urged this cleric to stand up for the One he claimed to believe in . . . instead of merely placating the monarchs.

*Faced Hard Times.* Alexander Macgregor of Nova Scotia learned that his brother, a missionary in the South Seas, had been murdered and his body desecrated by the very tribesmen to whom he had carried the Gospel. Alexander was a successful school teacher, but he left his teaching position and traveled halfway around the world to those same islands where his brother had met his death.

What was Alexander Macgregor's purpose? To avenge his brother's cruel end? No, he went to continue his brother's ministry among those same tribesmen. After some years, Alexander also fell victim to the tribe that had taken the life of his brother. But today there is a strong Christian church in those islands where the Macgregor brothers served so selflessly and sacrificially. Their faithful witness changed violent hearts. When Christians faithfully face hard times for the sake of Christ, it is never in vain.

*Questions for Students on the Next Lesson.* 1. What is the definition of faith in Hebrews 11? 2. Why are Noah and Abraham held up as great examples of faith? 3. Even if we have faith, will we always see our hopes realized in our lifetimes? 4. What persons in the past have inspired you to live in faith? 5. What particularly difficult occasions in your life have been times of remembering God's goodness in the past?

## TOPIC FOR YOUTH
### REMAIN TRUE

*Questions.* Michelle Holby was a lovely sophomore at Thomas Jefferson High School. She and her brothers went to school one October morning, and nothing seemed out of the ordinary. However, during gym class, as she ran a lap around the track, Michelle collapsed. Unknown to anyone, even to her parents, Michelle was an epileptic. She had a seizure on the track and stopped breathing. When the nurse and paramedics arrived, they discovered her epileptic condition and began artificial respiration. Unfortunately, her oxygen supply had been cut off too long. She was kept alive in the hospital's intensive care unit, although she was diagnosed as being brain dead. When her life support systems were removed, Michelle died.

Classmates, church friends, and family were crushed. They asked, "Why? What was the point of her life? Why would God permit such a thing?" Her mother and father's faith did not waver, however. Though numb with grief, they confidently assured Michelle's friends, stating that they were not to abandon their confidence in God but remain true. God had simply fulfilled His promised salvation to Michelle earlier than expected.

*Held to Commitment.* It was a misty, foggy Monday morning. The mother had picked up several neighborhood children and was taking them to school. The carefree children talked and laughed. The rural road on which they were driving crossed an unmarked railroad crossing. As the car crossed the tracks, an unseen train came out of the fog and hit it, spinning it around and off the tracks.

As the emergency medical personnel arrived to help, among the injured was one little girl in critical condition. She told one of the paramedics, "I'm so glad I confessed Jesus as my Lord and Savior last night at church."

In spite of her life hanging in the balance, she held fast to her confession of hope. Her faith did not waver. She knew God would care for her. In spite of her youth, this little girl trusted in God's promise of salvation. In a similar situation, would you have the faith to do and say the same?

*Eyes of the Beholder.* Art critics say that western artists tend to put more perspective into their drawings and paintings. Their distinctive style portrays the future-oriented outlook of Christianity. Oriental artists, on the other hand, do not place much emphasis on perspective. Buddhists and Confucians tend to focus only on the present.

While Christians may at times be pessimistic or have doubts about the future, we faithfully trust that God will fulfill His promises. We have confidence in God's promise of eternal salvation for His people.

*Questions for Students on the Next Lesson.* 1. What is faith? 2. Is your faith as strong as it could or should be? Why or why not? 3. Does God reward faith? If so, how? 4. What outstanding examples of faith were recalled by the writer of Hebrews? Why? 5. What promise has God made to you through these Scriptures?

# LESSON 12—AUGUST 17

## REMEMBER THE PAST

*Background Scripture:* Hebrews 11:1-40
*Devotional Reading:* Romans 4:1-15

### KING JAMES VERSION

HEBREWS 11:1 Now faith is the substance of things hoped for, the evidence of things not seen.

2 For by it the elders obtained a good report. . . .

6 But without faith it is impossible to please him: for he that cometh to God must believe that he is, and that he is a rewarder of them that diligently seek him.

7 By faith Noah, being warned of God of things not seen as yet, moved with fear, prepared an ark to the saving of his house; by the which he condemned the world, and became heir of the righteousness which is by faith.

8 By faith Abraham, when he was called to go out into a place which he should after receive for an inheritance, obeyed; and he went out, not knowing whither he went.

9 By faith he sojourned in the land of promise, as in a strange country, dwelling in tabernacles with Isaac and Jacob, the heirs with him of the same promise;

10 For he looked for a city which hath foundations, whose builder and maker is God. . . .

13 These all died in faith, not having received the promises, but having seen them afar off, and were persuaded of them, and embraced them, and confessed that they were strangers and pilgrims on the earth.

14 For they that say such things declare plainly that they seek a country.

15 And truly, if they had been mindful of that country from whence they came out, they might have had opportunity to have returned.

16 But now they desire a better country, that is, an heavenly: wherefore God is not ashamed to be called their God: for he hath prepared for them a city. . . .

39 And these all, having obtained a good report through faith, received not the promise:

40 God having provided some better thing of us, that they without us should not be made perfect.

### NEW REVISED STANDARD VERSION

HEBREWS 11:1 Now faith is the assurance of things hoped for, the conviction of things not seen. 2 Indeed, by faith our ancestors received approval. . . .

6 And without faith it is impossible to please God, for whoever would approach him must believe that he exists and that he rewards those who seek him. 7 By faith Noah, warned by God about events as yet unseen, respected the warning and built an ark to save his household; by this he condemned the world and became an heir to the righteousness that is in accordance with faith.

8 By faith Abraham obeyed when he was called to set out for a place that he was to receive as an inheritance; and he set out, not knowing where he was going. 9 By faith he stayed for a time in the land he had been promised, as in a foreign land, living in tents, as did Isaac and Jacob, who were heirs with him of the same promise. 10 For he looked forward to the city that has foundations, whose architecture and builder is God. . . .

13 All of these died in faith without having received the promises, but from a distance they saw and greeted them. They confessed that they were strangers and foreigners on the earth, 14 for people who speak in this way make it clear that they are seeking a homeland. 15 If they had been thinking of the land that they had left behind, they would have had opportunity to return. 16 But as it is, they desire a better country, that is, a heavenly one. Therefore God is not ashamed to be called their God; indeed, he has prepared a city for them. . . .

39 Yet all these, though they were commended for their faith, did not receive what was promised, 40 since God had provided something better so that they would not, apart from us, be made perfect.

*KEY VERSE: Faith is the assurance of things hoped for, the conviction of things not seen. Hebrews 11:1.*

HOME BIBLE READINGS

| Aug. | 11 | M. | Hebrews 11:17-22 | *The Faith of Abraham* |
|------|----|----|----|----|
| Aug. | 12 | T. | Hebrews 11:23-28 | *The Faith of Moses* |
| Aug. | 13 | W. | Hebrews 11:29-38 | *The Faith of the Israelites* |
| Aug. | 14 | T. | Romans 14:13-20 | *Abraham Gave God the Glory* |
| Aug. | 15 | F. | Galatians 3:15-22 | *God's Promise to Abraham* |
| Aug. | 16 | S. | Romans 9:27-33 | *Righteousness Comes through Faith* |
| Aug. | 17 | S. | James 2:18-26 | *Faith without Works Is Dead* |

BACKGROUND

Earlier in the letter, the writer of Hebrews had issued a call to his readers to be "God's house," that is, a living and holy community of believers among whom the Lord would dwell. The section of Hebrews from 3:1 through 4:16 deals with this theme.

The author of Hebrews then devoted considerable space to showing how Jesus Christ's great high priesthood has accomplished everything necessary to make believers right with God. No human priest was needed any longer. No elaborate system of sacrifices and ceremonies was necessary.

With the material in last week's lesson and the passages in this one—beginning with 10:19 and continuing through the remainder of the letter—Hebrews addresses our practical response to these great doctrinal proclamations. The Old Testament quotation appearing in Hebrews 10:38 is the springboard for the emphasis on the importance of faith in chapter 11. Those responding to the work of the great High Priest (explained in 4:14—10:18) walk in faith.

Chapter 11, the basis of this lesson, is the magnificent "faith chapter." This section opens with a superb summary of what faith is, and then lines up a magnificent array of heroes and heroines from sacred history. Each of these lives is actually a great story. But Hebrews was designed for more than entertainment. The writer held up these examples to call each reader to faith-filled living, no matter what daunting circumstance may threaten.

NOTES ON THE PRINTED TEXT

Most of us subscribe to the apostle Paul's definition of faith, emphasizing that it is a personal commitment to Christ, who makes the believer one with Him. The author of Hebrews supplied another, perhaps broader and fuller, addition. Here, faith is the confident assurance of God's providential care, which undergirds the believer's certainty of spiritual realities. *Now faith is the assurance of things hoped for, the conviction of things not seen* (11:1).

Faith, with its accompanying assurance and conviction, has always been crucial for God's people. *Indeed, by faith our ancestors received approval* (11:2). To prove the point, the author supplied a list of examples of individuals who were steadfast in their faith, in spite of not having seen all of God's promises come to fruition in their lifetimes. By faith Enoch was taken so that he did not experience death; and "he was not found, because God had taken him." For it was attested before he was taken away that "he had pleased God."

Noah provided an example of living by faith in spite of trying circumstances. Having been warned of God's coming judgment, he faithfully built the rectangular houseboat-like ark, even though there were no signs of danger. *By faith Noah, warned by God about events as yet unseen, respected the warning and built an ark to save his household; by this he condemned the world and became an heir to the righteousness that is in accordance with faith* (11:7).

Abraham, in a demonstration of faith, risked a venture into the unknown, trusting in God's promises. He departed Haran, trusting in the promise of land and descendants. *By faith Abraham obeyed when he was called to set out for a place that he was to receive as an inheritance; and he set out, not knowing where he was going. By faith he stayed for a time in the land he had been promised, as in a foreign land, living in tents, as did Isaac and Jacob, who were heirs with him of the same promise. For he looked forward to the city that has foundations, whose architect and builder is God* (11:8-10).

The author then summarized his lesson. Though these heroic people did not see their final hopes realized, they maintained their faith. They acknowledged that ultimate fulfillment was in the life beyond earthly existence. Abraham died seeking a homeland and a great city. He and his descendants found a land, but they were nomads there. He could have returned to Haran, but he trusted that God had a better city, a heavenly one, waiting for him. *All of these died in faith without having received the promises, but from a distance they saw and greeted them. They confessed that they were strangers and foreigners on the earth, for people who speak in this way make it clear that they are seeking a homeland. If they had been thinking of the land that they had left behind, they would have had the opportunity to return. But as it is, they desire a better country, that is, a heavenly one. Therefore God is not ashamed to be called their God; indeed, he has prepared a city for them* (11:13-16).

The writer continued, weaving into his letter the stories of Abraham, Isaac, Jacob, Moses, Rahab, and other personalities. In each instance, these faithful people of the Old Testament did not always receive the immediate reward for their faith. However, they were part of the community of the faithful who would eventually receive God's promise. *Yet, all these, though they were commended for their faith, did not receive what was promised, since God had provided something better so that they would not, apart from us, be made perfect* (11:39, 40).

## SUGGESTIONS TO TEACHERS

A friend of mine has a novel way of describing the essence of faith. She says faith is living for Christ with the "in-spite-of" factor. That is, faith means trusting in the Lord's mercy and obeying His will in spite of all problems—and in spite of all evidence that might be offered to explain away His existence.

You may want to open this lesson by recounting some "in spite of's" from your own life. Later, allow the great "roll call" of biblical personalities to provide inspiring illustrations of trust in spite of daunting obstacles.

1. REMINDER OF FAITH. The opening verse of Hebrews 11 contains more than enough grist for a great discussion. Go through the verse, examining the two sections in this great definition of faith. Note that the usual limitations of time and space do not hobble the trust of one centered on Jesus Christ. We realize the brevity of our earthly existence, and we know that all of God's plans will not be fulfilled our lifetimes. Yet, faith means confident living in the Lord, nevertheless.

2. ROLL CALL OF THE FAITHFUL. Hebrews 11 marches past our eyes a great parade of glorious Old Testament figures to show what faith actually means. Each of these persons held to God's assurances, in spite of severe trials and lack of any proof of God's presence.

You could, of course, build an entire lesson around almost any one of these biblical heroes. Because of time constraints, you will have to select a few to hold up as prime examples. Abraham and Moses, of course, are the two outstanding persons in the Hebrew tradition, and each lived by faith before the elaborate temple and sacrificial rituals were instituted. Show how faith was paramount for them. If possible, have class members relate episodes from their lives in which they, too, were able to trust "in spite of."

3. REWARD IN THE FUTURE. None of the faithful souls of the past had the benefit of knowing Jesus Christ, the great High Priest. Christians have more reason than any others to live with steadfast hope in God's victory.

Take time to reflect on the great words in verses 39 and 40, which summarize the writer's point. Faith's rewards may not be completely realized during our lifetimes, but through Jesus Christ, we catch a glimpse of the distant glory. The future is in God's hands.

## TOPIC FOR ADULTS
### REMEMBER THE PAST

*Too Young to Remember.* Half of all Americans alive today are too young to remember President John F. Kennedy's assassination and funeral. Two-thirds are not old enough to remember the Korean War. Nearly three-quarters living now cannot recall what it was like before television, because they hadn't been born. Eighty-five percent of the people in this country are not old enough to remember the collapse of the stock market in 1929.

The absence of memories of the past is so widespread among so many of our fellow citizens that some leaders have grave apprehensions about the future. In a culture where one-third of all those living in the United States feel that persons have always been on the moon, we must realize that we have a serious national case of poor memory.

How much greater the crisis when God's community fails to remember the great deeds of God and His people in the history of salvation! We Christians must constantly recall God's wondrous deeds for our own benefit and for the growth of our children.

*Shred of Memory.* During the nineteenth and early twentieth centuries, large numbers of Jews in central Europe eased their conflict with Christian and secular culture by integrating and assimilating into the society. They allowed memories of their Jewishness to fade. In Hungary, especially, full assimilation was the pattern for professionals living in urban communities.

Between 1870 and World War I, most of the Hungarian intelligentsia, including nearly all university professors, had repressed their Jewish background, though most were Jewish by birth. After the Second World War, Hungary's 100,000 Jewish survivors found themselves living under a communist regime that suppressed all religions. Deadly persecutions against Jews erupted across eastern Europe in 1953, when the Soviet authorities accused Jewish doctors of plotting to poison Stalin and other high-ranking Soviet leaders. The survivors of Nazism and communism throughout Hungary and other eastern European countries felt it best to renounce all traces of their Jewish heritage.

Matyas Eorsi, a member of Hungary's National Assembly, tells how his father even changed his name from the "Jewish-sounding" Schleiffer to the "Hungarian sounding" Eorsi. Matyas also says his father tried to hide his Jewish identity from his children.

One day, Matyas discovered his father weeping and uttering his first coherent words in months after declining into the late stages of Alzheimer's. The old man was repeating, "I am Jewish, I am Jewish." The younger Eorsi comments that this was the one fact that seemed to have survived in his father's ravaged mind.

Christ's people forget their heritage at their own peril. Although we have not had to suffer pogroms or repressive regimes in North America, other believers around the world endure the worst persecutions. We are apt to let the memories of our Christian forebears—who have often been required to exhibit great heroism—be obscured by our comfortable life-styles of assimilation. What will happen when the few elderly former church members mumble with sobs, "I am Christian, I am Christian"?

*What Do You Remember?* The memorization of Bible verses, poems, and famous literary passages is no longer common in education. No more are children taught to learn the Twenty-third Psalm by heart, for example.

Children continue to memorize, though, regardless of the theories of certain educators. Every kid seems to know the songs from the movie *The Lion King.* Teenagers memorize arcane lists of statistics about ball teams and sports heroes. But in their classrooms? A student in Dr. Milton Coalter's university class would invariably ask, everytime a new handout or material on the chalkboard was presented, "How much of this stuff do we have to remember?" This person represented a generation of students.

Significantly, such respected Christian leaders as Gregory the Great observed, "We ought to transform what we read into our very selves, so that when our mind is stirred by what it hears, our life may concur by practicing what has been heard."

*Remember the Past!* Deliberately remember how the Lord has been faithful in our past by memorizing and repeating passages from Scripture. As we recall the past by planting those memories in our minds, we may face the future with confidence.

*Questions for Students on the Next Lesson.* 1. How does God discipline us? 2. How would you explain God's discipline in light of His love and mercy? 3. What role models have influenced your life for good? 4. How has the Lord enabled you to deal with trials and temptations? 5. When is it most difficult for you to persevere in faith?

### TOPIC FOR YOUTH
### *REMEMBER THE PAST*

*Anxious Journey.* College used to be a place where young people could go and journey casually from youth to adulthood amidst stimulating academic discussions and study. It was a time of slow, exhilarating growth and carefree attitudes. Now, however, it is an anxious journey.

A survey of 200,000 college freshmen sponsored by the American Council of Education found that new students are wary and worried. Worries about finances top the list. Stress and anxiety characterize the journey, which is likened to an exercise in survival. A sense of hopelessness pervades.

What a contrast to the individuals in Hebrews 11! While none could see the end of the journey, each trusted God along the way. Faith, not anxiety, characterized these people. Hope, not hopelessness, triumphed.

*Support from the Past.* In 1968, the Dodgers' Don Drysdale pitched fifty-eight consecutive scoreless innings, a streak that was supposed to be one of baseball's unbreakable records. However, twenty years later another Dodger pitcher, Orel Hershiser, closed in on that record. On September 23, his scoreless string reached forty-nine. Five days later, Hershiser attempted to tie Drysdale's record against the San Diego Padres. Hershiser threw nine shutout innings. With the score tied at 0-0, Hershiser wanted to leave the game so that he could share the record with Drysdale. But Dodgers' Manager Tommy Lasorda spoke with Hershiser and persuaded him to try for the record.

Another baseball hero also lent support—Don Drysdale, who was watching the game! Drysdale said he would be upset if Orel didn't go for it. The young man went out and pitched a scoreless inning, setting down San Diego's three batters. With Drysdale's blessing, he went on to break the record and to become the World Series Most Valuable Player (as well as the Cy Young Award winner).

The writer of Hebrews spoke of the inspiration that can come to us from heroes of the past. As Drysdale encouraged Hershiser, so Moses and Abraham—and the others in the faith chapter—can spur us on to heroic deeds in the kingdom.

*Gradual Erosion. Time* magazine, January 30, 1995, reported that Judaism, while deeply rooted in the United States, is being eroded by secularization, low birth rates, and high levels of intermarriage. In fact, so great is the loss in numbers of believers that some experts are predicting that Muslims will outnumber Jews in the twenty-first century. The sad truth is that many young people from strong Jewish and Christian families have little interest in their faith.

The writer of Hebrews urged his readers to remember the past.

Countless numbers of God's people maintained their faith in spite of the temptations of the age. True fulfillment lay in God's great promises.

*Questions for Students on the Next Lesson.* 1. What was the "cloud of witnesses" that surrounded the believers? 2. In what ways was Jesus the "pioneer and perfecter of our faith"? 3. What role does discipline play in a Christian's life? 4. Do you feel you have ever been disciplined by God?

# LESSON 13—AUGUST 24

## *RENEW COMMITMENT*

*Background Scripture:* Hebrews 12:1-11
*Devotional Reading:* II Corinthians 4:7-17

### KING JAMES VERSION

HEBREWS 12:1 Wherefore seeing we also are compassed about with so great a cloud of witnesses, let us lay aside every weight, and the sin which doth so easily beset us, and let us run with patience the race that is set before us,

2 Looking unto Jesus the author and finisher of our faith; who for the joy that was set before him endured the cross, despising the shame, and is set down at the right hand of the throne of God.

3 For consider him that endured such contradiction of sinners against himself, let ye be wearied and faint in your minds.

4 Ye have not yet resisted unto blood, striving against sin.

5 And ye have forgotten the exhortation which speaketh unto you as unto children, My son, despise not thou the chastening of the Lord, nor faint when thou art rebuked of him:

6 For whom the Lord loveth he chasteneth, and scourgeth every son whom he receiveth.

7 If ye endure chastening, God dealeth with you as with sons; for what son is he whom the father chasteneth not?

8 But if ye be without chastisement, whereof all are partakers, then are ye bastards, and not sons.

9 Furthermore we have had fathers of our flesh which corrected us, and we gave them reverence: shall we not much rather be in subjection unto the Father of spirits, and live?

10 For they verily for a few days chastened us after their own pleasure; but he for our profit, that we might be partakers of his holiness.

11 Now no chastening for the present seemeth to be joyous, but grievous: nevertheless afterward it yieldeth the peaceable fruit of righteousness unto them which are exercised thereby.

### NEW REVISED STANDARD VERSION

HEBREWS 12:1 Therefore, since we are surrounded by so great a cloud of witnesses, let us also lay aside every weight and the sin that clings so closely, and let us run with perseverance the race that is set before us,

2 looking to Jesus the pioneer and perfecter of our faith, who for the sake of the joy that was set before him endured the cross, disregarding its shame, and has taken his seat at the right hand of the throne of God.

3 Consider him who endured such hostility against himself from sinners, so that you may not grow weary or lose heart. 4 In your struggle against sin you have not yet resisted to the point of shedding your blood.

5 And you have forgotten the exhortation that addresses you as children—"My child, do not regard lightly the discipline of the Lord. or lose heart when you are punished by him; 6 for the Lord disciplines those whom he loves, and chastises every child whom he accepts." 7 Endure trials for the sake of discipline. God is treating you as children; for what child is there whom a parent does not discipline? 8 If you do not have that discipline in which all children share, then you are illegitimate and not his children. 9 Moreover, we had human parents to discipline us, and we respected them. Should we not be even more willing to be subject to the Father of spirits and live? 10 For they disciplined us for a short time as seemed best to them, but he disciplines us for our good, in order that we may share his holiness. 11 Now, discipline always seems painful rather than pleasant at the time, but later it yields the peaceful fruit of righteousness to those who have been trained by it.

*KEY VERSE: Since we are surrounded by so great a cloud of witnesses, let us also lay aside every weight and the sin that clings so closely, and let us run with perseverance the race that is set before us.* Hebrews 12:1.

HOME BIBLE READINGS

| | | | | |
|---|---|---|---|---|
| *Aug.* | *18* | *M.* | James 3:13-18 | *Be Committed to Peace* |
| *Aug.* | *19* | *T.* | I Corinthians 9:19-27 | *In All Things Exercise Self-control* |
| *Aug.* | *20* | *W.* | James 1:1-11 | *Look to God for Wisdom* |
| *Aug.* | *21* | *T.* | James 1:12-18 | *Every Good Gift Is from God* |
| *Aug.* | *22* | *F.* | James 1:19-26 | *Act Out Your Beliefs* |
| *Aug.* | *23* | *S.* | Proverbs 3:1-12 | *Trust in the Lord* |
| *Aug.* | *24* | *S.* | Psalm 51 | *Pray for Renewal* |

## BACKGROUND

The author of Hebrews pleaded with those who were wavering in their commitment to the great High Priest. Previously, in chapter 11, he had reminded them of the long line of Old Testament heroes and heroines who had held true to the faith. In this chapter, the writer continued to encourage his readers to persevere, in response to what Christ's sacrificial death had accomplished for them.

Two vivid images come into play. The first was that of an athlete competing in a foot race. The second pictured a parent guiding and correcting a child. In both of these analogies, the point is that discipline is crucial. An athlete must expect to undergo rigorous training if he or she hopes to win. And a youngster must realize that a parent's discipline will encourage the development of character and maturity. A believer undergoes discipline in the race of life and accepts loving correction from the heavenly Father.

Underlying all the comments about persevering and enduring is the call to look to Jesus constantly, "the pioneer and perfecter of our faith" (12:12), who has persevered and suffered death for believers. The only genuine and lasting motivation for living a moral, faith-filled life until the end is Jesus Himself. Any person who has realized the meaning of Calvary's cross will be so affected that he or she will want to live for Christ in practical ways each day.

## NOTES ON THE PRINTED TEXT

*Therefore, since we are surrounded by so great a cloud of witnesses, let us also lay aside every weight and the sin that clings so closely, and let us run with perseverance the race that is set before us* (12:1). Nearing the end of his letter, the author called for renewed commitment. Believers were exhorted to see themselves as part of an immense group of faithful believers who had confessed Christ as their Lord. Anything that hindered that commitment had to be discarded, much like an athlete discarded the weights used in his training or his clothing before a race (athletes back then generally ran naked). Sin was to be discarded in the same manner. The race of life must be run in a disciplined manner.

As a runner competed by looking toward the finish line, the believer must keep *looking to Jesus, the pioneer and perfecter of our faith, who for the sake of the joy that was set before him endured the cross, disregarded its shame, and has taken his seat at the right hand of the throne of God* (12:2). Jesus was described as the perfect leader, or trailblazer for the faithful. He was perfect because He had made the eternal sacrifice that dealth with all sins. As one who willingly accepted the shame and pain of the cross, He now enjoyed the position of honor in God's kingdom.

Jesus is the ultimate example to whom believers can look for strength and courage in the face of trials. The Hebrews were called to calculate, or count up, all that Jesus had endured, lest they become discouraged by their own sufferings. *Consider him who endured such hostility against himself from sinners, so that you may not grow weary or lose heart* (12:3). While Christ had to endure death, the readers of Hebrews had not yet had to endure the shedding of their blood. *In your struggle against sin you have not yet resisted to the point of shedding your blood* (12:4).

If the reader-listeners had forgotten their lesson, the writer of Hebrews reminded them of earlier instruction. God did discipline out of love, just as a parent disciplined a child. Correction was part of development, and their persecutions and sufferings were demonstrations of discipline. Therefore, suffering should be accepted as valuable. The author quoted Proverbs 3:11, 12 as proof. *And you have forgotten the exhortation that addresses you as children—"My child, do not regard lightly the discipline of the Lord, or lose heart when you are punished by him; for the Lord disciplines those whom he loves, and chastises every child whom he accepts"* (12:5, 6).

Discipline is a necessity in good parenting, and God's correction served as proof of their relationship with Him. *Endure trials for the sake of discipline. God is treating you as children; for what child is there whom a parent does not discipline? If you do not have that discipline in which all children share, then you are illegitimate and not his children* (12:7, 8).

The writer continued the argument. Because believers had fathers who disciplined them and whom they respected, should not believers expect and accept discipline from God? *Moreover, we had human parents to discipline us, and we respected them. Should we not be even more willing to be subject to the Father of spirits and live?* (12:9). The human father acted to prepare his children for adulthood during the short period of childhood. God disciplined believers for their own good so that they might share in His purity and holiness forever. *For they disciplined us for a short time as seemed best to them, but he disciplines us for our good, in order that we may share his holiness* (12:10).

The writer compared the immediate with the future. While the present circumstances might seem difficult, the future would be far better. Discipline always feels painful at the time received; however, discipline from the Lord yields a great reward. *Now, discipline always seems painful rather than pleasant at the time, but later it yields the peaceful fruit of righteousness to those who have been trained by it* (12:11).

## SUGGESTIONS TO TEACHERS

How often have you heard someone respond to a request to serve in the church by saying, "I just don't want to commit myself to this." This lesson on renewing commitment may make us squirm a bit. In speaking of half-hearted allegiance, it may hit close to home.

1. RACING COMPETITIVELY. The writer of Hebrews holds up an arresting image, the picture of an athlete preparing to compete. In a sports-minded culture such as ours, this illustration grabs our attention immedi-

ately. You may want to select some examples from the sports pages to emphasize the necessity of discipline, training, and fitness for becoming a winner. The main point is that we Christians must think of ourselves as spiritual athletes. We are up against a ruthless opponent, evil in many forms. Our "running" to keep in shape spiritually is not a casual jogging for pleasure or self-gratification. Its purpose is to strengthen ourselves to stay the entire course of life without dropping out of the race from weariness.

2. REMEMBERING CHRIST. How do we maintain our commitment when we become weary of serving? By looking constantly to Jesus Christ! If we think of life as a long, grueling marathon and not as a short sprint, we must prepare ourselves to endure. That kind of commitment comes from keeping focused on Jesus, who is always out ahead of us to lead us onward. Jesus paces us and encourages us so that we are never alone in the long race.

3. RECEIVING CHASTENING. The author of Hebrews switched to another metaphor to demonstrate the place of discipline in holding on to the faith. He reminded his readers that as a human parent disciplines a child for his or her own good, so the loving Lord disciplines us for our own good. This does not mean that God is mean-spirited or fed up with us. Remember that the God we know has disclosed Himself in Jesus Christ, who treated people with love and mercy. Our God never capriciously metes out misery or finds perverse pleasure in punishing. Throughout all that we suffer, we can be certain of the love of God.

Discuss the presence of suffering in the life of a believer. Remind your students that enduring suffering in Christ's peace is a witness to the onlooking world.

## TOPIC FOR ADULTS
### RENEW YOUR COMMITMENT

"Our Lady of Exxon"? That's the name the local people often use to refer to the Arlington Temple United Methodist Church in Rosslyn, Virginia, a suburb of Washington. It's a place of worship for a dedicated, vibrant congregation. But it's also a gas station. When you drive past the tall structure, you see the familiar Exxon signs and gasoline pumps in a drive-through setting, on the street level under the building. Directly above the Exxon station is the sanctuary. A graceful steeple reaches above the building.

Newcomers to Rosslyn aren't sure what to make of the unusual arrangement. The church's pastor, Rev. Jack Sawyer says, "Where else can you get religious services upstairs and mechanical services downstairs?"

The oil company pays the church $2,000 a month to rent the space below the place of worship. But one cynical critic maintains that this unusual arrangement symbolizes what is wrong with the Christian church in North America today. This critic says that Christians aren't sure what they are, that churches cannot make up their mind what they stand for. Furthermore, he claims, churches have sold out their heritage to whatever interests have the most power or money.

Keep the Axe Sharp. Ole Svendsen, a big Swede from northern Wisconsin, was a champion in all the axe contests in his part of the world. For fifteen years, he won the tree-cutting contest. The sixteenth year he lost. Someone asked him why he didn't win as usual. Ole scratched his head and confessed, "Well, I guess I didn't take time to sharpen the axe."

Christians, too, must stay sharp, in order to compete in the contest of life. It requires discipline: Bible reading, prayer, giving, and constant fellowship.

*Come and Heal!* The early church historian Eusebius, who lived from about A.D. 265 to 339, told a charming story. The tale is legend, but it apparently was passed around in the centuries immediately after Jesus' sojourn on earth. In the account, a king named Abgar the Black (who actually lived from about A.D. 9 to 46) sent word from his small kingdom in Edessa to Jesus, asking Him "to come to me and heal the affliction I have."

In the legend, as related by Eusebius, the Lord Jesus answered King Abgar's messenger by explaining that He had to fulfill His mission in Palestine. But after His ascension He would send one of His followers to heal Abgar "and to give life to you and to those who are with you."

It is true that while Jesus is in heaven, before His Second Coming, we are the only hands and feet and mouth He has on earth. We must prepare ourselves well for the task of continuing His work. When we grow weary, let us encourage one another to renewed commitment.

*Questions for Students on the Next Lesson.* 1. Why is it so hard to show hospitality to strangers in our day? 2. What devotional practices do you follow to maintain spiritual growth? 3. How could your congregation help strengthen the marriages in your community? 4. What forms of ministry still need to be provided for the downtrodden in your community? Who is being overlooked? 5. In what sense is every Christian a priest?

## TOPIC FOR YOUTH
### *HAVE COURAGE*

*True Courage.* Do you remember the lion in *The Wizard of Oz*? In the classic motion picture he is first seen on the yellow brick road jumping out of the woods. He beats his chest, rants, raves, and growls ferociously trying to frighten Dorothy, Toto, and the scarecrow. Dorothy is not intimidated by his false bravado, though. She slaps his nose and he begins to cry.

Through this delightful scene, we discover that real courage requires more than outrageous acts of bravado. It demands commitment to a goal, such as shown by Dorothy, who persevered in going to see the Wizard.

The writer of Hebrews asserts that true courage shines forth in the lives of those who were committed to Christ through the toughest of circumstances. They trusted in God's will and love for them.

*God Proved Courage.* Near the end of her time of hiding from the Nazis, Anne Frank spoke with her friend Peter, who was also in the attic with her. Peter was depressed and feeling hopeless. He asked Anne how she could stand the captivity.

Anne responded that she thought of the outside often. She remembered the birds, the trees, the blue sky, and the sun. These remembrances supplied the hope she needed and enabled her to see the whole picture. Her sufferings were just a dot in time.

This viewpoint enabled Anne to endure suffering and despair. She could enjoy life in all circumstances, as long as there was breath within her. She trusted in the God of love being stronger than the force of death that surrounded her. This was the essence of her courage.

*Championship Role Model.* In an era when many professional athletes feel little responsibility to be a role model, the late heavyweight boxing champion Jack Dempsey is a refreshing contrast. He was an inspiration to many young athletes, having risen to the top of his sport despite many obstacles. He never received a formal education, but tirelessly lectured young people on the importance of completing school. This man recognized that he had to be an example for the youth of America.

As fine an example as Jack Dempsey provided, the writer of Hebrews urged his readers to look to Jesus for an even better mentor. He provides the real championship role model. All life-styles should be patterned after Him.

*Questions for Students on the Next Lesson.* 1. What Christian disciplines were the readers to develop? 2. Is the Lord truly your helper? How? 3. Do you "imitate" the faith of your leaders? Why, or why not? 4. How is Jesus the same yesterday, today, and forever? 5. What sacrifice did the writer advocate offering even in our day?

# LESSON 14—AUGUST 31

## ACCEPT RESPONSIBILITIES

*Background Scripture:* Hebrews 13:1-25
*Devotional Reading:* James 5:7-16

### KING JAMES VERSION

HEBREWS 13:1 Let brotherly love continue.

2 Be not forgetful to entertain strangers: for thereby some have entertained angels unawares.

3 Remember them that are in bonds, as bound with them; and them which suffer adversity, as being yourselves also in the body.

4 Marriage is honourable in all, and the bed undefiled: but whoremongers and adulterers God will judge.

5 Let your conversation be without covetousness; and be content with such things as ye have: for he hath said, I will never leave thee, nor forsake thee.

6 So that we may boldly say, The Lord is my helper, and I will not fear what man shall do unto me.

7 Remember them which have the rule over you, who have spoken unto you the word of God: whose faith follow, considering the end of their conversation.

8 Jesus Christ the same yesterday, and to day, and for ever.

9 Be not carried about the divers and strange doctrines. For it is a good thing that the heart be established with grace; not with meats, which have not profited them that have been occupied therein.

10 We have an altar, whereof they have no right to eat which serve the tabernacle.

11 For the bodies of those beasts, whose blood is brought into the sanctuary by the high priest for sin, are burned without the camp.

12 Wherefore Jesus also, that he might sanctify the people with his own blood, suffered without the gate.

13 Let us go forth therefore unto him without the camp, bearing his reproach.

14 For here have we no continuing city, but we seek one to come.

15 By him therefore let us offer the sacrifice of praise to God continually, that is, the fruit of our lips giving thanks to his name.

16 But to do good and to communicate forget not: for with such sacrifices God is well pleased.

### NEW REVISED STANDARD VERSION

HEBREWS 13:1 Let mutual love continue.
2 Do not neglect to show hospitality to strangers, for by doing that some have entertained angels without knowing it.
3 Remember those who are in prison, as though you were in prison with them; those who are being tortured, as though you yourselves were being tortured. 4 Let marriage be held in honor by all, and let the marriage bed be kept undefiled; for God will judge fornicators and adulterers. 5 Keep your lives free from the love of money, and be content with what you have; for he has said, "I will never leave you or forsake you." 6 So we can say with confidence, "The Lord is my helper; I will not be afraid. What can anyone do to me?"

7 Remember your leaders, those who spoke the word of God to you; consider the outcome of their way of life, and imitate their faith. 8 Jesus Christ is the same yesterday and today and forever. 9 Do not be carried away by all kinds of strange teachings; for it is well for the heart to be strengthened by grace, not by regulations about food, which have not benefited those who observe them. 10 We have an altar from which those who officiate in the tent have no right to eat. 11 For the bodies of those animals whose blood is brought into the sanctuary by the high priest as a sacrifice for sin are burned outside the camp. 12 Therefore Jesus also suffered outside the city gate in order to sanctify the people by his own blood. 13 Let us then go to him outside the camp and bear the abuse he endured. 14 For here we have no lasting city, but we are looking for the city that is to come. 15 Through him, then, let us continually offer a sacrifice of praise to God, that is, the fruit of lips that confess his name. 16 Do not neglect to do good and to share what you have, for such sacrifices are pleasing to God.

*KEY VERSE: Do not neglect to do good and to share what you have, for such sacrifices are pleasing to God. Hebrews 13:16.*

## HOME BIBLE READINGS

| | | | | |
|---|---|---|---|---|
| Aug. | 25 | M. | Ephesians 5:21-33 | *Be Responsible Husbands and Wives* |
| Aug. | 26 | T. | Ephesians 6:1-9 | *Be Responsible Parents and Children* |
| Aug. | 27 | W. | Matthew 22:15-22 | *Be Responsible Citizens* |
| Aug. | 28 | T. | Hebrews 4:1-10 | *Be Responsible to God* |
| Aug. | 29 | F. | Hebrews 13:17-25 | *Be Responsible Leaders* |
| Aug. | 30 | S. | James 3:1-12 | *Accept Responsibility for What You Say* |
| Aug. | 31 | S. | Luke 12:13-21 | *Use Your Wealth Responsibly* |

## BACKGROUND

The closing chapter of Hebrews finds the author offering down-to-earth advice about living together as a Christian community. After pleading for constant faithfulness to Christ, our writer ended his great letter with beautiful and helpful comments on what it means to respond to God's love by showing love. The dominant issue for Christ's family is love.

The author touches on six areas in which love must be shown: (1) the relationship with fellow believers in the Christian community; (2) the relationship to non-Christian outsiders; (3) the relationship to Christians suffering persecution; (4) the relationship with one's spouse; (5) the relationship with one's money and personal possessions; and (6) the relationship with church leaders.

Love must be shown not only to those within the Christian fellowship but also to those outside it. Compassion toward persons beyond one's family, clan, or ethnic group was unknown in those days. Caring for others indicates how profoundly Jesus Christ had affected those early believers.

The writer of Hebrews signed off with some of the most moving and memorable lines in the entire Bible (see 13:18-25). He referred to the God of peace, then spoke of Jesus as the great Shepherd of His people. This beautiful benediction is the writer's great final prayer that the Lord will continue to equip His sons and daughters to do the work outlined in previous parts of the letter.

## NOTES ON THE PRINTED TEXT

Hebrews concluded with the author's statements regarding the practice of faith. The comments were divided into two categories: social relations and spiritual relations. These two emphases form today's lesson.

*Let mutual love continue* (13:1). The people must exhibit love for one another. They were exhorted to care for each other's physical and material needs. For example, *do not neglect to show hospitality to strangers, for by doing that some have entertained angels without knowing it* (13:2). Jews and Christians were expected to feed and provide hospitality to travelers. As they did so, they fulfilled their responsibility—and might also entertain an angel in disguise.

*Remember those who are in prison, as though you were in prison with them; those who are being tortured, as though you yourselves were being tortured* (13:3). Within the Roman Empire, Christians and Jews were often considered subversives. Christians were to remember and care for those who were imprisoned for their faith. They were to identify with them by visiting them and sharing food and other necessities.

*Let marriage be held in honor by all, and let the marriage bed be kept undefiled; for God will judge fornicators and adulterers* (13:4). The writer also addressed the sanctity of marriage. Promiscuous behavior such as premarital and extramarital sex was forbidden.

Christians were also exhorted to be content with what they had and not be anxious about money. The author quoted two portions of Scripture (Deut. 31:6 and Psalm 118:6) in support of the truth that God provides for every need. *Keep your lives free from the love of money, and be content with what you have; for he has said, "I will never leave you or forsake you." So we can say with confidence, "The Lord is my helper; I will not be afraid. What can anyone do to me?"* (13:5, 6).

The readers were also encouraged to recall and emulate the faith of their Christian leaders. The Greek language here indicates that these leaders were dead, apparently martyred for their faith. They provided an excellent example to the believers. *Remember your leaders, those who spoke the word of God to you; consider the outcome of their way of life, and imitate their faith* (13:7). The believers were reminded that their greatest example was the Lord Jesus, who was always available to them. Perhaps the writer quoted an old Christian confession of faith. His example was timeless. *Jesus Christ is the same yesterday and today and forever* (13:8).

The writer warned about keeping the old Jewish law, particularly the food laws. The inner life is sustained by God's grace, not by ritual observances. *Do not be carried away by all kinds of strange teachings; for it is well for the heart to be strengthened by grace, not by regulations about food, which have not benefited those who observe them* (13:9). The readers must leave the comfort of the legalistic rituals, since the old ceremonies meant nothing. The Jewish priests had the exclusive right to eat certain offerings that were brought to the altar, while other people were excluded. The reverse was not true for believers. *We have an altar from which those who officiate in the tent have no right to eat* (13:10).

Under Levitical law, when the sin offering was made for atonement, the blood was sprinkled on the altar. Then the carcass of the animal was taken outside the city and burned. The person who handled the carcass was thus defiled and had to bathe for cleansing, in order to reenter the city. *For the bodies of those animals whose blood is brought into the sanctuary by the high priest as a sacrifice for sin are burned outside the camp* (13:11). Now came the comparisons: While the normal sacrifice took place within the city, Jesus was killed outside the city. The blood of the sacrificial victim atoned for those within the city, while Jesus cleansed those outside the city. *Therefore Jesus also suffered outside the city gate in order to sanctify the people by his own blood* (13:12).

The believers were urged to identify with Jesus and be willing to suffer dishonor and abuse as He did. *Let us then go to him outside the camp and bear the abuse he endured* (13:13). Faithfully enduring the suffering would ultimately bring God's reward. *For here we have no lasting city, but we are looking for the city that is to come* (13:14).

As priests who understood God's forgiveness and grace, Christians were to offer praise to God as their sacrifice, along with compassionate acts of goodness and generosity. *Through him, then, let us continually offer a sacrifice of praise to God, that is, the fruit of lips that confess his name. Do not neglect to do good and to share what you have, for such sacrifices are pleasing to God* (13:15, 16).

## SUGGESTIONS TO TEACHERS

If you were asked to offer five or six practical suggestions about living as a Christian in your community today, what would you say? In what areas are fellow believers finding it difficult to live responsibly? You may wish to start your lesson by asking class members to make a list of concerns. Then compare yours and theirs with the areas the writer of Hebrews highlights.

1. HOSTILITY TO HOSPITALITY. Hebrews 13 opens with a plea for Christians to reach out to outsiders, especially strangers and prisoners in the community. Think together about who, specifically, such "strangers" and "prisoners" may be in your community today. What about the homeless? Single mothers on welfare? Migrant farm workers? The unemployed? Does anyone visit those in your local jail? Living responsibly as Christ's community requires compassion and practical concern that reaches outside the fellowship.

2. FALSENESS TO FIDELITY. Hebrews also touches on the matter of sex and marriage. Our culture has glamorized infidelity. The affairs and sexual escapades are apparently considered normal. Hebrews 13:4 may seem like a verse out of touch with modern society, but God's Word on responsible sexual relationships will be ignored at our peril.

3. GREED TO CONTENTMENT. Does contentment come from acquiring and possessing? The shopping mall has replaced the church on Sundays for countless families. Hebrews' words about being preoccupied by "the love of money" provides a clue to true contentment. Note that money itself is not evil; it's the love of money that undercuts trust in God.

Hebrews 13:5, 6, and 16 should be studied carefully in today's lesson. Point to the sense of discontent that seems so widespread in our day. Hebrews connects such discontent with the love of money. Do your class members agree? What evidence do they see?

4. DETACHMENT TO DEVOTION. Hebrews' writer was also concerned about responsibility toward church leaders (see 13:7, 17, 18). Although many leaders have revealed dismaying flaws, we must not imagine that we can live without them. Our society shows disturbing signs of rampant individualism. Leaders are almost automatically suspected of wrongdoing. How well does your congregation support its pastors and church officers? Without setting these folks on pedestals or glorifying them as infallible, are you praying for and helping them?

5. CONFUSION TO CONCENTRATION. Focus on the closing benediction (13:9-15). By concentrating on Jesus Christ, every Christian is adequately equipped to serve. Throughout this chapter, the writer encourages each believer to bring glory to the Lord.

## TOPIC FOR ADULTS
### *LIVE RESPONSIBLY*

*Gracious Winner.* The Dallas Cowboys and the Buffalo Bills met in 1994's Super Bowl XXVIII, in which the Bills suffered their fourth straight Super Bowl loss. The Bills' great player Thurman Thomas had fumbled three times, contributing to Buffalo's defeat. After the game, Thomas sat on the bench with his face buried in his hands.

Walking up to him, and carrying his little goddaughter, was Emmitt Smith of the Cowboys. The Dallas Cowboy running back had just been named Most Valuable Player for the Super Bowl. Emmitt Smith said to the little girl in his arms, "Honey, I want you to meet the greatest running back in the National Football League, Mr. Thurman Thomas."

That kind gesture by Smith brought comfort to Thomas, and reflected a Christian sense of responsibility—to care about people, even when it would be easier to just walk away.

*Renewing Responsible Commitment.* Jim and Joan were acquaintances of mine. Jim was the son of an Episcopal rector. Joan was the daughter of a Presbyterian minister. They occasionally attended our worship services. When I called on them, they laughingly told me that as PKs (preachers' kids) they knew all about church life. Their cynicism about the faith and the Christian community was barely concealed in the hilarious accounts of their childhoods in parsonages.

They were not inclined to unite with any congregation, they said, because they really didn't have any confidence that "anyone up there is really interested in the show down here," as Jim put it. Occasionally, Jim and Joan would drop in to a morning worship service and greet me afterward with a flippant remark about how it was nice to know "you preachers are still dishing out the same old stuff." We would chuckle, but their attitude troubled me.

One morning, Joan called to ask if they could see me. We met that evening. Joan tried to control herself as she spoke of their current marital problems. Jim, she said, was encouraging a flirtatious relationship with a woman in his law office. Annoyed, Jim replied that it was all quite innocent. A few lunches, some drinks after work, but no adultery. "So what's the big deal? So I've taken an interesting woman out to lunch; I haven't slept with her."

"Yet!" snapped Joan, almost before Jim finished his protest. Then she turned away. Smarting from the selfishness and indifference reflected in Jim's words and attitude, she retreated into an angry, sullen silence.

I tried to nudge the conversation toward the possibilities of healing through Christ, but Jim cut me off: "Hey, Padre, don't get pious with us. Remember, we're preachers' kids, and we've heard all that stuff backward and forward." But reluctantly, Jim and Joan agreed to give their relationship "another shot," as Jim put it. Obviously, however, neither thought that the Lord could do much for them. As they left that evening, Joan sighed, "How can I be sure that God is going to make things any different for us in the future?"

Another failed attempt at significant pastoral counseling, I told myself. I didn't see them in church or socially in the next months, and I assumed I would never hear from them again. Yet three months later, Jim called. His wisecracks were as sharp as before. "Padre, Joan's headaches and blood pressure are bad news, and she's probably right that I'm drinking too much. Our family doctor told us we should see either a psychiatrist or a divorce lawyer . . . or our minister." Jim laughed again. "You come cheaper. When can we see you?"

This time in my office, we finally got down to basics, brushing aside the flimsy evasions and excuses of "too much religion when I was young." We talked, we listened, we cried. And we prayed. We remembered Jesus—the promise of God in human flesh, who has given us His word that He will stay by us, now and in the future.

The evening ended with Jim tenderly taking Joan's hand and saying softly, "Joan, please forgive me for hurting you. I want to be covenanted with you again, and for always." Joan responded, "Jim, please forgive me for being so unforgiving. I want to be covenanted with you again, and for always."

*Refusal to Exploit Kids.* Today's star athletes are known for lending their names to expensive sportswear companies. But one basketball star could not stand to see fellow sports heroes hawking sneakers at high prices to youngsters who can ill afford them. Houston Rockets' center Hakeem Olajuwon decided that a pair of Air Jordans or Shaqs at $125 to $150 a pair was exploitive. Olajuwon insisted on a deal with Spaulding in which he would endorse athletic shoes to be sold at mass merchandisers for no more than $60.

Hakeem Olajuwon's representative, Ralph Greene stated, "Hakeem is hung up on the price issue. He feels $100 or $200 for a pair of shoes is a backward thing to do. And he didn't want just another deal where they gave him a check and the company did what they wanted."

## TOPIC FOR YOUTH
### BE RESPONSIBLE

*Compassion and Understanding.* Imagine having a school holiday, and instead of sleeping in or loafing, you work in a soup kitchen, a homeless shelter, or a center for abused women! The United Way of Allegheny County, Pennsylvania, takes sixty teenagers each holiday into a program called "Youth Celebrating Service." It is a day-long project that serves the needy. Students arrive in the early morning to sort clothing and bag toiletries before dividing into teams that work at kitchens and shelters.

Jonnet Solomon, an eighteen-year-old senior from Keystone Oaks High School worked at Bethlehem Haven, a shelter for women. Why? She said she could remember her own family being at the bottom and needing help before they experienced better times. Jonnet recognized her responsibility to reach out.

*Gloom and Doom Sells.* For many teens, death makes a chic and sexy fashion statement. Today's look is built around wearable items from rock groups. The best-sellers, according to Andrew Rich of San Francisco's Winterland Productions, are skull, skeleton, and demon-festooned shirts from heavy metal groups such as Slayer, Metallica, Megadeath, and Ozzy Osbourne. Teenage males, especially, favor the death-rock variety of items.

Rock merchandise was almost a 500-million-dollar industry last year. While the music itself tends to glorify violence, sexuality, and Satan, many young people do not listen to the music. They tend to focus on the fashion clothing, which glorifies death and destruction.

Various organizations are banding together in an effort to point out the negative and harmful effects of such music and clothing. The Parents' Music Resource Center (founded by the Vice President's wife, Tipper Gore, and Susan Baker, the wife of the former Secretary of State), the National Parent Teacher Association, and the American Academy of Pediatrics have joined high school principals in urging that these negative influences be removed because they lead to a view of the world that glorifies violence.

The writer of Hebrews urges you to remember the example of Jesus. Life is so much more than gloom, doom, death, and destruction. In Christ, life is grace, goodness, and generosity. You are to demonstrate this, even in your dress. Don't be irresponsibly influenced by the fashion world.

*Inspiration.* Over twenty years ago, Henry Aaron broke Babe Ruth's record of 715 home runs with a new record of 755, earning himself a place in the Baseball Hall of Fame. While most people know about his baseball accomplishments, they may not know how much more there is to Henry Aaron. He has spent years tirelessly caring for children through the Big Brother and Big Sister programs. Above all, he has been involved in the fight for equal rights for Black Americans in baseball.

As he grew up, Aaron was profoundly influenced by the example of Jackie Robinson. When Robinson died, Aaron felt it was his job to continue the fight and finish the struggle.

Aaron draws on a lifetime of experiences. He started his baseball career in the old Negro League. In fact, when he retired from the Atlanta Braves, he was the last Negro Leaguer still in the majors. He remembers those uneasy days of barnstorming through a segregated nation. He says, in fact, it was easier then, when open segregation did not hide the bigotry. As he closed in on Babe Ruth's record, Aaron received ugly hate mail and death threats. Many people did not want a black man to beat the Babe's record.

Experiences like these led Aaron to make a documentary for TBS television. He wanted to let another generation see what he and others went through. It might keep them from writing ugly letters or generating such terrible feelings toward other black stars like Barry Bonds or Bobby Bonilla. Perhaps young people would find an inspiration from Hank Aaron.

You, too, can work to improve social relations. In fact, it is a responsibility of all citizens, especially Christians, who are to care for all people. Follow the advice of the author of Hebrews. Remember the example of your leaders and imitate their faith.